The Database Experts' Guide to Database 2

Bruce L. Larson

Intertext Publications
McGraw-Hill Book Company
New York, N.Y.

Library of Congress Catalog Card Number 87-83098

10 9 8 7 6 5 4 3 2 1

ISBN 0-07-023267-9 [Paperback]
ISBN 0-07-036488-5 [Hardcover]

Intertext Publications/Multiscience Press, Inc.
McGraw-Hill Book Company
1221 Avenue of the Americas
New York, NY 10020

Panels may have been edited for publication purposes and are subject to changes when new releases of these products become available.

Composition by Context, Inc.

Table of Contents

Preface

The Database Experts' Guide to Database 2 is a comprehensive, applications-oriented users' guide to Database 2. Intended for EDP Managers, Database 2 Administrators, Analysts, and Programmers, this book features a practical, working approach to learning relational database technology in general, and Database 2 in particular.

The Database Experts' Guide to Database 2 first provides a working foundation in relational databases, then establishes an effective and thorough overview of Database 2 itself, and finally details for the reader the many specific areas of interest integral to the database. All material is presented in a highly pragmatic manner. For example, guidelines and installation issues are identified to assist the reader in avoiding many of the frustrations that may be encountered without careful planning. Helpful hints are found in every chapter and on every subject. The SQL language, which is used to communicate to Database 2 and other relational software, is explored extensively. The powerful Query Management Facility is covered to clarify the management of queries and report writing. The role of each of the Database 2 utilities is discussed, and other products that compliment Database 2 and are considered essential to effective use are examined. Finally, since the best way of learning about a product such as Database 2 is through working examples, real-world, detailed examples will be found throughout the book.

The Database Experts' Guide to Database 2 is the product of many years of practical experience in using Database 2 in large corporate environments. I feel that this pragmatic knowledge can be of exceptional value to all users of relational databases.

Although I am grateful to many individuals for their support, I would especially like to thank Gregory H. Willmore for his assistance in reviewing much of the printed material. Also, special thanks goes to my wife Chris and our two children, Eric and Jackie, in their never-ending support.

1

Introduction

Welcome to the exciting era of relational database management systems. The data processing environment has entered an information age. The number of people employed in the industrial sectors of our economy has steadily declined for some time now, while the number of people employed in the services sector has been increasing and will probably continue to increase for some time to come. The database management systems that carried the workload through the "industrial" years are not necessarily the same ones that will provide the horsepower for the future. Rapid changes are occurring in both software and hardware to meet this challenge. It is my intention to provide enough information and assistance so that many of the frustrations commonly experienced when pioneering a new era of data processing will be eliminated. In addition, the reader will be exposed to relational concepts and terms, including a brief overview of the relational model. IBM's mainframe relational software product, called Database 2 or commonly referred to as DB2, is the focal point of the book. Tips on implementations as well as exposure to DB2's architecture will prove vital to a successful installation. You will be able to gain firsthand knowledge from someone responsible for overseeing several successful DB2 installations. Guidelines and tips will be presented throughout all chapters of this book. You will learn not only the language used to communicate with the relational database product, but also how to utilize related products that I consider a must. We will investigate the security aspects of DB2, as well as backup and recovery concepts. Equally important, many aspects affecting performance from design through implementation will be discussed. In addition, following the conclusion of each chapter the reader will be given the opportunity to answer questions intended to reinforce the material presented in the previous chapter.

Why are relational systems receiving so much attention? Relational systems are gaining popularity not only with EDP (Electronic Data Processing) professionals, but also with various levels of non-EDP management. A new wave of management has infiltrated the top decision-making ranks of many businesses. This new wave has previously been exposed to computers for decision making through the influx of personal computers. As a result, change is not viewed as a problem but rather as a necessity in today's business environment. Never before in the business world has the survival of so many firms depended so much on an accurate and timely decision-making process, with an emphasis on the timely. Today's management recognizes that placing more information in the hands of the decision makers is leading to more timely and accurate business decisions. Top management also recognizes the need to reduce the amount of time and money spent on developing new systems while curtailing the upwardly spiraling cost of maintaining existing ones. As a result, more pressure is being placed on EDP management to develop more applications while at the same time attempting to keep the ongoing costs of these applications to a minimum.

Relational Systems

While EDP managers are often under pressure to take on new projects, they are also being directed to enter the era of relational systems. Relational systems are being portrayed as tools that will improve the productivity of the application developer by allowing prototypes to be built quickly prior to committing major resource expenditures. EDP managers have also recognized that in order to take on more projects, a certain portion of the trivial tasks must be delegated to educated users (non-data processing professionals), thus freeing EDP management's staffs to concentrate on the more difficult tasks at hand, such as distributed data processing. *Distributed data processing*, although not easily achieved, can be simply defined as multiple computer processors having the capability to communicate with a central host processor. This communication link is a two-way street. Data can be sent and received on all the processors. The host processor or processors serve as the communications vehicle to achieve this. You may be asking what this has to do with relational systems on the host? Let's take a look into what is going on in the hardware and software technology areas. Many software products are available which allow both host and personal computers to access data stored in a host-based relational database management system (DBMS). This data can be retrieved in a variety of formats. The data can then be used by a multitude of personal computer software packages. Some of these software packages available on the personal computers are also relational. A few of these software packages have the capability to retrieve data from the host-based relational DBMS and place it in their relational DBMS on the personal computer. Thus, half of the distributed processing picture has been in place for some time. Currently, a good deal of effort is being extended into not only retrieving data from the host computer but also sending to the host. It appears that concentrated efforts are being made to make relational database systems the vehicle through which distributed data processing will be done. Soon relational applications and prototypes developed on the personal computer will be easily moved to the host computer, where they can be distributed to an endless number of other processors. This will become a common occurrence. The introduction of the IBM 3090 series of host-based computers complements relational database management systems nicely. Relational software packages have been developed to take advantage of new advances in the hardware design. Much of the new operating system software, including DB2, is designed to take advantage of this hardware technology. Before discussing a particular host-based relational database product, let's take a look at the relational model. The relational model consists of a series of abstract principles pertaining to data. These principles include how data is structured, how data is to be manipulated and, last but not least, how to address data integrity. It can be thought of as a model against which other relational software products can be measured. The relational model has several functional characteristics, with the first being *data independence*. A relational database management system should free the application from any concern about data structure, data positioning, data sorting, rules, closeness of the data to one another, etc. It should let the application program remain free of all the rules imposed by the relational database management system and allow the application program to concentrate solely on processing the data retrieved. *Communicability amongst users* is another function of the relational model. The structure of the data should be simplified so that it can be easily understood. Access and manipulation of the data should be easily performed and understood. *Set processing* is another function of the model. The relational database management system should remove the one-record-at-a-time processing concept. A lot of application program code is executed repeatedly solely for the purpose of one-record-at-a-time processing. The one-record-at-a-time processing concept has forced application programs to execute program logic after each record is retrieved to check for access errors. Also removed is the need to include program logic to handle first or last record processing or the discarding of unneeded records. The one-record-at-a-time processing concept is probably one of the hardest concepts for people to grasp. Developers have been processing one record at a time for so long that they have a tendency to attempt to process relational in the same manner. It works, but they are failing to capitalize on the real potential of relational systems. Part of the problem is that Cobol, Fortran and PL/I support only one-record-at-a-time processing.

The relational model has a *theoretical foundation* based on proven mathematical theory, unlike many of the database systems developed in the past. As a result, relational systems are very precise and predictable. *Removal of navigational programming* and *allowing the relational system to do the work* are also objectives of the model. The relational database management system should provide end users the best access to the data. The methods of accessing the data could vary. If different access paths are possible, then the relational database management system should choose the most efficient access path to the data. In some cases the number of access paths can reach into the thousands. The relational software product should be capable of choosing the best access path or strategy, since it has access to the characteristics of the data and how it is physically stored. The hardware design and the software design should work in harmony to perform efficiently.

The relational model along with functional characteristics has structural characteristics, such as relations. A *relation* is that entity for which you wish to collect information. All information in the relation describes the entity. It includes all the attributes, attribute names or columns, all rows or tuples or records of the relation expressed in tables. These tables are not ordinary tables. They have well-defined characteristics and should not to be confused with arrays. A row consists of columns that contain factual data or attributes about the entity being described in the table. Unlike arrays, no ordering between and among the rows is required. The rows in a relation or table are not required to be physically stored in any specific order. If the application requires that the rows be in sequence, then the relational database management system should select the desired rows, sort the selected rows, and then present them to the user in the requested sequence. There is no ordering between columns in a row either. The sequence in which the columns are defined within a row should not have any impact on an application. Whether a column is defined as the first field in a record or the last should have no bearing on an application.

The structural components of a relation, in addition to rows and columns, include items such as primary keys and foreign keys. The primary key is a unique identifier within a relation or table. It consists of one or more columns that uniquely differentiate a particular row from all other rows in the relation. In the following diagram, for example, "class name," "course credits," and "number of students allowed" are columns containing attributes that describe the entity called "class." The entity "class" in this case is a relation. The primary key in the following diagram is "class name," and the data contained in this column uniquely identifies a particular class(row) as opposed to all other classes (rows) in the relation.

class name	course credits	number of students allowed
algebra	3	35
science	2	60
music	2	120
chemistry	5	20
art	3	35

The degree of the relation refers to the number of columns in the table. In the above diagram, each class has one and only one row in the table. The number of rows in the table make up the cardinality of the relation. For example, a class table with 400 classes has a cardinality of 400, since it has 400 rows. In the diagram above, the cardinality of the table is five. Inevitably, you will have certain columns that must take on a value within some predefined pool of values. This pool of values represents what is called the *domain* for a column. For example, a column containing test scores might only be allowed to take values in the range of 0 to 100. A column like "course credits" might only be allowed to take on values of 2, 3 or 5. It is the combination of attributes or values in columns that distinguishes a row from all other rows in the relation. Together, these columns form the primary key of the relation. If the value of column C in table A is required to match the value of a primary key column D in another table B, then the column C in table A is termed a *foreign key*. Every value contained in column C of table A must be equal to a value in Column D of table B, or column C must be null (not present). Although every foreign key has to be contained in a primary key, not every value of the primary key has to exist in a foreign key, where foreign keys exist.

Table A

Table B

Col H	Col K	Col C
h1	k1	d1
h2	k2	d2
h3	k3	d3
h4	k4	d3
h5	k5	—

Col D	Col G	Col E
d1	g1	e1
d2	g2	e2
d3	g3	e3
d4	g4	e4
d5	g5	e5

Let's take a look at another example. In Figure 1-1 we see two relations or tables. One table contains information about an entity named students (STUDENT) while the other table contains information about classes (CLASS). Each row of the STUDENT table contains five columns while each row in the CLASS table contains four columns. The STUDENT table has six rows in it. The STUDENT row with a Student ID equal to 00020 has three columns with no data present. These columns are commonly referred to as being null. This student may have been absent for the final test and is awaiting a makeup test. The data there for student 00020 is valid, it's just that not all the data values are known at this time. The "Class No." column of the STUDENT table has data values that also exist in the CLASS table. This type of column is called a foreign key. If data is present in this column, the data value must exist as the primary key in the other table. In this case the "Class No." column of the STUDENT table is a foreign key reflecting a value present as a primary key in the "Class No." column of the CLASS table.

So far when discussing relations or tables, we have been referring to something called a base table. The base table is the logical representation of the stored data. There are other types of tables you may encounter. The first is the view table, which consists of one or more base tables. View tables may be restrictive by restricting access to specific columns in a base table, or they can encompass columns located in multiple base or view tables. Another table you might encounter is a query table. A query table is the result of a query into a base or view table. You can take the result from a query and continue to perform relational operations on it since the result of a query against a table is also a table.

There is a set of operations that make up what is called relational algebra. These operations are defined ways of manipulating tables together to yield yet another table. The relational model is mathematical in nature. The relational mathematical operators are meant to be simple operations that provide well-defined results. Relational assignment is a term that applies to the relational model. It is the ability to assign the result of any relational expression to another value. Since the relational model and relational algebra are closed entities, you can take the results from one relational operation and apply yet another relational operation against it. For example, you can combine the contents of two small tables into a large table. You could then take the large table and subtract rows from yet another table. It is the closure principle of the relational model that allows you, at any time, to operate on a table and always get a table of the results. The relational expression can be as long as you like. Since the result is always a table, you can perform another operation on it. There are eight relational algebraic operations you can perform on tables. In the following algebraic operations, it is assumed that when manipulating more than one table, the columns used to relate the tables are defined over the same domain.

SELECTION: Selection allows you to retrieve specific *rows* from a table. Only the rows that meet a specified set of requirements are returned to the requestor. If you had a table of employees involved in sales, you could select

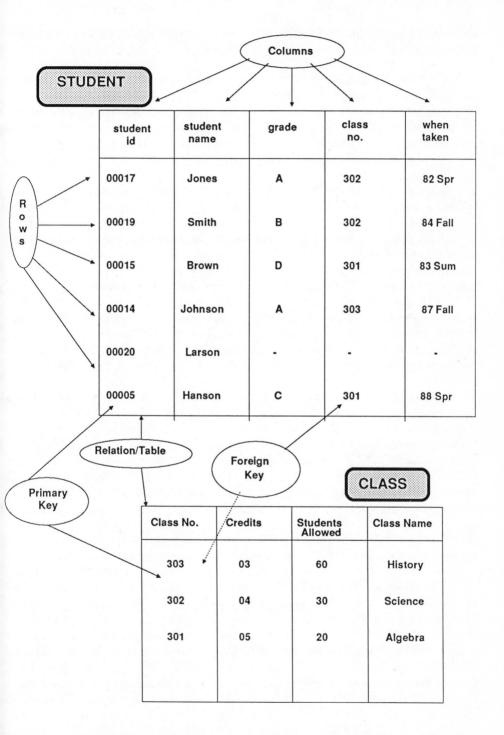

Figure 1-1 Relational Base Table Examples

only those rows from the relation where the salesperson is assigned a specific territory, like Northeast as seen in Figure 1-2.

PROJECTION: Projection allows you to retrieve certain *columns* from a table. If you had a table with four columns in it but you were only interested in three, you could retrieve just the three columns of interest and disregard the extra data. In Figure 1-3 we have an employee table with four columns, of which only three of the four are to be displayed in our results. Department number is to be discarded from the result.

CARTESIAN PRODUCT: A product is the multiplication of two or more tables. It does not produce any additional information. The multiplication is not the same as traditional math where you multiply one value times another yielding a third. Instead, each row of one table is combined with every row of another, one at a time. The resulting table has the same number of rows as the number of rows in the first table *times* the number of rows in the other tables. As seen in Figure 1-4A, the product of two tables produces many more rows. It is the product of the tables. As you might imagine, the results could potentially take up a lot of space and cause confusion. The Cartesian product is most commonly used in conjunction with other relational operations, as you will see in the case of the JOIN. Figure 1-4B shows a situation that might seem more practical.

UNION: This is where you take two or more tables over the same domain and combine them into one table. As you might guess, the tables need to have identical data types on the columns chosen for the union. For example, if you had 12 tables with identical data types, where each table contained historical data for one month, you could union all 12 tables into one table, producing a table containing historical data for an entire year. In Figure 1-5 two small tables each containing data for a specific department, are combined into one larger table.

INTERSECTION: The intersection operation allows you to find those rows in a table that correspond to rows in another table, as seen in Figure 1-6.

NATURAL JOIN: Consists of the Cartesian product followed by a selection followed by projection. In Figures 1-7A through 1-7C, we will go through the process of listing the salary and year-to-date (YTD) sales for employees in department 244. In Figure 1-7, we see that salary and year-to-date sales are in different tables. The first step is to take the Cartesian product of the two tables and thus produce a table as in Figure 1-7B. Next, select the rows from the table in Figure 1-7B where the employee's name equals the salesperson's name. These columns are the columns that match on the join condition. The rows selected are denoted by **. The results of this selection can be found in Figure 1-7C. In this table we apply the projection operation for just the columns we wanted (Employee, Salary, YTD Sales).

SELECTION

Salesperson	YTD Sales	Territory
Larson	80,000	Midwest
Black	90,000	Southeast
Parsons	50,000	Midwest
Smith	75,000	Southwest
Murphy	55,000	Northeast
Einerson	95,000	Northeast
Hughs	65,000	Southeast
Thompson	99,000	Northeast

Selecting rows from the above table where salesperson's territory must be equal to "Northeast" would produce the following results.

Salesperson	YTD Sales	Territory
Murphy	55,000	Northeast
Einerson	95,000	Northeast
Thompson	99,000	Northeast

Figure 1-2 Relational Model: SELECTION

PROJECTION

Employee	Dept	Salary	Bonus
Larson	244	35,000	2,000
Black	244	30,000	1,500
Parsons	244	45,000	2,250
Smith	244	60,000	3,500

Selecting employee, salary and bonus columns from the above table would give the following results.

Employee	Salary	Bonus
Larson	35,000	2,000
Black	30,000	1,500
Parsons	45,000	2,250
Smith	60,000	3,500

Figure 1-3 Relational Model: PROJECTION

PRODUCT

Col A	Col B	Col C	Col D
A1	B1	C1	D1
A2	B2	C2	D2
A3	B3	C3	D3
A4	B4	C4	D4

Table 1

Col E	Col F
E1	F1
E2	F2

Table 2

The product of table 1 and table 2 is 4 rows times 2 rows or 8 rows.
Every row in one table is combined with every row in the other table.
Thus the results would look like the following.

Col A	Col B	Col C	Col D	Col E	Col F
A1	B1	C1	D1	E1	F1
A1	B1	C1	D1	E2	F2
A2	B2	C2	D2	E1	F1
A2	B2	C2	D2	E2	F2
A3	B3	C3	D3	E1	F1
A3	B3	C3	D3	E2	F2
A4	B4	C4	D4	E1	F1
A4	B4	C4	D4	E2	F2

Figure 1-4A Relational Model: PRODUCT (Part 1)

PRODUCT

Employee	Dept	Salary	Bonus
Larson	244	35,000	2,000
Black	244	30,000	1,500
Parsons	244	45,000	2,250
Smith	244	60,000	3,500

Deptname	Deptmanager
Marketing	Jordan

Table 2

Table 1

The product of table 1 and table 2 is 4 rows times 1 row or still 4 rows.

Employee	Dept	Salary	Bonus	Deptname	Deptmanager
Larson	244	35,000	2,000	Marketing	Jordan
Black	244	30,000	1,500	Marketing	Jordan
Parsons	244	45,000	2,250	Marketing	Jordan
Smith	244	60,000	3,500	Marketing	Jordan

Figure 1-4B Relational Model: PRODUCT (Part 2)

UNION

Table 1	Employee	Dept	Salary	Bonus
	Larson	244	35,000	2,000
	Black	244	30,000	1,500
	Parsons	244	45,000	2,250
	Smith	244	60,000	3,500

Applying the union operator to table1 and table 2 defined over the same domain

Table 2	Employee	Dept	Salary	Bonus
	Murphy	245	37,000	2,700
	Einerson	245	39,000	3,700
	Hughs	245	45,000	4,200
	Thompson	245	66,000	6,600

Would produce the following results

Employee	Dept	Salary	Bonus
Larson	244	35,000	2,000
Black	244	30,000	1,500
Parsons	244	45,000	2,250
Smith	244	60,000	3,500
Murphy	245	37,000	2,700
Einerson	245	39,000	3,700
Hughs	245	45,000	4,200
Thompson	245	66,000	6,600

Figure 1-5 Relational Model: UNION

INTERSECTION

Employee
Sales
Table

Salesperson	Ytd Sales	Territory
Larson	80,000	Midwest
Black	90,000	Southeast
Parsons	50,000	Midwest
Smith	75,000	Southwest

Find employees in the Employee Salary Table that are in (intersect) the Employee Sales Table

Employee
Salary
Table

Employee	Dept	Salary	Bonus
Larson	244	35,000	2,000
Black	244	30,000	1,500
Parsons	244	45,000	2,250
Smith	244	60,000	3,500
Murphy	245	60,000	3,500
Einerson	245	65,000	3,750
Hughs	245	90,000	9,000
Thompson	245	99,000	9,750

Results
Table

Employee	Dept	Salary	Bonus
Larson	244	35,000	2,000
Black	244	30,000	1,500
Parsons	244	45,000	2,250
Smith	244	60,000	3,500

Figure 1-6 Relational Model: INTERSECTION

Employee
Sales
Table

Salesperson	Ytd Sales	Territory
Larson	80,000	Midwest
Black	90,000	Southeast
Parsons	50,000	Midwest
Smith	75,000	Southwest

List employee's salary and ytd sales if they work in Dept 244.
(Cartesian Product followed by selection followed by projection)

Employee
Sales
Table

Employee	Dept	Salary	Bonus
Larson	244	35,000	2,000
Black	244	30,000	1,500
Parsons	244	45,000	2,250
Smith	244	60,000	3,500
Murphy	245	60,000	3,500
Einerson	245	65,000	3,750
Hughs	245	90,000	9,000
Thompson	245	99,000	9,750

Figure 1-7A Relational Model: JOIN (Part 1)

Cartesian Product

Employee	Dept	Salary	Bonus	Salesperson	Ytd Sales	Territory
** Larson	244	35,000	2,000	** Larson	80,000	Midwest
Larson	244	35,000	2,000	Black	90,000	Southeast
Larson	244	35,000	2,000	Parsons	50,000	Midwest
Larson	244	35,000	2,000	Smith	75,000	Southwest
Black	244	30,000	1,500	Larson	80,000	Midwest
** Black	244	30,000	1,500	** Black	90,000	Southeast
Black	244	30,000	1,500	Parsons	50,000	Midwest
Black	244	30,000	1,500	Smith	75,000	Southwest
Parsons	244	45,000	2,250	Larson	80,000	Midwest
Parsons	244	45,000	2,250	Black	90,000	Southeast
** Parsons	244	45,000	2,250	** Parsons	50,000	Midwest
Parsons	244	45,000	2,250	Smith	75,000	Southwest
Smith	244	60,000	3,500	Larson	80,000	Midwest
Smith	244	60,000	3,500	Black	90,000	Southeast
Smith	244	60,000	3,500	Parsons	50,000	Midwest
** Smith	244	60,000	3,500	** Smith	75,000	Southwest
Murphy	245	60,000	3,500	Larson	80,000	Midwest
Murphy	245	60,000	3,500	Black	90,000	Southeast
Murphy	245	60,000	3,500	Parsons	50,000	Midwest
Murphy	245	60,000	3,500	Smith	75,000	Southwest
Einerson	245	65,000	3,750	Larson	80,000	Midwest
Einerson	245	65,000	3,750	Black	90,000	Southeast
Einerson	245	65,000	3,750	Parsons	50,000	Midwest
Einerson	245	65,000	3,750	Smith	75,000	Southwest
Hughs	245	90,000	9,000	Larson	80,000	Midwest
Hughs	245	90,000	9,000	Black	90,000	Southeast
Hughs	245	90,000	9,000	Parsons	50,000	Midwest
Hughs	245	90,000	9,000	Smith	75,000	Southwest
Thompson	245	99,000	9,750	Larson	80,000	Midwest
Thompson	245	99,000	9,750	Black	90,000	Southeast
Thompson	245	99,000	9,750	Parsons	50,000	Midwest
Thompson	245	99,000	9,750	Smith	75,000	Southwest

Figure 1-7B Relational Model: JOIN (Part 2)

JOIN

**SELECTION of rows that match on the join condition
(Employee column value = Salesperson column value)**

Employee	Dept	Salary	Bonus	Salesperson	Ytd Sales	Territory
Larson	244	35,000	2,000	Larson	80,000	Midwest
Black	244	30,000	1,500	Black	90,000	Southeast
Parsons	244	45,000	2,250	Parsons	50,000	Midwest
Smith	244	60,000	3,500	Smith	75,000	Southwest

followed by PROJECTION

Employee	Salary	Ytd Sales
Larson	35,000	80,000
Black	30,000	90,000
Parsons	45,000	50,000
Smith	60,000	75,000

Final Results

Figure 1.7.2

Figure 1-7C Relational Model: JOIN (Part 3)

DIFFERENCE: Subtract from one table the rows equivalent to the rows in a second table. In Figure 1-8 we see the results of subtracting one table from another.

DIVIDE: The relational divide consists of dividing a column from one table (divisor) into another table (dividend) to produce results (quotient). In Figure 1-9 you see Table 1 with two rows. The data values are Midwest and Northwest. Next you see Table 2 with columns Dept and Territory. Find the columns in Table 2 that have all of the attributes contained in Table 1. As indicated, only Departments 244 and 246 have territories of Midwest *and* Northwest.

In the relational model, no attribute or column participating in the primary key of a base relation is allowed to accept null values. Every table has a primary key. The primary key provides the only row level addressing mechanism within the relational model. You can reach any piece of data in any table by knowing the table's primary key and by naming the primary key attributes. It is totally independent of hardware and access methods.

Referential integrity is a term used with primary and foreign keys. If a base table includes a foreign key matching the primary key of some other base table, then every value for the foreign key must be equal to the value of the primary key in some row of another table, or it must be null in order to have referential integrity. If you recall, the domain for a column is the range of attributes that a column can contain. If the domain for the primary key is created first, then the relational system could ensure that when creating foreign keys the domain of the foreign key can be known, although this is not a requirement of the relational model. *User-defined integrity* is a must for future relational systems to provide. The relational product should allow users to define integrity aspects that are germane to their business needs. By allowing users to define the domain for some columns within the relational system, the system could then maintain domain integrity on the specific columns defined.

The last feature of relational systems to be discussed before discussing DB2 is a new computer language developed specifically for relational database systems. It is called SQL (Structured Query Language). SQL is considered a fourth-generation language, replacing in part third-generation languages such as COBOL, FORTRAN, PL/I, etc. The SQL language is very different from third-generation languages in that it allows the user to process many rows or records in one execution. The third-generation languages can only process one record at a time. Entire application programs have in some cases been replaced by a single SQL statement. Yet another generation of languages is on the horizon — fifth-generation languages. Companies such as Artificial Intelligence Corporation, with its product "Intellect" are rapidly addressing this area. Fifth-generation languages operate similarly to fourth-generation languages with one exception. They are considered "natural" languages. What this implies is that the doctor will request data in a language familiar to his or her medical profession. Meanwhile, the accountant will request data in terms familiar to an accountant. Thus the application systems

DIFFERENCE

Table 1

Employee	Dept	Salary	Bonus
Larson	244	35,000	2,000
Black	244	30,000	1,500
Parsons	244	45,000	2,250
Smith	244	60,000	3,500

Subtract the rows in table 1 from the rows in table 2 and show the difference from table 2.

Table 2

Employee	Dept	Salary	Bonus
Larson	244	35,000	2,000
Black	244	30,000	1,500
Parsons	244	45,000	2,250
Smith	244	60,000	3,500
Murphy	245	37,000	2,700
Einerson	245	39,000	3,700
Hughs	245	45,000	4,200
Thompson	245	66,000	6,600

Would yield the following set.

Employee	Dept	Salary	Bonus
Murphy	245	37,000	2,700
Einerson	245	39,000	3,700
Hughs	245	45,000	4,200
Thompson	245	66,000	6,600

Figure 1-8 Relational Model: DIFFERENCE

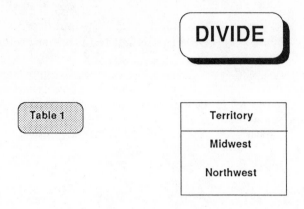

Territory
Midwest
Northwest

Table 1

Divide Table 1 into Table 2.   What depts in Table 2
have the same attributes as the column specified in table 1.
Dept 244 and 246 below are the only depts that have territory
equal to Midwest and Northwest.

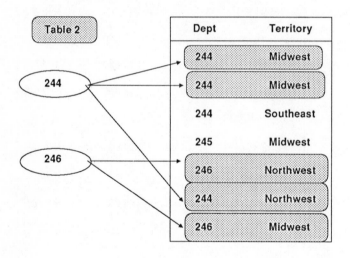

Would produce the following results

Dept
244
246

Figure 1-9 Relational Model: DIVIDE

of the future will seem very user friendly and require less end user training, since the user will be accessing data in terms relevant to his or her profession. You will see the natural language taken even further. On the not-too-distant horizon, the natural language will be expanded for verbal communication. You will be able to pose questions to a computer as part of a conversation with the machine.

Questions:

1. A relation or _____ describes an entity.
2. Attributes or _____ make up a record or _____.
3. The term that describes the column that uniquely distinguishes one row from all others is called a _____.
4. A column that contains no data is said to be _____.
5. The results of a query is always another _____.
6. The relational operator that allows you to combine one or more tables over the same domain is called _____.
7. The relational operator that allows you to retrieve a smaller subset of rows from a table is called _____.
8. The relational operator that allows you to retrieve a smaller subset of columns from a table is called _____.

True or False:

9. A column defined as a foreign key must always contain data.
10. SQL is a fourth-generation data processing language.
11. Relational database software products can run on personal computers as well as host computers.
12. The degree of a relation that has 400 rows and 3 columns per row is 1,200.

Answers:

1. Table
2. Columns, row
3. Primary key
4. Null
5. Table
6. Union
7. Selection
8. Projection
9. False, it may be null!
10. True
11. True
12. False, 3

2

IBM's Database 2

IBM's Database 2, commonly referred to as DB2, became generally available in the fall of 1984. DB2 was marketed as a relational database management system for the MVS operating system. It uses tables to represent the data that it manages. At the time, DB2 was considered an alternative to developing relational systems on personal computers. DB2 had the most potential of any host-based relational product as far as obtaining distributed processing. DB2 picked up where personal computers left off. It provided data sharing and relational development services to large groups of users at a time when relational systems on personal computers were limited to personal computer networks.

The early design of DB2 centered around providing relational development services for small personal applications on the host computer. Early users found the first release to contain many restrictions. The DB2 Catalog, which we will discuss later in this chapter, seemed to be the biggest bottleneck of all, in that it limited the number of concurrent users allowed. Sorting techniques were extremely inefficient and time-consuming. Other restrictions centered in its utility-based service programs. Early releases allowed for the reloading or refreshing of data in tables but required an extraordinary amount of work. One approach caused excessive logging of meaningless information, while another caused DB2 tables, including the security to use them, to be dropped.

Some users were lucky enough to circumvent the data load problem with a special execution of the reorganization utility. Developers also found that it was very difficult to manage the free space contained in tables when applications performed frequent insertions, because in Release 1, DB2's free space specification was predetermined and fixed. As a result, applications performing frequent insertions were forced into reorganizations more frequently than desired. Fortunately, all of the prior restrictions along with others not listed were addressed with Release 2 of DB2. Release 2 was categorized as a badly needed performance release. The DB2 Catalog, which was the source of many of the concurrency problems, was restructured. Performance was improved significantly. Options were introduced for specifying VSAM free space to reduce the need for frequent data reorganizations in many cases. Utilities that once required tables to be dropped prior to being refreshed with new data could now take advantage of the VSAM REUSE option.

Release 2

In Release 2, the row selection process performed by DB2 was also improved significantly. One of the requirements in the relational model is to have the relational DBMS system determine the access path to the data because it knows the characteristics of the data and how the data is stored. The portion of DB2 that performs this function was termed the DB2 Optimizer. The DB2 Optimizer has the task of analyzing every SQL statement and determining the best data access strategy. Users soon found out that the DB2 Optimizer had difficulty in determining the best access strategy at times. Release 2 was the first attempt at improving the access strategy process. The optimizer's decisions have a direct effect on your performance. In additon, after Release 2, DB2 tables were much easier to migrate to other DB2 systems.

Until Release 2, much of the development was done on relatively small and simple applications. The advent of Release 2 fueled development. The size and the complexity of the applications increased. Once again performance became a major concern, but on a more isolated level. Applications unable to attain the use of indexes were forced to scan entire tables causing unacceptable response times. Date- and time-sensitive applications found working with the existing data types for columns awkward. At the time, DB2 did not support arithmetic operations, conversions, or manipulations on dates and times.

Release 3

The introduction of Release 3 brought more needed function to the relational product. Release 3 allows users to capitalize on expanded storage available in the IBM 3090 Model 300E and 600E series. New data types (Date, Time, and Timestamp) and related operations for these new data types were added to assist users in ordering, converting, and manipulating date and time values. One of the important, but maybe not necessarily obvious, enhancements was the commitment to SQL consistency across multiple environments. By having a common interface to relational systems across processors, we are one step closer to obtaining distributed data processing.

The switch to relational application development is occurring very rapidly — perhaps a little too rapidly. Developers that arbitrarily picked DB2 for every application found themselves experiencing performance problems. They found themselves having to make a choice of either reverting back to a traditional DBMS for predictable performance or forging ahead with DB2 in the hope that new releases would address their problems. With each new release, DB2 has become a viable option for more and more types of applications. Soon, DB2 will begin to take on the characteristics of a major database management product capable of processing the type of applications that were traditionally targeted for other database management systems such as IMS.

How will applications developed on traditional DBMS systems migrate to DB2? In three words I would say, "Not very easily." This is not an easy task to complete. Software packages that allow traditional DBMS applications to bridge to relational are currently in high demand. Although the demand is high, it might be years before any complete bridge is seen, if ever. Even if one is developed, it may not be equipped to handle all types of applications. One of the biggest problems is the complexity that surrounds many of the applications developed in the traditional DBMS systems. These applications may not be suitable for relational. This has caused many users to look into the emergence of application code generators, some being capable of interfacing with DB2. Application code generators could play an even greater role in the migration. Before you invest too heavily in application code generators, keep in mind that applications of the future may not require as much, or in some instances any, program code. Much of the application program code today is written to sustain domain and referential integrity. It will only be a matter of time before DB2 will maintain both as part of its database services.

Without any bridge, an application integrated with other applications could go through several phases of migration before it becomes totally free of the traditional DBMS system. Figure 2-1 shows the phases an application might go through in conversion from a traditional DBMS to DB2. In Phase 1, an application has been identified as a candidate for relational. In Phase 2, you will see the data existing in both the traditional DBMS and DB2. This data will be maintained on the traditional DBMS but not on DB2. The data in the tables will be refreshed periodically from the traditional DBMS. The relational data will be used to satisfy the ad hoc requests of users as well as provide user training on relational methods. In Phase 3, maintenance applications will be revised to maintain the data in both DBMS systems. Applications on the traditional DBMS and the relational DBMS require that the data be kept up to date. Phase 3, or parallel processing, will continue until all the related applications needing current up-to-date data have been migrated. In Phase 4,

Phase 1

Identify applications
dependent on applica-
tion being targeted for
the relational DBMS.

| Traditional DBMS | Inquiry |
| | Maint | Traditional Database |

Phase 2

Place database in
relational system
for inquiry and user
education/training.

| Relational DBMS | Inquiry | Relational Database |

| Traditional DBMS | Inquiry | |
| | Maint | Traditional Database |

Phase 3

Change applications to
maintain databases in
both while related
applications are
migrated. Best if
this phase is short
lived due to duplication
of maintenance func-
tions

| Relational DBMS | Inquiry | |
| | Maint | Relational Database |

| Traditional DBMS | Inquiry | |
| | Maint | Traditional Database |

Phase 4

Remove traditional
database system when
all related applications
have been migrated or
have become obsolete.

| Relational DBMS | Inquiry | |
| | Maint | Relational Database |

Figure 2-1 Migration to Relational Phases

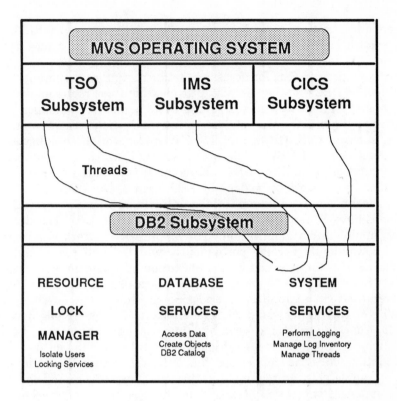

Figure 2-2 DB2 Subsystem Components

the final phase, the applications left on the traditional DBMS have either been migrated or become obsolete. All processing on the old system is terminated, and the application then resides only on the relational DBMS.

DB2's architecture is designed to interface with several subsystems in the MVS operating system environment. Unlike database management systems of the past, DB2 can be accessed by all major transaction processors. This includes TSO, IMS, and CICS. A table can be accessed by all three concurrently. Therefore, DB2 can serve as a database manager for a larger group of users than traditional database management systems. Now you have a choice as to which transaction processor you wish to use. On the other hand, you also have to make a choice, whereas in the past your options may have been limited. In the past, IMS and CICS served as the main transaction managers for many installations. TSO is now posed to handle transaction processing that at one time was processed strictly on IMS and CICS. TSO cannot be overlooked. Many of the products that will become an integral part of your environment run only under TSO. Many of the user's ad hoc requests are easiest to resolve through products developed to be executed under TSO.

DB2's architecture, as illustrated in Figure 2-2, can be separated into three areas. These areas consist of a resource lock manager, a database services manager, and a system services manager. The lock manager (IRLM — IMS Resource Lock Manager) is also used by DB2 to isolate DB2 users from each other and DB2 resources from other MVS subsystems. The database services manager provides services for accessing data, creating relational objects, and managing the DB2 Catalog. It also provides data set management, buffer management, and utility functions. The system services manager provides logging as well as performing services to maintain connections to other subsystems, such as IMS, CICS, and TSO. When one of these subsystems requests the services of DB2, a "thread" is created, which is a connection between an application and the DB2 subsystem. It is initiated when an application requests some work to be done by DB2, such as the execution of a user's SQL statement. A thread is maintained until the application terminates and all changes have either been committed or rolled back. DB2 records all table changes made by an application. The application determines when the changed rows should become permanently updated and made available to other applications for processing. An application may determine that a unit of work has been performed representing a logical break in processing. Such might be the case in an application updating multiple orders for shipping. The processing of each order could represent a unit of work. It might be determined that once an order has been updated, it should be released as soon as possible to other applications for shipping, but only after the entire order has been updated. Once the application has determined that the updates to an order are complete, it can request that the unit of work be committed. Several things happen as the result of this. The changes made for the last unit of work, or order in this case, become permanent and the changed rows are now available to others. When changes are committed, DB2 logs the changes to its log files. This point in time represents a recoverable unit of work. Likewise, if the application determines that the changes are not to be kept (maybe the order is incomplete), it can request that all the changes done during this unit of work, or order, be rolled back to the last commit point or in this case to the last order processed successfully. Thus, any changes committed by an application are written out to the DB2 Logs and will be present in the advent of a recovery of the table.

DB2 as a database manager is required to manage data that is defined to it. DB2 uses tables to manage the data that it keeps. In addition to keeping track of every object defined in the relational system, information is recorded pertaining to who can create new objects or access the existing ones. All of these tables are grouped into what is known as the DB2 Catalog or the DB2 System Catalog. The DB2 Catalog contains approximately 30 tables.

Let's identify what some of these objects are that have to be managed by the database management system. The objects include buffer pools, storage groups, databases, tablespaces, tables, indexes, views, synonyms, and plans. DB2 keeps track of not only the objects just mentioned in the DB2 Catalog, but also who has access and control over these objects. In Chapter 3 we will discuss the SQL (Structure Query Language) statements that create these objects. The DB2 Catalog is very comprehensive, in that it contains all the information necessary to manage the objects previously mentioned. An IBM product, which we will discuss in detail in Chapter 5, can reconstruct all SQL statements used to create objects by accessing the DB2 Catalog. Information that DB2 needs internally is also contained in the DB2 Catalog.

As you would expect of any good database manager, there are many utilities available to assist in managing data. Execution of various DB2 utilities, such as Copy, Recovery, Reorganization, Load, Runstats, and Stospace, will either retrieve or update information contained in columns in one or more of the DB2 Catalog tables. If information from utility executions were only available in reports, these reports would be the only source for information. Since information from utilities is recorded in the DB2 Catalog tables, all authorized persons can view the information, including DB2. DB2 makes use of this information in its management of data. This information is valuable to DB2 when determining data access strategies and recovering tables. Recovering a table in DB2 is a simple task to perform. DB2 keeps an inventory of all changes made to a table and retains information about backups of tables. You tell DB2 where your table resides and how you want it recovered; DB2 knows the rest of the information necessary to perform the recovery. The DB2 Catalog tables are unlike normal tables, in that SQL operations to perform inserts, updates, or deletes are not allowed. Instead, the DB2 Catalog is updated indirectly through special SQL data definition statements ("create," "alter," and "drop"), which we will cover in the next chapter.

Let's pursue the DB2 objects mentioned earlier beginning with buffer pools. Buffer pools are areas of storage used to temporarily store data being manipulated in tablespaces and indexspaces (including the DB2 Catalog tables and indexes). They are also used by DB2 when building temporary tables to store data resulting from sorts and joins. There are only four buffer pools available. They are BP0, BP1, BP2 and BP32K. Earlier it was mentioned that the DB2 Catalog consists of tables also. DB2 uses BP0 to store its data pages. A page represents a block of either 4K or 32K bytes of storage. A 4K page represents approximately 4056 bytes of storage (4096 byte VSAM control interval minus the DB2 overhead). Each DB2 installation can determine their own buffer pool use strategy. Performance-critical applications can process in their own buffer pools such as BP1 or BP2. I strongly recommend that you stay away from the BP32K buffer pool for performance reasons. All buffers in a buffer pool are the same size. Thus every page in the BP32K buffer pool is 32K. Since rows will not span pages, look closely at any application requiring 32K page sizes and attempt to redesign the table so that the row length is reduced to 4K. Use of the 32K buffer pools could have an adverse effect on both your performance and storage usage. They should be used only if no other alternatives are available.

The next item to be discussed is the storage group (see Figure 2-3). Storage groups represent groups of DASD volumes. The same DASD volume may be included in more than one storage group. You can also define more than one storage group per DB2 system. The storage group names you use are unique to a DB2 System. They allow you to manage space as well as provide a means of categorizing data on the DB2 system. The ability to access a storage group can be controlled so that isolation of production data from test data is pos-

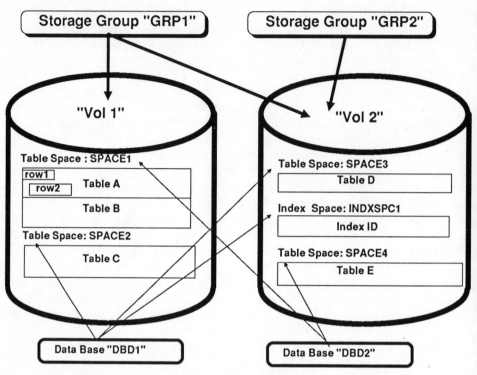

Storage Groups: "GRP1" and "GRP2"
        "GRP1" contains volumes "Vol1" and "Vol2"
        "GRP2" contains volume   "Vol2" only
Data Base "DBD1" contains:

        Tablespace: "SPACE2" in Storage Group "GRP1"
        Table: "C"
        Tablespace: "SPACE3" in Storage Group "GRP2"
        Table: "D"
        Indexspace: "INDXSPC3" in Storage Group "GRP2"
        Index: "ID"
Data Base "DBD2" contains:
        Tablespace: "SPACE1" in Storage Group "GRP1"
        Tables: "A" and "B:
        Tablespace: "SPACE4" in Storage Group "GRP2"
        Table: "E"

Figure 2-3 Storage Group Structure

sible. They can also allow you to organize data into different entities of your business. Data can be managed so that data belonging to the Payroll department or data in a major Customer Order Entry system are isolated and managed more effectively. Storage group usage is optional. The ability to generically specify volumes has allowed users to be removed from the detailed level of tracking volume serial numbers. Developers are also removed from having to come up with the VSAM control information necessary to create tablespace datasets. DASD volumes are now being managed at a much higher level of control. IBM's Data Facility Hierarchical Storage Manager (DFHSM) can play a major role in dataset management on volumes used in storage groups. Volumes can be added and removed from DB2 circulation through storage groups. Removing a DASD volume from a storage group will not delete or remove tablespaces on the removed volume, but no new datasets can be added to the volume. If a dataset is deleted and reallocated, it will automatically be placed on another volume defined in the storage group. Because storage groups can be managed, including who can access them, they can play a very important role in structuring your DB2 installation. Listed below are a variety of ideas on storage group management. Any combination or all of these could play a factor in your storage group management policy.

1. Distinguish between various levels of data sharing
   a. Highly shared
   b. Highly shared and distributed
   c. Limited sharing (Such as a department or group basis)
   d. Nonshared
   e. Personal
2. Distinguish data as it moves through your organization
   a. Feasibility prototypes
   b. Personal test data
   c. Distributed processing test data
   d. System test data
   e. Production parallel data
   f. Production permanent
   g. Distributed processing production data
3. Distinguish between different divisions within or throughout your organization
   a. Purchasing data
   b. Research data
   c. Accounting data
   d. Engineering data
   e. Corporate data
   f. Sales Branches
   g. Research Center
   h. Marketing Office

DB2 tables are stored in datasets called tablespaces. Indexes can be created to improve access to tables. Indexes are stored in datasets called indexspaces.

Tables, tablespaces, indexes, and indexspaces can all be associated by what is called the database. The database takes on a little different role in DB2 than in other DBMSs. It does not represent any physical component of a structure. Instead, it serves merely as a means of identifying a group of related tables, tablespaces, indexes, and indexspaces. The database can operationally control these objects from the standpoint of starting and stopping access. Each database name is unique per DB2 System. Certain privileges can be granted at this level rather than at the table or tablespace level. The creator of a database has control over everything associated to it.

The tablespace, where tables are placed, cannot be created unless the associated database is created first. Creation of a tablespace actually causes a physical dataset to be created on DASD. These datasets are specially formatted VSAM ESDS (Entry Sequenced Data Sets). Many of the utilities provided with DB2 operate on the tablespace dataset level. Tablespace datasets are organized into blocks (hopefully 4K, not 32K), called pages. Each page will hold one or more table rows. Once again, note that a table row can not span pages. Thus, if your table row exceeds 4K bytes, you will find the next largest page size allowed by DB2 to be 32K. The same tablespace name can be defined more than once per DB2 System, but only once within a specific database. The fully qualified name of a tablespace consists of Databasename.Tablespacename. In the situation of PAYROLL.HISTORY, PAYROLL is the name of the database and HISTORY is the name of the tablespace. This qualification is unique per DB2 system. If storage groups are being used, then the tablespace dataset will be created on one of the volumes defined in the specified storage group, otherwise you will have to give it the VSAM catalog to use and allocate the dataset yourself. One last comment about tablespaces: You could, if allowed at your installation, create a table without specifying a tablespace; DB2 will automatically generate a tablespace for you. This works but you will get some defaults in the tablespace definition that may be undesirable. We will discuss this more when discussing the Create Tablespace SQL statement.

Before a table can be created, the tablespace into which it is to be placed must already exist. It is highly recommended that you put only one table in each tablespace. There are several reasons for this. First, certain SQL statements may scan an entire tablespace to satisfy a user's request. If several tables are defined in the same tablespace, each table would be scanned, not just the desired table. Also, the tablespace is the lowest unit of start and stop. Starting or stopping a tablespace will start and stop all of the tables in the table space. Similarly, recovering or reorganizing the tablespace will impact all users of tables defined in the same tablespace. The more tables in a tablespace, the more impact one user has on others accessing tables in the same tablespace. By setting up guidelines of only one table per tablespace, you are converting tablespace scans into one table scans. You may also want to give serious consideration to restricting or eliminating the default database usage and not allowing DB2 developers to automatically generate tablespaces.

The table name by itself is not required to be unique within a DB2 System. The fully qualified name of a table consists of Creator.Tablename. Ten students taking a DB2 development class could create ten tables with identical names as long as each table had a different creator specified. Any time you access a table for which you are not listed as the creator, you must specify the creator as a prefix.

Let's review the object naming schemes for tablespaces and tables. The fully qualified name for a tablespace is Databasename.Tablespacename. The fully qualified name for a table is Creator.Tablename. Remembering this will help you avoid a lot of confusion later on. In DB2, it is possible to force the rows in a table to be unique. This is done by the next object, called the index.

Indexes are created in DB2 for three basic reasons: performance, uniqueness, and sequencing. Indexes cannot be created unless the table they reference has been created. An index can allow an application to access rows in a table without having to scan an entire tablespace. This will greatly improve performance. An index can also force uniqueness among the rows of a table. In order to force the primary key of a table to be unique, you must create an index specifying that the primary key columns are to be unique. An application attempting to insert or change the primary key to a value that already exists in another row will receive an error message stating that the insert or update will violate the index unique specification. The application's request is rejected. Indexes are also created to force rows to be stored in a specified physical sequence. This is not done automatically by DB2. It is not a requirement to have the rows stored in any particular sequence. This type of index is termed a clustered index. If an application needs to process a table sequentially by the columns specified in the clustered index, the application will not have to retrieve randomly from all over the tablespace to get the desired rows. The probability that the next row desired is in a page in the buffer pool is greatly increased. Thus, the amount of I/O processing is reduced.

It is possible to have multiple indexes on a table. In general, indexes increase retrieval performance at the expense of maintenance. If every column of a table is indexed, it is possible to spend more time maintaining the indexes than the actual table. You may not want to create an index for applications that run infrequently because of the expense of always having to maintain a seldom used index. It is possible to create an index for a seldom-used application before the application begins and delete the index after the application completes. Index creation at the time of table definition creation, however, is much more efficient than doing so after the data has been loaded into the table. The creation of an index is very similar to the creation of a table. Tables exist in tablespaces and indexes exist in indexspaces. There is one major difference in how this comes about. *You* create tablespaces for tables and *DB2* creates indexspaces for indexes automatically. DB2 will generate a unique indexspace name for you.

A very important point to note is how index usage is determined. As of the time of this writing, you have no direct control over index usage. DB2's optimizer has the final say in determining the access strategy. You could have the best of intentions in defining usable indexes only to find out that the optimizer decided not to use them. With an unused index, instead of improving performance, you may have decreased it by scanning a tablespace and maintaining an unuseable index. We will discuss later how to determine if an index will be utilized. Your options are limited. You could drop the index if not used and live with poor performance or attempt to get the optimizer to use the index. Getting the optimizer to use the index could vary from just restructuring the SQL statement to redesigning the entire application. In theory the optimizer sounds great because it knows the characteristics of your data and how the data is stored. Unfortunately, it isn't able to come up with the best decision every time. This unpredictability has caused confusion and concern. Index usage is a major concern of developers. Large applications unable to capitalize on indexes will struggle while running on DB2. Once index usage becomes predictable, DB2 will indeed be able to shoulder the bulk of the application development being done on the other database management systems used today.

Like the database, a view is not something that physically resides on DASD as do the tablespace, table, and index. A view is defined only in the DB2 Catalog and serves the purpose of providing an alternative to accessing tables directly. It is similar, conceptually, to the logical database in IMS. A view can be restrictive by limiting the rows and/or the columns that can be extracted from a table. For example, if Salary was a column in your table, you could restrict access to Salary by leaving it out of the view. Thus, by allowing applications to process against the view instead of the base table you are assured that Salary data is still confidential. If new columns are added to a base table, applications processing the view (not sensitive to the new columns) are unaffected, assuming the columns added to the base table allow for null values. Views can also be used to represent several tables joined together. The user is unaware in his or her request that several base tables had to be accessed.

The last DB2 object to be discussed is the Synonym. Synonyms are created by an individual for his or her own use. They allow you to refer to a specific table by another name. Synonyms allow you to change the table name you wish to specify in your SQL statements. For example, let's take a table with the name AZRTZKKXEEKBEILMKO. Would you like to have to remember a table name like that? Instead, by creating a synonym of A for table AZRTZKKXEEKBEILMKO, you can now reference that table simply as A in your SQL query statements. Synonyms also allow you to access someone else's table without having to specify the table creator. For example, creating a synonym TAB01 for table AAA.TAB01 (where AAA is the creator of the table) will allow you to access table AAA.TAB01 simply as TAB01 in your SQL statements. Lets take this thought one step farther. Suppose you have two tables where AAA.TAB01 is the test table and BBB.TAB01 represents the production table. You can use the same SQL query statements to access the production table or the test table simply by changing the synonym TAB01 to point to a different table. One last comment about synonyms — you cannot create a synonym with the same name as a table you have created. In other words, you cannot have a synonym TAB01 if you also have a table named TAB01.

In the following scenario let's assume that users AAA and BBB each created a table called TAB01. Assuming you are user CCC and you wish to process both tables with the same select:

- CREATE SYNONYM TAB01 FOR AAA.TAB01
- SELECT COL1, COL2, COL3 FROM TAB01
- The above select SELECT will access data in table AAA.TAB01 for columns COL1, COL2 and COL3
- DROP SYNONYM TAB01
- CREATE SYNONYM TAB01 FOR BBB.TAB01
- If you issue the SELECT again, you will be accessing data in table BBB.TAB01 for columns COL1, COL2 and COL3.

An object not yet discussed, called the PLAN, pertains basically to application programming so we will discuss it in the application programming chapter.

In summary, DB2 provides facilities that allow you to manage system resources such as storage groups, buffer pools, and DB2 logs. It also gives you the capability to control access to development functions, such as who can create databases, tablespaces, tables, views, and indexes. It allows creators of these objects the ability to control who can access them. DB2 also provides utilities to perform backup and recovery functions. DB2 contains an object dictionary called the DB2 Catalog, which has a record of all objects defined to the DB2 system and who is authorized to access them. DB2 allows you to perform relational operations on tables.

Now that we have identified what is included with DB2, let's take a look at some installation issues that need to be addressed prior to the DB2 installation.

This is not an exhaustive list of items, but is simply included as a set of topics that must be addressed. Since every installation will be a little different, you will want to replace or build upon these issues.

- DASD — DB2 will require slightly more storage than your traditional DBMS because of the DB2 Catalog table allocations. Over estimate your calculations for the DB2 Catalog tables. An expansion of any of these tables will potentially stop your entire operation.
- RACF protection — If you are using IBM's Resource Access Control Facility (RACF) you will want to determine what kind of security is required for tablespace datasets. Datasets can be protected by DB2 when under DB2 control, but what about the situations when the tablespace or database might be stopped? RACF or a similar system may be needed in these situations.
- Determine DFHSM usage — If you are using IBM's Data Facility Hierarchical Storage Manager, you should decide whether you want to have DB2 data volumes under its control and, if so, in what manner. Currently, when a migrated tablespace dataset is requested, the application gets a SQL

return code and has to take action. This may not be desirable. Should application programs abend because the dataset being accessed was migrated?

- Problem resolution — If you have a problem resolution scheme in process today, you will want to determine if the DB2 problem-solving process will fit the same scheme. DB2 can be used by developers with greatly varying skills. Do you direct users/developers to the Information Center? DB2 Administrators? DB2 may require altering your current methods.
- Determine operational support for DB2. Unless you are getting rid of work, your staff will increase to support DB2.
- What subsystems will be attached to DB2? IMS? CICS?
- Operation procedures need to be reviewed? DB2 is different from other data base management systems, in that DB2 *has* to be operational to perform backups using the DB2 utilities. How is DB2 availability going to be handled, since it is tied into IMS, CICS, and TSO, and they each might have different availability schedules?
- Set up backups for the DB2 Catalog tables. Who and when should they be run? DB2's operation centers around the DB2 Catalog.
- Determine who can develop. Do you want a controlled environment initially? When will you relax the controls, if ever?
- Determine application development support. Undoubtedly, you will have people developing their first application and need assistance. Will you hold design reviews?
- Determine user support? Is your Information Center trained and staffed to handle the additional load?
- Determine method/products needed to migrate data into DB2 from your exiting files. DXT Data Extract is an IBM product available to assist in data transferring. Initially you will find tables loaded out to DB2 from your current DBMS where ad hoc queries can be performed.
- Education on DB2 development and usage. Are you going to design your own classes, purchase, or attend vendors? What kinds of classes do you need?
  - introduction
  - development
  - DB2 administration related functions
- Determine who and how backup and recovery functions will be performed on application tablespaces. Backup and recovery functions are not nearly as complex as those in other DBMS systems.
- Develop disaster backup policy. How do you get a DB2 system intact to your disaster recovery site?
- Determine how and who is to handle DB2 Security and authorizations:
  - for application development
  - for production data access
  - for DB2 administration
- Determine TSO userid strategy. Will you allow system implementation under a personal TSO userid? Generic userid? If generic or functional TSO userids are your preference, how do you address accountability for multiple

users using the same TSO userid? TPX (Terminal Productivity Executive) is a product by DUQUESNE Systems that assists in addressing this area.
* Determine what other products are needed and who is to support them? (QMF, DBEDIT, DBMAUI — all offered by IBM)
* Determine strategy for access to and from mini/microprocessors and DB2.
* Determine storage group use strategy.
* Determine how to distinguish test from production, noncritical from critical, and shared from nonshared data. Can they be on the same DB2 system?
* Determine how to manage temporary data as might be the case from QMF's SAVE DATA.
* Guidelines and procedures for moving DB2 objects from test into production.
* Determine naming standards for DB2 objects.
    — storage groups
    — databases
    — tablespaces
    — tables
    — indexes
    — views
    — plans
* Develop or purchase performance monitoring tools. IBM's DB2PM?
* Determine and set DB2 lock limits. The installation can control the amount of resources that an application can control.
* Determine first major application and track cautiously. Determine if you want to keep DB2 application objects separate from existing environments.
    — programs
    — ISPF dialog panels, messages, skeletons etc.
    — CLISTS
    — DCLGENs verses COBOL 01 levels
    — transaction classes
* Determine procedures to implement applications that cross transaction managers. Such would be the case if a portion of the application runs under TSO and another portion runs under IMS or CICS. Do you have an implementation process that can integrate IMS/CICS/TSO?

Questions:

1. The unit of recovery is at the _____ level.
2. _____ are created to improve performance.
3. DB2 keeps track of all the objects it has to manage in the _____.
4. A connection from a subsystem to DB2 due to an application requesting the services of DB2 is called a _____.
5. _____ are used to temporarily hold pages of data until committed or rolled back.
6. DB2 tablespaces are allocated in 4K or 32K increments called _____.

7. A _____ index prevents any two rows from having the same primary key.

8. A _____ index is used to order the rows of a table into a specific physical sequence.

<u>True or False:</u>

9. DB2 can be accessed by more than one subsystem (TSO,IMS,CICS).
10. DB2 supports domain and/or referential integrity.
11. Tablespace name is unique per DB2 system.
12. Databases are a unit of start and stop.

<u>Answers:</u>

1. Tablespace
2. Indexes
3. DB2 Catalog or DB2 System Catalog or System Tables
4. Thread
5. Buffer pools
6. Pages
7. Unique
8. Clustered
9. True, it may be accessed by all three concurrently
10. False, maybe some time in the future
11. False, Databasename.Tablespacename
12. True

3

Structured Query Language

The data processing language used to communicate to DB2 is called SQL, which stands for Structured Query Language. This language is different from conventional computer languages. It is a language of its own, designed specifically for relational processing. It may be used by itself or in conjunction with other programming languages. Various SQL statements support specific functions, such as object creation, data manipulation, authorization, and others. The SQL statements can be subdivided into six functional groups as illustrated in Figure 3-1. Group 1 is referred to as DDL or Data Definition Language statements. This group is comprised of three types of statements. They are Create, Alter and Drop. Using this group, all DB2 objects are created, altered, or removed. This includes defining, altering and removing of storage groups, databases, tablespaces, tables, indexes, views, and synonyms.

Group 2 contains statements capable of manipulating the contents of tables. The SQL statements in this group are commonly referred to as DML or Data Manipulation Language statements. There are only four types of statements in this group. They are Select, Insert, Update, and Delete.

Group 3 SQL statements control the security and authorization aspects of DB2. There are only two types in this group, Grant and Revoke. Through these two types, creation and access to DB2 objects and tables are controlled.

DB2 with its relational processing did pose a problem for third-generation programming languages, since these languages are geared toward processing one record at a time where DB2 was designed for set processing. In order to access data stored in DB2 tables from third-generation application programs,

SQL STATEMENT GROUPS

Data Definition	Data Manipulation
Create	Select
	Insert
Alter	Update
Drop	Delete
1	**2**

Security & Authorization	Support 3rd Generation Lang
Grant	Close Whenever
	Declare Describe
Revoke	Fetch Execute
	Include Prepare
	Open
3	**4**

Data Control	Miscellaneous
Commit	Comment On
Lock	Explain
Rollback	Label On
5	**6**

Figure 3-1 SQL Statement Groups

the group of SQL statements contained in Group 4 were developed. Some were developed specifically to support one record at a time processing. This group pertains primarily to application programming languages such as COBOL, PL/I, FORTRAN and ASSEMBLER. This group consists of Close, Declare, Fetch, Include, Open, and Whenever statements as well as statements such as Describe, Execute, and Prepare, which are used exclusively in dynamic SQL. Group 4 SQL statements will be discussed in Chapter 6 since they can only exist in third-generation application programs.

SQL statements in Group 5 release or restrict use of data contained in tablespace pages. This group consists of Commit, Lock and Rollback. These data control statements provide functions allowing applications to commit changes so others can access updated rows, lock pages to ensure that applications have exclusive control over data, and roll back changes in a controlled manner should certain conditions be encountered.

The last group, Group 6, consists of statements which I have termed miscellaneous for lack of a a better name. Their roles range from putting comments about objects in the DB2 Catalog to explaining the access path chosen by the DB2 optimizer. SQL statements in Groups 1, 2, 5 and 6 will be discussed in this chapter. Groups 3 and 4 will be discussed in Chapters 9 and 6, respectively.

Group 1

Group 1 SQL statements pertain to the CREATE, ALTER and DROP of DB2 objects (DDL). Figure 3-2 shows the dependencies between DB2 objects. Objects dependent on other objects can be created only after the objects upon which they depend are created. For example, you cannot create an index on a table until the table being indexed has been created, nor can you create a tablespace until a database has been created. There are seven variations of CREATE and DROP SQL statements and four variations of the ALTER statement. The first DDL statement to be discussed in Group 1 is the CREATE.

CREATE STOGROUP: A storage group consists of a set of DASD volumes used by DB2 in the creation of tablespaces and indexspaces. When datasets are allocated for tablespaces or indexspaces, DB2 looks at volumes defined in the requested storage group and allocates the dataset in one of the designated volumes. The individual creating the dataset does not have to worry about setting up VSAM deletes and defines. The placement of datasets in the storage group is determined by DB2. Storage Groups allow you to manage not only the volumes used by DB2, but also who can create datasets on the volumes. Multiple storage groups can be defined to a DB2 system. Likewise, a volume could appear in more than one storage group. The removal of a volume from a storage group does not cause datasets on the removed volume to be deleted. All volumes specified in a storage group must be of the same device type. The following is the SQL format for creating a storage group.

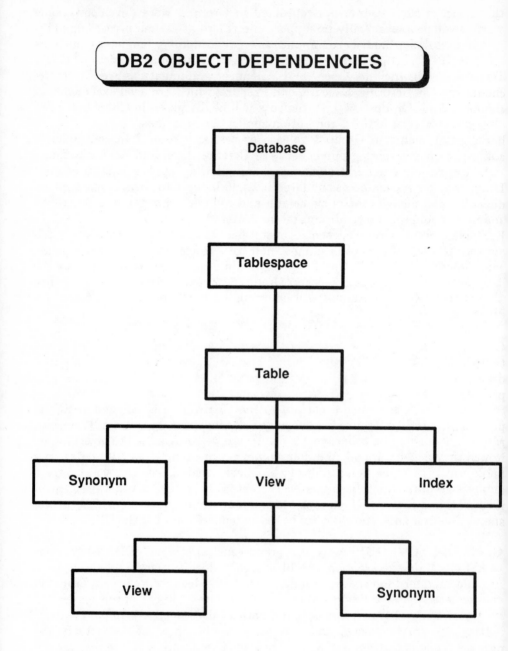

Figure 3-2 DB2 Object Dependencies

```
CREATE STOGROUP stogroup-name VOLUMES (volid1,...,volidN)
     VCAT vsam-catalog-name
     PASSWORD vsam-catalog-password
```

Stogroup-name is the name of the storage group. It can be up to eight characters, where the first character is alphabetic. The remaining positions can be alphabetic or numeric.

Volid(1 – N) is a list of the volume serial numbers of the DASD volumes to be included in the storage group. Maximum number of volumes that can be contained in a storage group is 133.

Vsam-catalog-password is the password that protects the VSAM catalog. DB2 uses this password to access VSAM datasets such as tablespaces and indexspaces. (Optional)

Example:

```
CREATE STOGROUP PROD0001 VOLUMES (VOL001,
     VOL002, VOL003) VCAT (DB2PROD)
```

CREATE DATABASE: This SQL statement defines a database in which tablespaces, tables and indexes can be associated. Information pertaining to a database will only be found in the DB2 Catalog and is not included in any physical structure of the table. The database serves as a unit of STOP and START within DB2. It is also a convenient way to grant authorizations that pertain to groups of tables and indexes at a much higher level. For these reasons, you should consider putting only tables with similar characteristics in one database. DB2 has a default database DSNDB04, which is used when tables are created without specifying a database or tablespace. The general availability of the default database should be restricted, if allowed at all, since it could prove to be unmanageable. The format for the CREATE DATABASE statement is:

```
CREATE DATABASE database-name STOGROUP storage-group-name
     BUFFERPOOL buffer-pool-name
```

Database-name is the name used to identify this database. The database name is unique per DB2 system.

Storage-group-name is the name of the storage group to be used if a tablespace is not specified when creating a table. If the storage group is not specified, the SYSDEFLT storage group is used. (Optional)

Buffer-pool-name refers to the buffer handling area used when retrieving and manipulating pages of tablespaces and indexspaces. The only allowable values are BP0 which is the default, BP1, BP2 and BP32K. (Optional)

Example:

```
CREATE DATABASE DBDNAM01 STOGROUP PROD0001
```

CREATE TABLESPACE: The tablespace is a specially formatted VSAM dataset. Creating the tablespace actually causes a dataset to be created on a volume in the specified storage group. Tablespaces contain the data stored in tables. More than one table can be stored in a tablespace, but it would be a wise choice to have only one table per tablespace if at all possible. Reorganization, Copy, and Recovery utilities operate on tablespaces as opposed to tables.

Tablespaces can also be subdivided into multiple datasets. Each of these datasets is called a partition. Partitioning allows large tables to be broken down into smaller, more manageable units. Tables that are in partitioned tablespaces are required to have clustered indexes. The index is used to determine in which of the tablespace partitions inserted rows are to be placed. Do not arbitrarily make a tablespace partitioned. When partitioning is used, other areas of data management can get a little more complicated. Some utilities can be run on one partition or on all partitions. Reorganizations can be run by partition, but all partitions will be unavailable to the users.

Nonpartitioned tablespace:

```
CREATE TABLESPACE tablespace-name in database-name
    USING VCAT vsam-catalog-name
```

or

```
    USING STOGROUP storage-group-name PRIQTY primary-quantity
                              SECQTY secondary-quantity
                  ERASE erase-parm
    FREEPAGE free-page
    PCTFREE percent-free
    BUFFERPOOL buffer-pool-size
    LOCKSIZE lock-size
    CLOSE    close-parm
    DSETPASS password
```

Partitioned tablespace:

```
CREATE TABLESPACE tablespace-name in database-name
      NUMPARTS no-of-partitions
            (PART 1 USING VCAT  vsam-catalog-name
```

or

```
                USING STOGROUP storage-group-name
                PRIQTY primary-quantity
                SECQTY secondary-quantity
                ERASE erase-parm
```

Structured Query Language 45

```
FREEPAGE   free-page PCTFREE percent-free,
                              .
                              .
                              .

PART partition-no USING VCAT vsam-catalog-name
```

r
```
                        USING STOGROUP storage-group-name
                        PRIQTY primary-quantity
                        SECQTY secondary-quantity
                        ERASE erase-parm
                        FREEPAGE free-page PCTFREE percent-free)
BUFFERPOOL buffer-pool
LOCKSIZE lock-size
CLOSE      close-parm
DSETPASS password
```

Tablespace-name is the name of the tablespace. It can be up to eight charac-ters. The first character has to be alphabetic. The remaining characters can be alphabetic or numeric.

Database-name is the database name this tablespace is to be associated with. If not specified the tablespace will be created in the default database DSNDB04.

Vsam-catalog-name is the name of your VSAM catalog. Specified if storage groups are not being used. User must create the VSAM dataset.

Storage-group-name is the name of the storage group that contains the volumes that your tablespace dataset should be allocated on.

Primary-quantity is the number of kilobytes (default is 12) to be allocated as the primary space for the tablespace. DB2 divides this number by either 4 or 32, depending on your page size, to come up with the number of pages your tablespace will contain. If not a whole number, then DB2 will round up to the next whole number.

Secondary-quantity is a number representing the amount of space in kilobytes (default is 12) to be used when secondary allocations are needed. Providing space is available in the storage group, a tablespace can have up to 119 secondary allocations. Like the primary space, DB2 divides this number by the page size and stores in terms of pages.

Erase-parm determines whether the tablespace dataset is to be erased when dropped. ERASE YES implies the tablespace area is to be zero filled. ERASE NO is the default.

Free-page tells DB2 how often a page is to be left completely empty. This parameter can be very important to applications with heavy insert activity. The default is to leave no empty pages. This parameter only has an effect when loading and reorganizing.

Percent-free tells DB2 what percentage (default is 5%) of each page is to be left available for insertions. Like *free pages*, this parameter is only utilized during loads and reorganizations.

Buffer-pool-size names the buffer pool to be used. Only BP0, BP1, BP2, and BP32K are allowed (default is the buffer pool specified in the database).

Lock-size tells DB2 at what level tablespaces are to be locked by applications. Your choices are ANY which is the default, PAGE, and TABLESPACE. ANY says let DB2 choose. The level of locks can vary between pages and tablespaces. DB2 may determine that an application is requesting too many page locks and will escalate the level up to the tablespace level. If not careful, you could have users locked out due to an application having its lock granularity increased to tablespace by DB2. PAGE locks are the smallest level or granularity of lock. This level of lock allows more concurrency than the others and is very popular for tablespaces having to support large numbers of users. Its main drawback is the overhead caused by DB2 lock management, and undoubtedly some applications will exceed the lock limits that an application can have (if specified at your installation). TABLESPACE will lock at the tablespace level (a good reason not to have more than one table per tablespace). Locking at the tablespace level is popular for tablespaces that are accessed by one user at a time. Applications that can lock at the tablespace level will have better performance since they will not have the overhead that goes with managing page locks. Nor will they be bumping into any lock limits defined at your installation.

Close-parm specifies whether the tablespace dataset is to be closed when no users are accessing it. *Yes* says to close when not being accessed. *No* means leave the dataset open. *No* gives the best performance. *Yes* is the default.

Password is the password given to VSAM when the datasets are accessed by DB2. You may decide not to use this and go with RACF protection. If you do use this, make sure that column DSETPASS is removed from visibility in DB2's SYSIBM.SYSTABLESPACE table so that users will not have access to this password. The password can be up to eight characters and is not scrambled.

No-of-partitions is an integer indicating how many tablespace datasets are to be created for this partitioned tablespace. If specified, this integer must be between 1 and 64.

Partition-no pertains to a specific partition dataset. Each dataset in a partitioned tablespace could have different attributes, such as primary quantity, secondary quantity, or storage group.

Example:

```
CREATE TABLESPACE SPACE001 IN DBDNAM01 LOCKSIZE PAGE
    USING STOGROUP PROD0001 PRIQTY 100 SECQTY 20
    FREEPAGE 20 PCTFREE 15

CREATE TABLESPACE SPACE001 IN DBDNAM01
    NUMPARTS 2 (PART 1 USING STOGROUP PROD0001
                    PRIQTY 100 SECQTY 20
```

```
              ERASE NO
              FREEPAGE 20 PCTFREE 15,
       PART 2 USING STOGROUP PROD0001
              PRIQTY  80 SECQTY 16
              ERASE NO
              FREEPAGE 25 PCTFREE 20)
  BUFFERPOOL BP0 LOCKSIZE PAGE CLOSE NO
```

CREATE TABLE: The table is the DB2 object that is accessed by applications. Databases and tablespaces are seldom if ever referenced by an application. It is through SQL DML statements that tables are accessed to retrieve and manipulate data. The table is also the unit from which access to data is commonly controlled. It is through the table-creation procedure that DB2 is told what columns are to be contained in a table and what the associated data types will be. Tables are placed in tablespace datasets, which in turn are associated with a database. Table names are uniquely identified by qualifying them with a creator. The CREATE TABLE statement is as follows.

```
CREATE TABLE table-name
     ( column-name1 data-type1,
       column-name2 data-type2 NOT NULL,
       column-name3 data-type3 NOT NULL WITH DEFAULT

           .        .
           .        .
           .       .)
     IN database-name.tablespace-name
```

Table-name is the name given to a table. Table name can be up to 18 characters, of which the first must be one of the following: A–Z,#,@,$. The remaining characters can be alphabetic, numeric, or underline (_). This is the name that users will reference in their SQL statements. If someone other than the creator is accessing the table, the table name must be prefixed by the ID of the creator (creator.table-name).

Column-name(1 – 3) represents the names given to the actual columns to be defined in the table. This name must be unique within the table and the sum of the column byte counts cannot exceed 4056 for 4K pages or 32714 for 32K pages.

Data-type(1 – 3) represents the data format to be used by DB2. There are four types used for numeric datas INTEGER, SMALLINT, FLOAT, and DECIMAL. All other format types refer to character data. They are CHAR, VARCHAR, LONG VARCHAR, GRAPHIC, VARGRAPHIC, LONG VARGRAPHIC, DATE, TIME, and TIMESTAMP. See Appendix B for explanations of each data type.

Null, Not Null, Not Null With Default control what action is to be taken if the data value is not present. If nothing is specified, it is assumed null, which implies data is not required to be present for this column when a row is being inserted into a table. *Not Null* implies a data value must be present for this column in order for the row to be inserted. *Not Null With Default* implies that, if the data value for a column is omitted, DB2 should set the column value equal to a default value. Thus, the column will not be considered null even though a user did not enter a value. Default values are zero for numeric data types and blanks for fixed-length character strings.

Database-name.tablespace-name represents the tablespace in which the table is to be contained. Database needs to be specified since tablespace alone is not unique. If you omit the tablespace-name, DB2 will automatically generate a tablespace for you but possibly with undesirable defaults.

There are several routines that can be specified about tables that I will just briefly mention, since they are modules that each installation would design and tailor to their own needs. They are EDITPROC (user-supplied edit routine), VALIDPROC (validation routine) and FIELDPROC (encoding data value routine). Make sure you have a real need for these, because they can add extra overhead to the DB2 system by being called every time a row is retrieved, inserted, or updated.

Example:

```
  CREATE TABLE TEST_TABLE
      (DEPT_NUMBER      INTEGER      NOT NULL,
       DEPT_NAME        CHAR(20)     NOT NULL,
       DEPT_MANAGER     CHAR(30)              ,
       AVERAGESALARY    DECIMAL(7,2)          ,
       AVERAGEAGE       SMALLINT              ,
       DEPTCHARTER      VARCHAR(200)          ,
       PC_WORKSTATIONS  INTEGER      NOT NULL WITH DEFAULT)
   IN DBDNAM01.SPACE001
```

CREATE INDEX: When an index is created, DB2 automatically generates an indexspace dataset in which to place it. Indexes are created on tables for four basic reasons. The first is for performance reasons. An index can be used to avoid scanning an entire tablespace dataset. Second, indexes are used to ensure that uniqueness among rows can be obtained. Applications attempting to insert duplicate rows into a table based on the columns defined in the index will receive an error condition. The third reason to use an index is to force rows to be stored in a certain physical sequence to reduce the I/O against tables when performing sequential processing of rows. The fourth and last reason is because of tablespace partitioning — partitioned tablespaces require a clustering index. The index is used to determine in which partitioned dataset the rows are to be placed and maintained.

When an application is updating a page of a table, all of the rows in the page are restricted from others until the application either commits, terminates, rolls back, or abends. With indexes the strategy is similar except you can define what are called subpages. Since an index page can contain pointers to many rows, a lock on an index page could potentially lock out many more users than locks on tablespace pages. Through subpages you can further divide the locks on index pages into smaller units (up to 16), and thus reduce lock contention problems. Keep in mind, the DB2 optimizer makes the final decision as to whether an index will be used or not. You should carefully review any index that has been created to ensure usage. Otherwise, you could be forcing DB2 to maintain an unusable index. Indexes are not copied for recovery purposes. Instead, they are dropped and reconstructed from the actual table during the recovery. It is more efficient to create indexes prior to the data being loaded. The following is the format for creating an index:

Nonpartitioned index:

    CREATE **UNIQUE** INDEX *index-name* ON *table-name*
      (*column-name1* ASC, *column-name2* DESC, ... *column-nameN*)
      CLUSTER
      USING VCAT *vsam-catalog-name*

or

      USING STOGROUP *stogroup-name* PRIQTY *primary-quantity*
                      SECQTY *secondary-quantity*
                      ERASE *erase-parm*

      FREEPAGE *free-page* PCTFREE *percent-free*
      SUBPAGES *sub-pages* BUFFERPOOL *buffer-pool*
      CLOSE *close-parm*   DSETPASS *password*
      ERASE *erase-parm*

Partitioned index:

    CREATE **UNIQUE** INDEX *index-name* ON *table-name*
      (*column-name1* ASC, *column-name2* DESC, ... *column-nameN*)
      CLUSTER
      (PART *part-number1* VALUES (*constants1*)
            USING VCAT *vsam-catalog-name*

or

            USING STOGROUP *stogroup-name*
            PRIQTY *primary-quantity*
            SECQTY *secondary-quantity*
            ERASE *erase-parm*
            FREEPAGE *free-page* PCTFREE *percent-free*,
              .
              .
              .
      PART *part-numberN* VALUES (*constantsN*)
      USING VCAT *vsam-catalog-name*

or

> USING STOGROUP *stogroup-name*
> PRIQTY *primary-quantity*
> SECQTY *secondary-quantity*
> ERASE *erase-parm*

> FREEPAGE *free-page* PCTFREE *percent-free*)
> SUBPAGES *sub-pages* BUFFERPOOL *buffer-pool*
> CLOSE *close-parm*   DSETPASS *password*
> ERASE *erase-parm*

UNIQUE: Indicates that values for columns in the index must be unique. An attempt to insert a row into a table that will generate an index entry with the same values as another index entry will be rejected.

CLUSTER: Indicates that the rows are to be physically sequenced in the table by the columns defined in the index. Only one clustering index can be defined per table.

Index-name is the name of the index being created. It can be up to 18 characters. Like table name, the first character should be alphabetic and the rest can be alphabetic, numeric, or contain the underscore.

Table-name names the table for which the index is created.

Column-name(1-N) names the columns of the table that are to be contained in the index. The first column name listed is the high order and so on down the list. The column name can be in ascending sequence (ASC) or descending (DESC). If left blank, ascending is assumed. If an application requests rows to be returned in the same sequence as defined in an index, a sort of the rows returned can be avoided.

Vsam-catalog-name is the name of your VSAM catalog. Use of this implies that storage groups are not used.

Stogroup-name is the name of the storage group that contains the volumes to be used when allocating an indexspace dataset.

Primary-quantity is the number of kilobytes to be allocated in the initial allocation of space for the indexspace dataset. This number is divided by 4K or 32K, depending on the buffer pool being used, rounded up to the next whole number, and is stored as pages in the DB2 Catalog.

Secondary-quantity is the number of kilobytes to be allocated should the indexspace dataset need more space. Each secondary allocation will be allocated with this amount. This number is divided by 4K or 32K, depending on the buffer pool being used, rounded up to the next whole number, and is stored as pages in the DB2 Catalog.

Free-page when loading or reorganizing the indexspace dataset, represents how often DB2 should leave a page totally empty. (Default is 0)

Percent-free indicates what percentage of every page is to be left empty when loading or reorganizing. (Default is 10)

Sub-pages represents the number of subpages in an index page. If the page size is 4K, subpages of 4 implies each page will have 4 subpages of 1K each.

Subpages of 16 implies each subpage will be 256 bytes. Likewise, 1 subpage implies the subpage size is one and the subpage and page are the same size. The larger the integer specified, the greater the concurrency and also overhead. If only one user will use the table or the table is very large, subpage of 1 is a good choice initially.

Close-parm specifies whether the indexspace dataset is be left open or closed when not in use. (Default is CLOSE YES)

Erase-parm specifies whether the indexspace dataset is to be zero filled whenever the dataset is dropped. (Default is ERASE NO).

Password is the VSAM dataset password to be passed to VSAM by DB2. (Optional)

Part-number(1-N) represents an individual partitioned indexspace dataset created to support a corresponding partition defined in the tablespace.

Constants(1-N) indicates in which of the partitioned indexspaces a particular index key should be placed. It also represents which of the appropriate tablespace partitions the row should be placed in. In the third example that follows, Values(100) implies that rows with a department less than or equal to 100 should be placed in partition 1. If the department number is greater than 100 and less than or equal to 200, it should be placed in partition 2. Since partition 2 is the last partition specified, all rows with a department greater than 200 will also be placed in this partition. If the column is a character string and not fully specified, it is padded with X'FF' if in ascending sequence and X'00' if descending. If an index contains more than one column, but only one is specified with a VALUE, the values for the other columns in the index are assumed to be X'FF's or X'00's, depending on the sequence (ASC or DESC).

Examples:

```
CREATE  INDEX INDX1_TEST_TABLE ON TEST_TABLE
        (DEPT_NUMBER,AVERAGESALARY DESC)
        USING STOGROUP PROD0001 PRIQTY 20 SECQTY 8
        PCTFREE 20

CREATE  UNIQUE INDX2_TEST_TABLE ON TEST_TABLE
        (DEPT_NUMBER)
        USING VCAT DB2PROD
        SUBPAGES 16
        BUFFERPOOL BP0
        CLOSE YES

CREATE  INDEX INDX3_TEST_TABLE ON TEST_TABLE
        (DEPT_NUMBER)
        CLUSTER
            (PART 1 VALUES (100) USING STOGROUP PROD0001,
             PART 2 VALUES (200) USING STOGROUP PROD0001)
        SUBPAGES 4 BUFFERPOOL BP0
        CLOSE NO
```

CREATE VIEW: Views are derived from tables and/or other views. Through a view, you can restrict the rows and columns users have access to. Views can also be used to simplify complicated joins of SQL statements. Since views can be restrictive, it would be appropriate to ensure that if someone was only allowed to update rows for department 100, they should not be able to change department number to a value which they cannot maintain and vice versa. This can be performed in views using the With Check Option. If this option is specified, all inserts and updates will be checked against the view definition to ensure that the view definition is not being violated. Views may or may not meet your needs, especially in the area of table maintenance. If a view is restrictive, in that it does not contain all the columns of a table and the columns omitted cannot be null, the view cannot be used for inserts.

The format for creating a view is as follows:

```
CREATE VIEW view-name ( column-name1 ,
                          .
                          .
                          .
                    column-nameN)
  AS subselect
  WITH CHECK OPTION
```

Subselect represents just about any valid SELECT statement excluding those with 'FOR UPDATE OF', 'ORDER BY', and 'UNION'. The SELECT statement defines the rows and columns to be retrieved when access to the data is performed using a named view rather than a table. The desired rows and/or columns will be retrieved from the specified tables and/or other views. There are lots of variations of SELECTs, but not all variations can be specified in a view. SELECTS specified in views to restrict column access may not be usable for inserts, updates and deletes. Careful consideration should be given to views that are intended to be used in maintaining data. We will discuss SELECT statements later in this chapter.

View-name is the name of the view. This name is referenced in the SQL statements rather than a table name.

Column-name(1-N) is a list of the columns that are to be available through this view. The columns listed in the subselect should correspond to the columns listed in the view. The column name referenced in the view may be different from the name of the actual table column used. A column named HIRE_DATE existing in a table could be called EMPL_START_DATE when referenced in a view. If column names are not specified, the view will contain the same column names as the actual table.

WITH CHECK OPTION forces all inserts and updates to be checked against the conditions in the subselect. With this you can give someone access to a view to maintain rows in their department. The WITH CHECK OPTION can be used to ensure that the user cannot change department number to a value that is not maintainable through the view. See the last view example for DEPT_NUMBER = 200.

Examples:

```
CREATE VIEW MYVIEW1
    AS SELECT * FROM USERID1.TEST_TABLE

CREATE VIEW MYVIEW2
    AS SELECT * FROM USERID1.TEST_TABLE
        WHERE DEPT_NUMBER = 100
            AND
            AVERAGESALARY > 50000

CREATE VIEW MYVIEW3
    AS SELECT DEPT_NUMBER,EMPLOYEE_NO,SALARY
        FROM USERID1.TEST_TABLE,USERID2.EMPLOYEE_TAB
            WHERE DEPT_NUMBER=EMPLOYEE_DEPT

CREATE VIEW MYVIEW4
    AS SELECT DEPT_NUMBER,AVERAGESALARY,AVERAGEAGE
        FROM USERID1.TEST_TABLE
    WHERE DEPT_NUMBER = 200
    WITH CHECK OPTION
```

CREATE SYNONYM: Synonyms give you the capability to reference a table by another name. Each user can have their own synonyms. A user cannot create a synonym with the same name of a table that already exists for the user. The format of the CREATE SYNONYM is as follows:

```
    CREATE SYNONYM synonym-name FOR authorization-id.table-name
```
or
```
    CREATE SYNONYM synonym-name FOR authorization-id.view-name
```

Synonym-name is the table or view name referenced in the SQL statements. *Authorization-id* is the recorded creator of the table or view for which the synonym is being created since table name and view name may not be unique. *Table-name* is the name of a table for which the synonym is being created. *View-name* is the name of a view for which the synonym has been created.

Examples:

```
    CREATE SYNONYM DT FOR USERID1.TEST_TABLE

    CREATE SYNONYM MY FOR USERID1.MYVIEW1
```

Once a DB2 object has been created it is possible to modify some of the attributes describing the object without dropping and recreating it. The SQL
DDL statement to alter attributes about objects is called the ALTER. The
ALTER statement only applies to indexes, storage groups, tables, and
tablespaces. It does not apply to databases, views, or synonyms.

ALTER INDEX: The following indicates what attributes of an index can be
altered. If you are not the creator of the index, you must have the appropriate
authority to perform the alter. This authority could come from being the
creator of the table or anyone granted database administration authority or
the database. The format of the ALTER INDEX is as follows:

```
ALTER INDEX index-name BUFFERPOOL buffer-pool-name
           CLOSE close-parm DSETPASS password
           PART partition-number FREEPAGE free-pages
           PCTFREE percent-free
```

Index-name is the name of the already existing index. If the ALTER is being
performed by other than the creator, prefix the index name with the creator's
userid.

Buffer-pool-name is the name of the buffer pool to be used. Your choices are
BP0, BP1, BP2 or BP32K.

Close-parm indicates whether the indexspace dataset is to be left open if not
being accessed (NO) or closed when not accessed (YES).

Password is the VSAM password that DB2 is to use when accessing the indexspace dataset.

Partition-number is the partition number (if partitioned) that is being altered. Each partition has a FREEPAGE and PCTFREE specification.

Free-pages indicates how often DB2 is to leave a page totally empty when
loading or reorganizing the indexspace dataset.

Percent-free represents the percentage of each page to be left empty when
loading or reorganizing the indexspace dataset.

Examples:

```
ALTER INDEX INDX1_TEST_TABLE CLOSE NO

ALTER INDEX INDX3_TEST_TABLE CLOSE YES
           BUFFERPOOL BP2
           PART 2 FREEPAGE 20 PCTFREE 20
```

ALTER STOGROUP: Since DASD volumes will need to be added and
removed from storage groups, the ALTER STOGROUP statement is designed

to do just that. If you are not the creator of the storage group, you must have SYSADM authority. SYSADM is an authority grouping designed for those who need to control the DB2 system. The number of people with this authority should be restricted since these individuals can create, alter, or drop any DB2 object. The format for the ALTER STOGROUP statement is as follows.

```
ALTER STOGROUP storage-group-name PASSWORD password
       ADD VOLUMES ( vol01, vol02, .... volON )
       REMOVE VOLUMES ( vol11, vol22, ... volNN )
```

Storage-group-name is the name of the storage group being altered.

Password is the password passed to VSAM when accessed by DB2. (Optional)

Vol(01-0N) are the volumes being added to the storage group. (Optional)

Vol(11-NN) are the volumes to be removed from the storage group. From this point on, when datasets are created, DB2 will avoid using the volumes mentioned in this list. The datasets already present on these volumes will still remain intact.

ALTER TABLE: Tables are altered for one basic reason — to add additional columns to the table. The columns being added to the table must allow for being null. After a table has been altered you should make sure that it is copied because the alter has caused the structure of every row to change. Although you can add columns to a table you cannot delete columns using the ALTER. To delete columns you will have to drop the table and recreate it. The format of the ALTER TABLE is as follows.

```
ALTER TABLE table-name
       ADD column-name data-type
```

Table-name is the name of the table that will have columns added to its structure.

Column-name is the name of the column to be added to the table.

Data-type is the data format to be used by DB2 for the corresponding column being added to the table. See Appendix B for a complete list of available data types. NOT NULL and NOT NULL WITH DEFAULT cannot be used.

Example:

```
ALTER TABLE TEST_TABLE
       ADD AVERAGE_BONUS DECIMAL(7,2)

ALTER TABLE TEST_TABLE ADD DEPT_SECRETARY CHAR(30)
```

ALTER TABLESPACE: Through this SQL statement certain attribute describing a tablespace can be altered. The attributes that are modifiable ar BUFFERPOOL, LOCKSIZE, CLOSE, DSETPASS, FREEPAGE an PCTFREE. If more than one partition of a tablespace is being modified, a separate alter statement is required for each partition. The format is:

```
ALTER TABLESPACE   database-name.tablespace-name
         BUFFERPOOL buffer-pool
         LOCKSIZE   locksize-parm
         CLOSE      close-parm
         DSETPASS   password
         PART        partition-number
         FREEPAGE free-page
         PCTFREE  percent-free
```

Database-name is the name of the database in which the tablespace resides Tablespace name alone is not required to be unique per DB2 system.

Tablespace-name is the name of the tablespace that is to be altered. (Re quired)

Buffer-pool is the buffer pool to be used. Your choices are BP0, BP1, BP2 and BP32K.

Locksize-parm is the unit at which locks are to be managed by DB2 on th tablespace. The choices are ANY, TABLESPACE and PAGE.

Close-parm determines whether the tablespace is to be closed when no being accessed (YES) or left open (NO).

Password is the password passed to VSAM by DB2 when accessing th tablespace dataset.

Partition-number represents the partition (if tablespace is partitioned) tha is to be altered.

Free-page represents how often DB2 is to leave a page totally empty whe loading or reorganizing.

Percent-free identifies the percentage of the page to be left empty during load or reorganization.

Examples:

```
ALTER TABLESPACE DBDNAM01.SPACE001
         BUFFERPOOL BP1
         LOCKSIZE TABLESPACE
         CLOSE NO
         FREEPAGE 20
         PCTFREE 15


ALTER TABLESPACE DBDNAM01.SPACE001
         PART 1 FREEPAGE 25 PCTFREE 15
```

The last of the DDL statements is the **DROP**. The DROP is very powerful,
n that all objects dependent on the object being dropped are also deleted. If a
able is dropped, the data is deleted from the tablespace and the description of
he table is removed from the DB2 Catalog. Any indexes defined on the table
ıre also removed including their definitions from the DB2 Catalog. If you drop
ı database, all tablespaces, tables, indexes, views, and synonyms dependent
)n the database are also removed. All authorizations to use the dropped ob-
ects are also removed. Tables created in partitioned tablespaces cannot be
lropped by the DROP TABLE statement. Instead, the table must be dropped
)y either dropping the database or the tablespace. The format of the DROP is
ıs follows:

```
)ROP  DATABASE  database-name
)ROP  TABLESPACE  database-name.tablespace-name
)ROP  TABLE  table-creator.table-name
)ROP  INDEX  index-creator.index-name
)ROP  VIEW   view-name
)ROP  SYNONYM  synonym-name
)ROP  STOGROUP  stogroup-name
```

Database-name is the name of the database that is being dropped or, in the
:ase of tablespaces, the database in which the tablespace resides.

Tablespace-name is the name of the tablespace name to be dropped.

Table-creator.table-name is the name of the creator of the table followed by
.) and the name of the table. Table name alone is not required to be unique
per DB2 System. The fully qualified name consists of (creator.tablename).

Index-creator.index-name like table name, is not required to be unique per
DB2 System. It is unique when qualified by creator.

View-name is the name of the view to be dropped.

Synonym-name is an alternate name given to a table. This DROP statement
would be done by the creator of the synonym since it pertains only to the in-
lividual that created it.

Stogroup-name is the name of a storage group defined to DB2. Before a
storage group can be dropped, all indexspaces and tablespaces in the storage
group must be moved to another storage group or deleted.

Examples:

```
)ROP  DATABASE  DBDNAM01
)ROP  TABLESPACE  DBDNAM01.SPACE001
)ROP  TABLE  USERID1.TEST_TABLE
)ROP  INDEX  USERID1.INDX_TEST_TABLE
)ROP  SYNONYM  DT
)ROP  VIEW  MYVIEW1
)ROP  STOGROUP  PROD001
```

Group 2

The next group of SQL statements pertain to data manipulation. They are called DML (Data Manipulation Language) statements. These operate on rows in tables and are the statements most familiar to DB2 users. Although SQL stands for Structured Query Language it by no means restricts users from updating, inserting, or deleting of rows. There are only four types of statements in this group. They are SELECT, INSERT, UPDATE, and DELETE. The first one to be discussed will be the SELECT.

SELECT: The SELECT is the command that drives relational processing. The SELECT allows users to retrieve a set of rows. They are issued against either tables or views. Since the result can be stored in a table in the case of IBM's Query Management System (QMF), additional relational operations may be performed on the result. In order for this to occur, the person issuing the select must have authority to access the data being requested. This authority could come from several different sources. It could come from grants on the table, view or execution authority for an application program containing SQL statements. Selects contain clauses. The available clauses are FROM, WHERE, GROUP BY, HAVING and ORDER. If present they must be specified in the sequence listed below. The FROM clause is the only required clause. The format of the SELECT is as follows:

```
SELECT all-or-distinct    selected-column-list
   FROM table-name1-or-view-name1 , ... ,table-nameN-or-view-nameN
   WHERE where-search-conditions
   GROUP BY group-by-columns
   HAVING    having-search-conditions
   ORDER BY order-by-column-list
```

All-or-distinct determines how duplicate rows, if encountered, will be returned in the results. ALL, which is the default, will return duplicate rows if found. Duplicate, in this case, refers to the situations where the column values of one row are identical to those of one or more other rows selected. If DISTINCT is specified, only one row will be returned, even though several rows may have qualified for selection.

Selected-column-list is the list of columns to be returned from the row. There may be many columns in a row, but this list identifies only the columns that will be returned from the row. If * is specified, all columns from the selected rows will be returned. It is also possible to select the same column name more than once in the selected-column-list.

Table-name-or-view-name(1-N) represents tables or views from which the rows are to be selected. Multiple tables may be included in the FROM clause

Having more than one table or view in the FROM clause by definition is a JOIN.

Where-search-conditions is the clause which determines what conditions must be met in the search. Use of the WHERE clause is optional. To assist you in coming up with selection criteria, DB2 has made several operators available. They are '=', 'not equal', '<', '>', '<=', '>=', 'Not >', 'Not <', '+', '-', '*' and '/'. The Boolean operators AND, OR and NOT are also available. Special keywords such as BETWEEN and IN are available for use in where clauses. These special keywords allow you to shorten expressions. DEPT=100 or DEPT=101 or DEPT=102 or DEPT=105 or DEPT=954 could be simply stated as DEPT IN (100,101,102,105,954). AVERAGESALARY >= 30000 and AVERAGESALARY <= 50000 can also be presented as AVERAGESALARY BETWEEN 30000 AND 50000.

Another keyword is the LIKE which pertains to characters. You could express DEPT_NAME='ACCOUNTING' as DEPT_NAME LIKE 'ACCOUNTING'. Partial search capabilities are available with the LIKE function through use of '%' and '_'. The % symbol allows you to search for any character string of any length. For example, LIKE '%SMITH%'would search a column's contents for the characters SMITH no matter where placed. The _ is very similar except that it represents a place holder. For example, LIKE '_ _JONES' would search a column and accept rows if the column had ED-JONES or MCJONES but skip rows where the column contained JONES or EDJONESS. The % and the _ can be included in the same LIKE. Coding a LIKE statement similar to LIKE '_ _JONES%' would be acceptable.

Group-by-columns is a list of columns used to group rows to retrieve a summary result instead of returning individual rows in the result. You could group all employees by department and return the average salary, minimum salary, maximum salary, and salary sum for each department as well as all departments. Individual rows are not returned, just the columns involved in the GROUP BY clause. Use of the GROUP BY clause is optional.

Having-search-condition goes hand in hand with the GROUP BY clause. The HAVING clause gives you flexibility in selecting which groups are to be in the results. You can discard groups of rows that were comprised of less than two rows or discard groups of rows that have an average salary < 1,000. The HAVING clause like the GROUP BY is optional.

Order-by-column-list tells DB2 that the results are to be in sequence. The columns used in determining the sequence are specified here. The first column specified is the high order sort field. Ascending sequence, ASC, is the default. If descending is required, follow the column with DESC. Sometimes it is not possible to specify a column name because it may be derived from a computation, consist of a constant, or be nonunique in the select list. When this occurs, specify the sequence number of the column from the selected list of columns. For example, ORDER BY 1,3,4 would order the results by the first column in the select list followed by the third column and then the fourth column. Use of the ORDER BY is optional.

Table 3-1 Department Table Contents

DEPT NO	DEPT NAME	DEPT MANAGER	AVERAGE SALARY	AVER AGE	DEPTCHARTER	PC WORK STATIONS
100	ACCOUNTING	JONES	50000.00	35	CORPORATE ACCOUNTING	15
101	PURCHASING	-	45000.00	-	PURCHASE FROM VENDOR	4
202	ENGINEERING	SMITH	51000.00	32	PRODUCT ENGINEERING	40
303	PERSONNEL	SMITH	53000.00	45	SET PERSONNEL POLICI	3
103	PAYROLL	BLACK	45000.00	29	PERFROM ALL PAYROLL	4
105	MAIL	MCJONES	15000.00	20	DELIVER MAIL	0
954	BLDG MAINT	EDJONES	17000.00	27	MAINTAIN BUILDING EX	1
500	GUEST SERVICES	JONESS	12000.00	23	MAKE GUEST ARRANGEME	3
401	APPL DEVELOP	SMITHONEAN	42000.00	31	COMPUTER APPL DEVELO	89
402	GROUNDS MAINT	GREEN	8900.00	18	GARDENING	0

The following selects are based on Table 3-1:

Problem: Retrieve information about all departments.

```
SELECT * FROM TEST_TABLE
```

DEPT NO	DEPT NAME	DEPT MANAGER	AVERAGE SALARY	AVER AGE	DEPTCHARTER	PC WORK STATIONS
100	ACCOUNTING	JONES	50000.00	35	CORPORATE ACCOUNTING	15
101	PURCHASING	-	45000.00	-	PURCHASE FROM VENDOR	4
202	ENGINEERING	SMITH	51000.00	32	PRODUCT ENGINEERING	40
303	PERSONNEL	SMITH	53000.00	45	SET PERSONNEL POLICI	3
103	PAYROLL	BLACK	45000.00	29	PERFROM ALL PAYROLL	4
105	MAIL	MCJONES	15000.00	20	DELIVER MAIL	0
954	BLDG MAINT	EDJONES	17000.00	27	MAINTAIN BUILDING EX	1
500	GUEST SERVICES	JONESS	12000.00	23	MAKE GUEST ARRANGEME	3
401	APPL DEVELOP	SMITHONEAN	42000.00	31	COMPUTER APPL DEVELO	89
402	GROUNDS MAINT	GREEN	8900.00	18	GARDENING	0

Problem: Find all information about department 100.

```
SELECT * FROM TEST_TABLE
        WHERE DEPT_NUMBER = 100
```

```
                                                      PC
DEPT DEPT                DEPT     AVERAGE AVER         WORK
  NO NAME                MANAGER  SALARY  AGE  DEPTCHARTER        STATIONS
---- ----------         -------  -------- ---- -------------------- --------
100  ACCOUNTING          JONES    50000.00  35 CORPORATE ACCOUNTING       15
```

Problem: Find department number, department name and average age
         where the average age column has a value >30.

```
SELECT DEPT_NUMBER,
       DEPT_NAME
       AVERAGEAGE
    FROM TEST_TABLE
       WHERE AVERAGEAGE > 30
```

```
DEPT    DEPT
NUMBER  NAME                AVERAGEAGE
------  ------------        ----------
   100  ACCOUNTING                  35
   202  ENGINEERING                 32
   303  PERSONNEL                   45
   401  APPL DEVELOP                31
```

ORDER BY DESC
Retrieve department number and department name from the table.
Return the rows by department number in descending sequence.
The ORDER BY clause does not affect the order of columns in
the result.

```
SELECT DEPT_NUMBER,DEPT_NAME
FROM TEST_TABLE
ORDER BY DEPT_NUMBER DESC
```

```
DEPT    DEPT
NUMBER  NAME
------  ----------------
   954  BLDG MAINT
   500  GUEST SERVICES
   402  GROUNDS MAINT
   401  APPL DEVELOP
   303  PERSONNEL
   202  ENGINEERING
   105  MAIL
   103  PAYROLL
   101  PURCHASING
   100  ACCOUNTING
```

ORDER BY

Select rows from the table and sequence the results first by average salary in descending order and then by department number in ascending sequence within average salary.

```
SELECT DEPT_NUMBER,
       AVERAGESALARY,
       AVERAGEAGE
     FROM TEST_TABLE
       ORDER BY AVERAGESALARY DESC,
               DEPT_NUMBER ASC
```

DEPT NUMBER	AVERAGESALARY	AVERAGEAGE
303	53000.00	45
202	51000.00	32
100	50000.00	35
101	45000.00	-
103	45000.00	29
401	42000.00	31
954	17000.00	27
105	15000.00	20
500	12000.00	23
402	8900.00	18

LIKE, '_'

Select rows from the table where the department manager's name must have 'J O N E S' in the third through seventh position of the column.
Note: The _ is positional and indicates that any character can exist in this position. The % represents that JONES can be followed by any character string of any length.

```
SELECT DEPT_NUMBER,DEPT_NAME,DEPT_MANAGER
FROM TEST_TABLE
WHERE DEPT_MANAGER LIKE '__JONES%'
```

DEPT NUMBER	DEPT NAME	DEPT MANAGER
105	MAIL	MCJONES
954	BLDG MAINT	EDJONES

```
************************************************************
*                      LIKE, '_'                          *
*   Select rows from the table where the department manager's  *
*   name is like '_ _ J O N E S'.                         *
*   Note: The _ is positional and indicates that any character  *
*   can exist in this position. Since the % was not used,  *
*   the column must contain 'JONES' in the third through seventh *
*   positions with no characters following. No rows were   *
*   found that met this condition.                        *
************************************************************
```

```
SELECT DEPT_NUMBER,DEPT_NAME,DEPT_MANAGER
FROM TEST_TABLE
WHERE DEPT_MANAGER LIKE '__JONES'
```

```
 DEPT   DEPT               DEPT
NUMBER  NAME               MANAGER
------  ----------         --------
```

The '_' is positional!

```
************************************************************
*                      LIKE, '_'                          *
*   Same as previous select, only 'JONES' can be followed by  *
*   any characters in positions 8 through 30.             *
************************************************************
```

```
SELECT DEPT_NUMBER,DEPT_NAME,DEPT_MANAGER
FROM TEST_TABLE
WHERE DEPT_MANAGER LIKE '__JONES                      '
```

```
 DEPT   DEPT               DEPT
NUMBER  NAME               MANAGER
------  ----------         --------
   105  MAIL               MCJONES
   954  BLDG MAINT         EDJONES
```

```
************************************************************
*                        IN                               *
*   Select rows where the department number is in a specified  *
*   list of values.                                       *
************************************************************
```

```
SELECT DEPT_NUMBER,DEPT_NAME,DEPT_MANAGER
FROM TEST_TABLE
WHERE DEPT_NUMBER IN (100,101,102,105,954,1000)
ORDER BY DEPT_NUMBER
```

```
DEPT      DEPT
NUMBER    NAME               MANAGER
------    ----------         ---------
 100      ACCOUNTING         JONES
 101      PURCHASING         -
 105      MAIL               MCJONES
 954      BLDG MAINT         EDJONES
```

```
*******************************************************************
*                    (BETWEEN,  ORDER BY)                         *
*  Select rows where the contents of the AVERAGESALARY column is  *
*  greater than or equal to 30,000 and less than or equal to      *
*  50,000.                                                        *
*  Note:If 30,000 and 50,000 are to be excluded from the range,   *
*  you have to specify greater than (>) and less than (<).        *
*******************************************************************
```

```
SELECT DEPT_NUMBER,DEPT_NAME,AVERAGESALARY
FROM TEST_TABLE
WHERE AVERAGESALARY BETWEEN 30000 AND 50000
ORDER BY AVERAGESALARY DESC
```

```
DEPT      DEPT
NUMBER    NAME               AVERAGESALARY
------    ------------       -------------
 100      ACCOUNTING          50000.00
 101      PURCHASING          45000.00
 103      PAYROLL             45000.00
 401      APPL DEVELOP        42000.00
```

INSERT: The insert statement can be used to insert rows into tables. The tables do not have to be empty. The data to be inserted can be included in the insert statement or exist in another table. The format for the INSERT is as follows:

```
INSERT INTO table-name-or-view-name
     ( column-name1, ... ,column-nameN )
        VALUES (column-name1-value, ... ,column-nameN-value)
```
or
```
INSERT INTO table-name-or-view-name
     ( column-name1, ... ,column-nameN )
     SELECT insert-column-name1, ... ,column-nameN
          FROM from-table
          WHERE where-conditions
```

Table-name-or-view-name is the name of the table or view in which rows are to be inserted.

Column-name(1-N) is a list of the columns being inserted. This parameter goes hand in hand with the VALUES clause. If the VALUES clause is present, then the order of values in the VALUES clause must match the sequence of the columns specified in this list. If this list is omitted and the VALUES clause is present, the values in the VALUES clause are assigned to columns in the order in which they were defined in the table or view. This parameter is optional.

Column-name(1-N)-values is the list of values to be assigned to the columns. If the previous parameter is omitted then the values are assumed to be in the same sequence as defined in the table. Enclose values for character, date, time, and timestamp columns within quotes.

Insert-column-name(1-N) are the columns to be used from another table. Rows from other tables may be inserted into a table. The column names do not have to match, but the data types do. There must be a one to one relationship between column-name and insert-column-name.

From-table is the table name from which rows are retrieved when inserting from another table. The table name listed in the FROM cannot be the same as the table name listed in the INTO.

Where-conditions specifies which rows from another table are to be inserted. You can thus insert a subset of rows from one table into another.

Examples:

```
INSERT INTO TEST_TABLE
   (DEPT_NUMBER,DEPT_NAME,
    AVERAGESALARY,
    AVERAGEAGE,
    DEPT_MANAGER,
    PC_WORKSTATIONS,
    DEPT_CHARTER)
   VALUES(100,'ACCOUNTING',50000.00,35,'JONES',
          15,'CORPORATE ACCOUNTING')
 INSERT INTO TEST_TABLE
   VALUES(101,'PURCHASING',NULL,45000.00,NULL,
          'PURCHASE FROM VENDORS',4)
```

Note: These values correspond to the sequence in which the columns were defined.

```
INSERT INTO TEST_TABLE
      SELECT DEPT_NUMBER,DEPT_NAME,MANAGER,AVGSAL,AVGAGE,
             CHARTER,WORKSTATIONS
      FROM AUDIT_TABLE
      WHERE DEPT_NUMBER > 99 AND DEPT_NUMBER < 999
```

DELETE: The DELETE SQL statement should not be confused with the DROP statement. The DROP statement drops DB2 objects, such as databases, tablespaces, and tables, while the DELETE statement removes rows from tables. The results from the DELETE could vary from deleting zero rows to deleting all rows in a table. The format of the DELETE is as follows:

```
DELETE FROM table-name
      WHERE search-condition
```
or
```
DELETE FROM view-name
      WHERE search-condition
```

Table-name is the table from which rows are to be deleted if they meet the search conditions.

Search-condition are the conditions that must be met prior to a row being deleted. This could also be a SELECT statement. (Optional)

View-name is the name of a view, rather than table, against which deletes can be issued.

Examples:

```
DELETE FROM TEST_TABLE                -- will delete all rows
DELETE FROM TEST_TABLE                -- will delete rows that have
   WHERE DEPT_NUMBER = 100            -- DEPT_NUMBER = 100 or 101
      OR DEPT_NUMBER = 101
DELETE FROM TEST_TABLE                -- will delete rows that have
   WHERE DEPT_MANAGER='SMITH'         -- DEPT_MANAGER='SMITH' and
      AND AVERAGESALARY > 50000       -- an AVERAGESALARY column
                                      -- value > 50000
DELETE FROM TEST_TABLE X              -- will delete rows from
   WHERE NOT EXISTS                   -- TEST_TABLE where the
   SELECT * FROM EMPLOYEE_TABLE       -- DEPT_MANAGER value is
      WHERE  EMPLOYEE_NAME = X.DEPT_MANAGER
                                      -- not in the EMPLOYEE_TABLE.
```

UPDATE: The last of the DML statements is the UPDATE. The UPDATE allows the user to update one or many rows with one SQL UPDATE statement. If a table contained a price column, one simple statement could increase price in every row by ten percent. The format of the UPDATE is as follows:

```
UPDATE  table-name-or-view-name
        SET column-name1 = expression
                        .

                        .
                        .
                column-nameN = expression
        WHERE where-search-condition
```

Table-name-or-view-name is the table or view name to be updated.

Column-name(1-N) are the columns being updated in the table or view. The number of columns updated can vary from one to all columns in a table.

Expression is the value a column is to be set to. It can be a simple value such as SALARY = 100 or it can be derived like SALARY = SALARY * 1.10. You cannot set a column equal to column values of another table.

Where-search-condition specifies in which rows the columns are to be updated.

Examples:

```
UPDATE PART_TABLE                          -- will increase contents of
  SET PART_PRICE = PART_PRICE * 1.10       -- PART_PRICE by 10% if
  WHERE PART_GROUP = 'BEARINGS'            -- PART_GROUP='BEARINGS'
UPDATE PART_TABLE                          -- will set PART_PRICE
  SET PART_PRICE = 500.00                  -- equal to 500 if the
  WHERE PART_NUMBER = 'AEIW006'            -- PART_NUMBER='AEIW006'
UPDATE PART_TABLE                          -- will set PART_PRICE
  SET PART_PRICE = 500                     -- equal to 500 in every
                                           -- row.

UPDATE TEST_TAB                            -- Set 2 columns = to null
  SET AVERAGESALARY=NULL                   -- value if DEPT_NUMBER = 100
      AVERAGEAGE=NULL
        WHERE DEPT_NUMBER=100.
```

Group 5

The fifth group of SQL statements regulate the duration of locks placed on data used by applications. Every SQL statement, when executed, will lock pages of data in a tablespace. Locks are used by an application to control in what manner pages or tablespaces used by the application will be available to other applications. These locks vary in nature. An application can issue SQL statements to lock pages or tablespaces in such a manner that other applications are only allowed to perform inquiries against the same data. An application can also lock pages or tablespaces so it has exclusive control, and no other application can access the pages or tablespaces. In addition to establishing locks, SQL statements can be executed to release the locks held. There are three types of SQL statements that can either acquire, release, or commit locks. The first one is:

LOCK: This SQL statement is frequently used in application programs. When an application issues a LOCK statement, it is acquiring locks on all the pages in the tablespace. This is another reason to have only one table per tablespace. In the BIND process, to be discussed in Chapter 6, an application can request that the locks not be released until the tablespace dataset is deallocated by the application program. The default is to have locks released when the application program issues a COMMIT SQL statement to save all changes made or when the application terminates normally. The format of the SQL statement is as follows:

```
LOCK TABLE table-name IN SHARE MODE
```

```
LOCK TABLE table-name IN EXCLUSIVE MODE
```

Table-name is the name of the table upon which the locks are acquired. The lock is actually acquired against the tablespace.

SHARE MODE allows other applications to process against the named table in read-only mode. Any application issuing a lock with update intent will be refused access.

EXCLUSIVE MODE prevents other applications from obtaining access to the table even if their locks are for inquiry.

Examples:

```
LOCK TABLE TEST_TABLE IN SHARE MODE
```

```
LOCK TABLE TEST_TABLE IN EXCLUSIVE MODE
```

COMMIT: The COMMIT SQL statement releases all locks that have been acquired by an application. It is only available to applications running in the TSO and CICS environments. When executed, the pages acquired by an application are available to other applications. Also, once the commit process is done the changes made to the data will be written to the DB2 Logs. This creates what is called a commit-point. It represents a unit of recovery. All changes made up to this point can be included in a recovery of the tablespace. Changes after a commit and before the next commit are not recoverable. Normal termination of an application program is also a commit-point. If an application program performs updates, deletes, or inserts of rows in a table and does not commit after doing so, the changes will be kept only if the program terminates successfully. If the program abends, all of the changes made will be backed out, and the tablespace will appear as it did prior to the execution of the application program. A COMMIT executed from an application program will cause all positioning used to process rows of a table to be lost. The format of the COMMIT statement follows:

```
COMMIT
```

ROLLBACK: Rollback is available in the TSO and CICS environments. The ROLLBACK is used to undue modifications made by an application. It forces all changes made to the tablespaces involved in the application to be backed out. All table positioning held by the application is removed. Like the COMMIT, it represents a unit of recovery. All changed pages held in buffers are deleted and will not be included in the event of a recovery. After the SQL statement is executed, the tablespaces will be returned to a prior point of consistency. This could be a point prior to the application executing or, if COMMITs were issued, back to the last commit-point. The format is as follows:

```
ROLLBACK
```

Group 6

COMMENT ON: This SQL statement allows the executor to place and maintain comments in a REMARKS column in the DB2 Catalog tables for tables and columns. This REMARKS column is updated by this statement. The catalog tables that can be updated are SYSIBM.SYSCOLUMNS and SYSIBM.SYSTABLES. The format of the statement is as follows:

```
COMMENT ON TABLE table-or-view-name IS '254-characters-of-user
    comment'
```
or
```
COMMENT ON COLUMN
        table-or-view-name.column-name
    IS '254-characters-of-user-comment'
```
or
```
COMMENT ON table-or-view-name
    (column-name1 IS '254-characters-of-user-comment',
                 .
                 .
    column-nameN IS '254-characters-of-user-comment')
```

Table-or-view-name is the name of the table or view for which this SQL statement is to add or revise comments.

254-characters-of-user-comment is the actual comment that you wish to have placed on either the table, view, or column.

Column-name(1-N) is the name of the table column whose REMARKS column is being updated (SYSIBM.SYSCOLUMNS).

Examples:

```
COMMENT ON TABLE TEST_TABLE
        IS 'TEST TABLE FOR BENCHMARKING'

COMMENT ON COLUMN TEST_TABLE.DEPT_NUMBER
        IS 'DEPARTMENT NUMBER FOR ACCOUNTING PURPOSES'

COMMENT ON TEST_TABLE
        (DEPT_NAME IS 'NAME OF THE DEPARTMENT',
        DEPT_MANAGER IS 'NAME OF THE CURRENT DEPARTMENT MANAGER',
        AVERAGE_SALARY IS 'THIS IS THE AVERAGE SALARY IN THE DEPT')
```

```
COMMENT ON TABLE MYVIEW IS 'THIS IS THE VIEW OF TEST_TABLE AND IS
     USED THROUGH OUT MY EXAMPLES'
```

EXPLAIN: Early DB2 users found that their requests could be satisfied by coding SQL statements in various ways. Even though different SQL statements could provide the correct results, users found that some SQL statements performed far better than others. The EXPLAIN statement was provided with Release 2 of DB2 to assist individuals in determining which SQL statements provide the best performance for a specific function. The EXPLAIN gathers information about the methods to be used in accessing data along with the processing sequences for a SQL statement. This information is stored in a user table called PLAN_TABLE. The columns contained in the PLAN_TABLE can be found in Appendix C. Each person executing an EXPLAIN statement must have their own PLAN_TABLE. When an EXPLAIN statement is executed, DB2 analyzes the SQL statement or SQL statements in the case of an application program and inserts one or more rows into the PLAN_TABLE with information about each of the SQL statements.

There are two basic modes of operation with the EXPLAIN. The first is where you EXPLAIN the SQL statement you want analyzed. The following examples are of this mode. The second is through an option in the BIND process of preparing application programs for execution. In the BIND process, one only needs to specify an option to get each of the SQL statements in an application program analyzed. This option will be discussed in the program preparation process discussed in Chapter 6.

Since the PLAN_TABLE can contain rows explaining multiple SQL statements, it will be necessary to decipher which rows go with the SQL statement you want explained. To do this you can code a query number, or in the case of an application program, a PLAN name established during the BIND process. SQL statements contained in programs can be found in the DB2 Catalog as a result of the BIND. The DB2 table SYSIBM.SYSSTMTS can be viewed to associate a SQL statement with a query number. You can Select rows from the PLAN_TABLE using the query number or in the case of application programs by either query number or plan name. At this point you have identified the query being explained. The next step is to analyze the contents of each row in the PLAN_TABLE that corresponds to this QUERYNO. The EXPLAIN is frequently executed to determine whether or not an index is useable. If the access method involves an index, DB2 will determine if the index itself is sufficient to satisfy the request. When tables are joined together in SQL statements, it may be necessary for DB2 to build several interim tables before producing the final result table. Information pertaining to the sequence in which the interim tables are built may also be found in the PLAN_TABLE. Clauses such as ORDER BY, DISTINCT and GROUP BY may dictate to DB2 how interim tables will be processed. The explain statement provides information on how these clauses impact the access method. The following examples do not apply to application programs. These examples cause rows to be inserted into a table named PLAN_TABLE. The user must issue SELECT statements to view the contents in the PLAN_TABLE.

```
   EXPLAIN PLAN SET QUERYNO = query-number
               FOR executable-sql-statement
or
   EXPLAIN PLAN FOR executable-SQL-statement
```

Query-number is an integer assigned by the person executing the EX-PLAIN. This number can then be used when accessing the PLAN_TABLE to locate the desired rows.

Executable-sql-statement is the executable SELECT, UPDATE, DELETE, or INSERT statement that is to be explained.

Note: If SET QUERYNO is not used, DB2 will assign a number. In the following examples, QUERYNO = 1,2,3 are user controlled. The user can view the rows in PLAN_TABLE for the corresponding QUERYNO. It is up to the user to try to remember what the query looked like being explained. In Example 3, the user did not specify a QUERYNO, so one was assigned by DB2 (1690).

Examples:

```
1) EXPLAIN PLAN SET QUERYNO = 1
            FOR SELECT * FROM TEST_TABLE
2) EXPLAIN PLAN SET QUERYNO = 2
            FOR SELECT * FROM TEST_TABLE
3) EXPLAIN PLAN FOR DELETE FROM TEST_TABLE
            WHERE DEPT_NUMBER = 100 OR DEPT_NUMBER = 101
4) EXPLAIN PLAN SET QUERYNO = 3
            FOR SELECT * FROM EMPLOYEES_TABLE
            WHERE EMPLOYEE_NO = 415 OR EMPLOYEE_NO = 200
```

The content of the PLAN_TABLE is as follows after the preceding EX-PLAIN statements. The following rows were inserted into the PLAN_TABLE as a result of the previously explained SQL statements. The QUERYNO column identifies the rows that correspond to the previous SQL statements. Appendix C describes the contents of each of the columns. Columns of particular importance are:

ACCESSTYPE	(I, indicates that access is by index listed in AC-CESSNAME.)
	(R, indicates that access is by a scan of all data pages.)
MATCHCOLS	(Represents the number of columns in the index that can be used in the access strategy.)
ACCESSNAME	(The name of the index used. Blank if index not used.)
INDEXONLY	(Y, indicates that only the index will be used to satisfy the request. No reference to the data pointed to by the index is necessary.)
SORT....	(Y, indicates that the Sort Utility will be invoked to complete the request. The sort may be needed to ORDER rows,

to resolve whether rows are DISTINCT, to JOIN rows between tables, or to assist in GROUPing rows. Even though a SQL statement has requested a function appearing to need the sort, it may not always be necessary due to the sequence of the data and available indexes. Performance can be improved if the Sort is not invoked.)

QUERYNO	QBLOCKNO	APPLNAME	PROGNAME	PLANNO	METHOD	CREATOR	TNAME
3	1		DSQIESQL	1	0	USERID1	EMPLOYEES_TABLE
1690	1		DSQIESQL	1	0	USERID1	TEST_TABLE
2	1		DSQIESQL	1	0	USERID1	TEST_TABLE
1	1		DSQIESQL	1	0	USERID1	TEST_TABLE

(Continued)

TABNO	ACCESSTYPE	MATCHCOLS
1	I	1
1	R	0
1	R	0
1	R	0

(Continued)

ACCESSCREATOR	ACCESSNAME	SORTN INDEXONLY	SORTN UNIQ	SORTN JOIN	SORTN ORDERBY	SORTN GROUPBY
USERID1	X_EMPLOYEES_TABLE	N	N	N	N	N
		N	N	N	N	N
		N	N	N	N	N
		N	N	N	N	N

(Continued)

SORTN JOIN	SORTN ORDERBY	SORTN GROUPBY	SORTC UNIQ	SORTC JOIN	SORTC ORDERBY	SORTC GROUPBY	TSLOCKMODE
N	N	N	N	N	N	N	IS
N	N	N	N	N	N	N	X
N	N	N	N	N	N	N	S
N	N	N	N	N	N	N	S

(Continued)

```
TIMESTAMP          REMARKS
----------         --------------------------------
1987071321552736
1987071321534340
1987071321530054
1987071321524163
```

The EXPLAIN statement may indicate what the access method will be, but it does not indicate why the access method was chosen. To get a total picture, you need to also view columns used in the DB2 Catalog by the optimizer. There are products available that collect all the information into easy to interrupt reports. These are well worth the effort to obtain.

LABEL ON: This SQL statement allows users to add or replace data in the LABEL column of the DB2 Catalog tables SYSIBM.SYSCOLUMNS and SYSIBM.SYSTABLES. Similar to the COMMENT ON statement, the LABEL ON statement allows you to add up to 30 characters to describe a column name. Some of the DB2 functions allow the data in the LABEL column to be used in column headings during report writing. If the column names are not very descriptive, the contents of the LABEL column can be used to replace the column name in the report headings. DB2 will, unless told otherwise, use the column name as the column heading in reports generated. The column name is limited to 18 characters, whereas the LABEL column can be up to 30 characters. DB2 will generate COBOL 01 Levels to be included in application programs through a utility called DCLGEN. These 01 Levels are used to store rows during application program processing. This utility can be directed to pass the contents of the LABEL column as comments so that additional documentation can be included in the program describing the tables and views being processed. The format of the LABEL ON statement is as follows.

```
    LABEL ON TABLE table-or-view-name IS '30-characters-of-user-
       comment'
or

    LABEL ON COLUMN
                table-or-view-name.column-name
             IS '30-characters-of-user-comment'
or

    LABEL ON table-or-view-name
       (column-name1 IS '30-characters-of-user-comment',
                    .
                    .
                    .
       column-nameN IS '30-characters-of-user-comment' )
```

Table-or-view-name identifies the name of the table or view for which this SQL statement is to add or revise comments.

'30-characters-of-user-comment' is the actual comment that you wish to have placed on either the table, view, or column.

Column-name(1-N) is the column name that is to have its LABEL column updated. This applies to the LABEL column in SYSIBM.SYSCOLUMNS.

Examples:

```
LABEL ON TABLE TEST_TABLE
      IS 'SAMPLE TABLE FOR ILLUSTRATION'

LABEL ON COLUMN TEST_TABLE.AVERAGESALARY
      IS 'AVERAGE SALARY'
LABEL ON TEST_TABLE
   (DEPT_CHARTER IS 'DEPARTMENT CHARTER',
    DEPT_MANAGER IS 'DEPARTMENT MANAGER',
    AVERAGEAGE IS 'AVERAGE AGE')

LABEL ON TABLE MYVIEW2 IS 'VIEW DEPT 100 & SAL  5000'


*****************************************************************
* Select using DB2I report writer (without LABEL column values  *
* loaded).                                                      *
*****************************************************************


SELECT DEPT_NUMBER,DEPT_MANAGER,AVERAGEAGE,
   DEPTCHARTER FROM TEST_TABLE
```

```
---------+---------+-------------+---------+---------+---------+----
DEPT_NUMBER  DEPT_MANAGER   AVERAGEAGE    DEPTCHARTER
---------+---------+-------------+---------+---------+---------+---+
100          JONES            35          CORPORATE ACCOUNTING
101          ----------    ----------     PURCHASE FROM VENDORS
202          SMITH            32          PRODUCT ENGINEERING
303          SMITH            45          SET PERSONNEL POLICIES
103          BLACK            29          PERFROM ALL PAYROLL FUNC
105          MCJONES          20          DELIVER MAIL
954          EDJONES          27          MAINTAIN BUILDING EXTER
500          JONESS           23          MAKE GUEST ARRANGEMENTS
401          SMITHONEAN       31          COMPUTER APPL DEVELOPME
402          GREEN            18          GARDENING
```

```
************************************************************************
*   Same select using DB2I (with the LABEL column values loaded)    *
*   Note the difference in the column heading!  Since DEPT column   *
*   did not have a LABEL created, it has no heading in the report.*
************************************************************************
```

```
SELECT DEPT_NUMBER,DEPT_MANAGER,AVERAGEAGE,
       DEPTCHARTER FROM TEST_TABLE
```

	DEPARTMENT MANAGER	AVERAGE AGE	DEPARTMENT CHARTER
100	JONES	35	CORPORATE ACCOUNTING
101	---------	------	PURCHASE FROM VENDORS
202	SMITH	32	PRODUCT ENGINEERING
303	SMITH	45	SET PERSONNEL POLICIES
103	BLACK	29	PERFROM ALL PAYROLL FUNC
105	MCJONES	20	DELIVER MAIL
954	EDJONES	27	MAINTAIN BUILDING EXTE
500	JONESS	23	MAKE GUEST ARRANGEMENT
401	SMITHONEAN	31	COMPUTER APPL DEVELOPM
402	GREEN	18	GARDENING

```
************************************************************************
* COBOL output from DB2I's DCLGEN utility if LABELS are not used.*
************************************************************************
```

```
01  DCLTEST-TABLE.
    10 DEPT-NUMBER          PIC S9(9) USAGE COMP.
    10 DEPT-NAME            PIC X(20).
    10 DEPT-MANAGER         PIC X(30).
    10 AVERAGESALARY        PIC S99999V99 USAGE COMP3.
    10 AVERAGEAGE           PIC S9(4) USAGE COMP.
    10 DEPTCHARTER.
       49 DEPTCHARTER-LEN   PIC S9(4) USAGE COMP.
       49 DEPTCHARTER-TEXT  PIC X(200).
    10 PC-WORKSTATIONS      PIC S9(9) USAGE COMP.
```

```
************************************************************************
*  COBOL output from the DCLGEN utility if LABELS are specified. *
************************************************************************
```

```
  01   DCLTEST-TABLE.
*      **********************************************************
      10   DEPT-NUMBER           PIC S9(9) USAGE COMP.
*      **********************************************************
```

(Continued)

```
10   DEPT-NAME                PIC X(20).
*    ********************************************************
*                        DEPARTMENT MANAGER
10 DEPT-MANAGER              PIC X(30).
*    ********************************************************
*                        AVERAGE SALARY
10 AVERAGESALARY             PIC S99999V99 USAGE COMP3.
*    ********************************************************
*                        AVERAGE AGE
10 AVERAGEAGE                PIC S9(4) USAGE COMP.
*    ********************************************************
*                        DEPARTMENT CHARTER
10 DEPTCHARTER.
   49 DEPTCHARTER-LEN    PIC S9(4) USAGE COMP.
   49 DEPTCHARTER-TEXT   PIC X(200).
*    ********************************************************
10 PC-WORKSTATIONS           PIC S9(9) USAGE COMP.
```

Advanced SQL Statements

The following SQL statements are based on the tables identified in Tables
3-2, 3-3, and 3-4. The following SQL statements display many of the features
of the SQL language. They will provide you with a basis upon which you can
build your expertise.

Table 3-2 Employees Table Contents

```
LIST OF COLUMNS FOR TABLE (EMPLOYEES_TABLE)


            SYSIBM.SYSCOLUMNS (DB2 CATALOG)
```

COLUMN NAME	COLUMN NUMBER	COLUMN TYPE	COLUMN LENGTH	SCALE	NULLS ALLOWED
EMPLOYEE_NO	1	INTEGER	4	0	N
EMPLOYEE_NAME	2	CHAR	16	0	N
ADDRESS_STATE	3	CHAR	2	0	N
DEPT	4	CHAR	4	0	N
SALARY	5	DECIMAL	7	2	N

EMPLOYEES_TABLE

EMPLOYEE NO	EMPLOYEE NAME	ADDRESS STATE	DEPT	SALARY
200	LARSON	IL	D890	60000.00
300	SMITH	WI	D900	50000.00
175	MURPHY	IA	D900	40000.00
400	BLACK	MO	D600	60000.00
150	JONES	UT	D600	70000.00
500	EINERSON	UT	D890	80000.00
250	CASPER	MN	D890	70000.00
600	GRAVES	CA	D890	30000.00
350	JORDAN	FL	D890	50000.00
415	THOMPSON	MN	D400	80000.00
425	WASHINGTON	NY	D400	40000.00
450	NICKELS	OH	D500	35000.00
495	GREEN	ND	D700	40000.00
550	WILLMORE	TX	D500	45000.00
700	ROCKY	SC	D890	40000.00
800	KENNEDY	OH	D400	30000.00
900	SHANK	NY	D700	35000.00
850	NELSON	IL	D700	35000.00
750	GRAY	TX	D500	45000.00
650	SMITH	NC	D500	40000.00

Table 3-3 Life Insurance Sales Table Contents

LIST OF COLUMNS FOR TABLE (LIF_INS_SALES)

SYSIBM.SYSCOLUMNS (DB2 CATALOG)

COLUMN NAME	COLUMN NUMBER	COLUMN TYPE	COLUMN LENGTH	SCALE	NULLS ALLOWED
SALESPERSONS_NO	1	INTEGER	4	0	N
REGION	2	CHAR	9	0	N
YTD_SALES	3	DECIMAL	9	2	N
BONUS	4	DECIMAL	7	2	N

```
                         LIF_INS_SALES

SALESPERSONS                     YTD
      NO      REGION           SALES       BONUS
------------  ---------   ------------   ----------
     200      MIDWEST       120000.00      1200.00
     300      MIDWEST       600000.00      6000.00
     175      MIDWEST       700000.00      7000.00
     400      SOUTHEAST    1000000.00     10000.00
     150      NORTHWEST     990000.00      9900.00
     500      NORTHWEST     800000.00      8000.00
     250      MIDWEST       800000.00      8000.00
     600      SOUTHWEST     122000.00      1200.00
     350      SOUTHEAST     750000.00      7500.00
     700      SOUTHEAST     400000.00      4000.00
```

Table 3-4 Auto Insurance Sales Table Contents

```
        LIST OF COLUMNS FOR TABLE (AUTO_INS_SALES)

            SYSIBM.SYSCOLUMNS (DB2 CATALOG)

COLUMN              COLUMN   COLUMN    COLUMN            NULLS
NAME                NUMBER   TYPE      LENGTH   SCALE   ALLOWED

------------------  ------   --------  ------   ------  -------
SALES_PERSON_NO       1      INTEGER     4        0       N
SALES_REGION          2      CHAR        9        0       N
YTD_SALES             3      DECIMAL     9        2       N
BONUS                 4      DECIMAL     7        2       N


                    AUTO_INS_SALES

     SALES
     PERSON      SALES         YTD
       NO        REGION       SALES        BONUS
-----------   ---------   ------------   ----------
415           MIDWEST      200000.00      2000.00
800           MIDWEST      500000.00      5000.00
425           NORTHEAST    750000.00      7500.00
500           NORTHWEST   1000000.00     10000.00
350           SOUTHEAST    500000.00      5000.00
```

```
******************************************************************
                    UNQUALIFIED JOIN                            *
   If you join two tables and fail to qualify the join you get  *
   the Cartesian Product (each row of the first table combined  *
   with each row of the second table). In this case, a 10-row   *
   table X a 20-row table = 200-row result table.               *
******************************************************************
```

```
ELECT EMPLOYEE_NO,  EMPLOYEE_NAME, ADDRESS_STATE, DEPT ,
      SALESPERSONS_NO, REGION
    FROM EMPLOYEES_TABLE, LIF_INS_SALES
```

MPLOYEE AME	ADDRESS STATE	DEPT	SALESPERSONS NO	REGION	EMPLOYEE NO
-------------	-------	----	------------	---------	--------
ARSON	IL	D890	200	MIDWEST	200
ARSON	IL	D890	300	MIDWEST	200
ARSON	IL	D890	175	MIDWEST	200
ARSON	IL	D890	400	SOUTHEAST	200
ARSON	IL	D890	150	NORTHWEST	200
ARSON	IL	D890	500	NORTHWEST	200
ARSON	IL	D890	250	MIDWEST	200
ARSON	IL	D890	600	SOUTHWEST	200
ARSON	IL	D890	350	SOUTHEAST	200
ARSON	IL	D890	700	SOUTHEAST	200
MITH	WI	D900	200	MIDWEST	300
MITH	WI	D900	300	MIDWEST	300
MITH	WI	D900	175	MIDWEST	300
MITH	WI	D900	400	SOUTHEAST	300
MITH	WI	D900	150	NORTHWEST	300
MITH	WI	D900	500	NORTHWEST	300
MITH	WI	D900	250	MIDWEST	300
MITH	WI	D900	600	SOUTHWEST	300
MITH	WI	D900	350	SOUTHEAST	300
MITH	WI	D900	700	SOUTHEAST	300
			.		
			.		
MITH	NC	D500	200	MIDWEST	650
MITH	NC	D500	300	MIDWEST	650
MITH	NC	D500	175	MIDWEST	650
MITH	NC	D500	400	SOUTHEAST	650
MITH	NC	D500	150	NORTHWEST	650
MITH	NC	D500	500	NORTHWEST	650

SMITH	NC	D500	250	MIDWEST	650
SMITH	NC	D500	600	SOUTHWEST	650
SMITH	NC	D500	350	SOUTHEAST	650
SMITH	NC	D500	700	SOUTHEAST	650

```
                                        =======
                                          200
```

```
****************************************************************
*                     QUALIFIED JOIN #1                        *
*  Problem: Find all employees selling life insurance and their *
*  corresponding sales region. Since the sales region is not    *
*  contained in the EMPLOYEES_TABLE, a join is performed between *
*  EMPLOYEES_TABLE and LIF_INS_SALES to get all of the required  *
*  information. By qualifying the above join by EMPLOYEE_NO AND  *
*  SALESPERSONS_NO, the total number of rows returned is 10      *
*  rather than 200.                                             *
****************************************************************
```

```
SELECT EMPLOYEE_NO,  EMPLOYEE_NAME, ADDRESS_STATE, DEPT, REGION
FROM EMPLOYEES_TABLE, LIF_INS_SALES
WHERE EMPLOYEE_NO=SALESPERSONS_NO
```

EMPLOYEE NO	EMPLOYEE NAME	ADDRESS STATE	DEPT	REGION
200	LARSON	IL	D890	MIDWEST
300	SMITH	WI	D900	MIDWEST
175	MURPHY	IA	D900	MIDWEST
400	BLACK	MO	D600	SOUTHEAST
150	JONES	UT	D600	NORTHWEST
500	EINERSON	UT	D890	NORTHWEST
250	CASPER	MN	D890	MIDWEST
600	GRAVES	CA	D890	SOUTHWEST
350	JORDAN	FL	D890	SOUTHEAST
700	ROCKY	SC	D890	SOUTHEAST

```
****************************************************************
*                     QUALIFIED JOIN #2                        *
*  Problem:  Find all employees that sell both life insurance   *
*  and auto insurance. Display name, employee number, and year- *
*  to-date sales for both life and auto insurance. Since        *
*  YTD_SALES column exists in both tables, it has to be fully    *
*  qualified by the table name in order for DB2 to distinguish   *
*  which table column is being referring to. If the column name  *
*  (YTD_SALES) selected is not unique, DB2 will make them unique *
*  in the results.                                             *
****************************************************************
```

```
ELECT EMPLOYEE_NO, EMPLOYEE_NAME, LIF_INS_SALES.YTD_SALES,
      AUTO_INS_SALES.YTD_SALES
   FROM EMPLOYEES_TABLE, LIF_INS_SALES, AUTO_INS_SALES
   WHERE EMPLOYEE_NO =  SALESPERSONS_NO AND
   EMPLOYEE_NO = SALES_PERSON_NO
```

MPLOYEE NO	EMPLOYEE NAME	YTD SALES	YTD SALES1
500	EINERSON	800000.00	1000000.00
350	JORDAN	750000.00	500000.00

```
***************************************************************
                  JOIN USING TABLE DESIGNATORS                *
   Problem:  Find all employees that sell both life insurance  *
   and auto insurance. Display name, employee number, and year- *
   to-date sales for both life and auto insurance. This is the *
   same problem as the previous example. Note how YTD_SALES    *
   column is qualified. In the FROM clause A and B are         *
   considered table designators and allow you to shorten the   *
   table names, as opposed to specifying the entire table name *
   every time a column name has to be fully qualified.         *
***************************************************************
```

```
ELECT EMPLOYEE_NO, EMPLOYEE_NAME, A.YTD_SALES,
      B.YTD_SALES
   FROM EMPLOYEES_TABLE, LIF_INS_SALES A, AUTO_INS_SALES B
   WHERE EMPLOYEE_NO = A.SALESPERSONS_NO AND
         EMPLOYEE_NO = B.SALES_PERSON_NO
RDER BY B.YTD_SALES
```

EMPLOYEE NO	EMPLOYEE NAME	YTD SALES	YTD SALES1
350	JORDAN	750000.00	500000.00
500	EINERSON	800000.00	1000000.00

```
***************************************************************
                  GROUP BY, AVG, MAX, MIN                     *
   Problem:  Find the maximum, minimum, and average salary for *
   employees in each department. The individual detail for each *
   row is not available when using the built-in summary        *
   functions. If both detail and summary information are desired,*
   consider selecting all rows and use QMF to group and compute *
   average, maximum, and minimum values.                       *
***************************************************************
```

```
SELECT DEPT, AVG(SALARY), MAX(SALARY),MIN(SALARY)
FROM EMPLOYEES_TABLE
GROUP BY DEPT
```

	AVERAGE	MAXIMUM	MINIMUM
DEPT	SALARY	SALARY	SALARY
----	----------	----------	---------
D400	50000.00	80000.00	30000.00
D500	41250.00	45000.00	35000.00
D600	65000.00	70000.00	60000.00
D700	36666.67	40000.00	35000.00
D890	55000.00	80000.00	30000.00
D900	45000.00	50000.00	40000.00

```
********************************************************************
*                    GROUP BY, HAVING, AVG, MAX, MIN              *
* Problem:  Find the maximum, minimum and average salary for      *
* employees  in each department. Display only departments having  *
* more than three people working in the department. HAVING        *
* allows you to discard groups.                                   *
********************************************************************
```

```
SELECT DEPT, AVG(SALARY), MAX(SALARY),MIN(SALARY)
FROM EMPLOYEES_TABLE
GROUP BY DEPT
HAVING COUNT(*) > 3
```

	AVERAGE	MAXIMUM	MINIMUM
DEPT	SALARY	SALARY	SALARY
----	----------	----------	---------
D500	41250.00	45000.00	35000.00
D890	55000.00	80000.00	30000.00

```
********************************************************************
*                    COUNT, AVG, MAX, MIN, SUM                    *
*  Problem: Find the maximum salary, minimum salary, average      *
*  salary, and sum of all salaries for all employees. Also count  *
*  the number of employees in the table.                          *
********************************************************************
```

```
SELECT COUNT(*), AVG(SALARY), MAX(SALARY), MIN(SALARY),
                 SUM(SALARY)
FROM EMPLOYEES_TABLE
```

NUMBER OF EMPLOYEES	AVERAGE SALARY	MAXIMUM SALARY	MINIMUM SALARY	SALARY SUM
20	48750.00	80000.00	30000.00	975000.00

```
************************************************************
                    COUNT DISTINCT                        *
  Problem:  Count the number of distinct salaries in the table. *
************************************************************
```

ELECT COUNT(DISTINCT SALARY)
ROM EMPLOYEES_TABLE

```
NUMBER OF
DISTINCT
SALARIES
----------
   8
```

```
************************************************************
                  DISTINCT column-name                    *
  Problem:  Display all the salaries in the employee table. *
  If the same salary is present more than once, display it only *
  once.                                                   *
************************************************************
```

ELECT DISTINCT SALARY
ROM EMPLOYEES_TABLE
RDER BY SALARY DESC

```
ALARY
---------
0000.00
0000.00
0000.00
0000.00
5000.00
0000.00
5000.00
0000.00
```

```
************************************************************
                   UNION, ORDER BY                        *
  The UNION combines the results from two or more SELECTS into *
  one result table.                                       *
  Problem: Combine life and auto insurance sales employees *
  together. Note what happens to employees 500 and 350, which *
```

```
*   are in both tables. LIF_INS_SALES table had 10 rows and      *
*   AUTO_INS_SALES table had 5. If each value in the result row   *
*   is equal to a corresponding value of a row in another result  *
*   table, the duplicate row will be eliminated from the final    *
*   result. If you use ORDER BY, use the position number in the   *
*   select for the columns you want the results sequenced by.     *
*   Note: If you do not want duplicate rows eliminated, replace    *
*   UNION with UNION ALL.                                          *
*   Note: All SELECTs involved in the UNION must have the same    *
*   number of columns specified.                                   *
********************************************************************


SELECT SALESPERSONS_NO,REGION
FROM LIF_INS_SALES
    UNION
SELECT SALES_PERSON_NO,SALES_REGION
 FROM AUTO_INS_SALES
ORDER BY 1


SALESPERSONS
      NO        REGION
------------    ---------
     150        NORTHWEST
     175        MIDWEST
     200        MIDWEST
     250        MIDWEST
     300        MIDWEST
     350        SOUTHEAST
     400        SOUTHEAST
     415        MIDWEST
     425        NORTHEAST
     500        NORTHWEST
     600        SOUTHWEST
     700        SOUTHEAST
     800        MIDWEST


********************************************************************
*     UNION, CHARACTER CONSTANTS, NUMERIC CONSTANTS, ORDER BY      *
*   Problem: Rank the life insurance sales employees by their     *
*   sales performance. Place employees selling over $700,000 in   *
*   a group called high performers. Place employees selling       *
*   from $400,000 to $700,000 into a group called average         *
*   performers. Employees selling less than 400,000 should be     *
*   placed in a low performing group. List the employees by       *
```

```
their ranking and within the ranking list them by their      *
YTD-SALES in descending sequence.                            *
                                                             *
Note: If you are deriving a column by performing a           *
      computation or by specifying a constant, DB2 will      *
      assign the column a name in the results. In this       *
      example, the first and fifth columns specified in the  *
      SELECT list are constants ( COL1 , COL2 ).             *
*****************************************************************
```

```
ELECT 1,SALESPERSONS_NO,EMPLOYEE_NAME,YTD_SALES,
              'HIGH PERFORMING    '
ROM EMPLOYEES_TABLE,LIF_INS_SALES
    WHERE YTD_SALES > 700000 AND SALESPERSONS_NO=EMPLOYEE_NO
NION
ELECT 2,SALESPERSONS_NO,EMPLOYEE_NAME,YTD_SALES,
              'AVERAGE PERFORMING'
ROM EMPLOYEES_TABLE,LIF_INS_SALES
      WHERE YTD_SALES BETWEEN 400000  AND 700000 AND
              SALESPERSONS_NO=EMPLOYEE_NO
NION
ELECT 3,SALESPERSONS_NO,EMPLOYEE_NAME,YTD_SALES,
              'LOW PERFORMING    '
ROM EMPLOYEES_TABLE,LIF_INS_SALES
  WHERE YTD_SALES < 400000 AND SALESPERSONS_NO=EMPLOYEE_NO
RDER BY 1,4 DESC
```

	SALES PERSONS	EMPLOYEE	YTD	
OL1	NO	NAME	SALES	COL2
---	-------	------------	------------	-------------------
1	400	BLACK	1000000.00	HIGH PERFORMING
1	150	JONES	990000.00	HIGH PERFORMING
1	500	EINERSON	800000.00	HIGH PERFORMING
1	250	CASPER	800000.00	HIGH PERFORMING
1	350	JORDAN	750000.00	HIGH PERFORMING
2	175	MURPHY	700000.00	AVERAGE PERFORMING
2	300	SMITH	600000.00	AVERAGE PERFORMING
2	700	ROCKY	400000.00	AVERAGE PERFORMING
3	200	LARSON	120000.00	LOW PERFORMING
3	600	GRAVES	122000.00	LOW PERFORMING

The next series of SQL statements contain what are called Subselects. To urther assist in explaining subselects, I have included a SELECT to calculate he average salary of all employees in the employee table. This computed verage salary will be useful in verifying the results in the following exercise.

```
****************************************************************
*   Problem:   Select the average salary for all employees in the
*   employee table. Keep this computed average salary in mind.
****************************************************************
```

SELECT AVG(SALARY) FROM EMPLOYEES_TABLE

```
  AVERAGE
  SALARY
----------
  48750.00
```

```
****************************************************************
*                        SUBSELECT
*   Problem: Select employees from the employee table making
*   more than the average employee.
*   This SQL statement contains a subselect. The subselect or
*   inner SELECT is executed once and is completed prior to the
*   outer SELECT being executed. The inner SELECT is replaced by
*   the results.
*           SALARY   (SELECT AVG(SALARY) FROM EMPLOYEES_TABLE)
*                    is replaced by
*           SALARY   48750.00
*                    and then the outer select is performed.
****************************************************************
```

SELECT EMPLOYEE_NO,EMPLOYEE_NAME,DEPT,SALARY
 FROM EMPLOYEES_TABLE
WHERE SALARY >
     (SELECT AVG(SALARY) FROM EMPLOYEES_TABLE)

EMPLOYEE NO	EMPLOYEE NAME	DEPT	SALARY
200	LARSON	D890	60000.00
300	SMITH	D900	50000.00
400	BLACK	D600	60000.00
150	JONES	D600	70000.00
500	EINERSON	D890	80000.00
250	CASPER	D890	70000.00
350	JORDAN	D890	50000.00
415	THOMPSON	D400	80000.00

```
****************************************************************
*                     SUBSELECT, ALL
*   Problem:  Find employees who have a salary greater than
*   everyone's salary working in department 500. Skip employees
```

```
that work in department D500 or D400.                              *
This subselect is a little different from the previous one.        *
In the previous subselect only one value AVG(SALARY) was           *
returned. In this subselect more than one value may be             *
returned. Should that be the case, you need to indicate what       *
to do if that happens. Three keywords come into play here.         *
They are (ALL,ANY,IN). ALL implies that whatever condition         *
you are checking for must be true for all values returned          *
from the subselect. ANY implies that the condition you are         *
checking for can be true for any of the values returned from       *
the subselect. IN implies that the condition you are checking      *
for must be equal to one of the values returned from the           *
subselect. In the following subselect, the returned values         *
are: 35000, 45000, 45000, 40000.                                   *
Employees not working in D500 and D400 are checked to see if       *
their salary is greater than all of the values returned.           *
Employees making more than 45000 will be selected if not in        *
D500 or D400.                                                      *
**********************************************************************
```

```
SELECT EMPLOYEE_NO,EMPLOYEE_NAME,DEPT,SALARY
FROM EMPLOYEES_TABLE
WHERE SALARY > ALL
        (SELECT SALARY FROM EMPLOYEES_TABLE
            WHERE DEPT = 'D500')
AND DEPT ¬= 'D500' AND DEPT ¬= 'D400'
```

```
EMPLOYEE    EMPLOYEE
     NO        NAME     DEPT      SALARY
--------   --------    ----   ----------
     200   LARSON      D890    60000.00
     300   SMITH       D900    50000.00
     400   BLACK       D600    60000.00
     150   JONES       D600    70000.00
     500   EINERSON    D890    80000.00
     250   CASPER      D890    70000.00
     350   JORDAN      D890    50000.00
```

Another Solution:

```
SELECT EMPLOYEE_NO,EMPLOYEE_NAME,DEPT,SALARY FROM EMPLOYEES_TABLE
WHERE SALARY >
        (SELECT MAX(SALARY) FROM EMPLOYEES_TABLE WHERE DEPT = 'D500')
            AND DEPT ¬= 'D500' AND DEPT ¬= 'D400'
```

```
************************************************************************
*                      SUBSELECT, ANY                                 *
*  Problem: Find employees with a salary greater than someone         *
*  working in department D500. Skip employees working in              *
*  department D500.                                                   *
*  In the previous select the salary had to be greater than           *
*  all of the values returned from the inner select. In this          *
*  situation, salary in the outer select only has to be               *
*  greater than any of the values returned from the inner             *
*  select. Once again the values returned from the inner select       *
*  are: 35000, 45000, 45000, 40000.                                   *
*  In this situation more employees qualify, since they make          *
*  more than 35000.                                                   *
************************************************************************
```

```
SELECT EMPLOYEE_NO,EMPLOYEE_NAME,DEPT,SALARY
FROM EMPLOYEES_TABLE
WHERE SALARY > ANY
     (SELECT SALARY FROM EMPLOYEES_TABLE
          WHERE DEPT='D500')
       AND DEPT ¬= 'D500'
```

```
EMPLOYEE  EMPLOYEE
    NO      NAME     DEPT     SALARY
--------  --------   ----   ----------
     200  LARSON     D890    60000.00
     300  SMITH      D900    50000.00
     175  MURPHY     D900    40000.00
     400  BLACK      D600    60000.00
     150  JONES      D600    70000.00
     500  EINERSON   D890    80000.00
     250  CASPER     D890    70000.00
     350  JORDAN     D890    50000.00
     415  THOMPSON   D400    80000.00
     425  WASHINGT   D400    40000.00
     495  GREEN      D700    40000.00
     700  ROCKY      D890    40000.00
```

Another Solution:

```
SELECT EMPLOYEE_NO,EMPLOYEE_NAME,DEPT,SALARY FROM EMPLOYEES_TABLE
WHERE SALARY > (SELECT MIN(SALARY) FROM EMPLOYEES_TABLE
                  WHERE DEPT='D500')
AND DEPT ¬= 'D500'
```

```
SELECT EMPLOYEE_NO,EMPLOYEE_NAME,DEPT,SALARY
FROM EMPLOYEES_TABLE
WHERE SALARY   IN
      (SELECT SALARY FROM EMPLOYEES_TABLE
            WHERE DEPT='D500')
      AND DEPT  ¬= 'D500'
```

EMPLOYEE NO	EMPLOYEE NAME	DEPT	SALARY
175	MURPHY	D900	40000.00
425	WASHINGTON	D400	40000.00
495	GREEN	D700	40000.00
700	ROCKY	D890	40000.00
900	SHANK	D700	35000.00
850	NELSON	D700	35000.00

The next type of SELECT to be reviewed is the Correlated Subselect. To further assist you in understanding the Correlated Subselect, the following select statement computes the average salary for each department. These values will be helpful in understanding the following Correlated Subselect.

```
SELECT DEPT,AVG(SALARY)
FROM EMPLOYEES_TABLE
GROUP BY DEPT
ORDER BY DEPT
```

```
AVERAGE
 DEPT     SALARY
 ----    ----------
 D400     50000.00
 D500     41250.00
 D600     65000.00
 D700     36666.67
 D890     55000.00
 D900     45000.00
```

```
**************************************************************
*                    CORRELATED SUBSELECT                    *
*    Problem: Find employees having a salary greater than the *
*    average salary for their department Again we have a      *
*    subselect, but this time it is a little different. In this *
*    situation the subselect is executed once for each row    *
*    retrieved by the outer SELECT. You may have guessed that *
*    this will be more expensive to run. In the FROM clause of *
*    the outer SELECT we see XXX, which is a table designator. *
*    It allows us to correlate columns of an outer SELECT with *
*    columns in the inner subselect. "XXX.DEPT"is the outer   *
*    column used in the inner subselect for comparisons. In the *
*    process of executing this query, a row is read by the outer *
*    select, and the department number is passed to the inner  *
*    SELECT where the inner SELECT is executed to determine the *
*    average  salary for the department in the outer row. This *
*    type of subselect is called a Correlated Subselect.      *
**************************************************************
```

```
SELECT EMPLOYEE_NO,EMPLOYEE_NAME,DEPT,SALARY
FROM EMPLOYEES_TABLE XXX
WHERE SALARY >
      (SELECT AVG(SALARY) FROM EMPLOYEES_TABLE
            WHERE DEPT=XXX.DEPT)
ORDER BY DEPT,EMPLOYEE_NO
```

```
EMPLOYEE   EMPLOYEE
   NO        NAME         DEPT      SALARY
--------   ---------      ----    ----------
     415   THOMPSON       D400     80000.00
     550   WILLMORE       D500     45000.00
     750   GRAY           D500     45000.00
     150   JONES          D600     70000.00
     495   GREEN          D700     40000.00
     200   LARSON         D890     60000.00
```

```
250   CASPER          D890    70000.00
500   EINERSON        D890    80000.00
300   SMITH           D900    50000.00
```

```
*********************************************************************
*                  EXISTS, CORRELATED SUBSELECT                    *
*   Find employees who sell both life and auto insurance.  In      *
*   the following select the EXISTS keyword is used. It allows      *
*   you to check the results of the inner subselect without         *
*   being concerned about the actual values returned. If any        *
*   rows are selected by the inner SELECT, it is considered a       *
*   true condition. If no rows are returned by the inner            *
*   SELECT, the condition is considered false. In this SELECT        *
*   we are looking at the life insurance table and the              *
*   employee table. If someone in the life insurance sales          *
*   table exists in the auto insurance sales table, the inner       *
*   select is considered true and the row in the outer select       *
*   is selected. The '*' is specified in the inner SELECT,          *
*   since no columns are actually returned. As soon as one          *
*   match is found in the inner SELECT, a true condition is          *
*   returned and the search is terminated.                         *
*********************************************************************
```

```
SELECT SALESPERSONS_NO,EMPLOYEE_NAME
     FROM LIF_INS_SALES X,EMPLOYEES_TABLE
        WHERE SALESPERSONS_NO = EMPLOYEE_NO AND
          EXISTS (SELECT * FROM AUTO_INS_SALES
                     WHERE SALES_PERSON_NO=X.SALESPERSONS_NO)
```

```
SALES
PERSONS   EMPLOYEE
   NO       NAME
-------   --------
   350   JORDAN
   500   EINERSON
```

```
*********************************************************************
*                          NOT EXISTS                              *
*   Find employees that do not sell either life or auto            *
*   insurance. In addition to using the EXISTS to check for true   *
*   conditions, you can also check for false conditions. This is   *
*   done by coding NOT EXISTS. In the following select we will      *
*   check to see if employees exist in either the life or auto     *
*   insurance tables. If they don't (NOT EXIST), then they         *
*   should be selected.                                            *
*********************************************************************
```

```
SELECT EMPLOYEE_NO,EMPLOYEE_NAME
      FROM EMPLOYEES_TABLE X
          WHERE NOT EXISTS
                      (SELECT * FROM AUTO_INS_SALES
                            WHERE SALES_PERSON_NO=X.EMPLOYEE_NO)
              AND
                  NOT EXISTS
                      (SELECT * FROM LIF_INS_SALES
                            WHERE SALESPERSONS_NO=X.EMPLOYEE_NO)


    EMPLOYEE     EMPLOYEE
        NO       NAME
-----------  ----------------
        450  NICKELS
        495  GREEN
        550  WILLMORE
        900  SHANK
        850  NELSON
        750  GRAY
        650  SMITH
```

```
**************************************************************************
*                 DELETE, CORRELATED SUBSELECT                          *
*  Delete employees from EMPLOYEES table who are not in the             *
*  LIFE_INSURANCE table. This one SQL statement will delete             *
*  half of the employees in the EMPLOYEES table.                        *
**************************************************************************
```

```
DELETE FROM EMPLOYEES X
    WHERE NOT EXISTS
      (SELECT * FROM LIFE_INSURANCE
        WHERE SALESPERSONS_NO=X.EMPLOYEE_NO)


          EMPLOYEES (Table before delete)


    EMPLOYEE  EMPLOYEE          ADDRESS
        NO    NAME              STATE   DEPT    SALARY
-----------  ----------------  -------  ----  ----------
        200  LARSON            IL       D890   60000.00
        300  SMITH             WI       D900   50000.00
        175  MURPHY            IA       D900   40000.00
        400  BLACK             MO       D600   60000.00
        150  JONES             UT       D600   70000.00
        500  EINERSON          UT       D890   80000.00
        250  CASPER            MN       D890   70000.00
        600  GRAVES            CA       D890   30000.00
        350  JORDAN            FL       D890   50000.00
```

```
415   THOMPSON        MN        D400      80000.00
425   WASHINGTON      NY        D400      40000.00
450   NICKELS         OH        D500      35000.00
495   GREEN           ND        D700      40000.00
550   WILLMORE        TX        D500      45000.00
700   ROCKY           SC        D890      40000.00
800   KENNEDY         OH        D400      30000.00
900   SHANK           NY        D700      35000.00
850   NELSON          IL        D700      35000.00
750   GRAY            TX        D500      45000.00
650   SMITH           NC        D500      40000.00
```

EMPLOYEES (Table after delete)

```
EMPLOYEE   EMPLOYEE            ADDRESS
NO         NAME                STATE   DEPT    SALARY
--------   ----------------    -------  ----   ----------
     200   LARSON              IL       D890   60000.00
     300   SMITH               WI       D900   50000.00
     175   MURPHY              IA       D900   40000.00
     400   BLACK               MO       D600   60000.00
     150   JONES               UT       D600   70000.00
     500   EINERSON            UT       D890   80000.00
     250   CASPER              MN       D890   70000.00
     600   GRAVES              CA       D890   30000.00
     350   JORDAN              FL       D890   50000.00
     700   ROCKY               SC       D890   40000.00
```

Table 3-5 Null Values Table Contents

```
                          NULL_VALUES_TABLE

                    S  S
                    M  M   I    I
                    A  A   N    N
                    L  L   T    T
C   C               L  L   E    E
H   H               I  I   G    G
A   A               N  N   E    E
R   R   VAR    VAR  T  T   R    R DECIMAL DECIMAL
1   2   CHAR1  CHAR2 1  2  1    2   1       2     FLOAT1    FLOAT2
--  --  ------- ------- -- -- --- ---- ------ ------ --------- ---------
AA  AB  ABCDEFG ABCDEFG 11 12 123 1234 123.12 123.12 4.000E+03 4.000E+02
AA  AB  ABCDEFG ABCDEFG 11 12 123 1234 123.12 123.12 4.000E+03 4.000E+02
AB  BB  BBBBBBB BBBBBBB 22 22 222 2222 222.22 222.22 2.222E+03 2.220E+02
CC  CC  CCCCCCC CCCCCCC 33 33 333 3333 333.33 333.33 3.333E+03 3.330E+02
```

```
DD DD DDDDDD DDDDDD 44 44 444 4444 444.44 444.44 4.444E+03 4.440E+02
EE EE EEEEEE EEEEEE 55 55 555 5555 555.55 555.55 5.555E+03 5.550E+02
-    -                -  0  -  0    -   0.00          - 0.000E+00
- SS SS       SS      0  0  0  0  0.00   0.00 0.000E+00 0.000E+00
```

The following SQL statements are based on Table 3-5.

```
*************************************************************************
*                              NULLS                                    *
*      When grouping by a column that contains nulls, the null          *
*      will be considered a group.                                      *
*************************************************************************
```

```
SELECT CHAR1,COUNT(*)
FROM NULL_VALUES_TABLE
GROUP BY CHAR1
```

```
         COUNT OF ROWS
CHAR1    IN GROUP
-----    --------------
AA             2
AB             1
CC             1
DD             1
EE             1
-              2
```

```
*************************************************************************
*                              NULLS                                    *
* Null values are omitted from AVG, SUM, MAX, MIN, and COUNT            *
* DISTINCT.                                                             *
* Nulls are included in counts.                                        *
*************************************************************************
```

```
SELECT AVG(INTEGER1),MAX(INTEGER1),MIN(INTEGER1),
SUM(INTEGER1),COUNT(*),
COUNT(DISTINCT CHAR1)
FROM NULL_VALUES_TABLE
```

```
                                        COUNT
AVERAGE MAXIMUM MINIMUM    SUM   COUNT DISTINCT
------- ------- ------- ------- ------- --------
257     555       0      1800     8       5
```

```
*********************************************************************
*                              NULLS                               *
*    Nulls do not participate in comparisons.                      *
*********************************************************************
```

```
SELECT CHAR1, CHAR2, VARCHAR1, VARCHAR2
     , SMALLINT1, SMALLINT2, INTEGER1
     , INTEGER2
FROM NULL_VALUES_TABLE
WHERE SMALLINT1 < 22 OR SMALLINT1 > 44
```

				SMALL	SMALL		
CHAR1	CHAR2	VARCHAR1	VARCHAR2	INT1	INT2	INTEGER1	INTEGER2
AA	AB	ABCDEFG	ABCDEFG	11	12	123	1234
AA	AB	ABCDEFG	ABCDEFG	11	12	123	1234
EE	EE	EEEEEE	EEEEEE	55	55	555	5555
-	SS	SS	SS	0	0	0	0

```
*********************************************************************
*                         NULLS, UPDATE                            *
*    The following select indicates the results of performing      *
*    computations on columns containing null values. Any           *
*    calculation that involves a NULL value produces a Null        *
*    value.                                                        *
*********************************************************************
```

```
UPDATE NULL_VALUES_TABLE SET
       SMALLINT1=SMALLINT1*100
     , SMALLINT2=SMALLINT2*100
     , INTEGER1=INTEGER1+1000
     , INTEGER2=INTEGER2+1000
     , DECIMAL1=DECIMAL1/10
     , DECIMAL2=DECIMAL2/10
```

CHAR1	CHAR2	SMALLINT1	SMALLINT2	INTEGER1	INTEGER2	DECIMAL1	DECIMAL2
AA	AB	1100	1200	1123	2234	12.31	12.31
AA	AB	1100	1200	1123	2234	12.31	12.31
AB	BB	2200	2200	1222	3222	22.22	22.22
CC	CC	3300	3300	1333	4333	33.33	33.33
DD	DD	4400	4400	1444	5444	44.44	44.44
EE	EE	5500	5500	1555	6555	55.55	55.55
-	SS	0	0	1000	1000	0.00	0.00
-	-	-	0	-	1000	-	0.00

Questions:

1. List the order in which the following DB2 objects should be created if interdependent.
Index
Table
Database
Storage Group
Tablespace
2. List the four types of DML SQL statements.
3. List the three types of DDL SQL statements.
4. What are the two levels at which data is locked from other applications?
5. Applications wanting to free held locks should issue _____ frequently.
6. An application that is updating large volumes of data, when no other applications are processing against the tables, could issue _____ for better performance.
7. The _____ statement should be used to assist in determining which access strategy the DB2 Optimizer has chosen.
8. _____ can be used to reference a table by another name.
9. Applications wishing to undo changes rather than commiting should issue the _____ statement.
10. Large tablespaces can be further divided into _____ for ease of managing.

True or False:

11. An index setup to prevent duplicate rows from being inserted into a table is said to be CLUSTERED.
12. Pages of free space can be placed throughout the tablespace by the PCTFREE parameter.
13. Columns can be added and removed from a table by using the ALTER statement.
14. Dropping a database removes all dependant objects, such as tablespaces, tables, and indexes.
15. Specifying two tables in the FROM clause constitutes a JOIN.
16. The ORDER BY clause determines the sequence in which columns are to be returned.
17. The EXISTS does not return any rows.
18. The WHERE, ORDER BY, HAVING, and GROUP BY clauses can be in any sequence, as long as they follow the FROM clause.
19. CHAR, VARCHAR, and DATE are all valid DB2 character data types.
20. The same disk volume may be specified in more than one storage group.

Answers:

1. Storage Group, Database, Tablespace, Table, Index

2. SELECT, UPDATE, INSERT, DELETE
3. CREATE, ALTER, DROP
4. Page, Tablespace
5. COMMITs
6. LOCK TABLE
7. EXPLAIN
8. SYNONYMS
9. ROLLBACK
10. Partitions
11. False, (UNIQUE)
12. False, (FREEPAGE)
13. False, Only added
14. True
15. True
16. False; the sequence is determined by the sequence specified in the selected column list. ORDER BY determines the sequence in which the rows are returned.
17. True
18. False; if specified, they must be in the following sequence: WHERE, GROUP BY, HAVING, and ORDER BY.
19. True
20. True

Query Management Facility (QMF)

The Query Management Facility (QMF) is a licensed interactive product offered by IBM to supplement DB2 in the TSO environment. QMF is a must because it allows each user to manage his or her SQL statements. To many users, QMF is inseparable from DB2. QMF provides the user-friendly interface to DB2 necessary to make DB2 usable by nonprofessionals and professionals alike. The user can develop, test, and store SQL queries for future use. QMF displays the rows retrieved in reports or charts. The user can then modify the report to suit his or her own needs. Not only will QMF allow users to execute stored queries, it allows users to share queries with others. Queries can be developed to serve multiple functions by allowing the development of SQL statements in such a manner that the user is prompted for variables to complete the query. One query could serve the needs of many users, thus reducing redundant development. Through QMF variables, different tables can be accessed by the same stored query. QMF allows a person to select a subset of rows from a large table, save the selected rows in a new table, and proceed to analyze the new table. QMF is also suitable for ad hoc user requests. With little assistance, users can be trained to use QMF to satisfy their own requests.

QMF allows the user to create queries in two different languages. The first is SQL to which you have already been exposed. The second language is referred to as QBE, which stands for Query By Example. QBE allows the user to construct a query by creating examples of the items to be to be queried.

QMF contains several system tables. Availability of the system tables will vary according to the controls placed by the installation. The content and use of these tables are outlined below.

Q.COMMAND_SYNONYMS — allows the installation to make additional commands available to users. QMF has commands to assist the user in managing queries. Commands such as SAVE and ERASE allow users to save and remove their stored queries. In addition to executing QMF system commands, additional commands can be developed by the installation to complement or replace the ones provided. These commands may be stored in this table or in installation defined tables.

Q.ERROR_LOG — is used automatically by QMF to record information when a user encounters resource, system, or QMF program errors. Should the user go to report a problem and not have all the documentation pertaining to the error, this table can be inquired against to display the error message received by the user.

Q.OBJECT_DATA — contains information describing the item stored. A stored item could be a procedure, form, or query.

Q.OBJECT_DIRECTORY — describes what kind of object is being stored and whether others are allowed to access the stored object.

Q.OBJECT_REMARKS — gives the individual saving the query the ability to record comments about the stored object.

Q.PROFILES — contains information about how an individual's QMF session is to be structured. This includes items such as PFKEY definitions, commands available, language to be used (SQL or QBE), whether changes require confirmation or not, and others. The information contained in the profile is used during the entire QMF session unless the user modifies it. This information can be modified temporarily during a session or recorded permanently.

Q.RESOURCE_TABLE — is a table allowing individuals responsible for QMF administration a method of treating QMF users differently. Through this table, users can be restricted in various ways. The methods of control varies from not allowing some users to use certain commands to not allowing others to use QMF during prime shift operations.

When a user invokes QMF, work areas are established for the user. In these work areas, the user develops and views the results of SQL statements and QMF Commands. The information placed in the work areas, whether by

QMF or the user, will reside in the work areas until the user either exits from QMF or performs another task overlaying the contents in the work areas. Thus, a user can execute a query in the work area and proceed to test it until it is working as desired. The user can then save the query for future use. Saved queries, procedures, and forms can be retrieved, modified, and resaved at any time.

```
QMF HOME PANEL                              Query
                                            Management
                                            Facility

(c) Copyright IBM Corp.


                        ******    **    **      **********
                      **    **  **  ***   ***    **
                      **    **  **** ****    *******
                      **    **  ** ** ** **    **
                    **   * **  **  ****  **  **
                    ******    **    **    ** **
                        *


Type command on command line or use PF keys.
For help, press PF1 or type HELP.

1=Help      2=List    3=Exit     4=        5=Chart   6=Query
7=Retrieve  8=  9=Form   10=Proc   11=Profile   12=Report
OK, you may enter a command.
COMMAND === DISPLAY QUERY
```

This is the QMF HOME PANEL. In the basic set of QMF panels, the bottom line is the Command Line. From it, you can enter commands to assist you in the construction, saving, and execution of queries, as well as navigation to the various work areas of QMF. Commands should be entered following COMMAND ===. The line just above the Command Line is the Message Line. This line is used by QMF to relay information to you regarding your interactive session. QMF will return to the user the status of the last command given. Above the Message Line are PFKEYS, which can be used in place of entering a command on the Command Line. The PFKEYS can be user defined or system defined. Several work areas are established when the QMF session is initiated. The top line of the QMF panel portrays which of the QMF work areas you are viewing. Information placed in the work areas will reside there until the session is terminated, the user requests the work area to be reset, or the user executes a command causing it to be overlaid. The work areas are as follows:

```
QUERY  (SQL or QBE)
DATA   (REPORT)
FORM
PROC
PROFILE
LIST
```

The following scenario of panels illustrates some of the potential uses of QMF. To begin, lets enter the command DISPLAY QUERY on the Command Line and press ENTER as seen on the QMF HOME PANEL. Pressing PF6 will also execute the DISPLAY QUERY command. Both direct QMF to the QUERY work area.

```
SQL QUERY                                    LINE 1




*** END ***




1=Help      2=Run      3=End    4=Print   5=Chart    6=Draw
7=Backward 8=Forward 9=Form 10=Insert 11=Delete 12=Report

COMMAND ===>                           SCROLL ===> PAGE
```

The above panel shows an empty SQL QUERY work area. On this panel SQL statements are constructed within QMF.

```
SQL QUERY                            MODIFIED    LINE 1


-- ANYTHING THAT FOLLOWS TWO DASHES PLACED ANY WHERE ON A
      -- LINE IS TREATED AS A COMMENT.
-- YOU CAN SELECT THE SAME COLUMN MORE THAN ONCE IN A SELECT.
-- IF YOU ORDER BY A COLUMN USED MORE THAN ONCE IN THE SELECT,
-- USE THE POSITION IN THE SELECT COLUMN LIST.
SELECT EMPLOYEE_NO, EMPLOYEE_NAME
      , ADDRESS_STATE, DEPT, SALARY, SALARY,SALARY
FROM EMPLOYEES_TABLE
ORDER BY DEPT,5 DESC




1=Help     2=Run     3=End    4=Print   5=Chart    6=Draw
7=Backward 8=Forward 9=Form 10=Insert 11=Delete 12=Report
COMMAND ===>                                SCROLL ===> PAGE
```

The above SQL statement was constructed to access the EMPLOYEES_TABLE. Note that the 5 DESC in the ORDER BY clause refers to the first of three SALARY fields in the SELECT list.

```
SQL QUERY                              MODIFIED     LINE 1

-- ANYTHING THAT FOLLOWS THE TWO DASHES IS TREATED AS A COMMENT.
-- YOU CAN SELECT THE SAME COLUMN MORE THAN ONCE IN A SELECT.
-- IF YOU ORDER BY A COLUMN USED MORE THAN ONCE IN THE SELECT,
-- USE THE POSITION IN THE SELECT COLUMN LIST.
SELECT EMPLOYEE_NO, EMPLOYEE_NAME
     , ADDRESS_STATE, DEPT, SALARY, SALARY,SALARY
FROM EMPLOYEES_TABLE
ORDER BY DEPT, 5 DESC




1=Help      2=Run     3=End    4=Print   5=Chart   6=Draw
7=Backward 8=Forward 9=Form 10=Insert 11=Delete 12=Report
OK, QUERY is displayed.
COMMAND ===> save query as employee_q1          SCROLL ===> PAGE
```

Should you wish to save the query, enter a QMF command called SAVE and the name by which you wish to refer to this stored query. The query name can be up to 18 characters, similar to table name. In this case, the saved query is called employee_q1. The query is stored in the QMF system tables as a result of the save.

```
SQL QUERY            EMPLOYEE_Q1                          LINE 1

-- ANYTHING THAT FOLLOWS THE TWO DASHES IS TREATED AS A COMMENT.
-- YOU CAN SELECT THE SAME COLUMN MORE THAN ONCE IN A SELECT.
-- IF YOU ORDER BY A COLUMN USED MORE THAN ONCE IN THE SELECT,
-- USE THE POSITION IN THE SELECT COLUMN LIST.
SELECT EMPLOYEE_NO, EMPLOYEE_NAME
      , ADDRESS_STATE, DEPT, SALARY, SALARY,SALARY
FROM EMPLOYEES_TABLE
ORDER BY DEPT,5 DESC




1=Help      2=Run     3=End    4=Print   5=Chart    6=Draw
7=Backward 8=Forward 9=Form 10=Insert 11=Delete 12=Report
OK, QUERY was saved as EMPLOYEE_Q1 in the data base.
COMMAND ===> run query                       SCROLL ===> PAGE
```

When QMF completes the task, a message indicating that the query was saved is returned to you. If you wish to run the query, enter RUN QUERY on the Command Line and press enter or just press PF2. Since a query name was not specified with the run command, the query in the present QUERY work area will be executed.

```
REPORT                              LINE 1        POS 1      79


EMPLOYEE EMPLOYEE   ADDRESS
    NO     NAME     STATE DEPT    SALARY     SALARY1    SALARY2
-------- ---------- ------- ---- ---------- ---------- ----------
     415 THOMPSON   MN    D400   80000.00   80000.00   80000.00
     425 WASHINGTON NY    D400   40000.00   40000.00   40000.00
     800 KENNEDY    OH    D400   30000.00   30000.00   30000.00
     550 WILLMORE   TX    D500   45000.00   45000.00   45000.00
     750 GRAY       TX    D500   45000.00   45000.00   45000.00
     650 SMITH      NC    D500   40000.00   40000.00   40000.00
     450 NICKELS    OH    D500   35000.00   35000.00   35000.00
     150 JONES      UT    D600   70000.00   70000.00   70000.00
     400 BLACK      MO    D600   60000.00   60000.00   60000.00
     495 GREEN      ND    D700   40000.00   40000.00   40000.00
     900 SHANK      NY    D700   35000.00   35000.00   35000.00
     850 NELSON     IL    D700   35000.00   35000.00   35000.00
     500 EINERSON   UT    D890   80000.00   80000.00   80000.00
1=Help    2=      3=End        4=Print       5=Chart     6=Query
7=Backward 8=Forward  9=Form 10=Left    11=Right      12=
OK, REPORT is displayed.
COMMAND === display form                    SCROLL === PAGE
```

Executing the query causes the above panel to be displayed. You are viewing a report as indicated on the top line of the panel. You do not view data
directly. If the entire report will not fit on a single screen, you can use the
PFKEYS to scroll backward, forward, left, or right in the report. QMF uses
what is called a FORM to format a report for the data retrieved. What you see
in this report is the result of using a default FORM automatically generated
by QMF. To display this FORM and optionally change the report layout, enter
DISPLAY FORM on the Command Line or press PF9. You will then see the
default FORM placed in the FORM work area.

```
FORM.MAIN

COLUMNS:              Total Width of Report Columns: 82
  NUM  COLUMN HEADING                 USAGE   INDENT  WIDTH  EDIT
  ---  --------------------------     -------  ------  -----  -----
    1  EMPLOYEE_NO                       2       11     L
    2  EMPLOYEE_NAME                     2       16     C
    3  ADDRESS_STATE                     2       7      C
    4  DEPT                              2       4      C
    5  SALARY                            2       10     L2


PAGE:   HEADING ===>
        FOOTING ===>
FINAL:  TEXT ===>
BREAK1:   NEW PAGE FOR BREAK? === NO
          FOOTING ===>
BREAK2:   NEW PAGE FOR BREAK? ===> NO
          FOOTING ===>
OPTIONS:  OUTLINE? ===> YES       DEFAULT BREAK TEXT? ===> YES

  1=Help 2=Check 3=End 4=Form.Columns 5=Form.Options 6=Query
  7=Backward 8=Forward 9=Form.Page 10=Form.Final 11=Form.Break1
 12=Report
OK, FORM is displayed.
  COMMAND === forward                     SCROLL === PAGE
```

This is the FORM.MAIN PANEL in the FORM work area. As indicated by
the PFKEYs, several other FORM panels can be referenced to further specify
report options. Pressing PF8 or entering FORWARD on the Command Line of
this panel allows you to view the additional columns referenced in the Select.

```
FORM.MAIN

COLUMNS:                    Total Width of Report Columns: 82
NUM   COLUMN HEADING                USAGE    INDENT  WIDTH  EDIT
---   --------------------------    -------  ------  -----  -----
  6   SALARY1                                  2      10     L2
  7   SALARY2                                  2      10     L2
      *** END ***
      PAGE:  HEADING ===>
      FOOTING ===>
FINAL:  TEXT ===>
BREAK1:  NEW PAGE FOR BREAK? ===> NO
         FOOTING ===>
BREAK2:  NEW PAGE FOR BREAK? ===> NO
         FOOTING ===>
OPTIONS:  OUTLINE? ===> YES          DEFAULT BREAK TEXT? ===> YES


 1=Help 2=Check 3=End 4=Form.Columns  5=Form.Options  6=Query
 7=Backward 8=Forward  9=Form.Page 10=Form.Final    11=Form.Break1
12=Report


COMMAND === display report                    SCROLL === PAGE
```

If the same column is selected more than once, QMF uniquely identifies the column name in the COLUMN HEADING. The first SALARY retained the column heading SALARY. The second and third SALARY columns had headings of SALARY1 and SALARY2, respectively. The column heading in the report is the same as the column name unless overridden in the form. Should the column heading not be sufficient for your report, you can replace it with whatever you desire in the COLUMN HEADING column for the selected columns being displayed. The COLUMNS: NUM column refers to the column position in regard to the select statement. When the report is displayed again, all the changes made to the form will be reflected. PF12 or entering DISPLAY REPORT on the Command Line will redisplay the report. It was not necessary to run the query again just to alter the report FORM, since the data is still in the DATA work area. The columns are presented in the FORM in the same sequence as coded on the query. Their sequence in the report may vary depending on the type of USAGE specified. For example, if you request the

eport to break on certain columns, these columns will appear on the left side
f the report regardless of their order specification in the SELECT. Likewise,
olumns having a USAGE of SUM and COUNT will appear on the right side
f the report.

```
FORM.MAIN                                        MODIFIED

COLUMNS:                Total Width of Report Columns: 47
  NUM  COLUMN HEADING             USAGE    INDENT  WIDTH  EDIT
  ---  ------------------------------   ------  -----  -----
    1  EMPLOYEE_NO                          1       8     L
    2  EMPLOYEE_NAME               OMIT     1      10     C
    3  ADDRESS_STATE               OMIT     1       7     C
    4  DEPT                        BREAK1   1       4     C
    5  SALARY                      SUM      1      10     L2

PAGE:  HEADING ===> DISPLAY MAXIMUM & MINIMUM SALARY
       FOOTING ===> ** CONFIDENTIAL REPORT **
FINAL:  TEXT ===>
BREAK1:  NEW PAGE FOR BREAK? ===> NO
         FOOTING ===>
BREAK2:  NEW PAGE FOR BREAK? === NO
         FOOTING ===>
OPTIONS:  OUTLINE? ===> YES        DEFAULT BREAK TEXT? ===> YES
1=Help  2=Check  3=End  4=Form.Columns  5=Form.Options  6=Query
7=Backward 8=Forward 9=Form.Page 10=Form.Final 11=Form.Break1
12=Report
OK, BACKWARD performed, Please Proceed.
COMMAND ===> forward                       SCROLL ===> PAGE
```

Through the USAGE column, you can OMIT columns from the report, place
control BREAKs in the report and SUM the values for numeric columns.
Pressing PF8 or entering FORWARD on the command line and pressing
ENTER will display additional columns if present. Likewise pressing PF7 or
entering BACKWARD will display previous columns. Note the message
generated by QMF following a BACKWARD COMMAND. Also note, the
columns are listed in the FORM in the same sequence in which they were
specified in the SELECT statement.

```
FORM.MAIN                                          MODIFIED


COLUMNS:              Total Width of Report Columns: 47
  NUM  COLUMN HEADING                USAGE     INDENT  WIDTH  EDIT
  ---  --------------------------    -------   ------  -----  -----
    6  MINIMUM_SALARY                MINIMUM   1       10     L2
    7  MAXIMUM_SALARY                MAXIMUM   1       10     L2
       *** END ***




PAGE:  HEADING ===> DISPLAY MAXIMUM & MINIMUM SALARY
       FOOTING ===> ** CONFIDENTIAL REPORT **
FINAL: TEXT ===>
BREAK1: NEW PAGE FOR BREAK? ===> NO
        FOOTING ===>
BREAK2: NEW PAGE FOR BREAK? ===> NO
        FOOTING ===>
OPTIONS:  OUTLINE? ===> YES          DEFAULT BREAK TEXT? ===> YES


1=Help 2=Check 3=End    4=Form.Columns  5=Form.Options  6=Query
7=Backward 8=Forward  9=Form.Page  10=Form.Final 11=Form.Break1
12=Report
OK, FORWARD performed. Please proceed.
=== display form.page              SCROLL === PAGE
```

You can specify maximum and minimum values to be determined for a
column. If the headings or footings you wish to include on the report do not fit
on the one line provided on the FORM.MAIN panel, press PF9 or enter DIS-
PLAY FORM.PAGE and you will be directed to a FORM.PAGE panel for including additional information about headings and footings.

```
FORM.PAGE                                               MODIFIED


Blank Lines Before Heading ===>0 Blank Lines After Heading ===>2
LINE   ALIGN    PAGE HEADING TEXT
----   ------   -------------------------------------------------
1      CENTER   DISPLAY MAXIMUM & MINIMUM SALARY
2      CENTER   PER DEPARTMENT
3      CENTER   DATE: &DATE      TIME: &TIME
4      CENTER
5      CENTER


Blank Lines Before Footing ===>2 Blank Lines After Footing ===>0
LINE   ALIGN    PAGE FOOTING TEXT
----   ------   -------------------------------------------------
1      LEFT     ** CONFIDENTIAL REPORT **
2      CENTER
3      CENTER
4      CENTER
5      CENTER


1=Help  2=Check 3=End   4=Form.Columns  5=Form.Options   6=Query
7=  8=  9=Form.Main   10=Form.Final   11=Form.Break1   12=Report
OK, FORM.PAGE is displayed.
COMMAND ===> display report
```

Up to five lines can be included in report headings and footings. If you wish
to include values from one of the columns selected in the heading or footing,
specify &n, where n is the column number from the FORM.MAIN panel. This
is commonly used when a new page is desired when a column changes values.
The columns whose values are to be placed in heading and/or footings can be
omitted from the report detail if desired. Information in headings and footings
can be left justified, centered, or right justified. In addition to including
column data in the report headings and footings, QMF has several system
variables that may be included. &DATE and &TIME are two of the most
popular. They allow you to timestamp the reports generated. The date and
time the report was generated will be, in this case, placed on the third line of
the report heading. PF12 or entering DISPLAY REPORT on the Command
Line will redisplay the report with the altered FORM.

```
REPORT                                LINE 1      POS 1      79

                      DISPLAY MAXIMUM & MINIMUM SALARY
                             PER DEPARTMENT
                      DATE: 87/07/17    TIME: 19:31

         EMPLOYEE                 MINIMUM     MAXIMUM
DEPT       NO       SALARY        SALARY      SALARY
----    --------  ----------   ----------  ----------
D400      415     80000.00     80000.00     80000.00
          425     40000.00     40000.00     40000.00
          800     30000.00     30000.00     30000.00

                  ----------   ----------  ----------
           *     150000.00     30000.00     80000.00

D500      550     45000.00     45000.00     45000.00
          750     45000.00     45000.00     45000.00
          650     40000.00     40000.00     40000.00
          450     35000.00     35000.00     35000.00
1=Help    2=          3=End        4=Print       5=Chart   6=Query
7=Backward    8=Forward      9=Form   10=Left   11=Right      12=
OK, REPORT is displayed.
COMMAND ===>                                    SCROLL ===> PAGE
```

Since a report could be multiple pages, PF8 or the command FORWARD will take you to the next page while PF7 will take you back one page. Should you prefer to go to the bottom of the report, enter BOTTOM on the Command Line and press ENTER. Likewise, TOP on the command line will take you to the first page of the report. Note that the DEPT column, which was specified as a BREAK column, is displayed only when its value changes.

```
REPORT                                  LINE 19      POS 1      79
        EMPLOYEE                MINIMUM   MAXIMUM
  DEPT    NO        SALARY      SALARY    SALARY
+----+--------+----------+----------+----------+++++++++++++++++++
              *  165000.00  35000.00  45000.00

  D600    150    70000.00  70000.00  70000.00
          400    60000.00  60000.00  60000.00
                ---------- ---------- ----------
              *  130000.00  60000.00  70000.00

  D700    495    40000.00  40000.00  40000.00
          900    35000.00  35000.00  35000.00
          850    35000.00  35000.00  35000.00
                ---------- ---------- ----------
              *  110000.00  35000.00  40000.00

  D890    500    80000.00  80000.00  80000.00
1=Help    2=       3=End      4=Print     5=Chart         6=Query
7=Backward         8=Forward  9=Form     10=Left    11=Right   12=
OK, FORWARD performed. Please proceed.
COMMAND ===> forward                           SCROLL ===> PAGE
```

```
REPORT                               LINE 34      POS 1      79
        EMPLOYEE                MINIMUM     MAXIMUM
  DEPT     NO        SALARY     SALARY      SALARY
  +----+--------+----------+----------+----------+++++++++++++++++++
  D890      250    70000.00   70000.00    70000.00
            200    60000.00   60000.00    60000.00
            350    50000.00   50000.00    50000.00
            700    40000.00   40000.00    40000.00
            600    30000.00   30000.00    30000.00
                   ----------  ----------  ----------
              *   330000.00   30000.00    80000.00


  D900      300    50000.00   50000.00    50000.00
            175    40000.00   40000.00    40000.00
                   ----------  ----------  ----------
              *    90000.00   40000.00    50000.00
                   ==========  ==========  ==========
                  975000.00   30000.00    80000.00


  ** CONFIDENTIAL REPORT **
  *** END ***

  1=Help    2=      3=End       4=Print       5=Chart   6=Query
  7=Backward    8=Forward      9=Form     10=Left   11=Right   12=
  OK, FORWARD performed. Please proceed.
  COMMAND ===> FORM                         SCROLL ===> PAGE
```

Note the summary line after the last row printed. Grand total sum, as wel
as minimum and maximum values for all salaries were determined. QMF
provided this, not DB2. The footings are also included. Should you actually
print this out, you would find the headings and footings on every page of the
report. Entering FORM on the Command Line or PF9 takes us once again to
the FORM work area, where you will see the last form used.

```
FORM.MAIN                                              MODIFIED

COLUMNS:                   Total Width of Report Columns: 47
  NUM  COLUMN HEADING                 USAGE    INDENT  WIDTH  EDIT
  ---  --------------------------    -------  ------  -----  -----
    6  MINIMUM_SALARY                MINIMUM  1        10     L2
    7  MAXIMUM_SALARY                MAXIMUM  1        10     L2
       *** END ***




PAGE:  HEADING ===> DISPLAY MAXIMUM & MINIMUM SALARY
       FOOTING ===> ** CONFIDENTIAL REPORT **
FINAL:  TEXT ===>
BREAK1:  NEW PAGE FOR BREAK? ===> NO
         FOOTING ===>
BREAK2:  NEW PAGE FOR BREAK? ===> NO
         FOOTING ===>
 OPTIONS:  OUTLINE? ===> YES        DEFAULT BREAK TEXT? ===> YES


1=Help    2=Check  3=End  4=Form.Columns  5=Form.Options  6=Query
7=Backward 8=Forward  9=Form.Page  10=Form.Final   11=Form.Break1
12=Report
OK, FORM.MAIN is displayed.
COMMAND ===> save form as employee_f1          SCROLL ===> PAGE
```

If you wish to save the FORM for future use, enter SAVE on the Command Line. Include the type of QMF object you are saving (FORM) and the name to be given to the saved object (EMPLOYEE_F1). The FORM will be stored in the QMF tables with the name of EMPLOYEE_F1. If you END or EXIT out of QMF without first saving the query and form, the form and query you worked so hard to create are gone, since they resided only in the QMF work areas.

```
FORM.MAIN              EMPLOYEE_F1


COLUMNS:                Total Width of Report Columns: 47
  NUM  COLUMN HEADING                USAGE      INDENT  WIDTH  EDIT
  ---  --------------------------    -------    ------  -----  -----
    6  MINIMUM_SALARY                MINIMUM  1         10     L2
    7  MAXIMUM_SALARY                MAXIMUM  1         10     L2
       *** END ***




PAGE:  HEADING ===> DISPLAY MAXIMUM & MINIMUM SALARY
       FOOTING ===> ** CONFIDENTIAL REPORT **
FINAL:  TEXT ===>
BREAK1:  NEW PAGE FOR BREAK? ===> NO
         FOOTING ===>
BREAK2:  NEW PAGE FOR BREAK? ===> NO
         FOOTING ===>
OPTIONS:  OUTLINE? ===> YES        DEFAULT BREAK TEXT? ===> YES


1=Help    2=Check   3=End   4=Form.Columns  5=Form.Options  6=Query
7=Backward 8=Forward  9=Form.Page 10=Form.Final    11=Form.Break1
12=Report
OK, FORM was saved as EMPLOYEE_F1 in the data base.
COMMAND ===>                                   SCROLL ===> PAGE
```

QMF will return the results of the SAVE command execution on the Message Line. We can now reference this form when running a query to display
the data using this form rather than the default form provided by QMF.

```
FORM.MAIN                                           MODIFIED

COLUMNS:              Total Width of Report Columns: 55
 NUM  COLUMN HEADING                  USAGE    INDENT  WIDTH  EDIT
 ---  --------------------------      -------  ------  -----  -----
   6  AVERAGE_SALARY                  AVERAGE  2       10     L2
   7  PERCENT_SALARY                  PCT      2       10     L2
      *** END ***




PAGE:   HEADING ===> THIS FORM DISPLAYS WHAT PERCENT AN EMPLOYEES
        FOOTING ===>
FINAL:  TEXT ===>
BREAK1: NEW PAGE FOR BREAK? ===> NO
        FOOTING ===>
BREAK2: NEW PAGE FOR BREAK? ===> NO
        FOOTING ===>
OPTIONS:  OUTLINE? ===> YES         DEFAULT BREAK TEXT? ===> YES


1=Help    2=Check   3=End   4=Form.Columns  5=Form.Options  6=Query
7=Backward 8=Forward  9=Form.Page    10=Form.Final 11=Form.Break1
12=Report
OK, FORWARD performed. Please proceed.
COMMAND ===> DISPLAY FORM.PAGE                 SCROLL ===> PAGE
```

After saving a form, you can still make alterations in the Form work area. The column headings for SALARY1 and SALARY2 were changed to AVERAGE_SALARY and PERCENT_SALARY. Also, the column usage has been changed to AVERAGE and PCT, respectively. This allows you to display the average salary per department, since there is a BREAK specified on department in the FORM. When individual employee rows are displayed, the PERCENT_SALARY value is the percentage of the department's salary that an individual's salary represents. For department breaks, PER-CENT_SALARY is that percentage the sum of all salaries in a department represents of the total salaries for all departments. Before displaying the report, let's make changes to the report headings. Enter PF9 or DISPLAY FORM.PAGE.

```
FORM.PAGE                                            MODIFIED


Blank Lines Before Heading ===>0 Blank Lines After Heading ===>2
 LINE  ALIGN PAGE HEADING TEXT
 ----  ----- -----------------------------------------------------

  1     LEFT  THIS FORM DISPLAYS WHAT PERCENT AN EMPLOYEES SALARY
  2     LEFT  IS OF THE DEPARTMENT TOTAL AND WHAT PERCENT THE SUM OF
  3     LEFT  ALL SALARIES IN A DEPARTMENT REPRESENTS IN TERMS OF
  4     LEFT  ALL SALARIES FOR ALL DEPARTMENTS. THE AVERAGE SALARY
  5     LEFT  PER DEPARTMENT IS ALSO COMPUTED.

Blank Lines Before Footing ===>2 Blank Lines After Footing ===>0

 LINE  ALIGN   PAGE FOOTING TEXT
 ----  ------  -----------------------------------------------------

  1     CENTER
  2     CENTER
  3     CENTER
  4     CENTER
  5     CENTER

1=Help   2=Check  3=End  4=Form.Columns  5=Form.Options  6=Query
7=   8=  9=Form.Main   10=Form.Final   11=Form.Break1   12=Report
OK, FORM.PAGE is displayed.
COMMAND ===> display report
```

The column headings entered are to be left justified rather than centered
PF12 or entering DISPLAY REPORT on the command line will redisplay the
data using this modified FORM.

```
REPORT                              LINE 1      POS 1      79

THIS FORM DISPLAYS WHAT PERCENT AN EMPLOYEES SALARY
IS OF THE DEPARTMENT TOTAL AND WHAT PERCENT THE SUM OF
ALL SALARIES IN A DEPARTMENT REPRESENTS IN TERMS OF
ALL SALARIES FOR ALL DEPARTMENTS. THE AVERAGE SALARY
PER DEPARTMENT IS ALSO COMPUTED.

          EMPLOYEE                  AVERAGE       PERCENT
DEPT         NO        SALARY       SALARY        SALARY
----      ----------- -----------  -----------   -----------
D400          415     80000.00     80000.00        53.33
              425     40000.00     40000.00        26.67
              800     30000.00     30000.00        20.00
                      -----------  -----------   -----------

                *     150000.00    50000.00        15.38

D500          550     45000.00     45000.00        27.27
              750     45000.00     45000.00        27.27
1=Help    2=        3=End        4=Print        5=Chart  6=Query
7=Backward    8=Forward       9=Form        10=Left    11=Right 12=
OK, REPORT is displayed.
COMMAND ===> forward                          SCROLL ===> PAGE
```

This is the report from the modified FORM. Press PF8 or enter FORWARD
on the Command Line and press ENTER to view additional pages of the
report.

```
REPORT                               LINE 19      POS 1      79
                EMPLOYEE             AVERAGE      PERCENT
    DEPT          NO      SALARY     SALARY       SALARY
++----++-----------++----------++----------++----------+++++++++
    D500          650    40000.00    40000.00      24.24
                  450    35000.00    35000.00      21.21
                        ----------  ----------  ----------
                   *    165000.00    41250.00      16.92

    D600          150    70000.00    70000.00      53.85
                  400    60000.00    60000.00      46.15
                        ----------  ----------  ----------
                   *    130000.00    65000.00      13.33

    D700          495    40000.00    40000.00      36.36
                  900    35000.00    35000.00      31.82
                  850    35000.00    35000.00      31.82
                        ----------  ----------  ----------
                   *    110000.00    36666.67      11.28
1=Help      2=        3=End       4=Print       5=Chart   6=Query
7=Backward     8=Forward     9=Form      10=Left  11=Right   12=
OK, FORWARD performed. Please proceed.
COMMAND ===> forward                      SCROLL ===> PAGE
```

```
REPORT                              LINE 34      POS 1       79
              EMPLOYEE              AVERAGE    PERCENT
   DEPT         NO       SALARY     SALARY     SALARY
++----++-----------++----------++----------+----------+++++++++
   D890         500    80000.00    80000.00      24.24
                250    70000.00    70000.00      21.21
                200    60000.00    60000.00      18.18
                350    50000.00    50000.00      15.15
                700    40000.00    40000.00      12.12
                600    30000.00    30000.00       9.09
                       ----------  ----------  ----------
                  *   330000.00    55000.00      33.85

   D900         300    50000.00    50000.00      55.56
                175    40000.00    40000.00      44.44
                       ----------  ----------  ----------
                  *    90000.00    45000.00       9.23
                       ==========  ==========  ==========
                      975000.00    48750.00     100.00

*** END ***


1=Help      2=       3=End       4=Print       5=Chart    6=Query
7=Backward    8=Forward     9=Form      10=Left    11=Right    12=
OK, FORWARD performed. Please proceed.
COMMAND ===> display form                   SCROLL ===> PAGE
```

DISPLAY FORM takes you back to the FORM work area.

```
FORM.MAIN                                          MODIFIED


COLUMNS:                 Total Width of Report Columns: 55
 NUM   COLUMN HEADING                USAGE     INDENT  WIDTH  EDIT
 ---   --------------------------    -------   ------  -----  -----
   6   AVERAGE_SALARY                AVERAGE   2       10     L2
   7   PERCENT_SALARY                PCT       2       10     L2
       *** END ***


PAGE:   HEADING ===> THIS FORM DISPLAYS WHAT PERCENT AN EMPLOYEES
        FOOTING ===>
FINAL:  TEXT ===>
BREAK1:  NEW PAGE FOR BREAK? ===> NO
         FOOTING ===>
BREAK2:  NEW PAGE FOR BREAK? ===> NO
         FOOTING ===>
 OPTIONS:  OUTLINE? ===> YES          DEFAULT BREAK TEXT? ===> YES


 1=Help    2=Check   3=End  4=Form.Columns  5=Form.Options  6=Query
 7=Backward 8=Forward  9=Form.Page  10=Form.Final  11=Form.Break1
12=Report
OK, FORM.MAIN is displayed.
COMMAND ===> save form as employee_f2            SCROLL ===> PAGE
```

This form will be saved as employee_f2 in the QMF system tables.

```
FORM.MAIN              EMPLOYEE_F2


COLUMNS:                 Total Width of Report Columns: 55
  NUM  COLUMN HEADING              USAGE    INDENT  WIDTH  EDIT
  ---  --------------------------  -------  ------  -----  -----
    6  AVERAGE_SALARY              AVERAGE     2      10    L2
    7  PERCENT_SALARY              PCT         2      10    L2
       *** END ***




PAGE:  HEADING ===>THIS FORM DISPLAYS WHAT PERCENT AN EMPLOYEES
       FOOTING ===>
FINAL:  TEXT ===>
BREAK1:  NEW PAGE FOR BREAK? ===> NO
         FOOTING ===>
BREAK2:  NEW PAGE FOR BREAK? ===> NO
         FOOTING ===>
OPTIONS:  OUTLINE? ===> YES         DEFAULT BREAK TEXT? ===> YES


1=Help   2=Check  3=End 4=Form.Columns  5=Form.Options  6=Query
7=Backward 8=Forward  9=Form.Page  10=Form.Final  11=Form.Break1
12=Report
OK, FORM was saved as EMPLOYEE_F2 in the data base.
COMMAND ===>                              SCROLL ===> PAGE
```

QMF confirmed that the form was saved in the QMF tables. You do not
have direct control over the width of your report. You can control the report
width indirectly by omitting columns, changing the spaces between columns
(INDENT), changing the column width (WIDTH), and changing the format in
which the data is displayed (EDIT). The INDENT column in the form determines how many spaces will be placed between the columns in the report. The
total width of the column is specified in the WIDTH column of the form. If you
shorten the width of a character data type column so that there is more data
than that which can be displayed, the data is truncated on the right. If the
column is numeric, it is filled with '*' instead of being truncated to avoid misleading results. The EDIT column can be used to specify how data is to be displayed. For example, a character column of 120 bytes could be displayed using

a WIDTH of 30 and an EDIT type of CT. This combination instructs QMF to wrap the column data printed out to multiple lines according to the characters contained in the column being printed and the column width specified. QMF would format up to 30 characters on a line and attempt to avoid breaking on other than blanks. Thus, long text data can be printed on multiple lines without truncating words. There are many EDIT types available for character, numeric, and graphic data.

```
SQL QUERY                               MODIFIED    LINE 1


SELECT SALESPERSONS_NO, REGION, YTD_SALES
      , BONUS
FROM LIF_INS_SALES
ORDER BY REGION,YTD_SALES




*** END ***



1=Help      2=Run       3=End       4=Print    5=Chart    6=Draw
7=Backward  8=Forward   9=Form  10=Insert  11=Delete    12=Report

COMMAND ===>                            SCROLL ===> PAGE
```

Construct a SQL statement to retrieve all rows from the LIF_INS_SALES table. Run SQL statement by pressing PF2.

```
REPORT                                    LINE 1      POS 1     79


SALESPERSONS                  YTD
    NO      REGION          SALES         BONUS
------------  ---------   ------------   ----------
        200  MIDWEST       120000.00      1200.00
        300  MIDWEST       600000.00      6000.00
        175  MIDWEST       700000.00      7000.00
        250  MIDWEST       800000.00      8000.00
        500  NORTHWEST     800000.00      8000.00
        150  NORTHWEST     990000.00      9900.00
        700  SOUTHEAST     400000.00      4000.00
        350  SOUTHEAST     750000.00      7500.00
        400  SOUTHEAST    1000000.00     10000.00
        600  SOUTHWEST     122000.00      1200.00


*** END ***
1=Help    2=       3=End      4=Print       5=Chart        6=Query
7=Backward        8=Forward   9=Form    10=Left   11=Right      12=
OK, REPORT is displayed.
COMMAND ===>                                  SCROLL ===> PAGE
```

This is the report from executing the SQL statement. Since no FORM was specified, QMF set up a default FORM. Press PF9 to display the default FORM.

```
FORM.MAIN                                          MODIFIED


COLUMNS:                  Total Width of Report Columns: 37
 NUM  COLUMN HEADING                  USAGE     INDENT  WIDTH  EDIT
 ---  --------------------------    -------   ------  -----  -----
   1  SALESPERSONS_NO                OMIT      2       12     L
   2  REGION                         GROUP     2       9      C
   3  YTD_SALES                      SUM       2       12     L2
   4  BONUS                          AVERAGE   2       10     L2
      *** END ***


PAGE:  HEADING ===>
       FOOTING ===>
FINAL:  TEXT ===>
BREAK1:  NEW PAGE FOR BREAK? ===> NO
         FOOTING ===>
BREAK2:  NEW PAGE FOR BREAK? ===> NO
         FOOTING ===>
OPTIONS:  OUTLINE? ===> YES         DEFAULT BREAK TEXT? ===> YES


1=Help    2=Check   3=End   4=Form.Columns   5=Form.Options   6=Query
7=Backward 8=Forward 9=Form.Page   10=Form.Final   11=Form.Break1
12=Report
OK, FORM is displayed.
COMMAND ===> display report                    SCROLL ===> PAGE
```

The Select statement ordered the rows returned by Region and Salary. You can use the FORM to summarize a group of rows (different than GROUP BY CLAUSE of SELECT) by the sorted column, such as region in this case. The USAGE column above specifies that only summary information is to be displayed for department rather than the detail for every row. Summary information should include the sum of all salaries for employees in a department and a determination of the average bonus for employees in the same department. The individual row for each employee is not desired. DISPLAY REPORT will redisplay the rows in the DATA work area with this modified FORM.

```
REPORT                               LINE 1      POS 1     79

                   SUM
                   YTD       AVERAGE
        REGION     SALES     BONUS
        ---------- --------- ----------

        MIDWEST    2220000.00   5550.00
        NORTHWEST  1790000.00   8950.00
        SOUTHEAST  2150000.00   7166.67
        SOUTHWEST   122000.00   1200.00
                   =========== ==========
                   6282000.00   6280.00

*** END ***



1=Help      2=        3=End      4=Print    5=Chart       6=Query
7=Backward        8=Forward      9=Form    10=Left     11=Right   12=
OK, REPORT is displayed.
COMMAND ===>                                  SCROLL ===> PAGE
```

This is the result from redisplaying the data with the modified FORM.

```
FORM.MAIN                                            MODIFIED

COLUMNS:                 Total Width of Report Columns: 37
  NUM  COLUMN HEADING                   USAGE    INDENT  WIDTH  EDIT
  ---  -------------------------        -------  ------  -----  -----
   1   SALESPERSONS_NO                  OMIT     2       12     L
   2   REGION                           GROUP    2       9      C
   3   YTD_SALES                        SUM      2       12     L2
   4   BONUS                            AVERAGE  2       10     L2
       *** END ***


PAGE:   HEADING ===>
        FOOTING ===>
FINAL:  TEXT ===>
BREAK1:  NEW PAGE FOR BREAK? ===> NO
         FOOTING ===>
BREAK2:  NEW PAGE FOR BREAK? ===> NO
         FOOTING ===>
OPTIONS:  OUTLINE? ===> YES          DEFAULT BREAK TEXT? ===> YES


1=Help  2=Check    3=End  4=Form.Columns  5=Form.Options  6=Query
7=Backward 8=Forward  9=Form.Page  10=Form.Final   11=Form.Break1
12=Report
OK, FORM is displayed.
COMMAND ===> save form as life_insurance_f1    SCROLL ===> PAGE
```

The modified FORM, including the USAGE alterations, is saved into the QMF tables.

There are many types of USAGE options available. Following is a list of available options.

ACROSS — used only if one or more columns have a USAGE of GROUP. The summary line for each group may contain several sets of results from the columns. This will allow you to display across the page the values in the column.

AVERAGE — computes the average of the values in the column.

COUNT — count of rows returned.

CPCT — the cumulative percentage for each value in a column.

CSUM — the cumulative sum for each of the values in a column.

FIRST — the first value in the column.

GROUP — display only one line of summary for each set of values in the column.

LAST — the last value in the column.

MAXIMUM — the maximum value in the column.

MINIMUM — the minimum value in the column.

OMIT — do not display this column in the report.

PCT — the percentage of the total that each value is.

STDEV — the standard deviation of the values in the column.

SUM — the sum of the values in the column.

TCPCT — the total cumulative percentage for each value in a column.

TPCT — the percentage of the column total that each value is.

BREAK, BREAK1 – BREAK6 — use when you want to show a control break in the report each time the value of the control break columns change. At these control breaks you can also display other USAGE types for non-BREAK columns. You can have up to six levels of breaks specified in the form. In the following example, Sales Region is the highest control level break (1) followed by Sales Territory (2) and Sales Zone (3). A control break also triggers all control breaks below it. For example, Control Break 1 forces control breaks 2 through 6, 2 forces 3 through 6, etc.

```
    SALES          SALES        SALES        SALES       GROSS
    REGION         TERRITORY    ZONE         TYPE        SALES
    #####################################################
    U.S.A.         MIDWEST                   AUTO INS    50,000
                                             LIFE INS    45,000
                                                         ------
                                 TOTAL FOR ZONE -- A     95,000

                                             AUTO INS    50,000
                                             LIFE INS    25,000
                                                         ------
                                 TOTAL FOR ZONE -- B     75,000

                      TOTAL FOR MIDWEST ------------- 170,000

    U.S.A          SOUTHEAST                 AUTO INS    40,000
                                             LIFE INS    40,000
                                                         ------
                                 TOTAL FOR ZONE -- A     80.000
```

```
                                        AUTO INS    25,000
                                        LIFE INS    25,000
                                                    ------
                          TOTAL FOR ZONE -- B       50,000


                 TOTAL FOR SOUTHEAST -----------    130,000


       TOTAL FOR U.S.A. ------------------------    300,000



       CANADA     NORTHEAST    A      AUTO INS      45,000
                                      LIFE INS      20,000
                                                    ------
                          TOTAL FOR ZONE -- A       65,000
                                            .
                                            .
                                            .
```

```
REPORT                                LINE 1      POS 1      79
                     SUM
                     YTD        AVERAGE
    REGION           SALES      BONUS
    ----------    -------------  ----------

    MIDWEST        2220000.00     5550.00
    NORTHWEST      1790000.00     8950.00
    SOUTHEAST      2150000.00     7166.67
  , SOUTHWEST       122000.00     1200.00
                  =============  ==========
                   6282000.00     6280.00

*** END ***


1=Help      2=     3=End     4=Print     5=Chart        6=Query
7=Backward        8=Forward  9=Form     10=Left  11=Right      12=
OK, REPORT is displayed.
COMMAND ===> print report                    SCROLL ===> PAGE
```

PF4 or entering PRINT REPORT on the Command Line will instruct QMF to place the report in a dataset for printing purposes. Additional PRINT REPORT commands will cause the report being printed to be added to the end of the existing print dataset.

```
REPORT                               LINE 1       POS 1      79

                 SUM
                 YTD      AVERAGE
  REGION         SALES    BONUS
  ---------   ------------  ----------

  MIDWEST     2220000.00    5550.00
  NORTHWEST   1790000.00    8950.00
  SOUTHEAST   2150000.00    7166.67
  SOUTHWEST    122000.00    1200.00
              ============  ==========
              6282000.00    6280.00

*** END ***

1=Help        2=      3=End       4=Print      5=Chart   6=Query
7=Backward    8=Forward   9=Form   10=Left   11=Right      12=
OK, REPORT is printed.
COMMAND ===> display proc                  SCROLL ===> PAGE
```

QMF will notify the user upon putting the report in the print dataset. The next topic to be discussed is the QMF Procedure or PROC. Enter DISPLAY PROC on the Command Line and press ENTER to go to the PROC work area.

```
PROC                                    MODIFIED    LINE 1


RUN EMPLOYEE_Q1 (FORM=EMPLOYEE_F1)
PRINT REPORT
DISPLAY  EMPLOYEES_TABLE
PRINT REPORT
RUN LIFE_INSURANCE_Q1 (FORM=LIFE_INSURANCE_F1)
PRINT REPORT






1=Help      2=Run       3=End       4=Print   5=Chart     6=Query
7=Backward  8=Forward   9=Form     10=Insert  11=Delete   12=Report
OK, PROC is displayed.
COMMAND ===> run proc                           SCROLL ===> PAGE
```

The QMF PROC work area is used to construct what are called QMF Procedures. Only one query can be executed from the QUERY work area or from a stored QUERY. If you need to run multiple queries together, you can perform them from a procedure. In addition to executing queries, you can also execute QMF commands, such as PRINT REPORT, in the procedure. RUN EMPLOYEE_Q1 (FORM=EMPLOYEE_F1) will execute a stored query called EMPLOYEE_Q1 and display the report using the FORM EMPLOYEE_F1. Since we immediately want to run another query, we place this report in the print dataset by executing the next command, PRINT REPORT. DISPLAY EMPLOYEES_TABLE is not the name of a stored query, proc, or form. It is the name of our table. Thus, the actual table is displayed using the QMF default FORM. As we did with the first report, we will print this report with a PRINT REPORT as the next statement in our proc. RUN LIFE_INSURANCE_Q1 (FORM=LIFE_INSURANCE_F1) runs query LIFE_INSURANCE_Q1 using form LIFE_INSURANCE_F1. The QMF print dataset will contain three reports following the execution of this procedure.

```
PROC                                    MODIFIED    LINE 1


RUN EMPLOYEE_Q1 (FORM=EMPLOYEE_F1)
PRINT REPORT
DISPLAY EMPLOYEES_TABLE
PRINT REPORT
RUN LIFE_INSURANCE_Q1 (FORM=LIFE_INSURANCE_F1)
PRINT REPORT




1=Help     2=Run      3=End     4=Print   5=Chart     6=Query
7=Backward 8=Forward  9=Form 10=Insert  11=Delete     12=Report
OK, PROC is displayed.
COMMAND ===> save proc as proc_empl_life      SCROLL ===> PAGE
```

QMF procedures or PROCS can also be saved in the QMF tables for future use, as noted above. In addition to executing stored queries and procs from the PROC and QUERY work areas, you can also execute them from the Command Line. For example, RUN LIFE_INSURANCE_Q1 (FORM=LIFE_IN-SURANCE_F1) could have been entered on the Command Line to run the stored query using the stored form as well.

```
SQL QUERY              EMPLOYEE_Q2                        LINE 1

-- YOU CAN PLACE VARIABLES IN THE SELECT STATEMENT.
-- YOU CAN THEN ENTER THE VARIABLE WHEN RUNNING THE QUERY OR
-- LET QMF PROMPT THE USER FOR THE VALUE.
SELECT EMPLOYEE_NO, EMPLOYEE_NAME
       DEPT, SALARY              -- .EMPLOYEES_TABLE
FROM EMPLOYEES_TABLE
WHERE EMPLOYEE_NO= &EMPLNO



1=Help     2=Run     3=End     4=Print   5=Chart    6=Draw
7=Backward  8=Forward  9=Form  10=Insert  11=Delete  12=Report
OK, QUERY was saved as EMPLOYEE_Q2 in the data base.
COMMAND ===>                                    SCROLL ===> PAGE
```

The above query was designed to allow the user to inquire into the employee table and retrieve information for one particular employee. When the above query was constructed, the WHERE clause was designed to contain a QMF variable &EMPLNO. QMF variable names begin with &. If enclosed by quotes, they will not be treated as variables. For example, '&EMPLNO' would be interpreted as a constant. When the query is executed, QMF prompts the executor for a value for variable &EMPLNO. Thus, this same query can return different rows from the table based on the value supplied for the variable. This query was saved with the name of EMPLOYEE_Q2 for future use.

```
SQL QUERY                                 MODIFIED     LINE 1

SELECT SALESPERSONS_NO, REGION, YTD_SALES
     , BONUS
FROM LIF_INS_SALES
WHERE SALESPERSONS_NO = &PERSON
*** END ***


1=Help      2=Run      3=End     4=Print   5=Chart     6=Draw
7=Backward  8=Forward  9=Form  10=Insert  11=Delete  12=Report


COMMAND ===> save query as life_insurance_q2    SCROLL ===> PAGE
```

The above query was saved as LIFE_INSURANCE_Q2. In this query, the QMF variable is &PERSON. To run this query, you could press PF2 or on the Command Line enter either RUN QUERY or RUN LIFE_INSURANCE_Q2. If you do not provide values for the variables when executing the query, QMF will provide you with a RUN Command Prompt panel to enter the values for the variables.

```
              RUN Command Prompt -- Values of Variables


Your RUN command runs a query or procedure with variables
that need values. Fill in the value for each variable
named below, after the arrow.

&PERSON              ===> 200
                     ===>
                     ===>
                     ===>
                     ===>
                     ===>
                     ===>
                     ===>
                     ===>
                     ===>


Then press ENTER to execute the command from this panel.

PF13=Help      15=End
Please give a value for each variable name.
ISPF Command ===>
```

Entering the value 200 for the employee number allows &PERSON in the query to be replaced with 200 prior to being executed. If RUN LIFE_IN-SURANCE_Q2 (&PERSON=200) had been entered on the Command Line, the prompt panel would have been bypassed.

```
REPORT                                  LINE 1      POS 1      79


SALESPERSONS                    YTD
    NO        REGION            SALES         BONUS
------------   ---------    ------------    ----------
        200   MIDWEST       120000.00        1200.00


*** END ***


1=Help     2=       3=End      4=Print      5=Chart     6=Query
7=Backward    8=Forward    9=Form    10=Left      11=Right    12=
OK, this is the REPORT from your RUN command.
COMMAND ===>                                 SCROLL ===> PAGE
```

This is the result of running the query where the &PERSON variable was set to 200. Assume employee numbers are contained in yet another table, and a query named EMPLOYEE_Q2 was constructed in such a manner as to prompt for employee number using a query variable called &EMPLNO. As you can see, there is a similarity between the QMF variables &PERSON and &EMPLNO. In this case, the employee number is in both tables. Assuming the same employee is being requested from both tables by queries in the same procedure, the user would be prompted twice for the employee number, once for &PERSON and once for &EMPLNO. By assigning query variables to proc variables, you can eliminate the user from having to enter the employee number more than once. The next panel will show how that can be accomplished.

```
PROC                                    MODIFIED    LINE 1
--  NOTE: && REPRESENTS A QUERY VARIABLE.
--  NOTE: &  REPRESENTS A PROC VARIABLE.
--
RUN LIFE_INSURANCE_Q2 (&&PERSON=&EMPLYNO
PRINT REPORT
RUN EMPLOYEE_Q2        (&&EMPLNO=&EMPLYNO
PRINT REPORT
1=Help      2=Run      3=End      4=Print    5=Chart     6=Query
7=Backward  8=Forward  9=Form    10=Insert  11=Delete   12=Report
OK, PROC is displayed.
COMMAND ===>                                 SCROLL ===> PAGE
```

In the above PROC, note the difference between query variables and proc variables. In a Procedure, double ampersands indicate query variables and single ampersands indicate proc variables. It is not necessary to save the proc before testing it, but the queries being executed from the proc must have previously been saved. PF2 or RUN PROC caused the following panel to be displayed.

```
          RUN Command Prompt -- Values of Variables
Your RUN command runs a query or procedure with variables
that need values. Fill in the value for each variable
named below, after the arrow.

&EMPLYNO            ===> 200

Then press ENTER to execute the command from this panel.
PF13=Help      15=End
Please give a value for each variable name.
ISPF Command ===>
```

There is now only one variable entered to satisfy both query variables in the proc. A user can be allowed to enter as many as 10 variables through the prompt panels.

```
SQL QUERY                                    MODIFIED      LINE 1

SELECT EMPLOYEE_NO, EMPLOYEE_NAME
     , ADDRESS_STATE, DEPT, SALARY
FROM EMPLOYEES_TABLE
WHERE DEPT = '&DEPT'

*** END ***

1=Help      2=Run        3=End        4=Print     5=Chart      6=Draw
7=Backward  8=Forward    9=Form     10=Insert    11=Delete  12=Report
OK, QUERY is displayed.
COMMAND ===>                                   SCROLL ===> PAGE
```

In the above select we have what at first appears to be a QMF query variable.

```
REPORT                           LINE 1       POS 1        79

    EMPLOYEE   EMPLOYEE            ADDRESS
       NO        NAME             STATE    DEPT     SALARY
    ----------- -----------------  -------  ----  ----------


*** END ***

1=Help        2=         3=End        4=Print     5=Chart   6=Query
7=Backward    8=Forward     9=Form    10=Left     11=Right     12=
OK, this is the REPORT from your RUN command.
COMMAND ===>                                   SCROLL ===> PAGE
```

This is the report displayed as a result of executing the query. Your question may be why the user was not prompted for the &DEPT query variable? The user was not prompted because the variable was placed between quotes and was therefore interpreted as a literal.

```
SQL QUERY                                    MODIFIED   LINE 1

SELECT EMPLOYEE_NO, EMPLOYEE_NAME
    , ADDRESS_STATE, DEPT, SALARY
FROM EMPLOYEES_TABLE
WHERE DEPT = &Q&DEPT&Q

*** END ***

1=Help      2=Run       3=End       4=Print   5=Chart   6=Draw
7=Backward  8=Forward   9=Form    10=Insert  11=Delete 12=Report

COMMAND ===>                                 SCROLL ===> PAGE
```

In the above Select, the quotes entered in the previous example have been replaced by variables themselves. Now the query has two distinct variables &Q and &DEPT. No matter how many times the same variable name appears in a query or proc, the user will only be prompted once for a value.

```
            RUN Command Prompt -- Values of Variables

Your RUN command runs a query or procedure with variables
that need values. Fill in the value for each variable
named below, after the arrow.

&Q                ===> '
&DEPT             ===> d400

Then press ENTER to execute the command from this panel.

PF13=Help     15=End
Please give a value for each variable name.
ISPF Command ===>
```

When the user enters both values, the query can be executed.

```
REPORT                              LINE 1       POS 1      79

   EMPLOYEE   EMPLOYEE             ADDRESS
      NO        NAME               STATE   DEPT      SALARY
  -----------  -----------------   -------  ----   ----------
         415   THOMPSON              MN     D400    80000.00
         425   WASHINGTON            NY     D400    40000.00
         800   KENNEDY               OH     D400    30000.00
*** END ***


1=Help      2=        3=End        4=Print       5=Chart    6=Query
7=Backward    8=Forward    9=Form    10=Left     11=Right    12=
OK, this is the REPORT from your RUN command.
COMMAND ===>                                  SCROLL ===> PAGE
```

The above is the report from the execution of the query where the rows containing department D400 are returned.

```
SQL QUERY                              MODIFIED     LINE 1

SELECT EMPLOYEE_NO, EMPLOYEE_NAME
    , ADDRESS_STATE, DEPT, SALARY
FROM EMPLOYEES_TABLE
WHERE DEPT = &Q&DEPT&Q

*** END ***


1=Help       2=Run        3=End       4=Print      5=Chart     6=Draw
7=Backward    8=Forward    9=Form   10=Insert   11=Delete   12=Report
OK, QUERY is displayed.
COMMAND ===> save query as employee_q3        SCROLL ===> PAGE
```

The generated SQL for the previous WHERE statement looks like WHERE DEPT = 'D400' after the variables are substituted. The query is saved as employee_q3 so it can be incorporated into a procedure.

```
PROC                                    MODIFIED    LINE 1


-- + IN COLUMN ONE INDICATES A CONTINUATION OF A PROC.
RUN EMPLOYEE_Q3
+ (FORM=EMPLOYEE_F3,
+ &&DEPT=&DEPT,&&Q='


1=Help      2=Run      3=End      4=Print    5=Chart    6=Query
7=Backward  8=Forward  9=Form   10=Insert  11=Delete  12=Report
OK, PROC is displayed.
COMMAND ===> save ?                              SCROLL ===> PAGE
```

The previously saved query is executed from a PROC this time. Query variables can be set equal to proc variables as well as constants. In this case, the query variable &&Q is set to a constant of quote in the PROC. When this PROC runs, the user is prompted for a proc variable &DEPT and is not required to surround it with quotes. Since the query variable &&Q is set in the PROC, the user is never prompted for it. Thus, character and numeric data can be entered by the user in the same manner.

If you enter ? after a QMF command, QMF will provide you with a panel upon which to enter the required parameters. Note "save ?."

```
                    SAVE Command Prompt
NAME ===> proc

        Type the name of the item that you want to save. It
        can be PROFILE, QUERY, DATA, FORM, or PROC to save the
        contents of the temporary storage area.

        Press ENTER to SAVE PROFILE, or to display the specified
        item's prompt panel for the SAVE command.

PF13=Help      15=End
Please tell what you want to SAVE.
ISPF Command ===>
```

```
                        SAVE COMMAND PROMPT

SAVE PROC
AS
NAME      ===> proc_empl_dept
              Type a name that the item will have in the data base.

CONFIRM ===> YES You can type YES or NO to indicate whether you
                want to be prompted before replacing an item in
                the data base.

SHARE    ===> yes You can type YES or NO to indicate whether you
                  to share this item. Leave this field blank
                  when replacing an item to keep existing SHARE
                  value.

COMMENT ===> display all the employees in a department.
             You can type a comment to be saved with the item.

Then press ENTER to execute the command from this panel.

PF13=Help      15=End
Complete your SAVE PROC command on this panel.
ISPF Command ===>
```

On the SAVE prompt panels, the user provides information about how the object being saved will be executed. It includes items such as the name to be used when executing the QMF object, whether you want to be prompted before replacing an already existing object, whether others can use this saved object, and a comment describing the object being saved.

```
SQL QUERY                                              LINE 1

*** END ***

1=Help    2=Run     3=End     4=Print    5=Chart     6=Draw
7=Backward  8=Forward  9=Form  10=Insert  11=Delete   12=Report
OK, QUERY is displayed.


COMMAND ===> employees_table                  SCROLL ===> PAGE
```

The DRAW command can be used to construct Select, Update, and Insert queries for a specific table or view. To tell QMF which type of SQL statement to generate, specify TYPE=SELECT, TYPE=UPDATE, or TYPE=INSERT. Select is the default TYPE. The SQL statement generated is for all columns in the table. You can remove columns not desired from the list. You can enter DRAW and the table or view name on the command line or just enter the table or view name on the Command Line and press PF6.

```
SQL QUERY                            MODIFIED    LINE 1

SELECT EMPLOYEE_NO, EMPLOYEE_NAME    -- USERID1.EMPLOYEES_TABLE
     , ADDRESS_STATE, DEPT, SALARY   -- USERID1.EMPLOYEES_TABLE
FROM USERID1.EMPLOYEES_TABLE


*** END ***

1=Help      2=Run      3=End      4=Print    5=Chart     6=Draw
7=Backward  8=Forward  9=Form    10=Insert  11=Delete   12=Report
OK, cursor positioned.
COMMAND ===>                                  SCROLL ===> PAGE
```

A Select statement was constructed by the DRAW command to retrieve all the columns from the EMPLOYEES_TABLE. The query can now be treated like any other query constructed in the query work area.

```
SQL QUERY                                 MODIFIED      LINE 1

SELECT EMPLOYEE_NO, EMPLOYEE_NAME      -- USERID1.EMPLOYEES_TABLE
     , ADDRESS_STATE, DEPT, SALARY     -- USERID1.EMPLOYEES_TABLE
FROM USERID1.EMPLOYEES_TABLE



*** END ***

1=Help     2=Run      3=End     4=Print    5=Chart     6=Draw
7=Backward 8=Forward  9=Form   10=Insert  11=Delete    12=Report


OK, cursor positioned.
COMMAND ===> reset query                        SCROLL ===> PAGE
```

The RESET command will reset a particular work area to the default work area setting. In the the case of QUERY and PROC, the work area will be cleared of the corresponding query or procedure.

```
SQL QUERY                                 MODIFIED      LINE 1



*** END ***

1=Help     2=Run      3=End     4=Print    5=Chart     6=Draw
7=Backward 8=Forward  9=Form   10=Insert  11=Delete    12=Report

COMMAND ===> draw employees_table (type=insert) SCROLL ===> PAGE
```

The above panel is the result of RESET QUERY. On the Command Line the DRAW command is entered to construct an insert query statement for the Employees_table.

```
SQL QUERY                                    MODIFIED     LINE 1

INSERT INTO USERID1.EMPLOYEES_TABLE (EMPLOYEE_NO, EMPLOYEE_NAME,
    ADDRESS_STATE, DEPT, SALARY)
    VALUES (
-- ENTER VALUES BELOW COLUMN NAME      DATA TYPE     LENGTH    NULLS
                , -- EMPLOYEE_NO       INTEGER                 NO
                , -- EMPLOYEE_NAME     CHAR           16       NO
                , -- ADDRESS_STATE     CHAR           2        NO
                , -- DEPT              CHAR           4        NO
                ) -- SALARY            DECIMAL       ( 7, 2)   NO


*** END ***



1=Help    2=Run    3=End     4=Print    5=Chart      6=Draw
7=Backward  8=Forward  9=Form 10=Insert 11=Delete    12=Report
OK, cursor positioned.
COMMAND ===>                                SCROLL ===> PAGE
```

The above INSERT statement is the result of the DRAW command using
TYPE=INSERT.

```
SQL QUERY                                    MODIFIED      LINE 1

INSERT INTO          EMPLOYEES_TABLE (EMPLOYEE_NO, EMPLOYEE_NAME,
   ADDRESS_STATE, DEPT, SALARY)
   VALUES (
-- ENTER VALUES BELOW    COLUMN NAME      DATA TYPE  LENGTH  NULLS
100                  , -- EMPLOYEE_NO     INTEGER             NO
'JOHNSON'            , -- EMPLOYEE_NAME   CHAR        16      NO
'TX'                 , -- ADDRESS_STATE   CHAR         2      NO
'D400'               , -- DEPT            CHAR         4      NO
65000                ) -- SALARY          DECIMAL   ( 7, 2)   NO



*** END ***



1=Help      2=Run       3=End      4=Print     5=Chart      6=Draw
7=Backward  8=Forward   9=Form    10=Insert   11=Delete    12=Report
OK, 1 rows in the data base were modified.
COMMAND ===>                                  SCROLL ===> PAGE
```

The user can enter the values for a row and insert them by running the query.

```
SQL QUERY                                           LINE 1



*** END ***

1=Help      2=Run       3=End       4=Print    5=Chart      6=Draw
7=Backward  8=Forward   9=Form      10=Insert  11=Delete    12=Report
OK, this is an empty SQL QUERY panel.
COMMAND ===> draw employees_table (type=update) SCROLL ===> PAGE
```

This DRAW command will construct a query to update rows in the employees_table.

```
SQL QUERY                                  MODIFIED    LINE 1

UPDATE USERID1.EMPLOYEES_TABLE SET
-- COLUMN NAME   ENTER VALUES BELOW    DATA TYPE     LENGTH   NULLS
   EMPLOYEE_NO=                        -- INTEGER                NO
,  EMPLOYEE_NAME=                      -- CHAR          16      NO
,  ADDRESS_STATE=                      -- CHAR          2       NO
,  DEPT=                               -- CHAR          4       NO
,  SALARY=                            -- DECIMAL     ( 7, 2)    NO
   WHERE

*** END ***

1=Help      2=Run       3=End       4=Print    5=Chart      6=Draw
7=Backward  8=Forward   9=Form      10=Insert  11=Delete    12=Report
OK, update query for table EMPLOYEES_TABLE drawn.
COMMAND ===>                                     SCROLL ===> PAGE
```

This is the result of DRAWing with TYPE=UPDATE. The user is expected to complete the query as necessary.

```
SQL QUERY                                    MODIFIED    LINE 1


UPDATE USERID1.EMPLOYEES_TABLE SET
-- COLUMN NAME    ENTER VALUES BELOW    DATA TYPE    LENGTH    NULLS
   EMPLOYEE_NO=                      -- INTEGER                  NO
 , EMPLOYEE_NAME=                    -- CHAR          16         NO
 , ADDRESS_STATE=                    -- CHAR          2          NO
 , DEPT=                             -- CHAR          4          NO
 , SALARY=                           -- DECIMAL      ( 7, 2)     NO
WHERE


*** END ***


1=Help     2=Run     3=End     4=Print    5=Chart     6=Draw
7=Backward  8=Forward  9=Form  10=Insert  11=Delete    12=Report
OK, update query for table EMPLOYEES_TABLE drawn.
COMMAND ===> edit query                          SCROLL ===> PAGE
```

You have two options in completing the query. You can make the change
on this panel (using PF10 and PF11 respectively, to add and delete lines t
the query when necessary) or you can use the PDF Editor by entering EDI*
QUERY on the Command Line and thus have all the functions of the PD*
Editor available. In this example we have chosen to use the PDF editor t
finish constructing the query.

```
EDIT ---- SYS87199.T092903.RA000.USERID1.R0000051 COLUMNS 001 072
****** **************************** TOP OF DATA ***************
000001 UPDATE USERID1.EMPLOYEES_TABLE SET
000002 -- COLUMN NAME   ENTER VALUES BELOW DATA TYPE     LENGTH
000003    SALARY= 70000                  -- DECIMAL      ( 7, 2)
000004 WHERE EMPLOYEE_NO = 100
****** **************************** BOTTOM OF DATA *************



PF13=Help 14= 15=End    16=SQL Help 17=R Find   18=R Change
PF19=Backward 20=Forward 21=   22=Left   23=Right    24=Cursor


COMMAND ===> end                          SCROLL ===> CSR
```

When finished editing the query, enter END or PF15 to keep the changes
made or CANCEL to return without saving the changes. The query or proc
will be placed back in their respective work area. The changed query or proc
is not saved in the QMF tables. If you want the query saved, use the QMF
SAVE command.

```
SQL QUERY                          MODIFIED     LINE 1

UPDATE USERID1.EMPLOYEES_TABLE SET
-- COLUMN NAME    ENTER VALUES BELOW  DATA TYPE   LENGTH   NULLS
   SALARY= 70000              -- DECIMAL   ( 7, 2)    NO
WHERE EMPLOYEE_NO = 100
*** END ***


1=Help    2=Run     3=End    4=Print    5=Chart     6=Draw
7=Backward 8=Forward 9=Form 10=Insert 11=Delete   12=Report
OK, EDIT performed. Please proceed.
COMMAND ===>                          SCROLL ===> PAGE
```

The execution of the above query caused the next panel to be displayed.

```
                          RUN CONFIRMATION

WARNING -- your RUN command is about to modify
              1         rows in the data base.

DO YOU WANT TO MAKE THIS CHANGE? ===> YES
                                      Type YES or NO.

        YES -- The changes made by your query will be made
               permanent in the data base.

        NO  -- The table will be restored to what it was before
               the query was run. No changes will be made.

Press ENTER to continue after responding to the question.
Press END at any time to cancel your QMF command and return
to the original QMF panel.

PF13=Help      15=End
ISPF Command ===>
```

In QMF you can request to be prompted before making changes permanent ly to the table. This panel is the result of requesting a confirmation prior to actually committing the changes. The pages containing the rows being up dated are locked from other users until you respond to this prompt panel.

```
SQL QUERY                                             LINE 1

*** END ***

1=Help     2=Run      3=End      4=Print    5=Chart     6=Draw
7=Backward 8=Forward  9=Form    10=Insert  11=Delete   12=Report
OK, this is an empty SQL QUERY panel.
COMMAND ===> display employees_table           SCROLL ===> PAGE
```

The DISPLAY command can be used to display the results of a table without constructing a query. Execution of the above causes the following to occur.

```
REPORT        USERID1.EMPLOYEES_TABLE           LINE 1   POS 1  79

   EMPLOYEE  EMPLOYEE          ADDRESS
        NO   NAME              STATE   DEPT      SALARY
   ---------- ----------------  ------- ----  ----------
        200  LARSON            IL      D890    60000.00
        300  SMITH             WI      D900    50000.00
        175  MURPHY            IA      D900    40000.00
        400  BLACK             MO      D600    60000.00
        150  JONES             UT      D600    70000.00
        500  EINERSON          UT      D890    80000.00
        250  CASPER            MN      D890    70000.00
        600  GRAVES            CA      D890    30000.00
        350  JORDAN            FL      D890    50000.00
        415  THOMPSON          MN      D400    80000.00
        425  WASHINGTON        NY      D400    40000.00
        450  NICKELS           OH      D500    35000.00
        495  GREEN             ND      D700    40000.00
1=Help     2=          3=End      4=Print       5=Chart  6=Query
7=Backward 8=Forward   9=Form    10=Left       11=Right     12=
OK, EMPLOYEES_TABLE is displayed.
COMMAND ===>                                    SCROLL ===> PAGE
```

```
REPORT          USERID1.EMPLOYEES_TABLE          LINE 1       POS 1   79


    EMPLOYEE   EMPLOYEE              ADDRESS
        NO     NAME                 STATE   DEPT      SALARY
  -----------  -----------------    -------  ----  ----------
          200  LARSON               IL      D890     60000.00
          300  SMITH                WI      D900     50000.00
          175  MURPHY               IA      D900     40000.00
          400  BLACK                MO      D600     60000.00
          150  JONES                UT      D600     70000.00
          500  EINERSON             UT      D890     80000.00
          250  CASPER               MN      D890     70000.00
          600  GRAVES               CA      D890     30000.00
          350  JORDAN               FL      D890     50000.00
          415  THOMPSON             MN      D400     80000.00
          425  WASHINGTON           NY      D400     40000.00
          450  NICKELS              OH      D500     35000.00
          495  GREEN                ND      D700     40000.00
1=Help      2=        3=End     4=Print       5=Chart    6=Query
7=Backward  8=Forward   9=Form   10=Left      11=Right       12=
OK, REPORT is displayed.
COMMAND ===> export ?                          SCROLL ===> PAGE
```

QMF allows you to export items in the work areas to TSO datasets. Item
that can be exported include QUERY, PROC, FORM, and DATA. Since th
user did not specify from which work area the item is to be exported, QMl
will prompt the user to obtain the required information.

```
                        EXPORT Command Prompt

EXPORT DATA
TO
DATA SET NAME ===> employee.table

                Type the name of the TSO data set into which the
                item is to be copied.


MEMBER          ===>         If the TSO data set is a member of a
                        partitioned data set, type the member name.


CONFIRM         ===> YES You can type YES or NO to indicate if you
                        want to be prompted before replacing an
                             existing TSO data set.
        Then press ENTER to execute the command from this panel.


PF13=Help       15=End
Complete your EXPORT DATA command on this panel.
ISPF Command ===>
```

The dataset name exported to is shown as "Employee.table." Actually the dataset name is appended by the work area and prefixed by the userid performing the export. If you wish to explicitly specify the entire dataset name, enclose it within quotes. If the dataset name does not exist, QMF will attempt to allocate it for you. QMF's IMPORT command works very similar to the EXPORT. You can use the IMPORT to place queries, procs, data, and forms into QMF work areas from TSO datasets. Both the EXPORT and IMPORT work strictly with the work areas. To export a QMF object, you first need to display the object in the respective work area. Likewise, if you import an object, it will not be saved until you issue the SAVE command to save it from the work area. The next work area to be discussed is the PROFILE work area. This work area can be displayed by executing DISPLAY PROFILE from the command line and appears as follows.

```
PROFILE


General Operands:
     CASE       ===> UPPER     Enter UPPER, STRING, or MIXED.
     DECIMAL    ===> PERIOD    Enter PERIOD, COMMA, or FRENCH.
     CONFIRM    ===> YES       Enter YES or NO.
     LANGUAGE   ===> SQL       Enter SQL or QBE.


Defaults for printing:
     WIDTH      ===> 132       Number of characters per line.
     LENGTH     ===> 60        Number of lines per page.
     PRINTER    ===>           Printer to be used for output.


QMF Administration Operands:   (Not usually changed)
     SPACE      ===> "DBDNAM03"."SPACE008"
              Enter the name of DB2 DATABASE or TABLESPACE in which
              tables will be saved by the SAVE DATA command.
     TRACE      ===> NONE
              Enter ALL, NONE or a character string of function-id,
              trace-level pairs.
1=Help        2=Save       3=End       4=Print      5=Chart     6=Query
7=            8=           9=Form      10=          11=         12=Report
OK, PROFILE is displayed.
COMMAND ===>
```

Each QMF user has their own PROFILE. When you invoke QMF, your PROFILE is placed in the PROFILE work area. The parameters specified in the PROFILE apply to your entire QMF session unless overridden. You can temporarily change your PROFILE for a particular application if necessary. An item of particular interest is the CONFIRM. Confirm YES indicates the user is to be prompted for a confirmation before making any changes. This might sound like the desirable option until one takes into account that when updating rows, the rows will be locked from other users until the user responds to the prompt. Better hope the user did not go on a coffee break.

The next item of major interest is the LANGUAGE. So far, all queries were SQL queries. There is another language called QBE or Query By Example, which can perform similar functions. QBE operates by creating example elements of the tables to be examined. I mention it because it is a function allowed in QMF. I have not included any examples due to a decline in interest by its users. The popularity of QBE declined somewhat due to the introduction of the DRAW command for SQL queries. Many initial users thought QBE was nice because they did not have to understand the SQL language. As more sophisticated QBE queries were developed, users found QBE to be just as complicated. Also, QBE does not support creating, dropping, or altering of DB2 objects (DDL).

The last item to be discussed in the PROFILE is the SPACE. But before we do that, we need to discuss the SAVE DATA command. This command allows users to save the result rows from a Select by dynamically creating a new table and inserting the rows into the newly defined table. The user can perform further analysis or processing on the newly defined table. The user only specifies the name of the new table when executing the SAVE DATA command. When creating this table, QMF uses the database and tablespace specified in the PROFILE work area to determine the database and tablespace the table is to be placed in. The database and tablespace must exist prior to the SAVE DATA command being executed unless you have access to the default database. If the data types match, you can replace an existing table with the SAVE DATA command. Your profile can be temporarily changed in a QMF procedure and reset back to its original status at the completion. You can vary a report's width, change the number of lines per page, change the database and tablespace used by a SAVE DATA, and request all confirmation to be suppressed. The net result is a lot of flexibility.

Example of a Proc altering the User's Profile:

```
SET PROFILE  (WIDTH=80,SPACE=DBDNAM01.SPACE008,CONFIRM=NO)
RUN QUERY1   (FORM=QUERY1_F)
PRINT REPORT
SAVE DATA AS TEMP_TABLE
RESET PROFILE
```

```
SQL QUERY                              MODIFIED     LINE 1

DELETE FROM EMPLOYEES_TABLE
   WHERE EMPLOYEE_NO = 100
*** END ***


1=Help      2=Run        3=End       4=Print    5=Chart     6=Draw
7=Backward  8=Forward    9=Form     10=Insert  11=Delete   12=Report


COMMAND ===> run query                           SCROLL ===> PAGE
```

If CONFIRM YES is specified in the PROFILE, the user will be prompted before the actual delete is performed. The following prompt panel would be displayed.

```
                        RUN CONFIRMATION
      WARNING -- your RUN command is about to modify
             10,000   rows in the data base.

      DO YOU WANT TO MAKE THIS CHANGE? ===> NO
                                      Type YES or NO.
             YES -- The changes made by your query will be made
                    permanent in the data base.
             NO  -- The table will be restored to what it was before
                    the query was run. No changes will be made.
      Press ENTER to continue after responding to the question.
      Press END at any time to cancel your QMF command and return
      to the original QMF panel.

      PF13=Help      15=End
      ISPF Command ===>
```

Note that the number of rows to be deleted is displayed. If the user thought only 10 rows were to be deleted and 10,000 rows were shown here, the user may opt to enter NO and check the DELETE statement for its accuracy.

```
SQL QUERY                                                      LINE 1


*** END ***
1=Help      2=Run       3=End       4=Print    5=Chart    6=Draw
7=Backward  8=Forward   9=Form  10=Insert    11=Delete  12=Report
OK, this is an empty SQL QUERY panel.
COMMAND ===> list ?                            SCROLL ===> PAGE
```

The LIST command allows the QMF user to display a list of QMF objects stored in the QMF tables. The user is only allowed to display QMF objects to which he or she has access to. Unless a QMF object is saved specifying SHARELEVEL YES, it is only available to the creator or what QMF refers to as the owner of the object. List ? causes the following prompt panel to be displayed.

```
                        LIST   Command Prompt
TYPE     ===> all
             Enter the name of the item type you want to list. It
             can be QUERIES, PROCS, FORMS, TABLES, or ALL.
OWNER    ===> USERID1
             Type the owner id of the item named. The owner id can
             contain selection symbols "%" and "_" to specify like
             owners. To list all owners, type ALL.
NAME     ===> ALL
             Type the specific item name. The name can contain selection
             symbols "%" or "_" to specify like names. To list all items
             for specified user, type ALL.
  Then press ENTER to execute the command from this panel.
PF13=Help      15=End
Please tell what you want to LIST.
ISPF Command ===>
```

LIST ? tells QMF to provide a panel in which the user can specify additional criteria in selecting which QMF objects are to be displayed.

```
QMF                             Item     Item     Item
Command   Item Name             Owner    Type     Sub-Type Restricted
-------   ------------------    -------- -------- -------- ---------
display   AUTO_INS_SALES        USERID1  TABLE    T
          AUTO_INSURANCE_Q1     USERID1  QUERY    SQL      Y
          AUTO_INSURANCE_Q2     USERID1  QUERY    SQL      Y
          DEPT_TABLE            USERID1  TABLE    T
          EMPLOYEE_F1           USERID1  FORM              Y
          EMPLOYEE_F2           USERID1  FORM              Y
          EMPLOYEE_F3           USERID1  FORM              Y
          EMPLOYEE_Q1           USERID1  QUERY    SQL      Y
          EMPLOYEE_Q2           USERID1  QUERY    SQL      Y
          EMPLOYEE_Q3           USERID1  QUERY    SQL      Y
          EMPLOYEES_TABLE       USERID1  TABLE    T
          LIF_INS_SALES         USERID1  TABLE    T
          LIFE_INSURANCE_F1     USERID1  FORM              Y
          LIFE_INSURANCE_Q1     USERID1  QUERY    SQL      Y
          LIFE_INSURANCE_Q2     USERID1  QUERY    SQL      Y
          MYVIEW1               USERID1  TABLE    V
          MYVIEW2               USERID1  TABLE    V
          MYVIEW4               USERID1  TABLE    V
          NULL_VALUES_TABLE     USERID1  TABLE    T
          NULLS_FORM            USERID1  FORM              Y
          PLAN_TABLE            USERID1  TABLE    T
          PROC_EMPL_DEPT        USERID1  PROC              N
          PROC_EMPL_LIFE        USERID1  PROC              Y
          PROC_EMPL_LIFE_2      USERID1  PROC              Y
PF13=Help    14=   15=End List 16=SortName 17=SortOwnr 18=SortType
PF19=Backward 20=Forward 21=List ? 22=Clear 23=Refresh 24=Comment
OK, your data base item list is displayed.
ISPF Command ===>                              SCROLL ===> PAGE
```

This is the result of executing the LIST command. In addition to viewing the items displayed, the user can enter QMF commands under the QMF Command heading. In this example, the table AUTO_INS_SALES is to be displayed. This is the equivalent of entering DISPLAY AUTO_INS_SALES on the command line. The result of the DISPLAY follows.

```
REPORT                USERID1.AUTO_INS_SALES      LINE 1    POS 1   79

      SALES
      PERSON   SALES              YTD
        NO     REGION            SALES        BONUS
    -----------  ---------   -------------   ----------
           415   MIDWEST      200000.00       2000.00
           800   MIDWEST      500000.00       5000.00
           425   NORTHEAST    750000.00       7500.00
           500   NORTHWEST   1000000.00      10000.00
           350   SOUTHEAST    500000.00       5000.00
           415   MIDWEST      200000.00       2000.00
           800   MIDWEST      500000.00       5000.00
           425   NORTHEAST    750000.00       7500.00
           500   NORTHWEST   1000000.00      10000.00
           350   SOUTHEAST    500000.00       5000.00

*** END ***

1=Help      2=        3=End      4=Print     5=Chart       6=Query
7=Backward  8=Forward  9=Form    10=Left     11=Right       12=
OK, USERID1.AUTO_INS_SALES is displayed.
COMMAND ===> list                          SCROLL ===> PAGE
```

Once a LIST command has been executed, the results will remain in the LIST work area until the QMF session is terminated or until another LIST command is executed. Entering LIST on the Command Line will redisplay the LIST work area.

```
QMF                          Item      Item      Item
Command   Item Name          Owner     Type      Sub-Type  Restricted
--------  ------------------ --------  --------  --------  ---------
*DISPLAY  AUTO_INS_SALES      USERID1   TABLE     T
run       AUTO_INSURANCE_Q1   USERID1   QUERY     SQL       Y
          AUTO_INSURANCE_Q2   USERID1   QUERY     SQL       Y
          DEPT_TABLE          USERID1   TABLE     T
          EMPLOYEE_F1         USERID1   FORM                Y
          EMPLOYEE_F2         USERID1   FORM                Y
          EMPLOYEE_F3         USERID1   FORM                Y
          EMPLOYEE_Q1         USERID1   QUERY     SQL       Y
          EMPLOYEE_Q2         USERID1   QUERY     SQL       Y
          EMPLOYEE_Q3         USERID1   QUERY     SQL       Y
          EMPLOYEES_TABLE     USERID1   TABLE     T
          LIF_INS_SALES       USERID1   TABLE     T
          LIFE_INSURANCE_F1   USERID1   FORM                Y
          LIFE_INSURANCE_Q1   USERID1   QUERY     SQL       Y
          LIFE_INSURANCE_Q2   USERID1   QUERY     SQL       Y
          MYVIEW1             USERID1   TABLE     V
          MYVIEW2             USERID1   TABLE     V
          MYVIEW4             USERID1   TABLE     V
          NULL_VALUES_TABLE   USERID1   TABLE     T
          NULLS_FORM          USERID1   FORM                Y
          PLAN_TABLE          USERID1   TABLE     T
          PROC_EMPL_DEPT      USERID1   PROC                N
          PROC_EMPL_LIFE      USERID1   PROC                Y
          PROC_EMPL_LIFE_2    USERID1   PROC                Y
PF13=Help 14=    15=End List 16=SortName 17=SortOwnr 18=SortType
PF19=Backward 20=Forward 21=List ? 22=Clear 23=Refresh 24=Comment
 OK, your data base item list is displayed.
ISPF Command ===>                                 SCROLL ===> PAGE
```

Previously run commands will be denoted by '*'. The user can enter another command as shown above. The RUN command will, in this case, run a query called AUTO_INSURANCE_Q1.

Overall, QMF is a very powerful and flexible tool. Applications running under TSO/ISPF can be integrated with QMF to provide easily accessed QMF applications.

Questions:

1. QMF serves as both a _____ manager and a _____ writer.
2. _____ is the QMF Command used to extract data, queries, procs, and forms into TSO datasets.
3. QMF allows you to manage _____, _____, and _____.
4. If you are running someone else's query, it must be preceded by the _____.
5. Display _____ allows you to alter the format of a report.
6. OMIT, AVERAGE, COUNT, and SUM all pertain to form _____.

True or False:

7. The results of a query could be displayed several times using different forms without re-execution of the query.
8. QMF runs only with TSO.
9. QMF variables can be used in both Procs and Queries.
0. Confirm of YES should be used with caution.
1. A Proc can execute QMF Commands as well as queries.
2. The SQL statements Export, Import, Save, Draw, List, and Display can all be issued from QMF interactively.

Answers:

1. Query, Report
2. EXPORT
3. PROCS, QUERIES, and FORMS
4. Owner's ID
5. FORM
6. USAGE
7. True
8. True
9. True
0. True
1. True
2. False, they may be executed interactively, but they are QMF commands not SQL statements.

5

Database Migration Aid Utility I (DBMAUI)

The Data Base Migration Aid Utility I (DBMAUI) is an IBM program offering that is very popular among many DB2 installations. Installations using personal TSOIDs when creating DB2 objects sometimes find themselves in a position where DB2 objects are owned by an employee that is no longer with the installation or has transferred to another area with different responsibilities. DBMAUI allows the user to construct Data Definition Language (DDL) statements from the DB2 System Catalog. This can be very useful in renaming DB2 objects, moving DB2 objects to other DB2 systems, and copying or moving DB2 objects to another TSOID. In addition to constructing DDL, it can also unload data from a table into a flat file. The unloaded data can be read into the same DB2 system or any other. DBMAUI can also reconstruct the security placed on tables, views, plans, storage groups, buffer pools, and tablespaces, plus it can reconstruct system privileges granted to individuals for creating databases, storage groups, etc. It runs under TSO in either foreground or background. The SQL generated is placed in output datasets. If the datasets do not already exist, DBMAUI will create the required datasets. If the datasets exist, they are reused. A CLIST to invoke the program is provided with the DBMAUI product. The CLIST displays a menu that includes 11 functions. The following is the list of functions displayed per execution of the CLIST. The actual dataset-naming convention used by the CLIST may differ at your installation, but the functions remain the same.

```
DB MIGRATION UTILITY
ENTER ...
  FUNCTION NAME

        DBAS   - BUILD DATABASE CREATE DDL
        FLAT   - FLAT FILE TABLE DUMP AND LOAD CONTROL
        GRANT  - DUMP TABLE GRANTS
        PLAN   - DUMP PLAN GRANTS
        SPACE  - BUILD TABLESPACE CREATE DDL
        STORG  - BUILD STORAGE GROUP CREATE DDL
        TDEF   - BUILD TABLE AND INDEX CREATE DDL
        USE    - DUMP USE GRANTS
        VIEW   - BUILD VIEW CREATE DDL
        SYN    - BUILD SYNONYM CREATE DDL
        SYSP   - DUMP SYSTEM PRIVILEGE GRANTS


  .TSO < CMD > - TO EXECUTE TSO COMMANDS
  .Pxxxxxxxx   - TO SET TSO DSN PREFIX ID ( < USER ID > )
  QUIT         - TO EXIT
```

Following ".TSO" with a TSO command will allow the user to execute TSO commands while using the CLIST. For example, ".TSO LISTC LEVEL(USERID1)" issues a TSO command that will list dataset names that have USERID1 as the high level dataset name qualifier. The datasets created by the CLIST have a prefix set equal to the userid of the individual executing the CLIST. If you wish to have the prefix set to some other qualifier, specify ".P" followed by whatever prefix you wish to use. For example, .PUSERID2 and pressing ENTER will cause all datasets allocated by the CLIST to be prefixed by USERID2.

The following material illustrates the ease at which this utility program can be executed. Responses to direct the CLIST to perform specific functions are highlighted.

```
                    CREATE DATABASE DDL

DB MIGRATION UTILITY
ENTER ...
 FUNCTION NAME


        DBAS  - BUILD DATABASE CREATE DDL
        FLAT  - FLAT FILE TABLE DUMP AND LOAD CONTROL
        GRANT - DUMP TABLE GRANTS
        PLAN  - DUMP PLAN GRANTS
        SPACE - BUILD TABLESPACE CREATE DDL
        STORG - BUILD STORAGE GROUP CREATE DDL
        TDEF  - BUILD TABLE AND INDEX CREATE DDL
        USE   - DUMP USE GRANTS
        VIEW  - BUILD VIEW CREATE DDL
        SYN   - BUILD SYNONYM CREATE DDL
        SYSP  - DUMP SYSTEM PRIVILEGE GRANTS


 .TSO < CMD > - TO EXECUTE TSO COMMANDS
 .Pxxxxxxxx   - TO SET TSO DSN PREFIX ID ( < USER ID > )
 QUIT         - TO EXIT

dbas
```

Dbas is the function name for building database create DDL. After pressing ENTER, the user will be prompted to specify the databases for which DDL statements are to be constructed.

```
DATABASE DEFINITION DUMP
ENTER ...

   DATABASE NAME  - <OWNER.>DBNAME
   OWNER.         - FOR ALL DATABASES CREATED BY OWNER
                  - NOTE: . IS NECESSARY
   NULL(ENTER)    - FOR ALL DATABASES IN SYSTEM
   . O<DSN>       - TO SET ONE-TIME DATA SET NAME OVERRIDE


   QUIT           - TO EXIT

userid1.
```

The user can select the databases for which DDL statements are to be generated. If ENTER is pressed without entering a choice, then DDL for all databases defined to the DB2 system will be generated. If only the userid is entered, as shown above, DDL statements will be generated for all of the databases created by "userid1." In this execution, USERID1 has three databases DBDNAM01, DBDNAM02 and DBDNAM03. If DDL statements are only desired for database DBDNAM01, then DBDNAM01 can be specified instead.

```
DATA SET USERID1.DBDBAS.USERID1.$ALL$ NOT IN CATALOG OR CATALOG
CAN NOT BE ACCESSED
MISSING DATA SET NAME+

ALLOCATING A NEW DATA SET...
ALLOCATION COMPLETE--DATA SET NAME: DBDBAS.USERID1.$ALL$

DATABASE CREATE BUILD ENTERED ...
END OF FILE ON SYSDATABASE REACHED
SELECTED DATABASE CREATE(S) DUMPED

        3  DATABASE CREATE(S) DUMPED
COMMIT

   MORE REQUESTS ? ( Y/N)

n
```

The following is the contents of the dataset created by DBMAUI to construct DDL to build databases. Because the dataset did not previously exist, the DBMAUI CLIST allocated the dataset. "O.<DSN>" allows you to override the dataset name created if you wish to provide your own dataset name. Otherwise, DBMAUI will determine the dataset name for you. If the dataset already exists, it will be overlaid. The following is the contents of the dataset.

```
--
--      DBDBAS.USERID1.$ALL$
--
--   DATABASE(S) CREATED BY USERID1
--
CREATE DATABASE DBDNAM01     STOGROUP PROD0001    BUFFERPOOL BP0;
CREATE DATABASE DBDNAM02     STOGROUP SYSDEFLT    BUFFERPOOL BP0;
CREATE DATABASE DBDNAM03     STOGROUP PROD0001    BUFFERPOOL BP0;
```

```
                    CREATE TABLESPACE DDL

DB MIGRATION UTILIT
ENTER ...
  FUNCTION NAME :


        DBAS   - BUILD DATABASE CREATE DDL
        FLAT   - FLAT FILE TABLE DUMP AND LOAD CONTROL
        GRANT  - DUMP TABLE GRANTS
        PLAN   - DUMP PLAN GRANTS
        SPACE  - BUILD TABLESPACE CREATE DDL
        STORG  - BUILD STORAGE GROUP CREATE DDL
        TDEF   - BUILD TABLE AND INDEX CREATE DDL
        USE    - DUMP USE GRANTS
        VIEW   - BUILD VIEW CREATE DDL
        SYN    - BUILD SYNONYM CREATE DDL
        SYSP   - DUMP SYSTEM PRIVILEGE GRANTS


  .TSO < CMD > - TO EXECUTE TSO COMMANDS
  .Pxxxxxxxx   - TO SET TSO DSN PREFIX ID ( < USER ID > )
  QUIT         - TO EXIT

space
```

The space function allows the user to build DDL to define tablespaces.

```
TABLESPACE DEFINITION DUMP
ENTER ...

    TABLESPACE NAME  - <OWNER>.TSNAME
    OWNER.           - FOR ALL TABLESPACES CREATED BY OWNER
                     - NOTE: . IS NECESSARY
    NULL(ENTER)      - FOR ALL TABLESPACES IN SYSTEM
    .O<DSN>          - TO SET ONE-TIME DATA SET NAME OVERRIDE

    QUIT             - TO EXIT

useridl.
```

Since a specific tablespace name was not specified, DDL will be generated or all tablespaces created by USERID1. SPACE001 could be specified to renerate tablespace DDL for only tablespace SPACE001.

```
DATA SET USERID1.DBSPAC.USERID1.$ALL$ NOT IN CATALOG OR CATALOG
CAN NOT BE ACCESSED
MISSING DATA SET NAME+

ALLOCATING A NEW DATA SET...
ALLOCATION COMPLETE--DATA SET NAME: DBSPAC.USERID1.$ALL$

TABLESPACE CREATE BUILD ENTERED...
END OF FILE ON SYSTABLESPACE AND SYSTABLEPART REACHED
COMMIT

SELECTED TABLE SPACE CREATE(S) DUMPED
      6 TABLESPACE CREATE(S) DUMPED
COMMIT


  MORE REQUESTS ? ( Y/N)

n
```

The following dataset was created by DBMAUI to contain tablespace DDL.

```
--      DBSPAC.USERID1.$ALL$
-- TABLESPACE(S) CREATED BY USERID1
 CREATE TABLESPACE GDVEXPLN IN DBDNAM02
LOCKSIZE  PAGE       BUFFERPOOL BP0          CLOSE YES      USING
STOGROUP TEST0001     PRIQTY 12     SECQTY 12
ERASE  NO  ;
 CREATE TABLESPACE SPACE001 IN DBDNAM01
LOCKSIZE  TABLESPACE    BUFFERPOOL BP0      CLOSE NO    USING
STOGROUP PROD0001        PRIQTY 100      SECQTY 20
ERASE  NO     FREEPAGE      20     PCTFREE        15 ;
 CREATE TABLESPACE SPACE002 IN DBDNAM01
LOCKSIZE  PAGE       BUFFERPOOL BP0          CLOSE NO   NUMPARTS
2 (PART        1     USING     STOGROUP PROD0001        PRIQTY
100    SECQTY        20    ERASE  NO     FREEPAGE        20
PCTFREE      15, PART     2     USING    STOGROUP PROD0001
PRIQTY 80     SECQTY 16    ERASE  NO     FREEPAGE
PCTFREE      15, PART     2     USING     STOGROUP PROD0001
```

```
RIQTY 80      SECQTY 16     ERASE   NO        FREEPAGE
      25       PCTFREE         20 );
CREATE TABLESPACE SPACE003 IN DBDNAM01
OCKSIZE   PAGE      BUFFERPOOL BP0           CLOSE NO   NUMPARTS
 (PART        1     USING     STOGROUP PROD0001           PRIQTY
52     SECQTY         20     ERASE   NO        FREEPAGE       20
CTFREE       15, PART       2      USING      STOGROUP PROD0001
RIQTY 52     SECQTY 20     ERASE   NO        FREEPAGE
      25       PCTFREE         20 );
CREATE TABLESPACE SPACE004 IN DBDNAM01
OCKSIZE   PAGE      BUFFERPOOL BP0           CLOSE NO   NUMPARTS
 (PART        1     USING     STOGROUP PROD0001           PRIQTY
52     SECQTY         20     ERASE   NO        FREEPAGE       20
CTFREE       15, PART       2      USING      STOGROUP PROD0001
RIQTY 52     SECQTY 20     ERASE   NO        FREEPAGE
      25       PCTFREE         20 );
CREATE TABLESPACE SPACE005 IN DBDNAM01
OCKSIZE   ANY       BUFFERPOOL BP0           CLOSE NO       USING
TOGROUP PROD0001      PRIQTY 12      SECQTY 12
RASE   NO   ;
```

```
                    CREATE TABLE AND INDEX DDL


DB MIGRATION UTILITY
ENTER ...
   FUNCTION NAME :


           DBAS  - BUILD DATABASE CREATE DDL
           FLAT  - FLAT FILE TABLE DUMP AND LOAD CONTROL
           GRANT - DUMP TABLE GRANTS
           PLAN  - DUMP PLAN GRANTS
           SPACE - BUILD TABLESPACE CREATE DDL
           STORG - BUILD STORAGE GROUP CREATE DDL
           TDEF  - BUILD TABLE AND INDEX CREATE DDL
           USE   - DUMP USE GRANTS
           VIEW  - BUILD VIEW CREATE DDL
           SYN   - BUILD SYNONYM CREATE DDL
           SYSP  - DUMP SYSTEM PRIVILEGE GRANTS


   .TSO < CMD > - TO EXECUTE TSO COMMANDS
   .Pxxxxxxxx   - TO SET TSO DSN PREFIX ID ( < USER ID > )
   QUIT         - TO EXIT


tdef
```

The TDEF function will create the DDL for building tables and their corresponding indexes.

```
TABLE DEFINITION DUMP
ENTER ...

     TABLE NAME    - <OWNER.>TNAME
     OWNER.        - FOR ALL TABLES CREATED BY OWNER
                   - NOTE: . IS NECESSARY
     NULL(ENTER)   - FOR ALL TABLES IN SYSTEM
     .O<DSN>       - TO SET ONE-TIME DATA SET NAME OVERRIDE

     QUIT          - TO EXIT

useridl.
```

Since USERID1 was specified without any specific table, DDL will be generated for all tables created by USERID1. DBMAUI will build all the index DDL for the tables selected. SQL COMMENT and LABEL statements will also be generated for the selected tables.

```
COMMIT
DATA SET USERID1.DBDEF.USERID1.$ALL$ NOT IN CATALOG OR CATALOG
CAN NOT BE ACCESSED
MISSING DATA SET NAME+

ALLOCATING A NEW DATA SET...
ALLOCATION COMPLETE--DATA SET NAME: DBDEF.USERID1.$ALL$

EOF ON SYSTABLES
 CALLING BUILD FOR TABLE USERID1.AUTO_INS_SALES
 PROCESS SYSCOLUMNS DATA FOR USERID1.AUTO_INS_SALES
EOF ON SYSCOLUMNS
COMMENT ENTERED ...
                0 CREATE COMMENT STATEMENT(S) PRODUCED
LABEL ENTERED ...
                0 CREATE LABEL STATEMENT(S) PRODUCED
INDX ENTERED ...
```

```
EOF ON SYSINDEXES AND SYSKEYS

                  2 CREATE INDEX STATEMENT(S) PRODUCED
COMMIT
 CALLING BUILD FOR TABLE USERID1.EMPLOYEES_TABLE
 PROCESS SYSCOLUMNS DATA FOR USERID1.EMPLOYEES_TABLE
EOF ON SYSCOLUMNS
COMMENT ENTERED ...
                  0 CREATE COMMENT STATEMENT(S) PRODUCED
LABEL ENTERED ...
                  0 CREATE LABEL STATEMENT(S) PRODUCED
INDX ENTERED ...
EOF ON SYSINDEXES AND SYSKEYS
                  1 CREATE INDEX STATEMENT(S) PRODUCED
COMMIT
 CALLING BUILD FOR TABLE USERID1.LIF_INS_SALES
 PROCESS SYSCOLUMNS DATA FOR USERID1.LIF_INS_SALES
EOF ON SYSCOLUMNS
COMMENT ENTERED ...
                  0 CREATE COMMENT STATEMENT(S) PRODUCED
LABEL ENTERED ...
                  0 CREATE LABEL STATEMENT(S) PRODUCED
INDX ENTERED ...
EOF ON SYSINDEXES AND SYSKEYS
                  2 CREATE INDEX STATEMENT(S) PRODUCED
COMMIT
 CALLING BUILD FOR TABLE USERID1.NULL_VALUES_TABLE
 PROCESS SYSCOLUMNS DATA FOR USERID1.NULL_VALUES_TABLE
EOF ON SYSCOLUMNS
COMMENT ENTERED ...
                  0 CREATE COMMENT STATEMENT(S) PRODUCED
LABEL ENTERED ...
                  0 CREATE LABEL STATEMENT(S) PRODUCED
INDX ENTERED ...
EOF ON SYSINDEXES AND SYSKEYS
                  1 CREATE INDEX STATEMENT(S) PRODUCED
COMMIT
 CALLING BUILD FOR TABLE USERID1.PLAN_TABLE
```

```
PROCESS SYSCOLUMNS DATA FOR USERID1.PLAN_TABLE


EOF ON SYSCOLUMNS
COMMENT ENTERED ...
                0 CREATE COMMENT STATEMENT(S) PRODUCED
LABEL ENTERED ...
                0 CREATE LABEL STATEMENT(S) PRODUCED
INDX ENTERED ...
EOF ON SYSINDEXES AND SYSKEYS
                0 CREATE INDEX STATEMENT(S) PRODUCED
COMMIT
 CALLING BUILD FOR TABLE USERID1.TEST_TABLE
 PROCESS SYSCOLUMNS DATA FOR USERID1.TEST_TABLE
EOF ON SYSCOLUMNS
COMMENT ENTERED ...
                0 CREATE COMMENT STATEMENT(S) PRODUCED
LABEL ENTERED ...
                5 CREATE LABEL STATEMENT(S) PRODUCED
INDX ENTERED ...
EOF ON SYSINDEXES AND SYSKEYS
                1 CREATE INDEX STATEMENT(S) PRODUCED
COMMIT

SELECTED TABLE CREATE(S) DUMPED
                6 TABLE CREATE(S) DUMPED
COMMIT


MORE REQUESTS ? ( Y/N)

n
```

The following dataset was constructed and contains create DDL for all of
he tables that existed for USERID1.

```
--    DBDEF.USERID1.$ALL$
--    CREATE FOR TABLE USERID1.AUTO_INS_SALES FOLLOWS
CREATE TABLE USERID1."AUTO_INS_SALES" (
"SALES_PERSON_NO"   INTEGER NOT NULL,
```

```
"SALES_REGION"        CHAR(     9) NOT NULL,
"YTD_SALES"           DECIMAL(   9,      2) NOT NULL WITH DEFAULT
"BONUS"               DECIMAL(   7,      2) NOT NULL WITH DEFAULT
    ) IN DBDNAM01.SPACE004;
--   CREATE INDEXES FOR TABLE AUTO_INS_SALES
CREATE UNIQUE INDEX USERID1."X_AUTO_INS_SALES" ON
USERID1."AUTO_INS_SALES" ("SALES_PERSON_NO")
        USING STOGROUP PROD0001     PRIQTY    20      SECQTY 4
        8      ERASE NO     PCTFREE          20      SUBPAGES 16
BUFFERPOOL BP0           CLOSE YES ;
 CREATE INDEX USERID1."X_AUTO_SALES" ON USERID1."AUTO_INS_SALES"
("YTD_SALES")                               SUBPAGES 16
BUFFERPOOL BP0           CLOSE NO ;
--   CREATE FOR TABLE USERID1.EMPLOYEES_TABLE FOLLOWS
CREATE TABLE USERID1."EMPLOYEES_TABLE" (
 "EMPLOYEE_NO"         INTEGER NOT NULL,
 "EMPLOYEE_NAME"       CHAR(   16) NOT NULL,
 "ADDRESS_STATE"       CHAR(    2) NOT NULL,
 "DEPT"                CHAR(    4) NOT NULL,
 "SALARY"              DECIMAL(   7,      2) NOT NULL
    ) IN DBDNAM01.SPACE002;
--   CREATE INDEXES FOR TABLE EMPLOYEES_TABLE
 CREATE UNIQUE INDEX USERID1."X_EMPLOYEES_TABLE" ON
USERID1."EMPLOYEES_TABLE" ("EMPLOYEE_NO")
        CLUSTER (PART  1 VALUES ( 600)   USING STOGROUP PROD0001
        PRIQTY 20      SECQTY 12       ERASE NO , PART
        2    VALUES( 999)      USING STOGROUP PROD0001    PRIQTY
    12    SECQTY          12      ERASE NO )
        SUBPAGES 4       BUFFERPOOL BP0             CLOSE NO ;
--   CREATE FOR TABLE USERID1.LIF_INS_SALES FOLLOWS
CREATE TABLE USERID1."LIF_INS_SALES" (
 "SALESPERSONS_NO"     INTEGER NOT NULL,
 "REGION"              CHAR(     9) NOT NULL,
 "YTD_SALES"           DECIMAL(  9,    2) NOT NULL WITH DEFAULT,
 "BONUS"               DECIMAL(  7,    2) NOT NULL WITH DEFAULT
    ) IN DBDNAM01.SPACE003;
--   CREATE INDEXES FOR TABLE LIF_INS_SALES
 CREATE INDEX USERID1."X_LIF_SALES" ON USERID1."LIF_INS_SALES"
("SALESPERSONS_NO")                         USING STOGROUP
PROD0001    PRIQTY 12      SECQTY 12        ERASE NO
        SUBPAGES 4       BUFFERPOOL BP0              CLOSE NO ;
```

```
CREATE INDEX USERID1."X_LIFE_SALES" ON USERID1."LIF_INS_SALES"
("YTD_SALES")                              SUBPAGES 16
BUFFERPOOL BP0           CLOSE NO ;
--    CREATE FOR TABLE USERID1.NULL_VALUES_TABLE FOLLOWS
CREATE TABLE USERID1."NULL_VALUES_TABLE" (
 "CHAR1"                CHAR (    2),
 "CHAR2"                CHAR (    2) NOT NULL WITH DEFAULT,
 "VARCHAR1"             CHAR (   20),
 "VARCHAR2"             CHAR (   20) NOT NULL WITH DEFAULT,
 "SMALLINT1"            SMALLINT,
 "SMALLINT2"            SMALLINT NOT NULL WITH DEFAULT,
 "INTEGER1"             INTEGER,
 "INTEGER2"             INTEGER NOT NULL WITH DEFAULT,
 "DECIMAL1              "DECIMAL(  5,   2),
 "DECIMAL2"             DECIMAL(  5,   2) NOT NULL WITH DEFAULT,
 "FLOAT1"               FLOAT ,
 "FLOAT2"               FLOAT  NOT NULL WITH DEFAULT
     ) IN DBDNAM01.SPACE005;
--    CREATE INDEXES FOR TABLE NULL_VALUES_TABLE
CREATE INDEX USERID1."X_NULLVALUES_TABLE" ON
USERID1."NULL_VALUES_TABLE" ("CHAR1")
 USING STOGROUP PROD0001     PRIQTY     12      SECQTY
12       ERASE NO     SUBPAGES 4          BUFFERPOOL BP0        CLOSE
YES ;
--    CREATE FOR TABLE USERID1.TEST_TABLE FOLLOWS
CREATE TABLE USERID1."TEST_TABLE" (
 "DEPT_NUMBER"          INTEGER NOT NULL,
 "DEPT_NAME"            CHAR (   20) NOT NULL,
 "DEPT_MANAGER"         CHAR (   30),
 "AVERAGESALARY"        DECIMAL(   7,    2),
 "AVERAGEAGE"           SMALLINT,
 "DEPTCHARTER"          VARCHAR(  200),
 "PC_WORKSTATIONS"      INTEGER NOT NULL WITH DEFAULT
     ) IN DBDNAM01.SPACE001;
--    LABELS FOR TABLE TEST_TABLE
LABEL ON TABLE USERID1."TEST_TABLE" IS
     'SAMPLE TABLE FOR ILLUSTRATION';
LABEL ON COLUMN USERID1."TEST_TABLE"."DEPT_MANAGER" IS
     'DEPARTMENT MANAGER';
LABEL ON COLUMN USERID1."TEST_TABLE"."AVERAGESALARY" IS
     'AVERAGE SALARY';
```

```
LABEL ON COLUMN USERID1."TEST_TABLE"."AVERAGEAGE" IS
    'AVERAGE AGE';
LABEL ON COLUMN USERID1."TEST_TABLE"."DEPTCHARTER" IS
    'DEPARTMENT CHARTER';
--   CREATE INDEXES FOR TABLE TEST_TABLE
 CREATE INDEX USERID1."INDX1_TEST_TABLE" ON USERID1."TEST_TABLE"
("DEPT_NUMBER","AVERAGESALARY" DESC )
  USING STOGROUP PROD0001     PRIQTY  20     SECQTY
    8     ERASE NO     PCTFREE    20     SUBPAGES 4     BUFFERPOOL
BP0          CLOSE NO ;
```

```
                        CREATE VIEW DDL


  DB MIGRATION UTILITY
  ENTER ...
       FUNCTION NAME :

           DBAS  - BUILD DATABASE CREATE DDL
           FLAT  - FLAT FILE TABLE DUMP AND LOAD CONTROL
           GRANT - DUMP TABLE GRANTS
           PLAN  - DUMP PLAN GRANTS
           SPACE - BUILD TABLESPACE CREATE DDL
           STORG - BUILD STORAGE GROUP CREATE DDL
           TDEF  - BUILD TABLE AND INDEX CREATE DDL
           USE   - DUMP USE GRANTS
           VIEW  - BUILD VIEW CREATE DDL
           SYN   - BUILD SYNONYM CREATE DDL
           SYSP  - DUMP SYSTEM PRIVILEGE GRANTS

           .TSO < CMD > - TO EXECUTE TSO COMMANDS
           .Pxxxxxxxx    - TO SET TSO DSN PREFIX ID ( < USER ID > )
           QUIT          - TO EXIT

  view
```

VIEW is the function specified to create DDL statements for existing views.

```
VIEW DEFINITION DUMP
ENTER...

        VIEW NAME    - <OWNER.>VIEWNAME
        OWNER.       - FOR ALL VIEWS CREATED BY OWNER
                     - NOTE: . IS NECESSARY
        NULL(ENTER)  - FOR ALL VIEWS IN SYSTEM
        .O<DSN>      - TO SET ONE-TIME DATA SET NAME OVERRIDE

        QUIT         - TO EXIT

userid1.
```

Entering "USERID1." instructs DBMAUI to create DDL for all views created by userid1. Individual view names can be specified if desired.

```
DATA SET USERID1.DBVIEW.USERID1.$ALL$ NOT IN CATALOG OR CATALOG
CAN NOT BE ACCESSED
MISSING DATA SET NAME+

ALLOCATING A NEW DATA SET...
ALLOCATION COMPLETE--DATA SET NAME: DBVIEW.USERID1.$ALL$

VIEW CREATE BUILD ENTERED...
END OF FILE ON SYSVIEWS REACHED
         4 VIEW CREATE(S) DUMPED

COMMIT


 MORE REQUESTS ? ( Y/N)

n
```

The following dataset is the result of building DDL for all views created by user USERID1.

```
-- USERID1.DBVIEW.USERID1.$ALL$ --
--     DBVIEW.USERID1.$ALL$
--  VIEW(S) CREATED BY USERID1
        CREATE VIEW MYVIEW1 AS SELECT * FROM USERID1.TEST_TABLE;
        CREATE VIEW MYVIEW2 AS SELECT * FROM USERID1.TEST_TABLE
WHERE DEPT_NUMBER = 100 AND AVERAGESALARY > 50000;
        CREATE VIEW MYVIEW4 AS SELECT DEPT_NUMBER,AVERAGESALARY,
AVERAGEAGE FROM USERID1.TEST_TABLE WHERE DEPT_NUMBER =200
WITH CHECK OPTION;
            CREATE VIEW VIEWTEST AS SELECT * FROM EMPLOYEES_TABLE;
```

```
                        CREATE SYNONYM DDL


DB MIGRATION UTILITY
ENTER ...
    FUNCTION NAME :
            DBAS  - BUILD DATABASE CREATE DDL
            FLAT  - FLAT FILE TABLE DUMP AND LOAD CONTROL
            GRANT - DUMP TABLE GRANTS
            PLAN  - DUMP PLAN GRANTS
            SPACE - BUILD TABLESPACE CREATE DDL
            STORG - BUILD STORAGE GROUP CREATE DDL
            TDEF  - BUILD TABLE AND INDEX CREATE DDL
            USE   - DUMP USE GRANTS
            VIEW  - BUILD VIEW CREATE DDL
            SYN   - BUILD SYNONYM CREATE DDL
            SYSP  - DUMP SYSTEM PRIVILEGE GRANTS
    .TSO < CMD > - TO EXECUTE TSO COMMANDS
    .Pxxxxxxxx   - TO SET TSO DSN PREFIX ID ( < USER ID > )
    QUIT         - TO EXIT

syn
```

The SYN function allows the user to reconstruct CREATE SYNONYM statements.

```
SYNONYM DEFINITION DUMP
ENTER...

    SYNONYM NAME  - <OWNER.>SYNONYMNAME
    OWNER.        - FOR ALL SYNONYMS CREATED BY OWNER
                  - NOTE: . IS NECESSARY
    NULL(ENTER)   - FOR ALL SYNONYMS IN SYSTEM
    .O<DSN>       - TO SET ONE-TIME DATA SET NAME OVERRIDE

    QUIT          - TO EXIT

userid1.
```

All of the synonyms created by USERID1 will be reconstructed.

```
DATA SET USERID1.DBSYN.USERID1.$ALL$ NOT IN CATALOG OR CATALOG
CAN NOT BE ACCESSED
MISSING DATA SET NAME+

ALLOCATING A NEW DATA SET...
ALLOCATION COMPLETE--DATA SET NAME: DBSYN.USERID1.$ALL$

SYNONYM CREATE BUILD ENTERED...
END OF FILE ON SYSSYNONYMS REACHED
        2 SYNONYM CREATE(S) DUMPED

COMMIT

  MORE REQUESTS ? ( Y/N)

n
```

The following dataset contains the SYNONYM SQL.

```
-- USERID1.DBSYN.USERID1.$ALL$ --


--      DBSYN.USERID1.$ALL$
--   SYNONYM(S) CREATED BY USERID1
CREATE SYNONYM "DT" FOR USERID1 ."TEST_TABLE";
CREATE SYNONYM "MY" FOR USERID1 ."MYVIEW1";
```

```
                 GENERATE UNLOAD DATASET AND LOAD CONTROL CARDS


    DB MIGRATION UTILITY
    ENTER ...
        FUNCTION NAME :


               DBAS  - BUILD DATABASE CREATE DDL
               FLAT  - FLAT FILE TABLE DUMP AND LOAD CONTROL
               GRANT - DUMP TABLE GRANTS
               PLAN  - DUMP PLAN GRANTS
               SPACE - BUILD TABLESPACE CREATE DDL
               STORG - BUILD STORAGE GROUP CREATE DDL
               TDEF  - BUILD TABLE AND INDEX CREATE DDL
               USE   - DUMP USE GRANTS
               VIEW  - BUILD VIEW CREATE DDL
               SYN   - BUILD SYNONYM CREATE DDL
               SYSP  - DUMP SYSTEM PRIVILEGE GRANTS


        .TSO < CMD > - TO EXECUTE TSO COMMANDS
        .Pxxxxxxxx   - TO SET TSO DSN PREFIX ID ( < USER ID > )
        QUIT         - TO EXIT

    flat
```

The FLAT function allows data from a table to be unloaded to a sequentia
dataset.

```
FLAT FILE TABLE DUMP
ENTER...

     TABLE NAME   -   <OWNER.>TNAME
     .EX          -   TO EXECUTE SQL CMDS
     .BNNNNN      -   TO SET BLIP COUNT ( BLIP =        20 )
     .FNN         -   TO SET NUMERIC FIELD WIDTH 1-18 (WIDTH =12 )
     .LX          -   TO SET DELIMITER ( DELIMITER = : )
     .KX          -   TO SET LOCK OPT Y  N ( LOCK OPT = N )
     .TX          -   TO SET TERMINATOR ( TERMINATOR = ; )
     .NX          -   TO SET NULL OPT Y  N ( NULL OPT = Y )
     .GX          -   TO SET GEN OPT Y  N ( GEN  OPT  = N )
     .RNNNNNNN    -   TO SET ESTIMATED ROW COUNT ( DEFAULT =    0
     .O<DSN>      -   TO SET ONE-TIME DATA SET NAME OVERRIDE

     QUIT         -   TO EXIT

userid1.auto_ins_sales
```

This request is to unload the data contained in table AUTO_INS_SALES wned by USERID1.

```
ENTER WHERE ARGUMENT (TERMINATE WITH ; OR NULL)
     QUIT     -- RETURN TO MENU
     RESTART -- TO RE-SPECIFY
  >


;
```

; or ENTER without any changes implies that all of the rows are to be un-oaded from the table or tables.

```
BUILD
ALL1
COMMIT
DATA SET USERID1.DBFLAT.USERID1.AUTO@INS.$@SALES NOT IN CATALOG
     OR CATALOG CAN NOT BE ACCESSED
MISSING DATA SET NAME+

ALLOCATING A NEW DATA SET...
ALLOCATION COMPLETE--DSNAME: DBFLAT.USERID1.AUTO@INS.$@SALES

END OF FILE REACHED
COMMIT
5 ROWS FROM TABLE USERID1.AUTO_INS_SALES WERE SUCCESSFULLY DUMPED


  NEW TABLE ( Y / N ) ?

y
```

The following dataset was created and contains the unloaded data.

```
-- USERID1.DBFLAT.USERID1.AUTO@INS.$@SALES --

          415.MIDWEST  .   200000.00.    2000.00.;
          800.MIDWEST  .   500000.00.    5000.00.;
          425.NORTHEAST.   750000.00.    7500.00.;
          500.NORTHWEST.  1000000.00.   10000.00.;
          350.SOUTHEAST.   500000.00.    5000.00.;
```

```
FLAT FILE TABLE DUMP
ENTER...

       TABLE NAME   -   <OWNER.>TNAME
       .EX          -   TO EXECUTE SQL CMDS
       .BNNNNN      -   TO SET BLIP COUNT ( BLIP =  20 )
       .FNN         -   TO SET NUMERIC FIELD WIDTH 1-18 (WIDTH = 12 )
       .LX          -   TO SET DELIMITER ( DELIMITER = : )
       .KX          -   TO SET LOCK OPT Y  N ( LOCK OPT = N )
       .TX          -   TO SET TERMINATOR ( TERMINATOR = ; )
       .NX          -   TO SET NULL OPT Y  N ( NULL OPT = Y )
       .GX          -   TO SET GEN OPT Y  N ( GEN  OPT  = N )
       .RNNNNNNN    -   TO SET ESTIMATED ROW COUNT ( DEFAULT =  0 )
       .O<DSN>      -   TO SET ONE-TIME DATA SET NAME OVERRIDE

       QUIT         -   TO EXIT

userid1.employees_table
```

Employees_table is the name of the table to be unloaded. Userid1 is the name of the creator of the table.

```
ENTER WHERE ARGUMENT (TERMINATE WITH ; OR NULL)
       QUIT    -- RETURN TO MENU
       RESTART -- TO RE-SPECIFY
   >

where dept='d400' or dept='d890' or dept='d500';
```

You can unload the entire table or code in the predicates like the ones above to select certain rows.

```
BUILD
ALL1
COMMIT
DATA SET USERID1.DBFLAT.USERID1.EMPLOYEE.$S@TABLE NOT IN CATALOG
    OR CATALOG CAN NOT BE ACCESSED
MISSING DATA SET NAME+

ALLOCATING A NEW DATA SET...
ALLOCATION COMPLETE--DSNAME: DBFLAT.USERID1.EMPLOYEE.$S@TABLE

END OF FILE REACHED
COMMIT
13 ROWS FROM TABLE USERID1.EMPLOYEES_TABLE WERE SUCCESSFULLY
    DUMPED.

NEW TABLE ( Y / N ) ?

y
```

The following dataset contains the result from unloading the EMPLOYEES_TABLE where employees work in departments D400, D890, or D500.

```
-- USERD1.DBFLAT.USERID1.EMPLOYEE.$S@TABLE --

        200.LARSON          .IL.D890.     60000.00.;
        500.EINERSON        .UT.D890.     80000.00.;
        250.CASPER          .MN.D890.     70000.00.;
        600.GRAVES          .CA.D890.     30000.00.;
        350.JORDAN          .FL.D890.     50000.00.;
        415.THOMPSON        .MN.D400.     80000.00.;
        425.WASHINGTON      .NY.D400.     40000.00.;
        450.NICKELS         .OH.D500.     35000.00.;
        550.WILLMORE        .TX.D500.     45000.00.;
        700.ROCKY           .SC.D890.     40000.00.;
        800.KENNEDY         .OH.D400.     30000.00.;
        750.GRAY            .TX.D500.     45000.00.;
        650.SMITH           .NC.D500.     40000.00.;
```

In this illustration, we will investigate several of the options available when unloading a table. To change an option, enter the option plus the new value and press ENTER. Note that the new value entered appears for the option instead of the default. Repeat this process until all desired options have been set.

```
FLAT FILE TABLE DUMP
  ENTER...

       TABLE NAME    -   <OWNER.>TNAME
       .EX           -   TO EXECUTE SQL CMDS
       .BNNNNN       -   TO SET BLIP COUNT ( BLIP = 20 )   <========
       .FNN          -   TO SET NUMERIC FIELD WIDTH 1-18 (WIDTH = 12 )
       .LX           -   TO SET DELIMITER ( DELIMITER = : )
       .KX           -   TO SET LOCK OPT Y  N ( LOCK OPT = N )
       .TX           -   TO SET TERMINATOR ( TERMINATOR = ; )
       .NX           -   TO SET NULL OPT Y  N ( NULL OPT = Y )
       .GX           -   TO SET GEN OPT Y  N ( GEN  OPT  = N )
       .RNNNNNNN     -   TO SET ESTIMATED ROW COUNT ( DEFAULT = 0 )
       .O<DSN>       -   TO SET ONE-TIME DATA SET NAME OVERRIDE


       QUIT          -   TO EXIT

.b5
```

The .BNNNNN option allows the user to specify at what intervals messages are to be displayed indicating the number of rows unloaded. If 100 is specified, the user would see messages indicating that 100 rows unloaded, 200 rows unloaded, 300 rows unloaded, etc., until completion.

```
FLAT FILE TABLE DUMP
ENTER...

    TABLE NAME   -   <OWNER.>TNAME
    .EX          -   TO EXECUTE SQL CMDS
    .BNNNNN      -   TO SET BLIP COUNT ( BLIP = 5 ) <===============
    .FNN         -   TO SET NUMERIC FIELD WIDTH 1-18 (WIDTH = 12 )
    .LX          -   TO SET DELIMITER ( DELIMITER = : ) <===========
    .KX          -   TO SET LOCK OPT Y  N ( LOCK OPT = N )
    .TX          -   TO SET TERMINATOR ( TERMINATOR = ; )
    .NX          -   TO SET NULL OPT Y  N ( NULL OPT = Y )
    .GX          -   TO SET GEN OPT Y  N ( GEN  OPT  = N )
    .RNNNNNNN    -   TO SET ESTIMATED ROW COUNT ( DEFAULT =  0 )
    .O<DSN>      -   TO SET ONE-TIME DATA SET NAME OVERRIDE


    QUIT         -   TO EXIT

.L*
```

The .LX option allows the user to specify the symbol to be used as the delimiter between columns in the unload dataset. ":" is the default. In this example, we are changing the delimiter to *.

```
FLAT FILE TABLE DUMP
ENTER...

    TABLE NAME    -    <OWNER.>TNAME
    .EX           -    TO EXECUTE SQL CMDS
    .BNNNNN       -    TO SET BLIP COUNT ( BLIP =   5 )
    .FNN          -    TO SET NUMERIC FIELD WIDTH 1-18 (WIDTH = 12 )
    .LX           -    TO SET DELIMITER ( DELIMITER = * ) <===========
    .KX           -    TO SET LOCK OPT Y  N ( LOCK OPT = N )
    .TX           -    TO SET TERMINATOR ( TERMINATOR = ; )
    .NX           -    TO SET NULL OPT Y  N ( NULL OPT = Y )
    .GX           -    TO SET GEN OPT Y  N ( GEN  OPT  = N ) <========
    .RNNNNNNN     -    TO SET ESTIMATED ROW COUNT ( DEFAULT =  0 )
    .O<DSN>       -    TO SET ONE-TIME DATA SET NAME OVERRIDE

    QUIT          -    TO EXIT

.gy
```

The .GX parameter plays a key role in the unload process. It tells the program to generate the appropriate LOAD control cards for reloading the data unloaded. It will take into account columns that contain nulls and construct corresponding control cards to handle the null conditions.

```
FLAT FILE TABLE DUMP
ENTER...

    TABLE NAME   -   <OWNER.>TNAME
    .EX          -   TO EXECUTE SQL CMDS
    .BNNNNN      -   TO SET BLIP COUNT ( BLIP =  5 )
    .FNN         -   TO SET NUMERIC FIELD WIDTH 1-18 (WIDTH = 12 )
    .LX          -   TO SET DELIMITER ( DELIMITER = * )
    .KX          -   TO SET LOCK OPT Y  N ( LOCK OPT = N )
    .TX          -   TO SET TERMINATOR ( TERMINATOR = ; )
    .NX          -   TO SET NULL OPT Y  N ( NULL OPT = Y )
    .GX          -   TO SET GEN OPT Y  N ( GEN  OPT  = Y ) <=======
    .RNNNNNNN    -   TO SET ESTIMATED ROW COUNT ( DEFAULT =  0 ) <=
    .O<DSN>      -   TO SET ONE-TIME DATA SET NAME OVERRIDE


    QUIT         -   TO EXIT

.r50000
```

You can assist the CLIST when allocating datasets to ensure enough space exists in the unload dataset by providing an estimate of the number of rows to be unloaded from a table. This is done by specifying a value for .RNNNNNNN where the NNNNNNN is replaced by the number of rows to be unloaded.

```
FLAT FILE TABLE DUMP
ENTER...

    TABLE NAME   -   <OWNER.>TNAME
    .EX          -   TO EXECUTE SQL CMDS
    .BNNNNN      -   TO SET BLIP COUNT ( BLIP =    5 )
    .FNN         -   TO SET NUMERIC FIELD WIDTH 1-18 (WIDTH = 12)
    .LX          -   TO SET DELIMITER ( DELIMITER = * )
    .KX          -   TO SET LOCK OPT Y  N ( LOCK OPT = N )
    .TX          -   TO SET TERMINATOR ( TERMINATOR = ; )
    .NX          -   TO SET NULL OPT Y  N ( NULL OPT = Y )
    .GX          -   TO SET GEN OPT Y  N ( GEN  OPT  = Y )
    .RNNNNNNN    -   TO SET ESTIMATED ROW COUNT (DEFAULT = 50000)<=
    .O<DSN>      -   TO SET ONE-TIME DATA SET NAME OVERRIDE <======

    QUIT         -   TO EXIT

.olifeins.data
```

".O<DSN>" options allows you to override the dataset name that will be generated by the CLIST for the table unload. In this illustration, we want the dataset name of the flat file to be LIFEINS.DATA.

```
ENTER DSN OVERRIDE VALUE FOR CONTROL FILE:

life.cntl
```

If the unload dataset name or flat file has been overridden by the user, the user will be prompted for the dataset name to be used for the control card dataset if the GY option is also set. In this example, LIFE.CNTL is the dataset that will contain the load control cards. The load utility, which loads tables from flat files, requires control cards to describe the flat file records. These control cards can be generated by DBMAUI for use with the load utility.

```
FLAT FILE TABLE DUMP
ENTER...

    TABLE NAME   -   <OWNER.>TNAME
    .EX          -   TO EXECUTE SQL CMDS
    .BNNNNN      -   TO SET BLIP COUNT ( BLIP =  5 )
    .FNN         -   TO SET NUMERIC FIELD WIDTH 1-18 (WIDTH = 12)
    .LX          -   TO SET DELIMITER ( DELIMITER = * )
    .KX          -   TO SET LOCK OPT Y  N ( LOCK OPT = N )
    .TX          -   TO SET TERMINATOR ( TERMINATOR = ; )
    .NX          -   TO SET NULL OPT Y  N ( NULL OPT = Y )
    .GX          -   TO SET GEN OPT Y  N ( GEN   OPT  = Y )
    .RNNNNNNN    -   TO SET ESTIMATED ROW COUNT (DEFAULT = 50000)
    .O<DSN>      -   TO SET ONE-TIME DATA SET NAME OVERRIDE


    QUIT         -   TO EXIT

    OVERRIDE DSN: '<USERID>.LIFEINS.DATA'<===========================

useridl.lif_ins_sales
```

If all of the table unload options have been set, enter the name of the table to be unloaded. Other options: Option KY can be used to lock the table from other users. Option FNN can be used to override the default output width for numeric fields. Option NX allows the user to change the symbol used in the unloaded data to represent null values. The default is "?". Option TX allows the user to replace or omit the ";" used to terminate the SQL statements.

```
ENTER WHERE ARGUMENT (TERMINATE WITH ; OR NULL)
       QUIT    -- RETURN TO MENU
       RESTART -- TO RE-SPECIFY
  >


;


DATA SET USERID1.LIFE.CNTL NOT IN CATALOG OR CATALOG CAN NOT
BE ACCESSED MISSING DATA SET NAME+

ALLOCATING A NEW DATA SET...
ALLOCATION COMPLETE--DATA SET NAME: LIFE.CNTL

BUILD
ALL1
COMMIT

USING AN EXISTING DATA SET...
ALLOCATION COMPLETE--DATA SET NAME: LIFEINS.DATA

            5 RECORDS WRITTEN
           10 RECORDS WRITTEN
END OF FILE REACHED
COMMIT
10 ROWS FROM TABLE USERID1.LIF_INS_SALES WERE SUCCESSFULLY DUMPED
  NEW TABLE ( Y / N ) ?

Y
```

The following dataset contains the data that has been unloaded. The .L* option specified earlier indicated that column data should be separated by the asterisk.

```
-- USERID1.LIFEINS.DATA --
----+----10---+----20---+----30---+----40---+----50---

         200*MIDWEST   *   120000.00*    1200.00*;
         300*MIDWEST   *   600000.00*    6000.00*;
         175*MIDWEST   *   700000.00*    7000.00*;
         400*SOUTHEAST*  1000000.00*   10000.00*;
         150*NORTHWEST*   990000.00*    9900.00*;
         500*NORTHWEST*   800000.00*    8000.00*;
         250*MIDWEST   *   800000.00*    8000.00*;
         600*SOUTHWEST*   122000.00*    1200.00*;
         350*SOUTHEAST*   750000.00*    7500.00*;
         700*SOUTHEAST*   400000.00*    4000.00*;
```

The following dataset contains the control cards generated to reload the data based from the unload format.

```
-- USERID1.LIFE.CNTL --

LOAD DATA INDDN(SYSREC) RESUME(YES) LOG(NO)
INTO TABLE LIF_INS_SALES
("SALESPERSONS_NO"      POSITION(    1) INTEGER EXTERNAL(    12),
 "REGION"               POSITION(   14) CHAR(     9),
 "YTD_SALES"            POSITION(   24) DECIMAL EXTERNAL(    12),
 "BONUS"                POSITION(   37) DECIMAL EXTERNAL(    12))
```

```
FLAT FILE TABLE DUMP
ENTER...

     TABLE NAME    -    <OWNER.>TNAME
     .EX           -    TO EXECUTE SQL CMDS
     .BNNNNN       -    TO SET BLIP COUNT ( BLIP = 20 )
     .FNN          -    TO SET NUMERIC FIELD WIDTH 1-18 (WIDTH = 12 )
     .LX           -    TO SET DELIMITER ( DELIMITER = : )
     .KX           -    TO SET LOCK OPT Y  N ( LOCK OPT = N )
     .TX           -    TO SET TERMINATOR ( TERMINATOR = ; )
     .NX           -    TO SET NULL OPT Y  N ( NULL OPT = Y )
     .GX           -    TO SET GEN OPT Y  N ( GEN  OPT  = N )
     .RNNNNNNN     -    TO SET ESTIMATED ROW COUNT (DEFAULT =  0)
     .O<DSN>       -    TO SET ONE-TIME DATA SET NAME OVERRIDE

     QUIT          -    TO EXIT

.ex
```

The .EX option allows the user to enter SQL statements (except SELECT). The SQL statement will be executed prior to the unload. Only SQL statements that do not return rows are allowed.

```
ENTER SQL CMD (TERMINATE WITH ; OR NULL)
     QUIT     -- RETURN TO MENU
     RESTART -- TO RE-SPECIFY

delete from employees_table where dept='d400';
```

The above SQL statement is valid but probably not desirable. Rows will actually be deleted from the table prior to the unload, which in most cases is not what is desired.

DB2 security is administered through the GRANT and REVOKE SQL statements. The GRANT statement is used to issue privileges, while the REVOKE is used to remove privileges that have already been granted. The formats of the GRANT and REVOKE SQL statements are as following.

```
       GRANT authorization-specifications TO userids
or
       GRANT authorization-specifications TO PUBLIC
or
       GRANT authorization-specifications TO userids WITH GRANT OPTION

       REVOKE authorization-specifications FROM userids
or
       REVOKE authorization-specifications FROM PUBLIC
```

Authorization-specifications vary, depending on which DB2 object the authorizations are to be placed on. For example, CREATEDBA is a privilege that will allow a user to create new databases, where DBADM ON DATABASE DBDNAM01 is a privilege that allows a user to have complete control over all objects associated to a database named DBDNAM01. SELECT ON EMPLOYEES_TABLE is a privilege to retrieve rows and columns from a table.

Userids is a list of TSOIDs that are to receive privileges if a GRANT SQL statement, or lose privileges if a REVOKE SQL statement. PUBLIC implies that the privilege is to be given to everyone if a GRANT or removed from everyone if a REVOKE SQL.

WITH GRANT OPTION allows the person receiving the privilege the authority to grant the same privilege to others.

Authorizations will be covered in detail in a later chapter. DBMAUI has the ability to reconstruct the authorizations that were granted on a particular DB2 resource. In the following illustrations, assume that the following two GRANT statements have been issued.

1. The following grant is issued by USERID1. It allows userids USERID2, USERID3, USERID4 the ability to select rows from tables AUTO_INS_SALES, EMPLOYEES_TABLE, and LIF_INS_SALES owned by USERID1. Because the WITH GRANT OPTION is specified, these userids can grant the same privilege to others, as is seen in the second SQL statement:

```
GRANT SELECT ON USERID1.AUTO_INS_SALES,
               USERID1.EMPLOYEES_TABLE,
               USERID1.LIF_INS_SALES
          TO USERID2,USERID3,USERID4 WITH GRANT OPTION
```

2. The following grant is issued by USERID2 to grant the same privileges to USERID5, USERID6, and USERID7, only without the grant option.

```
GRANT SELECT ON USERID1.AUTO_INS_SALES,
               USERID1.EMPLOYEES_TABLE,
               USERID1.LIF_INS_SALES
          TO USERID5,USERID6,USERID7
```

```
                    CREATE AUTHORIZATION SQL


DB MIGRATION UTILITY
ENTER ...
        FUNCTION NAME :
                DBAS   - BUILD DATABASE CREATE DDL
                FLAT   - FLAT FILE TABLE DUMP AND LOAD CONTROL
                GRANT  - DUMP TABLE GRANTS
                PLAN   - DUMP PLAN GRANTS
                SPACE  - BUILD TABLESPACE CREATE DDL
                STORG  - BUILD STORAGE GROUP CREATE DDL
                TDEF   - BUILD TABLE AND INDEX CREATE DDL
                USE    - DUMP USE GRANTS
                VIEW   - BUILD VIEW CREATE DDL
                SYN    - BUILD SYNONYM CREATE DDL
                SYSP   - DUMP SYSTEM PRIVILEGE GRANTS


                .TSO < CMD > - TO EXECUTE TSO COMMANDS
                .Pxxxxxxxx   - TO SET TSO DSN PREFIX ID ( < USER ID > )
                QUIT         - TO EXIT
grant
```

The GRANT functions allow a user to build SQL statements to reconstruct the authority granted on tables. You can therefore regrant the authority on a dropped object once it has been reconstructed.

```
TABLE/VIEW PRIVILEGES GRANT DUMP
ENTER ...


    TABLE NAME   - <GRANTOR.>NAME
    GRANTOR.     - FOR ALL TABLES GRANTED BY GRANTOR
                 - NOTE: . IS NECESSARY
    NULL(ENTER)  - FOR ALL TABLE GRANTS IN SYSTEM
    .O<DSN>      - TO SET ONE-TIME DATA SET NAME OVERRIDE


    QUIT         - TO EXIT


userid1.auto_ins_sales
```

By specifying USERID1, all grants performed by USERID1 for table
AUTO_INS_SALES will be reconstructed. Observe in the result dataset that
not all of the authority granted on the table is reconstructed. Anyone who
received authority from USERID1 with the ability to grant it away and has
done so will not show up in the results.

This is the contents of the dataset created. Note that the grants by
USERID2 do not appear.

```
-- USERID1.DBGRNT.USERID1.AUTO@INS.$@SALES --
--
--      DBGRNT.USERID1.AUTO@INS.$@SALES
--
--
--    TABLE(S) GRANTED BY USERID1
--
GRANT SELECT ON USERID1."AUTO_INS_SALES" TO USERID4   WITH GRANT
OPTION;
GRANT SELECT ON USERID1."AUTO_INS_SALES" TO USERID3   WITH GRANT
OPTION;
GRANT SELECT ON USERID1."AUTO_INS_SALES" TO USERID2   WITH GRANT
OPTION;
```

```
TABLE/VIEW PRIVILEGES GRANT DUMP
ENTER ...

        TABLE NAME   - <GRANTOR.>NAME
        GRANTOR.     - FOR ALL TABLES GRANTED BY GRANTOR
                     - NOTE: . IS NECESSARY
        NULL(ENTER)  - FOR ALL TABLE GRANTS IN SYSTEM
        .O<DSN>      - TO SET ONE-TIME DATA SET NAME OVERRIDE


        QUIT         - TO EXIT

userid1.employees_table
```

Grants issued by USERID1 for table EMPLOYEES_TABLE will be generated.

```
DATA SET USERID1.DBGRNT.USERID1.EMPLOYEE.$S@TABLE NOT IN CATALOG
OR CATALOG CAN NOT BE ACCESSED
MISSING DATA SET NAME+

ALLOCATING A NEW DATA SET...
ALLOCATION COMPLETE--DSNAME: DBGRNT.USERID1.EMPLOYEE.$S@TABLE

END OF FILE ON SYSTABAUTH REACHED
SELECTED TABLE GRANT(S) DUMPED
        3 TABLE GRANT(S) DUMPED

COMMIT

 MORE REQUESTS ? ( Y/N)

y
```

The following dataset contains all the grants issued by USERID1 on table
EMPLOYEES_TABLES.

```
-- USERID1.DBGRNT.USERID1.EMPLOYEE.$S@TABLE --
--
--      DBGRNT.USERID1.EMPLOYEE.$S@TABLE
--
--   TABLE(S) GRANTED BY USERID1
--
GRANT SELECT ON USERID1."EMPLOYEES_TABLE" TO USERID4  WITH GRANT
OPTION;
GRANT SELECT ON USERID1."EMPLOYEES_TABLE" TO USERID3  WITH GRANT
OPTION;
GRANT SELECT ON USERID1."EMPLOYEES_TABLE" TO USERID2  WITH GRANT
OPTION;
```

```
TABLE/VIEW PRIVILEGES GRANT DUMP
ENTER ...


     TABLE NAME   - <GRANTOR.>NAME
     GRANTOR.     - FOR ALL TABLES GRANTED BY GRANTOR
                  - NOTE: . IS NECESSARY
     NULL(ENTER)  - FOR ALL TABLE GRANTS IN SYSTEM
     .O<DSN>      - TO SET ONE-TIME DATA SET NAME OVERRIDE


     QUIT         - TO EXIT

useridl.lif_ins_sales
```

Reconstruct all grants issued by USERID1 for table LIF_INS_SALES table.

```
DATA SET USERID1.DBGRNT.USERID1.LIF@INS@.$SALES NOT IN CATALOG
     OR CATALOG CAN NOT BE ACCESSED
MISSING DATA SET NAME+

ALLOCATING A NEW DATA SET...
ALLOCATION COMPLETE--DSNAME: DBGRNT.USERID1.LIF@INS@.$SALES

END OF FILE ON SYSTABAUTH REACHED
SELECTED TABLE GRANT(S) DUMPED
          3 TABLE GRANT(S) DUMPED
COMMIT

 MORE REQUESTS ? ( Y/N)

n
```

The following dataset contains the results from the previous request to construct the grants issued by USERID1 on table LIF_INS_SALES table.

```
-- USERID1.DBGRNT.USERID1.LIF@INS@.$SALES ---
--
--     DBGRNT.USERID1.LIF@INS@.$SALES
--
--
--    TABLE(S) GRANTED BY USERID1
--
GRANT SELECT ON USERID1.LIF_INS_SALES TO USERID4
     WITH GRANT OPTION;
GRANT SELECT ON USERID1.LIF_INS_SALES TO USERID3
     WITH GRANT OPTION;
GRANT SELECT ON USERID1.LIF_INS_SALES TO USERID2
     WITH GRANT OPTION;
```

```
DB MIGRATION UTILITY
ENTER ...
     FUNCTION NAME :
               DBAS  - BUILD DATABASE CREATE DDL
               FLAT  - FLAT FILE TABLE DUMP AND LOAD CONTROL
               GRANT - DUMP TABLE GRANTS
               PLAN  - DUMP PLAN GRANTS
               SPACE - BUILD TABLESPACE CREATE DDL
               STORG - BUILD STORAGE GROUP CREATE DDL
               TDEF  - BUILD TABLE AND INDEX CREATE DDL
               USE   - DUMP USE GRANTS
               VIEW  - BUILD VIEW CREATE DDL
               SYN   - BUILD SYNONYM CREATE DDL
               SYSP  - DUMP SYSTEM PRIVILEGE GRANTS

               .TSO < CMD > - TO EXECUTE TSO COMMANDS
               .Pxxxxxxxx   - TO SET TSO DSN PREFIX ID ( < USER ID > )
               QUIT         - TO EXIT

grant
```

```
TABLE/VIEW PRIVILEGES GRANT DUMP
ENTER ...

        TABLE NAME   - <GRANTOR.>NAME
        GRANTOR.     - FOR ALL TABLES GRANTED BY GRANTOR
                     - NOTE: . IS NECESSARY
        NULL(ENTER)  - FOR ALL TABLE GRANTS IN SYSTEM
        .O<DSN>      - TO SET ONE-TIME DATA SET NAME OVERRIDE


        QUIT         - TO EXIT

auto_ins_sales
```

By not specifying the grantor, you will get all grants made to table
AUTO_INS_SALES. Since table name is not unique, DBMAUI will
reconstruct the grants for all tables called AUTO_INS_SALES regardless of
who created the table. You should edit the dataset built and remove any of the
grants that do not apply to the desired table. You will be able to determine
this by the creator of the table in the SQL statements.

```
DATA SET USERID1.DBGRNT.$ALL$.AUTO@INS.$@SALES NOT IN CATALOG OR
      CATALOG CAN NOT BE ACCESSED
MISSING DATA SET NAME+

ALLOCATING A NEW DATA SET...
ALLOCATION COMPLETE--DSNAME: DBGRNT.$ALL$.AUTO@INS.$@SALES
END OF FILE ON SYSTABAUTH REACHED
SELECTED TABLE GRANT(S) DUMPED
        6 TABLE GRANT(S) DUMPED

COMMIT

 MORE REQUESTS ? ( Y/N)

y
```

This is the contents of the dataset generated by DBMAUI fo
AUTO_INS_SALES table. Note that there are more SQL statements in th
dataset because the grantor was not specified.

```
- USERID1.DBGRNT.$ALL$.AUTO@INS.$@SALES ----

--
--     DBGRNT.$ALL$.AUTO@INS.$@SALES
--
--
--   TABLE(S) GRANTED BY USERID1
--
GRANT SELECT ON USERID1."AUTO_INS_SALES" TO USERID4   WITH GRANT
OPTION;
GRANT SELECT ON USERID1."AUTO_INS_SALES" TO USERID3   WITH GRANT
OPTION;
GRANT SELECT ON USERID1."AUTO_INS_SALES" TO USERID2   WITH GRANT
OPTION;
--
--   TABLE(S) GRANTED BY USERID2
--
GRANT SELECT ON USERID1."AUTO_INS_SALES" TO USERID7 ;
GRANT SELECT ON USERID1."AUTO_INS_SALES" TO USERID6 ;
GRANT SELECT ON USERID1."AUTO_INS_SALES" TO USERID5 ;
```

```
TABLE/VIEW PRIVILEGES GRANT DUMP
ENTER ...

        TABLE NAME   - <GRANTOR.>NAME
        GRANTOR.     - FOR ALL TABLES GRANTED BY GRANTOR
                     - NOTE: . IS NECESSARY
        NULL(ENTER)  - FOR ALL TABLE GRANTS IN SYSTEM
        .O<DSN>      - TO SET ONE-TIME DATA SET NAME OVERRIDE


        QUIT         - TO EXIT


employees_table
```

```
DATA SET USERID1.DBGRNT.$ALL$.EMPLOYEE.$S@TABLE NOT IN CATALOG
     OR CATALOG CAN NOT BE ACCESSED
MISSING DATA SET NAME+

ALLOCATING A NEW DATA SET...
ALLOCATION COMPLETE--DSNAME: DBGRNT.$ALL$.EMPLOYEE.$S@TABLE

END OF FILE ON SYSTABAUTH REACHED
SELECTED TABLE GRANT(S) DUMPED
          6 TABLE GRANT(S) DUMPED

COMMIT

  MORE REQUESTS ?  ( Y/N)

y
```

```
- USERID1.DBGRNT.$ALL$.EMPLOYEE.$S@TABLE ---

-
-      DBGRNT.$ALL$.EMPLOYEE.$S@TABLE
-
-
-    TABLE(S) GRANTED BY USERID1
-
RANT SELECT ON USERID1."EMPLOYEES_TABLE" TO USERID4  WITH GRANT
PTION;
RANT SELECT ON USERID1."EMPLOYEES_TABLE" TO USERID3  WITH GRANT
PTION;
RANT SELECT ON USERID1."EMPLOYEES_TABLE" TO USERID2  WITH GRANT
PTION;
-
-    TABLE(S) GRANTED BY USERID2
-
RANT SELECT ON USERID1."EMPLOYEES_TABLE" TO USERID7 ;
RANT SELECT ON USERID1."EMPLOYEES_TABLE" TO USERID6 ;
RANT SELECT ON USERID1."EMPLOYEES_TABLE" TO USERID5 ;
```

```
TABLE/VIEW PRIVILEGES GRANT DUMP
ENTER ...
        TABLE NAME   - <GRANTOR.>NAME
        GRANTOR.     - FOR ALL TABLES GRANTED BY GRANTOR
                     - NOTE: . IS NECESSARY
        NULL(ENTER)  - FOR ALL TABLE GRANTS IN SYSTEM
        .O<DSN>      - TO SET ONE-TIME DATA SET NAME OVERRIDE
        QUIT         - TO EXIT


lif_ins_sales
```

```
DATA SET USERID1.DBGRNT.$ALL$.LIF@INS@.$SALES NOT IN CATALOG OR
      CATALOG CAN NOT BE ACCESSED
MISSING DATA SET NAME+

ALLOCATING A NEW DATA SET...
ALLOCATION COMPLETE--DSNAME: DBGRNT.$ALL$.LIF@INS@.$SALES

END OF FILE ON SYSTABAUTH REACHED
SELECTED TABLE GRANT(S) DUMPED
        6 TABLE GRANT(S) DUMPED
COMMIT

  MORE REQUESTS ? ( Y/N)

y
```

```
-- USERID1.DBGRNT.$ALL$.LIF@INS@.$SALES --
--     DBGRNT.$ALL$.LIF@INS@.$SALES
--     TABLE(S) GRANTED BY USERID1
GRANT SELECT ON USERID1."LIF_INS_SALES" TO USERID4
  WITH GRANT OPTION;
GRANT SELECT ON USERID1."LIF_INS_SALES" TO USERID3
  WITH GRANT OPTION;
GRANT SELECT ON USERID1."LIF_INS_SALES" TO USERID2
```

```
WITH GRANT OPTION;
  -   TABLE(S) GRANTED BY USERID2
RANT SELECT ON USERID1."LIF_INS_SALES" TO USERID7 ;
RANT SELECT ON USERID1."LIF_INS_SALES" TO USERID6 ;
RANT SELECT ON USERID1."LIF_INS_SALES" TO USERID5 ;
```

```
TABLE/VIEW PRIVILEGES GRANT DUMP
ENTER ...
        TABLE NAME   - <GRANTOR.>NAME
        GRANTOR.     - FOR ALL TABLES GRANTED BY GRANTOR
                     - NOTE: . IS NECESSARY
        NULL(ENTER)  - FOR ALL TABLE GRANTS IN SYSTEM
        .O<DSN>      - TO SET ONE-TIME DATA SET NAME OVERRIDE
        QUIT         - TO EXIT
useridl.
```

By just specifying the userid, SQL statements will be constructed for all
grants performed by USERID1 to all tables.

```
DATA SET USERID1.DBGRNT.USERID1.$ALL$ NOT IN CATALOG OR CATALOG
CAN NOT BE ACCESSED
MISSING DATA SET NAME+

ALLOCATING A NEW DATA SET...
ALLOCATION COMPLETE--DATA SET NAME: DBGRNT.USERID1.$ALL$

END OF FILE ON SYSTABAUTH REACHED
SELECTED TABLE GRANT(S) DUMPED
         9 TABLE GRANT(S) DUMPED


COMMIT

  MORE REQUESTS ? ( Y/N)
```

n

The following dataset contains all the grants that had been issued b；
USERID1.

```
-- USERID1.DBGRNT.USERID1.$ALL$ --

--
--      DBGRNT.USERID1.$ALL$
--
--
--      TABLE(S) GRANTED BY USERID1
--
GRANT SELECT ON USERID1."LIF_INS_SALES" TO USERID4   WITH GRANT
OPTION;
GRANT SELECT ON USERID1."LIF_INS_SALES" TO USERID3   WITH GRANT
OPTION;
GRANT SELECT ON USERID1."LIF_INS_SALES" TO USERID2   WITH GRANT
OPTION;
GRANT SELECT ON USERID1."EMPLOYEES_TABLE" TO USERID4   WITH GRANT
OPTION;
GRANT SELECT ON USERID1."EMPLOYEES_TABLE" TO USERID3   WITH GRANT
OPTION;
GRANT SELECT ON USERID1."EMPLOYEES_TABLE" TO USERID2   WITH GRANT
OPTION;
GRANT SELECT ON USERID1."AUTO_INS_SALES" TO USERID4   WITH GRANT
OPTION;
GRANT SELECT ON USERID1."AUTO_INS_SALES" TO USERID3   WITH GRANT
OPTION;
GRANT SELECT ON USERID1."AUTO_INS_SALES" TO USERID2   WITH GRANT
OPTION;
```

```
DB MIGRATION UTILITY
ENTER ...
    FUNCTION NAME :


        DBAS  - BUILD DATABASE CREATE DDL
        FLAT  - FLAT FILE TABLE DUMP AND LOAD CONTROL
        GRANT - DUMP TABLE GRANTS
        PLAN  - DUMP PLAN GRANTS
        SPACE - BUILD TABLESPACE CREATE DDL
        STORG - BUILD STORAGE GROUP CREATE DDL
        TDEF  - BUILD TABLE AND INDEX CREATE DDL
        USE   - DUMP USE GRANTS
        VIEW  - BUILD VIEW CREATE DDL
        SYN   - BUILD SYNONYM CREATE DDL
        SYSP  - DUMP SYSTEM PRIVILEGE GRANTS


        .TSO < CMD > - TO EXECUTE TSO COMMANDS
        .Pxxxxxxxx   - TO SET TSO DSN PREFIX ID ( < USER ID > )
        QUIT         - TO EXIT

quit
```

Questions:

1. DBMAUI is an IBM utility that performs three basic functions. What are they?
2. The output of DBMAUI is in the form of _____.
3. .GY option when creating flat files, will cause _____ _____ _____ to be generated.
4. FLAT, GRANT, and TDEF are all _____ of DBMAUI.

True or False

5. DBMAUI generates load control cards automatically when a table dump or unload is performed.
6. TSO commands can be executed from the DBMAUI main menu.
7. You can create DDL statements for more than one database at a time.
8. TDEF causes only table DDL statements to be created.

9. Null columns, when unloaded to a flat file, contain either blanks or nulls.
10. DBMAUI will load table data from the same or other DB2 systems.
11. SQL statements (excluding SELECTS) can be executed from DBMAUI.
12. DBMAUI output may be transferred to other DB2 systems.

Answers:

1. Create DDL, Create Authorization Grants, Unload Table Data
2. Datasets
3. Load Control Cards
4. Functions
5. False, an option needs to be specified
6. True
7. True
8. False; it also causes Index DDL, Labels, and Comments
9. False; ? is placed in the first position of the unloaded data to indicate that the column is null. This option can be overridden by the user
10. False; the Load utility or something similar must be used
11. True
12. True

6

Application Programming

o access DB2 data from application programs, one codes SQL statements in-
termingled with the "host language" program statements. Host programs is-
uing SQL statements may be written in PL/I, COBOL, FORTRAN, APL2 and
.SSEMBLER LANGUAGE. The SQL statements will be similar to what you
ave seen already, but there are some major differences. There are two
methods in which SQL statements can be executed in traditional application
rogramming languages. The first method is termed STATIC SQL. Static
QL statements do not change in structure between executions. The columns
nd tables referenced are the same for every execution of the SQL statement.
When using Static SQL, DB2 will determine an access path before execution
nd will save this information to use every time the SQL statement is ex-
cuted in the program.

With the second method, Dynamic SQL, the application does not know what
he SQL statements look like until the program is executing. The SQL statement is frequently constructed in the course of the program being executed.
•B2 has to determine an access path each and every time a Dynamic SQL
tatement is executed. QMF is an example of a program that executes SQL
ynamically. Before discussing SQL coding techniques, lets view how the ap-
lication program preparation process has changed to accommodate SQL
tatement processing.

Three additional steps in the program preparation process are available.
wo are required: PRECOMPILE and BIND. One is optional: DCLGEN, also
ferred to as Table Declaration. Their perspective location in the program

preparation process is identified in Figure 6-1. The first step, Table Declara tion, is optional and consists of two components. The first component, SQ Declaration, describes the table or view to be accessed in the program. Thi description is used by the DB2 Precompiler to verify that correct colum names and data types have been specified in the SQL statements. The secon component of the Table Declaration consists of a Host Language Declaration This component contains the input/output area to be used by the program fo processing rows. The two components can be manually constructed or, in th case of COBOL, generated for you by a product provided with DB2 entitle DB2I. Table Declarations can be stored in datasets and merged into th program source by the SQL INCLUDE statement at DB2 Precompile tim The following example illustrates how a COBOL Table Declaration, stored i dataset "USERID1.DCLGEN.COBOL(EMPLOYEE)," is placed in the applica tion source code during the program preparation process.

COBOL: PDS='USERID1.DCLGEN.COBOL' member = EMPLOYEE

```
*********************************************************************
*  DCLGEN  TABLE(EMPLOYEES_TABLE)                                   *
*          LIBRARY(USERID1.DCLGEN.COBOL(EMPLOYEE))                  *
*          ACTION(REPLACE)                                          *
*          QUOTE                                                    *
*  ... IS THE DCLGEN COMMAND THAT MADE THE FOLLOWING STATEMENTS     *
*********************************************************************

       EXEC SQL DECLARE EMPLOYEES_TABLE TABLE
       ( EMPLOYEE_NO                  INTEGER NOT NULL,
       EMPLOYEE_NAME                  CHAR(16) NOT NULL,
       ADDRESS_STATE                  CHAR(2) NOT NULL,
       DEPT                           CHAR(4) NOT NULL,
       SALARY                         DECIMAL(7, 2) NOT NULL
       ) END-EXEC.

*********************************************************************
*  COBOL DECLARATION FOR TABLE EMPLOYEES_TABLE                      *
*********************************************************************

       01  DCLEMPLOYEES-TABLE.
       10 EMPLOYEE-NO            PIC S9(9) USAGE COMP.
       10 EMPLOYEE-NAME          PIC X(16).
       10 ADDRESS-STATE          PIC X(2).
       10 DEPT                   PIC X(4).
       10 SALARY                 PIC S99999V99 USAGE COMP-3.

*********************************************************************
*  THE NUMBER OF COLUMNS DESCRIBED BY THIS DECLARATION IS 5         *
*********************************************************************
```

SQL and Host Languages

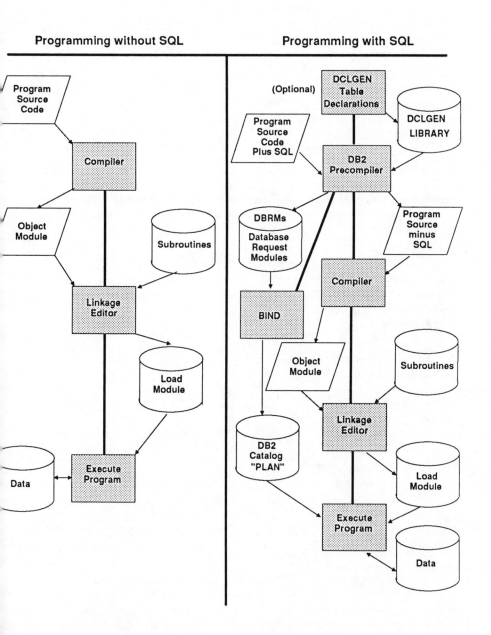

Programming without SQL | Programming with SQL

** gure 6-1 Programming Processes**

COBOL Source Code to include previous declaration:

```
ID DIVISION.
  PROGRAM-ID.   PROGRM1C.
  AUTHOR.       BRUCE LARSON
ENVIRONMENT DIVISION.
CONFIGURATION SECTION.
INPUT-OUTPUT SECTION.
FILE-CONTROL.
DATA DIVISION.
FILE SECTION.
WORKING-STORAGE SECTION.

    EXEC SQL
    INCLUDE EMPLOYEE
    END-EXEC.
```

Outputted COBOL Source Code from DB2 Precompiler:

```
ID DIVISION.
  PROGRAM-ID.   PROGRM1C.
  AUTHOR.       BRUCE LARSON
ENVIRONMENT DIVISION.
CONFIGURATION SECTION.
INPUT-OUTPUT SECTION.
FILE-CONTROL.
DATA DIVISION.
FILE SECTION.
WORKING-STORAGE SECTION.

*****EXEC SQL
*****   INCLUDE EMPLOYEE
*****END-EXEC.
****************************************************************
* DCLGEN TABLE(EMPLOYEES_TABLE)
*        LIBRARY(DVDB2ST.DCLGEN.COBOL(EMPLOYEE))
*        ACTION(REPLACE)
*        APOST
* ... IS THE DCLGEN COMMAND THAT MADE THE FOLLOWING STATEMENTS
****************************************************************
*****EXEC SQL DECLARE EMPLOYEES_TABLE TABLE
*****( EMPLOYEE_NO                 INTEGER NOT NULL,
*****  EMPLOYEE_NAME               CHAR(16) NOT NULL,
*****  ADDRESS_STATE               CHAR(2) NOT NULL,
*****  DEPT                        CHAR(4) NOT NULL,
*****  SALARY                      DECIMAL(7, 2) NOT NULL
*****) END-EXEC.
```

```
************************************************************
COBOL DECLARATION FOR TABLE EMPLOYEES_TABLE                *
************************************************************
01  DCLEMPLOYEES-TABLE.
    10 EMPLOYEE-NO          PIC S9(9) USAGE COMP.
    10 EMPLOYEE-NAME        PIC X(16).
    10 ADDRESS-STATE        PIC X(2).
    10 DEPT                 PIC X(4).
    10 SALARY               PIC S99999V99 USAGE COMP-3.
************************************************************
THE NUMBER OF COLUMNS DESCRIBED BY THIS DECLARATION IS 5   *
************************************************************
```

Input to the DB2 Precompiler consists of program source code, including QL statements. During the DB2 Precompile process, Table Declarations are etrieved from user-specified PDSs and placed where the corresponding SQL NCLUDE statement is specified. SQL statements in their current state ould be flagged as errors by any of the host language compilers. Therefore, he DB2 precompiler translates SQL statements into host language Call tatements and comments out the original imbedded SQL statements. The recompiler outputs a SQL statement summarization module called a Data ase Request Module (DBRM). This outputted module is later used as input the BIND step. Also outputted by the precompiler is program source that an be interpreted by a host language compiler. View Appendix F, for example, for programs containing SQL statements prior to the DB2 Precompile rocess. To ensure that the appropriate Data Base Request Module (DBRM) used with the corresponding object modules, both the DBRM and outputted ource code are timestamped. This timestamp is carried through the program reparation process and checked at execution time.

The next steps, COMPILE and LINKEDIT, require very little change. The ource code input to the Compiler or Assembler comes from the DB2 Precompile step. Since DB2 can interface with TSO, CICS, and IMS transaction rocessors, you are required to include the appropriate module for the transaction processor attachment used by the program. The following are the coresponding modules for the transaction processing subsystems:

Subsystems	Module Name	How Included
TSO	DSNELI	INCLUDE DSNELI
CICS	DSNCLI	INCLUDE DSNCLI
IMS	DFSLI000	INCLUDE DFSLI000

he output from the LINKEDIT process is an executable load module. Before e load module can actually be executed, the next step, BIND, must have een performed.

The Bind function uses the DBRM from the DB2 Precompile step as input nd produces what is called an application PLAN. The BIND checks the authority granted to the individual user issuing the BIND to ensure that the individual has the authority to perform the SQL statements contained in the program. During the BIND, SQL statements in the DBRM are validated. I the creator of the table is not specified in the SQL FROM clause, DB2 as sumes the SQL statements are against tables of the individual performing the BIND. The individual is checked to ensure that he or she has the proper authority to perform the SQL statements. DB2 also determines an access strategy for the static SQL statements summarized in the DBRM and record this information as a PLAN in the DB2 Catalog. The name of the PLAN may or may not be identical to the program name, depending on your execution en vironment. If the PLAN is going to be accessed using IMS, the PLAN name must match the program name. All of the object dependencies of the PLAN are recorded in the DB2 Catalog as a result of the Bind. These objects include tablespaces, indexes, views, tables, and synonyms. After the BIND and LINKEDIT steps are completed, the plan/program is executable. If one of the objects upon which the PLAN depends is dropped, the PLAN is marked as in valid and in some situations action will be required to make it executable.

For programs accessing DB2 through TSO, the DSN command is used to es tablish the connection or what is commonly referred to as a *thread*. The fol lowing examples illustrate establishing a TSO/DB2 connection and executing a program called PROGRM1C. The lower case entries represent the user' responses. Dbxx, in these examples, is the name given to the DB2 system while 'userid1.load' is the library where the executable load module wa placed. Progrm1C is also the name given to the PLAN.

TSO Foreground:

```
READY
dsn system(dbxx)
DSN
run program(progrm1c) plan(progrm1c) lib('userid1.load')
DSN
end
```

or

TSO Background:

```
//    EXEC PGM=IKJEFT01,REGION=1024K
//SYSOUT    DD SYSOUT=*
//SYSUDUMP  DD SYSOUT=*
//SYSTSPRT  DD SYSOUT=*
//SYSTSIN   DD *
DSN SYSTEM(DBXX)
RUN PROGRAM(PROGRM1C) PLAN(PROGRM1C) LIB('USERID1.LOAD')
END
/*
```

In the DB2 application programming environment it is necessary to check the status after each executable SQL statement is performed. An area must be specified in the program where DB2 can place the status of the SQL statement executed. This area is called the SQL Communication Area or SQLCA. The fields in the SQLCA area should be interrogated after executing all SQL statements except DECLARE and INCLUDE. DECLARE and INCLUDE do not request DB2 services during execution. The following SQLCA relates just to COBOL. Appendix E contains SQLCA areas for COBOL and other host languages. The SQL Communication Area is included in the same manner as Table Declarations.

COBOL:

```
01 SQLCA.
    05 SQLCAID    PIC X(8).
    05 SQLCABC    PIC S9(9) COMP-4.
    05 SQLCODE    PIC S9(9) COMP-4.
    05 SQLERRM.
        49 SQLERRML PIC S9(4) COMP-4.
        49 SQLERRMC PIC X(70).
    05 SQLERRP    PIC X(8).
    05 SQLERRD    OCCURS 6 TIMES
                  PIC S9(9) COMP-4.
    05 SQLWARN.
        10 SQLWARN0 PIC X.
        10 SQLWARN1 PIC X.
        10 SQLWARN2 PIC X.
        10 SQLWARN3 PIC X.
        10 SQLWARN4 PIC X.
        10 SQLWARN5 PIC X.
        10 SQLWARN6 PIC X.
        10 SQLWARN7 PIC X.
    05 SQLEXT     PIC X(8).
```

The SQLCA data field SQLCODE or SQLCOD, depending on host language, contains a value indicating the success of the SQL statement. This field should be interrogated after the SQL statement is executed. The value 0 indicates the SQL statement was successful, while < 0 return codes indicate an error condition occurred. A return code > 0 indicates a successful SQL execution but that an exceptional condition occurred. Following are some of the more frequent return codes you will encounter while processing SQL statements:

+100   No rows found (or no more available rows to process)
   0   Successful execution
-803   Unique index violated
-811   More than one row returned for a SELECT

-818   The DB2 Precompiler generated time stamp for the load module is different from the DBRM time stamp used as input into the BIND.

-904   Unavailable resource

-913   Unsuccessful execution caused by deadlock or timeout

When negative SQL return codes are encountered, the error message text data field SQLERRMC or SQLTXL, depending on the host language used, should be displayed as well as the SQL return code. Frequently, you will find that the SQL return code is insufficient by itself for problem resolution. The error message text data field in many situations further describes the probable cause of the problem. Data fields SQLWARN0-SQLWARN7 or SQLWRN(0)-SQLWRN(7) are flags useful in program debugging. These fields should be checked to determine if truncations, null values in built-in-functions were encountered or other exceptional conditions have occurred.

STATIC SQL: Static SQL implies the SQL statement does not change from one execution to the next. The SQL statements executed can be identified during the program preparation process. This does not imply that different rows cannot be returned from one execution of the SQL statement to the next. It implies that the table being accessed, along with the columns of the rows returned, do not change. Once DB2 determines an access strategy for the SQL statement, it will be used every time the SQL statement is executed.

Data fields from the program can be specified in SQL statements. These data fields are referred to as host variables. Whenever a data field is used in the SQL statement, it must be preceded by a colon. For example, :DEPT found in a SELECT represents a host variable defined in the program's data area. Likewise, DEPT referenced in a SQL statement refers to a column named DEPT in a table or view.

The Selects in the following examples work only if one or no rows are returned. If multiple rows are returned, SQL return code of -811 is returned to the application program. The SQL statements found in this chapter are coded irrespective to any specific host language. The EXEC SQL always precedes the SQL statement. The ending of the SQL statement varies depending on the host language. Programs PROGRM2C, PROGRM2F, and PROGRM2P in Appendix F should be referenced for the exact syntax used with the various host languages.

The INTO clause specifies where, in the program, the column data should be placed.

```
EXEC SQL
SELECT EMPLOYEE_NO,EMPLOYEE_NAME,
       ADDRESS_STATE, DEPT, SALARY
  INTO :DCLEMPLOYEES-TABLE
  FROM EMPLOYEES_TABLE
 WHERE DEPT = :HOST-DEPT AND EMPLOYEE_NO = 495
```

```
EXEC SQL
   SELECT EMPLOYEE_NO, EMPLOYEE_NAME,
      ADDRESS_STATE, DEPT, SALARY
   INTO :EMPLOYEE-NO, :EMPLOYEE-NAME, :ADDRESS-STATE,
      :DEPT , :SALARY
   FROM EMPLOYEES_TABLE
   WHERE DEPT = :HOST-DEPT AND EMPLOYEE_NO = 850
```

Multiple rows can be updated (or even deleted) by a single SQL statement, but not SELECTED.

```
EXEC SQL
   UPDATE EMPLOYEES_TABLE
      SET SALARY = SALARY - 1000.00
      WHERE DEPT='D700'

EXEC SQL
   DELETE FROM EMPLOYEES_TABLE
      WHERE DEPT='D900'

EXEC SQL
   INSERT INTO EMPLOYEES_TABLE
      (EMPLOYEE_NO,EMPLOYEE_NAME,EMPLOYEE_STATE,DEPT,SALARY)
      VALUES(:EMPLOYEE-NUMBER,'JACKSON','NY',:DEPT,0)
```

The next series of SQL examples display the strategy necessary to process SQL SELECTs returning multiple rows. Multiple row processing is controlled through what is called a CURSOR. The cursor identifies a particular SELECT statement declared in the program and its corresponding SQL statements, such as OPEN, FETCH, and CLOSE. A cursor is not defined in the program data area. It is only referenced in SQL statements. Multiple selects accessing multiple rows are allowed to process concurrently. The SELECTs could be against different tables or even the same table.

Multiple cursors may be specified in the same program. The cursor name can be up to 18 characters long. It must begin with a character and be followed by alpha/numerics. The following example indicates the process through which multiple rows are accessed by an application program using a cursor.

```
EXEC SQL
   DECLARE cursor-name CURSOR
   FOR
   SELECT col1, col2,...
      FROM table-name1, table-name2....
      WHERE conditions
```

```
                 ORDER BY col1,col2,....
                     .
                     .
                     .
        EXEC SQL
          OPEN cursor-name
                     .
                 . <...... until SQLCODE = +100..
                     .                          .
        EXEC SQL                                .
          FETCH cursor-name                     .
          INTO :host-val1, :host-val2,...       .
                     .                          .
                     ...............................
                     .
        EXEC SQL
          CLOSE cursor-name
```

The DECLARE cursor-name CURSOR statement, where cursor-name represents the name given to the cursor, does not cause any data to be returned. The SQL return code should *not* be checked after its execution. When selecting multiple rows, this is where the SQL statement is coded.

The OPEN cursor-name actually causes the SELECT to be executed. Any host variables used in the SELECT should be set to the required values prior to the OPENing of the cursor. After the OPEN, the program will be situated to return the first row when the first FETCH is executed. The FETCHed rows are placed in the program's input/output area. If you wish to execute the select again with different host values, you will need to CLOSE the cursor, set the host variables, and execute the OPEN again.

The FETCH places columns of the current row positioned on into the input/output area and moves the cursor to the next row to be SELECTed. If no more rows are found, the SQL return code is set to +100. The input/output area should have matching data types to the columns returned.

Once all rows have been FETCHed, the CLOSE should be processed prior to executing the OPEN again. If the application does not CLOSE the cursor, it will be closed automatically when the program terminates. Programs PROGRM1C, PROGRM1F, and PROGRM1P in Appendix F contain examples of SELECTs returning multiple rows.

DYNAMIC SQL: Occasionally you will find circumstances in which Static SQL does not satisfy your needs. The SQL statements being executed in the program may be too varied and difficult to construct without the user's input. Another reason might stem from the access path chosen by DB2 for the Static SQL statement. The access strategy, for a column whose values must be within a range, could vary depending on how large the range is. With Static SQL, the access strategy is chosen prior to the program being executed. DB2 does not know how large a range the user will be providing. DB2 may choose an access strategy that can handle 1 row as well as the entire table. As a result, suitable indexes may be over looked.

For example:

```
EXEC SQL
    SELECT * FROM EMPLOYEES_TABLE
        WHERE SALARY > :VALUE1 AND SALARY < :VALUE2
```

In this example, :VALUE1 = 00 and :VALUE2 =1000000 would appear to return a large subset of rows from the table. On the other hand, :VALUE1=11000 and :VALUE2=11500 would in most situations return a much smaller subset of rows. Since the values for :VALUE1 and :VALUE2 are not known in the case of Static SQL, the access path is chosen with regard to optimizer default assumptions. With Dynamic SQL, DB2 knows the exact values and can choose an access path on the actual values provided by the user. One execution of a SELECT might require an entire tablespace be scanned to return a large subset of rows, while another might use an index to retrieve a much smaller subset. One disadvantage of Dynamic SQL stems from the preparation and binding of the SQL statement on every execution. As a result, the user may experience slower response while DB2 validates and determines the access strategy for the SQL statement.

DYNAMIC FIXED-LIST-SELECTS: Dynamic SELECTS are divided into two categories, Fixed-List-Selects and Varying-List-Selects. Fixed-List-Selects are Dynamic SELECTs in which the columns returned can be placed into program data areas. The same columns must be selected for every execution of the SELECT. Because of this, the program can predefine a data area for the rows to be placed. Fixed-List-Selects are very similar to the previous SELECTs using cursors. Rather than coding the SQL statement in the DECLARE statement, it may be constructed during application program execution. The process of coding Dynamic Selects follows:

```
Construct SQL statement into :host-sql
    .
    .
    .

DECLARE cursor-name CURSOR FOR statement
    .
    . <.......... for next SELECT ..................
    .
PREPARE statement FROM :host-sql            .
    .                                       .
    .                                       .
    .
OPEN cursor-name                            .
```

```
                    .   <....... until SQLCODE=+100 ........    .
                    .                                           .
      FETCH cursor-name   INTO :host-IO                  .      .
                    .                                    .      .
                    ...........................................
                    .
      CLOSE cursor-name                                         .
                    .                                           .
                    ..........................................................
                    .
```

The DECLARE **cursor-name** CURSOR FOR statement, like the previous examples, requires a cursor-name to be specified. **Statement** is the name given to the PREPAREd SQL statement referenced by the PREPARE.

The PREPARE **statement** FROM :host-sql causes the SELECT statement to be prepared for execution. The SQL statement goes through the precompile and bind processes discussed earlier. It is ready for execution at this time. :host-sql is the data area in the program where the SELECT statement was constructed. **Statement** is the name used in the DECLARE.

The OPEN **cursor-name** causes the SELECT statement to be processed and as mentioned earlier, positions you for processing rows.

The FETCH **cursor-name** INTO :host-IO causes a row selected to be returned to a program data area **host-IO**.

The CLOSE **cursor-name** is required to be executed before the cursor is opened again. If the application constructs a different SELECT statement (retrieving the same columns), the entire process must be performed, including the PREPARE. Examples of executing Dynamic Fixed-List-Selects may be found in Appendix F, programs PROGRM3C, PROGRM3F, and PROGRM3P.

DYNAMIC SQL (Non-SELECT): The process of executing Non-Selects dynamically is less complicated. It consists of only one SQL statement, EXECUTE IMMEDIATE. This statement verifies the statement can be executed dynamically and proceeds to prepare and execute it. You can specify the SQL statement to be executed as a string of characters or as being contained in a host data area. Program examples PROGRM4C, PROGRM4F, and PROGRM4P in Appendix F illustrate the use of the EXECUTE IMMEDIATE. The format of the EXECUTE IMMEDIATE is as follows:

```
      EXECUTE IMMEDIATE string-expression
or
      EXECUTE IMMEDIATE :host-variable
```

DYNAMIC VARYING-LIST-SELECTS: If Dynamic SELECT statements cannot predict the number of columns or format of data to be retrieved, they are considered Varying-List-Selects. The process of executing this type of SQL statement is similar to the previous examples listed for dynamic Selects, ex-ept for an additional process. This new process consists of executing the SQL tatement called DESCRIBE. Varying-List-Selects require the application rogram set up a SQLDA (SQL Descriptor Area). This area is used to pass information to your program about an SQL statement. Appendix E contains a layout of the SQLDA data fields for PL/I.

Since Varying-List-Selects require storage to be allocated during execution, heir use is limited for the most part to PL/I and Assembler. It is not possible or the application program to retrieve rows without first analyzing the SELECT to be executed. From the SQLDA area, the program obtains information about how many columns are going to be retrieved and what their data types are. The following processes are required to execute Varying-List-Selects:

```
EXEC SQL INCLUDE SQLDA
         .
         .
EXEC SQL DECLARE statement1 STATEMENT
         .
         .
EXEC SQL DECLARE cursor-name CURSOR FOR statement1
         . <............ for next SELECT..................
         .                                               .
PREPARE statement1 FROM :host-string                     .
         .                                               .
         .                                               .
         .                                               .
DESCRIBE statement1 INTO SQLDA                            .
         .                                               .
         .                                               .
         .                                               .
OPEN cursor-name                                         .
         .                                               .
         . <......................................... .
         .                                             . .
FETCH cursor-name USING DESCRIPTOR  SQLDA              . .
         .                                             . .
         .                                             . .
         .                                             . .
Process rows returned in SQLDA Buffer                 . .
         .                                             . .
         .>........ until SQLCODE=+100 .............. .
         .                                               .
CLOSE cursor-name                                         .
         .                                               .
         ................................................
         .
```

UPDATING WITH A CURSOR: We have discussed the process of selecting multiple rows using cursors. We will now look at the process for updating columns in the rows retrieved. A FOR UPDATE OF clause appears with the SELECT statement indicating what columns can be updated when retrieved. An UPDATE statement referencing the cursor actually performs the update. Not every row selected has to be updated. The application can programatically control which of the rows selected need to be updated. The cursor-name is what ties all the SQL statements together. The columns to be updated must be listed in the FOR UPDATE OF clause of the DECLARE.

```
EXEC SQL
    DECLARE cursor-name CURSOR
    FOR
    SELECT col1,col2,...
        FROM table-name
        WHERE conditions
        FOR UPDATE OF col1,col2,....
            .
            .
            .

EXEC SQL
    OPEN cursor-name
            .
            .<.............. until SQLCODE=+100 ..........
            .                                                .
EXEC SQL                                                     .
    FETCH cursor-name                                        .
    INTO :host-val1, :host-val2,...                          .
                                                             .
            .                                                .
            .                                                .
            .                                                .
EXEC SQL                                                     .
    UPDATE table-name                                        .
        SET col1 = :host-value1 col2 = :host-value2 ...      .
        WHERE CURRENT OF cursor-name                         .
                                                             .
            .                                                .
            ...................................................
            .

EXEC SQL
    CLOSE cursor-name
```

DELETING WITH A CURSOR: The following process allows rows selected while using cursors to be deleted. Not every row selected has to be deleted. Like the update, the application can programmatically control which selected rows should be deleted. Note once again cursor-name is what ties all the SQL statements together.

```
EXEC SQL
   DECLARE cursor-name CURSOR
      FOR
      SELECT col1,col2,...
      FROM table-name
      WHERE conditions
         .
         .

EXEC SQL
   OPEN cursor-name

         .
         . <............ until SQLCODE=+100 ............
         .
EXEC SQL                                                    .
   FETCH cursor-name                                        .
   INTO :host-val1, :host-val2,...                          .
         .                                                  .
         .                                                  .
         .                                                  .

EXEC SQL                                                    .
   DELETE FROM table-name                                   .
   WHERE CURRENT OF cursor-name                             .
         .                                                  .
         ................................................
         .

EXEC SQL
   CLOSE cursor-name
```

LOCKING and UNLOCKING: Occasionally you will have an application requesting extensive locking. There is a certain amount of overhead associated
with page locking. If no other applications need the table for updating, you
can have the application issue a LOCK TABLE SQL statement. Depending on
the lock mode the application chooses, the table will be unavailable to other
applications for updating and possibly retrieval. An important point about the
LOCK SQL statement is that it actually locks at the tablespace level. Once
again, attempt to keep only one table per tablespace. The format of the LOCK
is as follows:

```
EXEC SQL
   LOCK TABLE table-name in SHARE MODE

or

   LOCK TABLE table-name in EXCLUSIVE MODE
```

Table-name is the name of the table upon which the lock should be applied.
In actuality, the tablespace is locked. This lock applies regardless of the
LOCK specifications used when creating the tablespace.

SHARE MODE allows other applications to issue read only locks.

EXCLUSIVE MODE prevents other applications from issuing any kind o lock. Even the SELECT issues a lock. Thus, the application issuing an EX CLUSIVE lock has total control over the tablespace.

If an application has updated pages or requested data pages not be avail able to other applications, it will have to issue a COMMIT before the resour ces or pages are available again. The SQL statement to free the resources is:

```
EXEC SQL
    COMMIT
```

Once an application issues a COMMIT, the pages updated are recoverable The COMMIT also causes all open cursors to be closed. It is up to the applica tion to save the information necessary to reposition on rows if further process ing is needed.

The ROLLBACK SQL statement also frees up resources. It works just th opposite of COMMIT. Instead of saving changes, all changes are backed ou to the last COMMIT point. If no COMMIT was issued, all changes made b the application are backed out. Like the COMMIT, all cursor positioning i lost. The application is required to save information needed to reposition i necessary. The format of the ROLLBACK is as follows:

```
EXEC SQL
    ROLLBACK
```

IMS PROGRAMS: Neither the COMMIT or the ROLLBACK statement is al lowed in application programs executing in the IMS environment. Instead, is suing IMS CHECKPOINT or getting from the MESSAGE QUE informs DB to COMMIT any changes made.

WHENEVER: This SQL statement determines the next statement to be ex ecuted if the execution of a SQL statement produces a special condition. Th format is as follows:

```
    EXEC SQL
        WHENEVER   NOT FOUND      CONTINUE
or
        WHENEVER   SQLERROR       CONTINUE
or
        WHENEVER   SQLWARNING     CONTINUE
or
        WHENEVER   NOT FOUND      GOTO  host-label
or
        WHENEVER   SQLERROR       GOTO  host-label
or
        WHENEVER   SQLWARNING     GOTO  host-label
```

NOT FOUND identifies conditions when the SQL return code = +100
SQLERROR identifies conditions when the SQL return code < 0.
SQLWARNING identifies conditions when SQLWARN = 'W'.
CONTINUE implies the next instruction should be executed.
GOTO or GO TO, depending on host language, specifies a host label to
which execution should be transferred.

Example:

```
EXEC SQL
    WHENEVER SQLERROR GO TO ERROR-ROUTINE.
```

INDICATOR VARIABLES: Indicator variables must be used if column
definitions allow for null values. If columns are allowed to be null, the application programming aspect becomes more complicated. Each column allowed to be null must have an indicator variable. The application program
must check all indicator variable contents after each row is retrieved. If the
indicator variable contains 0, data for the column was retrieved. If the indicator variable contains -1, no data was retrieved and the column is considered null. In the following example, assume SALARY and AGE can be null.

```
SELECT EMPLOYEE_NAME,EMPLOYEE_NO,SALARY,AGE
    INTO :EMPLOYEE-NAME,:EMPLOYEE-NO,
        :SALARY :INDVL1, :AGE :INDVL2
    FROM EMPLOYEES_TABLE
    WHERE EMPLOYEE_NO = :host-employee'
```

If INDVL1 and INDVL2 are both equal to -1, the employee does not have
any data for SALARY or AGE. You must define the host variables INDVL1
and INDVL2 in the program's data area. Indicator variables can be used to
set columns to null values. Set the indicator variable to -1 prior to the insert
or update and DB2 will set the column to null values. For example:

```
INDVL1 = -1
EXEC SQL
    INSERT INTO EMPLOYEES_TABLE
        VALUES (:EMPLOYEE-NO,EMPLOYEE-STATE,:ADDRESS-STATE,
            :DEPT, :SALARY :INDVL1)

INDVL1 = -1
EXEC SQL
    UPDATE EMPLOYEES_TABLE
        SET SALARY = :HSAL :INDVL1
        WHERE DEPT = :HDEPT
```

DB2I FOR PROGRAM PREPARATION: Included with DB2 is a product
allowing developers to interactively perform program preparation. This

product is called DB2 Interactive or DB2I. It is not a tool for end users. It is designed with the application developer and DB2 administrator in mind Several of the functions it performs center around the application preparation processes just discussed. It runs under TSO and can be invoked through a CLIST.

```
READY
db2i
```

Invoking DB2I provides the user with the following primary option menu. On this menu, option 3 allows you to perform the program preparation processes previously discussed.

```
                        DB2I PRIMARY OPTION MENU
    ===> 3


Select one of the following DB2 functions and press ENTER.

1  SPUFI                  (Process SQL statements)
2  DCLGEN                 (Generate SQL and source language declarations)
3  PROGRAM PREPARATION    (Prepare a DB2 application program to run)
4  PRECOMPILE             (Invoke DB2 precompiler)
5  BIND/REBIND/FREE       (BIND, REBIND, or FREE application plans)
6  RUN                    (RUN an SQL program)
7  DB2 COMMANDS           (Issue DB2 commands)
8  UTILITIES              (Invoke DB2 utilities)
D  DB2I DEFAULTS          (Set global parameters)
X  EXIT                   (Leave DB2I)


 PRESS:  END to exit          HELP for more information
```

```
                    DB2 PROGRAM PREPARATION
 ===>


 Enter the following:
 1  INPUT DATA SET NAME ....  ===> PROGRM1C.COBOL
 2  DATA SET NAME QUALIFIER   ===> TEMP (For building data set names)
 3  PREPARATION ENVIRONMENT   ===> FOREGROUND (FOREGROUND,
                                              BACKGROUND, EDITJCL)
 4  RUN TIME ENVIRONMENT ...  ===> TSO        (TSO, CICS, IMS)
 5  STOP IF RETURN CODE >=    ===> 8 (Lowest terminating return code)
 6  OTHER OPTIONS ===>


 Select functions:          Display panel?      Perform function?
 7  CHANGE DEFAULTS ........ ===> Y  (Y/N)       .............
 8  PL/I MACRO PHASE ....... ===> N  (Y/N)       ===> N  (Y/N)
 9  PRECOMPILE ............. ===> Y  (Y/N)       ===> Y  (Y/N)
10  CICS COMMAND TRANSLATION .... .  .....       ===> N  (Y/N)
11  BIND .................. ===> Y  (Y/N)        ===> Y  (Y/N)
12  COMPILE OR ASSEMBLE .... ===> Y  (Y/N)       ===> Y  (Y/N)
13  LINK .................. ===> Y  (Y/N)        ===> Y  (Y/N)
14  RUN ................... ===> Y  (Y/N)        ===> Y  (Y/N)



 PRESS:   ENTER to process  END to exit  HELP for more information
```

The user can select which processes are to be performed. Many of the program preparation processes require the user to enter certain parameters. By displaying the various panels used, you may enter required and optional parameters which apply to the program being prepared and possibly the majority of the programs you will be preparing. These options will be in effect until changed by you. In addition to setting parameters, the actual function can be performed. If you want to change or initially set the parameters, put Y for the appropriate process under the "*Display panel?*" column. If you want the function to be performed, place Y for the appropriate function under the "*Perform function?*" column. The above selections will cause the following panels to be displayed.

```
                        DB2I DEFAULTS
 ===>


Change defaults as desired:


1  DB2 NAME ............. ===> DBXX       (Subsystem identifier)
2  DB2 CONNECTION RETRIES ===> 0 (How many retries for DB2 connection)
3  APPLICATION LANGUAGE   ===> cobol (COBOL,COB2,FORT,ASM,ASMH,PLI)
4  LINES/PAGE OF LISTING  ===> 60        (A number from 5 to 999)
5  MESSAGE LEVEL ........ ===> I (Information,Warning,Error,Severe)
6  COBOL STRING DELIMITER ===> '          (DEFAULT, ' or ")
7  SQL STRING DELIMITER   ===> '          (DEFAULT, ' or ")
8  DECIMAL POINT ........ ===> .          (. or ,)


9  DB2I JOB STATEMENT:   (Optional if your site has a SUBMIT exit)
   ===>
   ===>
   ===>
   ===>


PRESS: ENTER to save and exit END to exit  HELP for more information
```

This is a panel used to describe the application programming language being used.

1. Name of your DB2 System. (DBXX)
2. Not used for program preparation.
3. Host language being used. (COBOL in this case)
4. Number of lines per page for the output listings.
5. I is recommended so all BIND messages are returned.
6. Specify what is appropriate for delimiting string data in the host language chosen.
7. Specify what is appropriate for delimiting string data in the SQL statements.
8. Specify what is appropriate for decimal points in the host language specified.
9. Specify job card information if you have a submit exit provided at your installation.

```
                          PRECOMPILE
===>


Enter precompiler data sets:
  1  INPUT DATA SET  ....  ===>  PROGRM1C.COBOL
  2  INCLUDE LIBRARY ...  ===>  DCLGEN.COBOL


  3  DSNAME QUALIFIER ..  ===>  TEMP      (For building data set names)
  4  DBRM DATA SET .....  ===>  DBRMLIB


Enter processing options as desired:
  5  WHERE TO PRECOMPILE ===>  FOREGROUND  (FOREGROUND, BACKGROUND,
                                           or EDITJCL)

  6  OTHER OPTIONS .....  ===>


PRESS:  ENTER to process  END to exit  HELP for more information
```

On this panel, you provide information required for the DB2 Precompile process.

1. The dataset containing the host language program source.
2. The name of the dataset containing table and host language declarations.
3. Precompiled source and listings go to datasets prefixed by what is specified here. Precompiler Source: TEMP.COBOL or TEMP.PLI or TEMP.FORT   Precompiler Listing: TEMP.PCLIST
4. The name of the dataset to contain the DBRMs outputted by this process.
5. Carried forward from the DB2 PROGRAM PREPARATION panel.
6. Any special precompiler options desired.

```
                              BIND
===>


Enter DBRM data set name(s):
 1  LIBRARY(s)    ===> DBRMLIB
 2  MEMBER(s)     ===> PROGRM1C
 3  PASSWORD(s) ===>


 4  MORE DBRMS? ===> NO                    (YES to list more DBRMs)


Enter options as desired:
 5  PLAN NAME ................ ===> PROGRM1C (Required to create plan)
 6  ACTION ON PLAN .......... ===> REPLACE   (REPLACE or ADD)
 7  RETAIN EXECUTION AUTHORITY ===> YES     (YES to retain user List)
 8  ISOLATION LEVEL ......... ===> CS       (RR or CS)
 9  PLAN VALIDATION TIME ..... ===> BIND     (RUN or BIND)
10  RESOURCE ACQUISITION TIME ===> USE       (USE or ALLOCATE)
11  RESOURCE RELEASE TIME .... ===> COMMIT    (COMMIT or DEALLOCATE)
12  EXPLAIN PATH SELECTION ... ===> YES       (NO or YES)


PRESS: ENTER to process    END to exit    HELP for more information
```

This panel defines the BIND options to be used.

1. The name of the library containing the DBRMs.
2. The list of DBRMs to be used as input to this process. If the program being prepared for execution calls subroutines containing SQL, the DBRMs from the subroutines executing SQL statements must also be included. DBRMs were outputted from the DB2 Precompile process.
3. Dataset passwords.
4. Enter YES if you have more DBRMs than what will fit on this panel.
5. Plan Name is unique on a DB2 System. Its naming convention is the same used for program names. Plan names the same as program names are allowed.
6. Specifies whether you are creating a new plan or changing an existing one. Specify ADD for new plans and REPLACE to replace existing plans. If REPLACE is specified for a new plan, it will be added.
7. Specifies the disposition of the privileges granted on an existing Plan. YES implies the existing privileges granted are to be retained. Specify NO if you wish to remove the privileges granted. These privileges include not only who can execute the PLAN but also who can prepare the application for execution.
8. Isolation level is either RR or CS. RR implies that pages read by the application program cannot be changed by other applications until a COM-

MIT is executed. CS implies that a page read by the application is available to other applications when the cursor positioning moves to another page. If the application updates a row in a page, the page is still not available to other applications until a COMMIT has been performed.

9. When do you want the authorizations checked against the person performing the bind and the existence of the tables referenced in the DBRMs? If you want authorizations checked at run time, specify RUN. If they are to be checked at Bind time, specify BIND.

10. When should the DB2 resources be acquired for the application? USE implies the resources, such as opens and tablespace locks are to be acquired when the resource is used. ALLOCATE implies the resources are to be acquired when the Plan begins execution. For example, do you want the tablespace opened when the Plan is allocated, or should it remain closed until used (if CLOSE YES specified on tablespace)?

11. When should the DB2 resources be released? COMMIT implies the resources should be freed at each commit point. DEALLOCATE implies the resources allocated should be freed when the execution of the Plan is completed.

12. Do you want the PLAN_TABLE updated with information about the SQL statements contained in the Plan? A table named PLAN_TABLE must already exist for the user issuing the Bind if YES is specified.

```
PROGRAM PREPARATION: COMPILE, LINK, AND RUN
===>


Enter compiler or assembler options:
 1  INCLUDE LIBRARY ===>
 2  INCLUDE LIBRARY ===>
 3  OPTIONS ....... ===>


Enter linkage editor options:
 4  INCLUDE LIBRARY ===>
 5  INCLUDE LIBRARY ===>
 6  INCLUDE LIBRARY ===>
 7  LOAD LIBRARY .. ===> 'userid1.load'
 8  OPTIONS ....... ===>


Enter run options:
 9  PARAMETERS .... ===>
10  SYSIN DATA SET  ===> TERM
11  SYSPRINT DS ... ===> TERM


PRESS: Enter to proceed  END to exit   HELP for more information
```

On this panel, enter the compile, link, and run options desired.

1. Dataset names containing COPY/INCLUDE members needed in th compile.
2. Same as 1.
3. List compile options desired.
4. List dataset names for libraries containing other modules needed for th LINKEDIT process.
5. Same as 4.
6. Same as 4.
7. Dataset name for library where the executable load module is to l placed.
8. List of LINKEDIT options desired.

The following three items pertain to executing the program as the next ste in the program preparation process.

9. Enter any PARM data required by the program if the program is goin to be executed from here.
10. Dataset name, if needed by the program, containing SYSIN data.
11. Dataset name, if needed by the program, for SYSPRINT.

Upon the completion of all the panels the processes are executed.

```
SOURCE STATISTICS
  SOURCE LINES READ: 145
  NUMBER OF SYMBOLS: 36
  SYMBOL TABLE BYTES EXCLUDING ATTRIBUTES: 2592
THERE WERE 1 MESSAGES FOR THIS PROGRAM.
THERE WERE 0 MESSAGES SUPPRESSED BY THE FLAG OPTION.
85416 BYTES OF STORAGE WERE USED BY THE PRECOMPILER.
RETURN CODE IS 0
       ======= PRECOMPILER FINISHED, RC =  0
       ======= LISTING IN TEMP.PCLIST =========================
       -  BIND FOR PLAN PROGRM1C SUCCESSFUL
       ======= BIND FINISHED, RC =  0 =========================
       ======= COBOL FINISHED, RC =  0
       ======= LISTING IN TEMP.LIST ==========================
              INCLUDE DSNHOBJ

       ======= LINK FINISHED, RC =  0
       ======= LISTING IN TEMP.LINKLIST ======================

***************** BEGIN EXECUTION OF PROGRM1C.*****************

OPEN CURSOR NAMED: CURSOR1

DISPLAY ROWS FETCHED FOR CURSOR NAMED = CURSOR1
EMPLOYEE NUMBER = 000000200
                  EMPLOYEE NAME = LARSON
                  STATE = IL
                  DEPARTMENT = D890
                  SALARY =  60000.00

EMPLOYEE NUMBER = 000000500
                  EMPLOYEE NAME = EINERSON
                  STATE = UT
                  DEPARTMENT = D890
                  SALARY =  80000.00

EMPLOYEE NUMBER = 000000250
                  EMPLOYEE NAME = CASPER
                  STATE = MN
                  DEPARTMENT = D890
                  SALARY =  70000.00

EMPLOYEE NUMBER = 000000600
                  EMPLOYEE NAME = GRAVES
```

```
                        STATE = CA
                        DEPARTMENT = D890
                        SALARY =   30000.00

EMPLOYEE NUMBER = 000000350
                        EMPLOYEE NAME = JORDAN
                        STATE = FL
                        DEPARTMENT = D890
                        SALARY =   50000.00

EMPLOYEE NUMBER = 000000700
                        EMPLOYEE NAME = ROCKY
                        STATE = SC
                        DEPARTMENT = D890
                        SALARY =   40000.00


SQLCODE = +00100

END OF FETCH USING CURSOR NAMED: CURSOR1.

CLOSE CURSOR NAMED: CURSOR1


******************* END EXECUTION OF PROGRM1C.*****************

DSNH740I ======= RUN FINISHED, RC =   0 ========================
```

Several of the program preparation processes can be performed individually
rom the DB2I Primary Option Menu such as the Precompile, Bind, and Run.
n addition to those, you can generate table and host language declarations.
ʼhe declarations can be generated only for COBOL. To generate COBOL dec-
arations, select option 2.

```
                    DB2I PRIMARY OPTION MENU
 ===> 2


 Select one of the following DB2 functions and press ENTER.

 1  SPUFI                 (Process SQL statements)
 2  DCLGEN                (Generate SQL and source language declarations)
 3  PROGRAM PREPARATION   (Prepare a DB2 application program to run)
 4  PRECOMPILE            (Invoke DB2 precompiler)
 5  BIND/REBIND/FREE      (BIND, REBIND, or FREE application plans)
 6  RUN                   (RUN an SQL program)
 7  DB2 COMMANDS          (Issue DB2 commands)
 8  UTILITIES             (Invoke DB2 utilities)
 D  DB2I DEFAULTS         (Set global parameters)
 X  EXIT                  (Leave DB2I)


 PRESS:  END to exit          HELP for more information
```

```
                                DCLGEN
===>


Enter table name for which declarations are required:
 1   SOURCE TABLE NAME ===> employees_table


Enter destination data set:      (Can be sequential or partitioned)
 2   DATA SET NAME ... ===> 'useridl.dclgen.cobol(employee)'
 3   DATA SET PASSWORD ===>        (If password protected)


Enter options as desired:
 4   ACTION .......... ===> REPLACE (ADD new or REPLACE old
                                     declaration)
 5   COLUMN LABEL .... ===> NO        (Enter YES for column label)
 6   STRUCTURE NAME .. ===>                      (Optional)
 7   FIELD NAME PREFIX ===>                      (Optional)


PRESS: ENTER to process    END to exit    HELP for more information
```

1. Enter the name of the table for which you want declarations.
2. Enter the name of the dataset where the declaration is to be placed. If a PDS, specify the member name also.
3. Dataset password if protected.
4. Enter ADD if first time declaration has been generated. Enter REPLACE if replacing an existing one.
5. If the SQL COMMENT statement was used to place comments about columns in the DB2 Catalog, you can have these comments placed in the declaration by entering YES. If you did not place comments in the DB2 Catalog or do not wish to list them in the declaration, enter NO.
6. You can override the name assigned to the COBOL 01 Level. If you do not specify anything here, the table or view name is prefixed by DCL.
7. If you wish to place a prefix in front of all generated COBOL data field in the 01 Level, place the prefix here.

You are not limited to DB2I for your program preparation processes. You can invoke your own CLIST or one provided with DB2 (DSNH) to accomplish the same tasks. Program preparation can also be performed from background.

Questions:

1. Dynamic Selects are of two types: _____ or _____.
2. A program must define _____ _____ in order to process null columns.

3. _____ is a product, provided with DB2, used to prepare programs for execution.
4. Host language data fields used in SQL statements are called _____ _____.
5. The _____ should be interrogated after every executable SQL statement to determine the success of the SQL statement.
6. Application Plans are created as a result of the _____ process.

True or False:

7. Cursors are used to process Selects returning multiple rows.
8. The output of the the DB2 Precompiler is a DBRM and source code minus the SQL statements.
9. The Bind cannot be done until the program has been compiled or the timestamp in the DBRM will not match the timestamp in the executable load module.
10. Before a cursor can be opened for repeated use, it must first be closed.
11. When a program issues a COMMIT, all cursors are closed.
12. Table and host language declarations specified by the SQL INCLUDE are merged into the source at DB2 Precompile time.

Answers:

1. Fixed-List-Selects, Varying-List-Selects
2. Indicator Variables
3. DB2I
4. Host Variables
5. SQLCA (SQL Communication Area)
6. BIND
7. True
8. True
9. False; the time stamps are generated at DB2 Precompile time. The Bind step can be performed any time after the DB2 Precompile since the DBRM is the only input.
10. True
11. True
12. True

7

DB2I and Utilities

In the previous chapter we reviewed DB2I options pertaining to the application programming environment. The remaining options, starting with option 1, will be discussed in this chapter.

SPUFI, or SQL Processor Using File Input, allows a user to construct SQL statements outside of an application program. Queries can be tested prior to being coded in an application program. The queries, constructed in TSO datasets, can be executed interactively. Multiple queries can be contained in the input dataset. Unlike QMF, you have the capability of running several queries before committing the results of any. Selecting 1 on the DB2I Primary Option Menu will direct you to the SPUFI Home Panel.

```
DB2I PRIMARY OPTION MENU
=== 1


Select one of the following DB2 functions and press ENTER.

  1   SPUFI                 (Process SQL statements)
  2   DCLGEN                (Generate SQL and source language declares)
  3   PROGRAM PREPARATION   (Prepare a DB2 application program to run)
  4   PRECOMPILE            (Invoke DB2 precompiler)
  5   BIND/REBIND/FREE      (BIND, REBIND, or FREE application plans)
  6   RUN                   (RUN an SQL program)
  7   DB2 COMMANDS          (Issue DB2 commands)
  8   UTILITIES             (Invoke DB2 utilities)
  D   DB2I DEFAULTS         (Set global parameters)
  X   EXIT                  (Leave DB2I)


PRESS:  END to exit          HELP for more information
```

```
                          SPUFI
===


Enter the input data set name:    (Can be sequential or partitioned)
1  DATA SET NAME ... === SPUFIIN.DATA(MEMBER1)
2  VOLUME SERIAL ... ===            (Enter if not cataloged)
3  DATA SET PASSWORD ===            (Enter if password protected)


Enter the output data set name:    (Must be a sequential data set)
4  DATA SET NAME ... === SPUFIOUT.DATA


Specify processing options:
5  CHANGE DEFAULTS   === YES  (Y/N - Display SPUFI defaults panel?)
6  EDIT INPUT ...... === YES  (Y/N - Enter SQL statements?)
7  EXECUTE ......... === YES  (Y/N - Execute SQL statements?)
8  AUTOCOMMIT ...... === YES  (Y/N - Commit after successful run?)
9  BROWSE OUTPUT ... === YES  (Y/N - Browse output data set?)


PRESS: ENTER to process   END to exit   HELP for more information
```

For the above items, enter the following:

1. The TSO dataset containing or that will contain the SQL statements. If the dataset is partitioned, enter the member name also. The member name can exist prior to this, or it can be new. The dataset name entered has to exist prior to using SPUFI.
2. If the dataset specified for item 1 is not cataloged, enter the volume where it resides here.
3. If the dataset is password protected, enter the password on this line.
4. This is the dataset browsed to review the query results. This dataset does not need to exist prior to using SPUFI.
5. You can specify default options that will pertain to all of your SPUFI sessions. Entering YES here, causes a default panel to be displayed. Unless you wish to change the default items, usually NO is specified for this item after initially being set.
6. If you wish to edit the dataset (member) specified for item 1 prior to executing the SQL statements contained in it, place YES for this item.

7. If you wish to execute the queries contained in the dataset specified for item 1, enter YES.

8. Specify YES for AUTOCOMMIT if you want all changes made as a result of executing SQL statements to be kept without being prompted. If you wish to receive confirmation, enter NO and you will be requested to respond. Be careful if you specify NO. Not responding causes the resources to be locked from other users.

   If AUTOCOMMIT of YES is specified and the SQL statements do not include a commit or rollback, all of the updates will be rolled back if one fails. To prevent the rollback from occurring, consider placing COMMIT between SQL statements. Commits also reduce contention on the resources being accessed by the SQL statements.

9. If you wish to be placed in browse mode on the results from the query executions, specify YES. The dataset browsed is the dataset specified for item 4.

Items 5 through 9 are considered processing options. They will be executed in the same sequence (5–9). Excluding AUTOCOMMIT, any item not specified as YES is bypassed. You can perform each item separately by placing a YES on the item to be performed and NO on all others. Specify YES for all items to EDIT the input dataset, execute it, confirm successful changes automatically and be placed in browse mode on the results. From the specifications on the previous panel, the following will occur.

```
                    CURRENT SPUFI DEFAULTS
===


Enter the following to control your SPUFI session:
 1 ISOLATION LEVEL    === CS  (RR=Repeatable Read,CS=Cursor Stability)
 2 MAX SELECT LINES  === 250     (Maximum number of lines to be
                                  returned from a SELECT)
Output data set characteristics:
 3 RECORD LENGTH ... === 4092    (LRECL=Logical record length)
 4 BLOCK SIZE ...... === 4096    (Size of one block)
 5 RECORD FORMAT ... === VB      (RECFM=F, FB, FBA, V, VB, or VBA
 6 DEVICE TYPE ..... === SYSDA   (Must be DASD unit name)


Output format characteristics:
 7 MAX NUMERIC FIELD === 20      (Maximum width for numeric fields)
 8 MAX CHAR FIELD .. === 80      (Maximum width for character fields)
 9 COLUMN HEADING .. === NAMES   (NAMES, LABELS, ANY or BOTH)

PRESS: ENTER to proceed   END to exit  HELP for more information
```

This is the SPUFI default panel. Enter the options recommended by your installation.

1.   Isolation level references the page locking scheme to be used while executing your queries. I have chosen CS over RR to reduce the number of locks held by my application. CS implies that once a cursor moves from one page to the next, the rows in the previous page are available to other users as long as no rows were updated in the page. RR implies that you may want to reprocess rows previously read and that no one should be allowed to change them until you commit.

2.   You can limit the maximum number of lines to be return by a select. The number specified here represents the maximum number of rows returned by any select.

3 – 6.   Describe the record length, block size, record format, and device type for the result dataset to be browsed

7.   The maximum width a numeric column can occupy in the displayed output.

8.   The maximum width a character column can occupy in the output.
9.   Column headings can consist of column names (NAMES), or colum
      label values if created by the LABEL query (LABELS), or bot
      (BOTH) if you wish to see both column names and column labels.
      you want column labels where they exist and column names whe
      the label values do not exist, specify (ANY).

Following the changes to the default panel, the next process to be pe
formed is the edit of the dataset or dataset(member) specified as the inpu
dataset. The member specified was new, and the following SQL statemen
were entered using the PDF editor. Each query must be separated by a sem
colon ;. Since no COMMIT was specified, both authorization GRANTS will k
rolled back if any one of the queries fails. Specify END if you wish to save ar
changes made and CANCEL if changes are not to be kept. When you exit, yc
are returned to the SPUFI home panel.

```
EDIT ---- USERID1.SPUFIIN.DATA(MEMBER1)
COMMAND ===         .                      SCROLL === CSR
****** ************* TOP OF DATA ******************************
000001 SELECT * FROM EMPLOYEES_TABLE
000002 ORDER BY EMPLOYEE_NO;
000003 GRANT SELECT ON EMPLOYEE_TABLE TO PUBLIC;
000004 SELECT * FROM AUTO_INS_SALES
000005 ORDER BY SALES_PERSON_NO;
000006 GRANT SELECT ON AUTO_INS_SALES TO PUBLIC;
****** ************* BOTTOM OF DATA **************************
```

Note that asterisks have been placed on the completed processes in the following panel. To continue to the next process, EXECUTE, press **enter**. END will allow you to exit out of SPUFI. By removing the asterisks and changing items to YES or NO, you can begin the process over if desired.

```
                            SPUFI
===

            EDIT SESSION HAS COMPLETED. PRESS ENTER TO CONTINUE
Enter the input data set name:      (Can be sequential or partitioned)
1  DATA SET NAME ... === SPUFIIN.DATA(MEMBER1)
2  VOLUME SERIAL ... ===                (Enter if not cataloged)
3  DATA SET PASSWORD ===                (Enter if password protected)


Enter the output data set name:      (Must be a sequential data set)
4  DATA SET NAME ... === SPUFIOUT.DATA

Specify processing options:
5  CHANGE DEFAULTS   === *       (Y/N - Display SPUFI defaults panel?)
6  EDIT INPUT ...... === *       (Y/N - Enter SQL statements?)
7  EXECUTE ......... === YES     (Y/N - Execute SQL statements?)
8  AUTOCOMMIT ...... === YES     (Y/N - Commit after successful run?)
9  BROWSE OUTPUT ... === YES     (Y/N - Browse output data set?)

PRESS: ENTER to process      END to exit      HELP for more information
```

Since AUTOCOMMIT of YES was specified, you are taken directly into browse mode on the results dataset. Each query executed should be reviewed. The SQLCODE is returned as well, as any messages that may indicate a problem has occurred. Like QMF, SPUFI executes queries dynamically. You may have entered a Select statement, but SPUFI may have had to use a cursor to obtain multiple rows. As a result, you will find +100 SQLCODE return values present indicating that the last row was fetched. Should an error occur, all of the queries following the one in error are bypassed. When you exit PDF browse, you are returned to the SPUFI home panel, where you can correct any errors, exit, or perform another unit of work.

```
BROWSE -- USERID1.SPUFIOUT.DATA --------------------
 COMMAND ===                                     SCROLL === CSR
********************** TOP OF DATA  *******************************
---------+---------+---------+---------+---------+---------+--------
SELECT * FROM EMPLOYEES_TABLE
ORDER BY EMPLOYEE_NO;
---------+---------+---------+---------+---------+---------+--------
EMPLOYEE_NO  EMPLOYEE_NAME    ADDRESS_STATE  DEPT     SALARY
---------+---------+---------+---------+---------+---------+--------
        150  JONES            UT             D600     70000.00
        175  MURPHY           IA             D900     40000.00
        200  LARSON           IL             D890     60000.00
        250  CASPER           MN             D890     70000.00
        300  SMITH            WI             D900     50000.00
        350  JORDAN           FL             D890     50000.00
        400  BLACK            MO             D600     60000.00
        450  NICKELS          OH             D500     35000.00
        495  GREEN            ND             D700     40000.00
        500  EINERSON         UT             D890     80000.00
        550  WILLMORE         TX             D500     45000.00
        600  GRAVES           CA             D890     30000.00
        650  SMITH            NC             D500     40000.00
        700  ROCKY            SC             D890     40000.00
        750  GRAY             TX             D500     45000.00
        850  NELSON           IL             D700     35000.00
        900  SHANK            NY             D700     35000.00
        NUMBER OF ROWS DISPLAYED IS 17
        STATEMENT EXECUTION WAS SUCCESSFUL, SQLCODE IS 100
---------+---------+---------+---------+---------+---------+--------
GRANT SELECT ON EMPLOYEE_TABLE TO PUBLIC;
---------+---------+---------+---------+---------+---------+--------
        STATEMENT EXECUTION WAS SUCCESSFUL, SQLCODE IS 0
---------+---------+---------+---------+---------+---------+--------
SELECT * FROM AUTO_INS_SALES
ORDER BY SALES_PERSON_NO;


---------+---------+---------+---------+---------+---------+--------
SALES_PERSON_NO  SALES_REGION    YTD_SALES      BONUS
---------+---------+---------+---------+---------+---------+--------
```

```
350  SOUTHEAST        500000.00    5000.00
415  MIDWEST          200000.00    2000.00
425  NORTHEAST        750000.00    7500.00
500  NORTHWEST       1000000.00   10000.00
800  MIDWEST          500000.00    5000.00
NUMBER OF ROWS DISPLAYED IS 5
STATEMENT EXECUTION WAS SUCCESSFUL, SQLCODE IS 100
---------+---------+---------+---------+---------+---------+---------
GRANT SELECT ON AUTO_INS_SALES TO PUBLIC;
---------+---------+---------+---------+---------+---------+--------
STATEMENT EXECUTION WAS SUCCESSFUL, SQLCODE IS 0
---------+---------+---------+---------+---------+---------+--------
---------+---------+---------+---------+---------+---------+--------
COMMIT PERFORMED, SQLCODE IS 0
STATEMENT EXECUTION WAS SUCCESSFUL, SQLCODE IS 0
---------+---------+---------+---------+---------+---------+--------
SQL STATEMENTS ASSUMED TO BE BETWEEN COLUMNS 1 AND 72
NUMBER OF SQL STATEMENTS PROCESSED IS 4
NUMBER OF INPUT RECORDS READ IS 6
NUMBER OF OUTPUT RECORDS WRITTEN IS 55
******************************* BOTTOM OF DATA ********************
```

In Chapter 6 we discussed executing the TSO DSN command, which in
return allowed us to execute DB2 subcommands, such as BIND and RUN
Also, through the program preparation processes, various DB2 subcommand
were executed for you by DB2I. Option 7 on the DB2I Primary Option Men
allows you to directly enter DB2 subcommands yourself from within DB2I
Subcommands can be used to display the current processing on the DB2 Sys
tem.

```
                         DB2I PRIMARY OPTION MENU
=== 7


Select one of the following DB2 functions and press ENTER.


   1  SPUFI                 (Process SQL statements)
   2  DCLGEN                (Generate SQL & source language declares)
   3  PROGRAM PREPARATION   (Prepare DB2 application program to run)
   4  PRECOMPILE            (Invoke DB2 precompiler)
   5  BIND/REBIND/FREE      (BIND, REBIND, or FREE application plans)
   6  RUN                   (RUN an SQL program)
   7  DB2 COMMANDS          (Issue DB2 commands)
   8  UTILITIES             (Invoke DB2 utilities)
   D  DB2I DEFAULTS         (Set global parameters)
   X  EXIT                  (Leave DB2I)


PRESS:  END to exit       HELP for more information
```

This is the DB2I panel from which DB2 Subcommands are entered. Only one command containing up to four lines of information can be entered on this panel. All commands have to preceded by a dash.

```
                            DB2 COMMANDS
  ===


Enter a single DB2 command on up to 4 lines below:


   1  ===
   2  ===
   3  ===
   4  ===


PRESS:  ENTER to process   END to exit   HELP for more information
```

Some commands pertain to individuals responsible for monitoring the DB2 system, while others pertain for the most part to application developers and Data Base Administrators. The following commands are frequently used by application developers or Data Base Administrators:

```
-DISPLAY DATABASE
-DISPLAY THREAD
-DISPLAY UTILITY
-START DATABASE
-STOP DATABASE
-TERM UTILITY
```

I have taken the familiar database, DBDNAM01, including all of its associated tablespaces, tables, indexes, and indexspaces, and constructed examples surrounding it. To assist you in understanding the examples, the following list of DB2 objects have been defined in database DBDNAM01. This information will be useful in the coming examples.

Database: **DBDNAM01**

TABLE SPACE	PARTITIONED	CONTAINS TABLE	CORRESPONDING INDEX	INDEXSPACE NAME
SPACE001	NO	TEST_TABLE	INDEX_TEST_TABLE	INDX1RTE
SPACE002	YES(2)	EMPLOYEES_TABLE	X_EMPLOYEES_TABLE	XREMPLOY
SPACE003	YES(2)	LIF_INS_SALES	X_LIF_SALES	XRLIFRSA
		LIF_INS_SALES	X_LIFE_SALES	XRLIFERS
SPACE004	YES(2)	AUTO_INS_SALES	X_AUTO_SALES	XRAUTORS
		AUTO_INS_SALES	X_AUTO_INS_SALES	XRAUTORI
SPACE005	NO	NULL_VALUES_TABLE	X_NULLVALES_TABLE	XRNULLVA

DISPLAY DATABASE COMMAND: Displays the status information about the database or databases being inquired on.

-DISPLAY DATABASE(DBDNAM01) will display the status of all tablespaces and indexspaces contained in the database DBDNAM01.

-DISPLAY DATABASE(DBDNAM01) SPACENAM(*) works the same as the previous display. '*' implies all tablespaces and indexspaces.

-DISPLAY DATABASE(DBDNAM01) SPACENAM(SPACE001) will display the status of a specific tablespace named SPACE001 in database DBDNAM01.

-DISPLAY DATABASE(DBDNAM01) SPACENAM(INDX1RTE) will display the status of a specific indexspace named INDX1RTE.

-DISPLAY DATABASE(DBDNAM01) LOCKS will display not only the status of all tablespaces and indexspaces in database DBDNAM01, but also the type of locks held by users.

-DISPLAY DATABASE(*) RESTRICT will display the status of all databases restricted in some manner or another. Any database not available for read/write is considered restricted.

In the following example, the DISPLAY DATABASE(DBDNAM01) command was entered. The result of the execution of this command immediately follows.

```
                        DB2  COMMANDS
===

Enter a single DB2 command on up to 4 lines below:

1   === -DISPLAY DATABASE(DBDNAM01)
2   ===
3   ===
4   ===


PRESS:  ENTER to process    END to exit   HELP for more information
```

```
            -    DATABASE = DBDNAM01   STATUS = RW
            -

NAME      TYPE PART STATUS
--------  ---- ---- ----------------
SPACE001  TS        RW
SPACE002  TS   001  RW
SPACE002  TS   002  RW
SPACE003  TS   001  RW
SPACE003  TS   002  RW
SPACE004  TS   001  RW
SPACE004  TS   002  RW
SPACE005  TS        RW
INDX1RTE  IX        RW
XRAUTORI  IX        RW
XRAUTORS  IX   001  RW
XRAUTORS  IX   002  RW
XREMPLOY  IX   001  RW
XREMPLOY  IX   002  RW
XRLIFERS  IX   001  RW
XRLIFERS  IX   002  RW
XRLIFRSA  IX        RW
XRNULLVA  IX        RW
******* DISPLAY OF DATABASE DBDNAM01 ENDED     *******************
```

The results returned from the DISPLAY DATABASE include the tablespace or indexspace NAME associated with the database, the TYPE of object it is such as tablespace or indexspace, the PARTition number, and its STATUS. TYPE is either TS for tablespace or IX for indexspace name. Since each partition of a tablespace or index is a dataset, you are displayed the status on each individually partitioned dataset. If the PART value is blank, the tablespace or indexspace is not partitioned. The last item, STATUS, gives you the disposition of the dataset. RW, in this example, indicates that the tablespace or indexspace is available for read/write.

The status of a tablespace or indexspace dataset can be altered through commands. The START DATABASE and STOP DATABASE commands control the accessibility of tablespaces and indexspaces. The status or mode of a tablespace or indexspace can be set to RO, RW, STOP, or UT.

RO status implies that the dataset is only available to "read only" users. Any application requesting an update will be denied access.

RW status implies that the dataset is available to users for both reading and updating.

STOP or STOPP status implies that the dataset has been stopped or a stop request is pending upon the completion of another task. The datasets involved are removed from DB2's control. They are not available to any DB2 users or utilities in this status.

UT status implies that the dataset is placed in DB2 utility mode where only DB2 utilities may process against it.

The status of tablespace or indexspace datasets can also be altered during the execution of utilities.

UTRO implies that a dataset in RW mode has been placed in RO mode due to utility processing.

UTRW indicates that a dataset is in RW mode while a utility is processing.

UTUT indicates that a dataset that was in RW mode has been placed in UT mode because a utility is processing and only utility access is allowed.

COPY implies that an image copy is required before this object can be updated.

The issuing of the next three commands will alter the availability of tablespaces SPACE001, SPACE004, and SPACE005. Following the three commands, another -DISPLAY DATABASE(DBDNAM01) is executed to display the status after these commands were executed.

```
-START DATABASE(DBDNAM01) SPACENAM(SPACE001) ACCESS(RO)
-START DATABASE(DBDNAM01) SPACENAM(SPACE004) ACCESS(UT)
-STOP DATABASE(DBDNAM01) SPACENAM(SPACE005)
```

The following command will display the status of the three tablespaces altered by the previous three commands.

```
-DISPLAY DATABASE(DBDNAM01) SPACENAM(SPACE001,SPACE004,SPACE005)
```

```
NAME      TYPE PART STATUS            PHYERRLO PHYERRHI CATALOG  PIECE
--------  ---- ---- ----------------  -------- -------- -------- -----
SPACE001 TS         RO                3        5        DBXX     001
SPACE004 TS    001  UT
SPACE004 TS    002  UT
SPACE005 TS         STOP
****** DISPLAY OF DATABASE DBDNAM01 ENDED      ********************
```

PHYERRLO is blank unless a tablespace or indexspace has physical I/O errors. If there is a number(hex) here, it represents the lowest page encountered containing I/O errors.

PHYERRHI is blank unless a tablespace or indexspace has physical I/O errors. If there is a number(hex) here, it represents the highest page encountered containing I/O errors.

CATALOG is the name of the catalog owning the dataset containing the I/O errors. Blank if no physical I/O errors exist. In this example, it is DBXX for tablespace SPACE001.

PIECE is a number constructed by taking the partition number and adding one to it. It is helpful in reconstructing the dataset name containing the errors. If a dataset is not partitioned the partition value is zero. The piece number is equal to the partition number +1 or 001 in this example.

From the above information, the actual dataset name containing the errors can be determined by replacing the following:

```
"CATALOG".DSNDBC.database-name.tablespace/indexspace.I0001.A"PIECE"
```

with the displayed values

```
DBXX.DSNDBC.DBDNAM01.SPACE001.I0001.A001
```

The following command can be issued to place the three tablespaces in read/write status again.

```
-START DATABASE(DBDNAM01) SPACENAM(*) ACCESS(RW)
```

The locks held by users against a database can also be displayed. This information is very important in trying to identify lock contention problems. You can determine who has the lock and the kind of lock issued. The following DISPLAY DATABASE command will display information about the locks obtained against a database by several users.

```
-DISPLAY DATABASE(DBDNAM011) LOCKS
```

```
      - ********************************************************
      - *  DISPLAY DATABASE SUMMARY
      *     GLOBAL LOCKS
      - ********************************************************
      -    DATABASE = DBDNAM011  STATUS = RW
      -
NAME      TYPE PART STATUS            CONNID    CORRID        LOCKINFO
--------  ---- ---- ----------------- --------  ------------  ---------
SPACE001  TS        RW
SPACE002  TS   001  RW
SPACE002  TS   002  RW
SPACE003  TS   001  RW                TSO       USERID2       H(IS,S,C)
SPACE003  TS   002  RW                TSO       USERID2       H(IS,S,C)
SPACE004  TS   001  RW
SPACE004  TS   002  RW
SPACE005  TS        RW                TSO       USERID3
INDX1RTE  IX        RW                TSO       USERID4
XRAUTORI  IX        RW
XRAUTORS  IX   001  RW
XRAUTORS  IX   002  RW                TSO       USERID4
XREMPLOY  IX   001  RW
XREMPLOY  IX   002  RW
XRLIFERS  IX   001  RW
XRLIFERS  IX   002  RW                TSO       USERID4
XRLIFRSA  IX        RW
XRNULLVA  IX        RW
******* DISPLAY OF DATABASE DBDNAM011 ENDED   ********************
```

CONNID identifies from where the connection originated. The valid values are BATCH, TSO, IMS, CICS, or blank.

CORRID identifies the requestor of the thread.

LOCKINFO identifies the kind of locks issued against the corresponding ablespace or indexspace dataset. The format for lock information is as folows:

```
"lock-qualifier"("lock-identifier","lock-unit","lock-duration")
```

Lock-qualifier:

H — for a held lock
W — for locks issued that are waiting on other locks to complete

Lock-identifier:

IS — user is requesting tablespace or indexspace lock with read intentions (Shared)
IX — requesting tablespace or indexspace lock with update intentions (Exclusive)
SIX — indicates requestor will issue tablespace or indexspace (Shared) locks when reading and (exclusive) locks while updating.
S — implies a lock with read intention.
X — implies an exclusive lock.

Lock-unit:

S — implies a tablespace or indexspace lock

Lock-duration (for held locks):

A — lock is freed at end of allocation
C — lock is freed at commit point
M — lock is freed by the system
D — lock is freed at deallocation

Lock-duration (for waiting locks):

Number representing requestor's position in the queue for obtaining locks

Let's analyze the previous lock: H(IS,S,C) on tablespace SPACE003 where locks are held by user USERID2.
USERID2 placed these locks through the TSO connection.

H — Locks are currently being held
IS — Tablespace lock with read intentions
S — Lock unit is a tablespace
C — Lock is freed at commit point

The command DISPLAY THREAD allows you to review the status of all DB2 threads or connections in process. This can be valuable in determining if a particular user is accessing a plan you are about to change. Coupled with the previous DISPLAY DATABASE LOCKS you can determine what application the user is running that is causing the lock problems. Before rebinding a Plan, you may want to display the active threads to determine if the Plan is in use. You cannot REBIND a Plan if someone is using it. The following are examples of the DISPLAY THREAD command:

```
-DISPLAY THREAD
-DISPLAY THREAD TYPE(ACTIVE)
-DISPLAY THREAD TYPE(*)
```

The following is from the -DISPLAY THREAD command:

```
          - DISPLAY THREAD REPORT FOLLOWS -
          - ACTIVE THREADS -
NAME   ST A   REQ ID          AUTHID   PLAN      ASID
TSO    N       1              USERID4            004B
TSO    T      263 USERID4     USERID4  INTR303D  004B
TSO    T        6 USERID5     USERID5  PROGRM4C  0059
TSO    T       22 USERID7     USERID7  PROGRM2C  002A
TSO    T     2006 USERIDA     USERIDA  PROGRM1C  001E
TSO    T     1988 USERID2     USERID2  PROGRM1C  0042
TSO    T     2716 USERID3     USERID3  PROGRM1C  0081
TSO    T        5 USERID6     USERID6  PROGRM2P  0071
TSO    T        7 USERID8     USERID8  PROGRM2C  0075
TSO    T  *     3 USERID1     USERID1            006B
TSO    T      994 USERID9     USERID9  PROGRM1C  0050
DISPLAY ACTIVE REPORT COMPLETE
    - NO INDOUBT THREADS FOUND FOR NAME=TSO
```

NAME lists the system from which the connection to DB2 was made.

ST is the status of the connection. T indicates the thread is established. If a plan is involved, the plan has been allocated. N indicates the thread is either being identified or going through the process of connecting to DB2.

"A" indicates whether the thread is active within DB2 (*) or not.

REQ indicates the number of requests sent through the thread since it was initially established. It does not indicate how many rows were updated, inserted, or deleted during the connection.

ID represents a recovery correlation-identifier associated to the established thread.

AUTHID is an authorization-identifier associated to the sign on.

PLAN, if specified, indicates the Plan associated with the thread. If blank, the user's thread is not yet established.

ASID is an internal address space identifier used by DB2 for the thread.

Later in this chapter we will review the available DB2 utilities. You can display the status of a utility in process. The DISPLAY UTIL command allows the user to view the current status of a utility executing on the DB2 System. All utilities are assigned a utility identifier. You can assign this utility identifier yourself or let DB2 assign one for you. If you know a utility's id, you can display the status of just the desired utility id.

-DISPLAY UTIL(*) will display the status of all utilities currently running on the DB2 system.

-DISPLAY UTIL(DB2BK*) displays the status of all utilities whose utility id begins with DB2BK.

-DISPLAY UTIL(USERID1.DB2BKUP) displays the status of a utility with an id of USERID1.DB2BKUP. Following are the results of executing this command for a copy utility whose processing has been stopped.

```
-- USERID = USERID1
UTILID = USERID1.DB2BKUP
PROCESSING UTILITY STATEMENT 3
UTILITY = COPY
PHASE = UTILINIT    COUNT = 0
STATUS = STOPPED
--DISPLAY UTIL' NORMAL COMPLETION
```

USERID = displays the user that submitted the utility.

UTILID = is the utility identifier. All utilities are run in background. If the submitter does not specify a utility id, DB2 will assign one equal to the individual userid submitting the job followed by (.) and the job name. For example, job JOBxxxx submitted by TSO user USERID2 would have a utility id of USERID2.JOBxxxx.

PROCESSING UTILITY STATEMENT indicates the progress of the utility running. In this case it indicates which control statement is currently being executed in a utility job containing multiple control cards. This is also true for a recovery.

UTILITY indicates the type of utility executing. Types of utilities will be discussed later.

PHASE indicates the utility phase currently executing. UTILINIT indicates that the utility is in an initial phase of preparing for execution. In the case of reorgs, you may have up to four additional phases.

1. UNLOAD — unload rows
2. RELOAD — reload rows
3. SORT — sort index work records
4. BUILD — build indexes

COUNT, in the case of reorgs and loads, displays the number of rows processed in the phase.

STATUS indicates the current status of the utility. STOPPED indicates the utility encountered problems and is stopped from further execution. The person submitting the utility should resolve the problem causing the utility to fail and restart it.

Occasionally you will encounter a problem with a utility that can not be resolved by restarting it. In these situations, you will need to terminate the utility in process. This should not be your first choice. In many instances, the problem causing the utility to fail can be resolved and the utility restarted. Care should be taken prior to terminating a utility to ensure that the tablespaces and indexspaces are not in a damaged or inconsistent state. Terminating a reorg during the reload phase would leave the tablespaces and indexes in a questionable state. Likewise, terminating a recovery could possibly leave objects in a questionable state. The TERM UTIL command is as follows:

-TERM UTIL(DB2BK*) will terminate all utilities beginning with DB2BK*.
-TERM UTIL(USERID1.DB2BKUP) will terminate a utility with an id of USERID1.DB2BKUP. The following is the result of executing this command for the previously displayed utility.

```
- COPY UTILITY,
UTILID = USERID1.DB2BKUP NOT EXECUTING,
CLEANUP COMPLETE
'-TERM UTIL' NORMAL COMPLETION
```

A good database manager should provide utilities to assist in servicing and managing data. DB2 is no exception to this. There are many such utilities available with DB2. Some utilities require DB2 to be operational, others do not. Some can be generated by DB2I, while others are not.

The following is a list of the utilities that can be generated using DB2I and their corresponding function. All of these utilities require DB2 to be operational.

Utility Name	Utility Function
CHECK	Validates index entries against the data pointed to
COPY	Creates copies of tablespaces for recovery purposes
LOAD	Loads data into DB2 tables from input datasets
MERGECOPY	Combines partial and full image copies
MODIFY	Removes recovery information from DB2 Catalog
RECOVER	Recovers a tablespace or index
REORG	Resequences rows of tables in tablespaces and removes space occupied by dropped tables
REPAIR	Fixes bad data or pointers (similar to ZAP)
RUNSTATS	Records information about data contained in tablespaces and indexes in the Catalog
STOSPACE	Records information about the space utilized in storage groups in the Catalog

All of the previously mentioned utilities require JCL to execute. Several approaches can be used to generate this JCL. One approach, as noted previously, is to use DB2I. Yet another is to use a CLIST, called DSNU, provided with DB2. By entering parameters, the CLIST can be instructed to generate JCL for the same utilities handled by DB2I. And, last but not least, you can generate the JCL yourself. Be careful whenever generating utility JCL. Few of the tools generating JCL assure you of JCL suitable for every situation. For instance, the JCL generators are not sensitive to the volume of data contained in the table. It is your responsibility to verify that enough sort work areas, unload space, backup space, etc. is available. Tools are very helpful in constructing skeleton JCL, but you should review the JCL for the particular application in mind for accuracy.

DB2I can be used to generate JCL for the LOAD, REORG, COPY, MERGECOPY, RECOVER, REPAIR, RUNSTATS, STOSPACE, CHECK, and MODIFY utilities. Each utility requires its own control cards. You have to construct the control cards. DB2I does not. I have constructed a PDS containing control cards for the execution of each of the previously mentioned utilities. Each member in the dataset USERID1.DB2I.CONTROL.CARDS contains control cards for a specific utility. From the DB2I Primary Option Menu, choosing option 8 invokes the utility generation feature of DB2I.

```
                       DB2I PRIMARY OPTION MENU
   === 8


   Select one of the following DB2 functions and press ENTER.

   1   SPUFI                (Process SQL statements)
   2   DCLGEN               (Generate SQL and source language declares)
   3   PROGRAM PREPARATION  (Prepare a DB2 application program to run)
   4   PRECOMPILE           (Invoke DB2 precompiler)
   5   BIND/REBIND/FREE      (BIND, REBIND, or FREE application plans)
   6   RUN                  (RUN an SQL program)
   7   DB2 COMMANDS         (Issue DB2 commands)
   8   UTILITIES            (Invoke DB2 utilities)
   D   DB2I DEFAULTS        (Set global parameters)
   X   EXIT                 (Leave DB2I)


   PRESS:   END to exit        HELP for more information
```

Utility Example: LOAD

The load utility is used to load rows into a table without using SQL. Load utility processing can consists of up to three distinct phases, depending on whether indexes are present or not. If indexes are not present, only the load phase exists. The phases are:

LOAD — data is actually written to the table in this phase. The data is found in the dataset referenced by ddname SYSREC. If indexes exit for the table, work records are written out to ddname SYSUT1 for the construction of the indexes in later phases.

SORT — in this phase, the index work records are sorted. The SYSUT1 file is sorted and placed in SORTOUT. SORTWK1 through SORTWK4 are used if the sort cannot be done in memory.

BUILD — the indexes are reconstructed from the work records sorted to SORTOUT. If the load is adding additional rows to an existing table, the index entries are inserted just for the rows loaded in the LOAD phase.

```
DB2 UTILITIES

===


Select from the following:


  1 FUNCTION  === EDITJCL (SUBMIT job, EDITJCL, DISPLAY, or TERMINATE)

  2 JOB ID    === USERID1         (A unique job identifier string)

  3 UTILITY   === LOAD        (LOAD,REORG,COPY,MERGECOPY,RECOVER,REPAIR,

                                RUNSTATS,STOSPACE,CHECK, or MODIFY)



  4 CONTROL CARDS DATA SET      === DB2I.CONTROL.CARDS(LOAD)

  5 RECDSN   (LOAD, REORG)      === LOAD.DATA

  6 DISCDSN  (LOAD)             ===

  7 COPYDSN  (COPY, MERGECOPY) ===


To RESTART a utility, specify starting point, otherwise enter NO.

  8 RESTART  === NO  (NO, At CURRENT position, or beginning of PHASE)


PRESS:  ENTER to process     END to exit    HELP for more information
```

1. The function to be performed. You can generate and edit utility JCL (EDITJCL), terminate an existing utility in process (TERMINATE), or display the status of a database (DISPLAY).
2. JOB ID is an identifier used to uniquely identify a utility during execution. No two utilities with the same identifier can be executing concurrently. If this is left blank, the associated Job Name becomes the identifier.

3. UTILITY identifies which of the 10 utilities JCL is being generated for. In this example, JCL for a LOAD is to be created.
4. CONTROL CARDS DATA SET is the dataset containing the control cards necessary for the utility's execution. The control card dataset is DB2I.CONTROL.CARDS(LOAD). The contents of the dataset is as follows:

```
LOAD DATA INDDN(SYSREC) RESUME(NO) LOG(NO)
INTO TABLE USERID1.EMPLOYEES_TABLE
("EMPLOYEE_NO"          POSITION(    1) INTEGER EXTERNAL(12),
 "EMPLOYEE_NAME"        POSITION(   14) CHAR(   16),
 "ADDRESS_STATE"        POSITION(   31) CHAR(    2),
 "DEPT"                 POSITION(   34) CHAR(    4),
 "SALARY"               POSITION(   39) DECIMAL EXTERNAL(22))
```

INDDN identifies the ddname of the dataset containing the load data. In this example, the ddname is SYSREC.

RESUME indicates whether you are loading to an empty table (NO) or you are loading rows to an already existing table (YES). RESUME(NO) REPLACE can also be specified. It resets a table containing rows to be empty prior to loading.

LOG reflects whether the changes to the table are to be logged for recovery purposes (YES) or not (NO). LOG(NO) will still allow you to restart the utility. If you specify LOG(NO), DB2 will request you to take an image copy before allowing updates. On large table loads, it is more efficient to specify LOG(NO) and run an image copy afterwards than specify LOG(YES) and force DB2 to log all changes.

INTO TABLE specifies the table where the data is to be loaded. (column-name position data-type) describes the input data to DB2. The first item (column-name) is the DB2 column name to receive the data, the second item (position) identifies the position in the load data where the data can be found, and the third item (data type) describes how the data is stored on the input load file. Both a beginning and ending position can be used to describe data positioning in the input file. For example, POSITION(1:2) implies a beginning position of 1 and an ending position of 12.

5. RECDSN datasets are required to be present if generating JCL for LOAD or REORG utilities. If a LOAD, it is the dataset containing the

data to be loaded into the table. If a REORG, it is the dataset to contain the unloaded rows. LOAD.DATA, in this case, contains the data to be loaded into a DB2 table.

6. DISCDSN is valid only for the LOAD and its use is optional. Rows containing inconsistent column data can be placed in this dataset rather than abending the utility's execution. If this dataset is not specified and bad data is encountered, the utility is abended. You would have to fix the bad data and restart the utility. If this dataset is specified, the bad rows (you set the limit on how many) are rejected and placed in the discard dataset for your review. The discarded rows can be fixed and reloaded in another execution.

7. COPYDSN is only used by the COPY and MERGECOPY utilities. This dataset will become the backup for the tablespace being image copied.

8. RESTART is used to re-establish a sync-point in restarting failed utilities. NO implies that the JCL being generated is not for restarting a failed utility. NO should be specified on the initial execution of any utility. CURRENT implies that JCL is being generated for a failed utility and the utility is being restarted at the point the failure occurred. PHASE, on the other hand, implies that the restart is to begin at the start of the phase in which the failure occurred.

If a utility failed in the reload phase, because the dataset containing the index work records became full, we could:

1. Rename the index work dataset
2. Allocate a larger index work dataset with the same name and on the *same* volume
3. Copy the data from the original dataset to the newly expanded dataset.
4. Add the following to the step's execution: ,UTPROC=RESTART
5. Resubmit the utility

If a utility fails in the sort phase, it is rather difficult to restart at the point of failure. Instead, we could restart the reorg at the beginning of the sort phase by specifying a PHASE restart.

```
,UTPROC='''RESTART(PHASE)'''
```

The following are messages received in the course of DB2I generating the LOAD utility JCL:

```
DSNU EXEC:
> LOAD UTILITY REQUESTED WITH
>    CONTROL=NONE, EDIT=SPF, COPYDSN=**NOT REQUIRED**,
>    INDSN=USERID1.DB2I.CONTROL.CARDS(LOAD),
>    RECDSN=USERID1.LOAD.DATA, RESTART=NO,
>    SYSTEM=DBXX, SUBMIT=NO, UID=USERID1,
>    UNIT=SYSDA, VOLUME="OMITTED", DB2I=YES,
>    DISCDSN="OMITTED".
> THE RESULTING JCL WILL BE WRITTEN TO DSNULOA.CNTL
>SPF EDITING FACILITY INVOKED TO EDIT DSNULOA.CNTL
> WHEN *** APPEAR, PLEASE PRESS ENTER
> TO TERMINATE SPF:
>    PRESS PF3    - RETURN TO CLIST WITH CHANGES
>    PRESS PF4    - RETURN TO CLIST WITH CHANGES THEN
>                   RETURN TO MAIN MENU
>    ENTER CANCEL - RETURN TO CLIST WITH NO CHANGES
```

Note that the JCL generated is placed in dataset DSNULOA.CNTL. Following this, you will be placed in EDIT mode on the JCL generated.

All utilities execute the same procedure DSNUPROC. UID represents the JOB ID specified on the DB2 UTILITIES panel for item 2. UTPROC is the result of specifying NO for RESTART. Note that the control cards in dataset DB2I.CONTROL.CARDS(LOAD) have been merged in stream.

```
EDIT ---- USERID1.DSNULOA.CNTL
COMMAND ===                                    SCROLL === CSR

000001 //JOBCARD ...
000005 //UTIL EXEC DSNUPROC,SYSTEM=DBXX,UID='USERID1',UTPROC=''
000006 //*
000007 //************************************************
000008 //*
000009 //*   GENERATING JCL FOR THE LOAD UTILITY
000010 //*   DATE:  01/01/88          TIME:  19:43:23
```

```
000011 //*
000012 //*************************************************
000013 //DSNUPROC.SORTWK01 DD DSN=USERID1.SORTWK01,
000014 //      DISP=(MOD,DELETE,CATLG),
000015 //      SPACE=(4000,(20,20),,,ROUND),
000016 //      UNIT=SYSDA
000017 //DSNUPROC.SORTWK02 DD DSN=USERID1.SORTWK02,
000018 //      DISP=(MOD,DELETE,CATLG),
000019 //      SPACE=(4000,(20,20),,,ROUND),
000020 //      UNIT=SYSDA
000021 //DSNUPROC.SORTWK03 DD DSN=USERID1.SORTWK03,
000022 //      DISP=(MOD,DELETE,CATLG),
000023 //      SPACE=(4000,(20,20),,,ROUND),
000024 //      UNIT=SYSDA
000025 //DSNUPROC.SORTWK04 DD DSN=USERID1.SORTWK04,
000026 //      DISP=(MOD,DELETE,CATLG),
000027 //      SPACE=(4000,(20,20),,,ROUND),
000028 //      UNIT=SYSDA
000029 //DSNUPROC.SYSREC DD DSN=USERID1.LOAD.DATA,
000030 //      DISP=(MOD,CATLG)
000031 //DSNUPROC.SYSUT1 DD DSN=USERID1.SYSUT1,
000032 //      DISP=(MOD,DELETE,CATLG),
000033 //      SPACE=(4000,(20,20),,,ROUND),
000034 //      UNIT=SYSDA
000035 //DSNUPROC.SORTOUT DD DSN=USERID1.SORTOUT,
000036 //      DISP=(MOD,DELETE,CATLG),
000037 //      SPACE=(4000,(20,20),,,ROUND),
000038 //      UNIT=SYSDA
000039 //DSNUPROC.SYSIN    DD  *
000040    LOAD DATA INDDN(SYSREC) RESUME(NO) LOG(NO)
000041    INTO TABLE USERID1.EMPLOYEES_TABLE
000042    ("EMPLOYEE_NO"       POSITION(    1) INTEGER EXTERNAL(12),
000043     "EMPLOYEE_NAME"        POSITION(  14) CHAR(   16),
000044     "ADDRESS_STATE"        POSITION(  31) CHAR(    2),
000045     "DEPT"                 POSITION(  34) CHAR(    4),
000046     "SALARY"               POSITION(  39) DECIMAL EXTERNAL(22))
000047 //
```

Utility Example: <u>REORG</u>

This DB2 Utility generation process creates JCL for a reorganization.

```
                          DB2 UTILITIES
===


Select from the following:


1 FUNCTION === EDITJCL (SUBMIT job, EDITJCL, DISPLAY, or TERMINATE)
2 JOB ID   === USERID1   (A unique job identifier string)
3 UTILITY  === REORG     (LOAD,REORG,COPY,MERGECOPY,RECOVER,REPAIR,
                          RUNSTATS,STOSPACE,CHECK, or MODIFY)
4 CONTROL CARDS DATA SET    === DB2I.CONTROL.CARDS(REORG)
5 RECDSN  (LOAD, REORG)     === REORG.UNLOAD.DATA
6 DISCDSN (LOAD)            ===
7 COPYDSN (COPY, MERGECOPY) ===


To RESTART a utility, specify starting point, otherwise enter NO.
8 RESTART  === NO  (NO, At CURRENT position, or beginning of PHASE)


PRESS:  ENTER to process    END to exit    HELP for more information
```

The following messages were generated in the process of creating reorg
CL.

```
=USERID1.DB2I.CONTROL.CARDS(REORG),
>    RECDSN=USERID1.REORG.UNLOAD.DATA, RESTART=NO,
>    SYSTEM=DBXX, SUBMIT=NO, UID=USERID1,
>    UNIT=SYSDA, VOLUME="OMITTED", DB2I=YES,
>    DISCDSN="OMITTED".
>  THE RESULTING JCL WILL BE WRITTEN TO DSNUREO.CNTL
>SPF EDITING FACILITY INVOKED TO EDIT DSNUREO.CNTL
>  WHEN *** APPEAR, PLEASE PRESS ENTER
>  TO TERMINATE SPF:
>     PRESS PF3     - RETURN TO CLIST WITH CHANGES
>     PRESS PF4     - RETURN TO CLIST WITH CHANGES THEN
>                     RETURN TO MAIN MENU
>     ENTER CANCEL  - RETURN TO CLIST WITH NO CHANGES
```

```
EDIT ---- USERID1.DSNUREO.CNTL
COMMAND ===                                    SCROLL ===CSR

************************* TOP OF DATA ********************
000001 //JOB CARD...
000005 //UTIL EXEC DSNUPROC,SYSTEM=DBXX,UID='USERID1',UTPROC=''
000007 //*******************************************
000008 //*
000009 //*  GENERATING JCL FOR THE REORGANIZATION UTILITY
000010 //*  DATE: 01/01/88           TIME:  19:44:42
000011 //*
000012 //*******************************************
000014 //DSNUPROC.SORTWK01 DD DSN=USERID1.SORTWK01,
000015 //      DISP=(MOD,DELETE,CATLG),
000016 //      SPACE=(4000,(20,20),,,ROUND),
000017 //      UNIT=SYSDA
000018 //DSNUPROC.SORTWK02 DD DSN=USERID1.SORTWK02,
000019 //      DISP=(MOD,DELETE,CATLG),
000020 //      SPACE=(4000,(20,,0),,,ROUND
000021 //      UNIT=SYSDA
000022 //DSNUPROC.SORTWK03 DD DSN=USERID1.SORTWK03,
```

```
000023 //       DISP=(MOD,DELETE,CATLG),
000024 //       SPACE=(4000,(20,20),,,ROUND),
000025 //       UNIT=SYSDA
000026 //DSNUPROC.SORTWK04 DD DSN=USERID1.SORTWK04,
000027 //       DISP=(MOD,DELETE,CATLG),
000028 //       SPACE=(4000,(20,20),,,ROUND),
000029 //       UNIT=SYSDA
000030 //DSNUPROC.SYSREC DD DSN=USERID1.REORG.UNLOAD.DATA,
000031 //       DISP=(MOD,CATLG),
000032 //       SPACE=(4000,(20,20),,,ROUND),
000033 //       UNIT=SYSDA
000034 //DSNUPROC.SYSUT1 DD DSN=USERID1.SYSUT1,
000035 //       DISP=(MOD,DELETE,CATLG),
000036 //       SPACE=(4000,(20,20),,,ROUND),
000037 //       UNIT=SYSDA
000038 //DSNUPROC.SORTOUT DD DSN=USERID1.SORTOUT,
000039 //       DISP=(MOD,DELETE,CATLG),
000040 //       SPACE=(4000,(20,20),,,ROUND),
000041 //       UNIT=SYSDA
000042 //DSNUPROC.SYSIN    DD   *
000043 REORG TABLESPACE DBDNAM01.SPACE001
000044       LOG NO
000045       UNLDDN SYSREC
000046       WORKDDN SYSUT1
000047       SORTDEVT SYSDA
000048       SORTNUM 4
000049       UNLOAD CONTINUE
000050 //
*********************** BOTTOM OF DATA ***********************
```

The REORG phases are identical to the load with one exception. The reorg
has an additional phase, called the UNLOAD. The reorg does serve a different
function than the load. The reorg reorganizes rows for all tables contained in
a tablespace. If clustering indexes are defined, the rows will be unloaded
using the clustering index and reloaded in the same sequence as the clustering index's key. If space in the tablespace is occupied by dropped tables, the
space occupied by the dropped tables is reclaimed. The PCTFREE and
FREEPAGE parameters specified during the tablespace definition will be applied when reloading. When a tablespace is reorganized, all of the associated
indexes for tables in the tablespace are rebuilt. Indexes can be reorganized

,eparately from the tablespace if desired. Note the dispositions of the datasets reated for utilities are geared for restart purposes. The space parameter for hese datasets is based on bytes. You can improve performance by increasing he blocking size to half track. Unless you are working with small tables and ablespaces, you should calculate how much space you actually need prior to submitting the utility JCL and reflect this in the JCL. To determine the space needed for index work records (SYSUT1 and SORTOUT), perform the following:

1. For each table in the tablespace, multiply the number of rows in the table by the number of indexes defined on the table.
2. Sum the products derived in step 1.
3. Multiply the sum by the largest index key + 7. This will give you the total number of bytes required.

For example:

Tablespace SPACE009 contains 3 tables.
Table 1 has 10,000 rows and 3 indexes (longest index key is 12)
Table 2 has 5,000 rows and 1 index (longest index key is 50)
Table 3 has 90,000 rows and 2 indexes (longest index key is 30)

1. 10,000 X 3 = 30,000
   5,000 X 1 = 5,000
   90,000 X 2 = 180,000
2. Sum of rows = 215,000
3. 215,000 X (50 + 7) = 12,255,000
4. SYSUT1 & SORTOUT must be able to contain approximately 12,255,000 bytes.

Contents of USERID1.DB2I.CONTROL.CARDS(REORG):

```
REORG TABLESPACE DBDNAM01.SPACE001
     LOG NO
     UNLDDN SYSREC
     WORKDDN SYSUT1
     SORTDEVT SYSDA
     SORTNUM 4
     UNLOAD CONTINUE
```

LOG is the same as for LOAD.

UNLDDN includes the ddname of the dataset used to unload the data contained in the tablespace. It is used in the reload phase as well.

WORKDDN includes the ddname pointing to the dataset where index records are written during the reload phase.

SORTDEVT is the device type to be used when allocating datasets.

SORTNUM is the number of sort work areas to be generated.

UNLOAD specifies whether the utility should just perform an unload (ONLY), stop after the unload so that the unload results can be verified (PAUSE), or continue to perform the reload after successfully completing the unload (CONTINUE). A utility specifying PAUSE will still be in process after the unload. To continue on with the reload, change the PAUSE to CONTINUE and resubmit the utility in restart mode.

Utility Example: COPY

In this example, JCL will be generated for copying the contents of a tablespace to a sequential dataset. The sequential dataset is considered a backup and would be used by the RECOVERY utility to restore a damaged tablespace. If all of the pages of a tablespace are copied, the sequential dataset is called a FULL copy. If only pages changed since the last copy execution are backed up, the sequential dataset is considered an INCREMENTAL copy.

```
                        DB2 UTILITIES
===


Select from the following:


 1 FUNCTION === EDITJCL (SUBMIT job, EDITJCL, DISPLAY, or TERMINATE)
 2 JOB ID   === USERID1 (A unique job identifier string)
 3 UTILITY  === COPY    (LOAD,REORG,COPY,MERGECOPY,RECOVER,REPAIR,
                         RUNSTATS,STOSPACE,CHECK, or MODIFY)


 4 CONTROL CARDS DATA SET    === DB2I.CONTROL.CARDS(COPY)
 5 RECDSN (LOAD, REORG)      ===
 6 DISCDSN (LOAD)            ===
 7 COPYDSN (COPY, MERGECOPY) === FULL.BACKUP.DATA
To RESTART a utility, specify starting point, otherwise enter NO.
 8 RESTART === NO (NO, At CURRENT position, or beginning of PHASE)


PRESS: ENTER to process     END to exit    HELP for more information
```

```
DSNU EXEC:
>  IMAGE COPY UTILITY REQUESTED WITH
>     CONTROL=NONE, EDIT=SPF, COPYDSN=USERID1.FULL.BACKUP.DATA,
>     INDSN=USERID1.DB2I.CONTROL.CARDS(COPY),
>     RECDSN=**NOT REQUIRED**, RESTART=NO,
>     SYSTEM=DBXX, SUBMIT=NO, UID=USERID1,
>     UNIT=SYSDA, VOLUME="OMITTED", DB2I=YES,
>     DISCDSN="OMITTED".
>  THE RESULTING JCL WILL BE WRITTEN TO DSNUCOP.CNTL
>SPF EDITING FACILITY INVOKED TO EDIT DSNUCOP.CNTL
>  WHEN *** APPEAR, PLEASE PRESS ENTER
>  TO TERMINATE SPF:
>     PRESS PF3    - RETURN TO CLIST WITH CHANGES
>     PRESS PF4    - RETURN TO CLIST WITH CHANGES THEN
>                    RETURN TO MAIN MENU
>     ENTER CANCEL - RETURN TO CLIST WITH NO CHANGES
```

```
EDIT ---- USERID1.DSNUCOP.CNTL
COMMAND ===                                      SCROLL === CSR
****** *************************** TOP OF DATA ********************
000001 //JOB CARD ...
000005 //UTIL EXEC DSNUPROC,SYSTEM=DBXX,UID='USERID1',UTPROC=''
000006 //*
000007 //*********************************************
000008 //*
000009 //* GENERATING JCL FOR THE IMAGE COPY UTILITY
000010 //* DATE:  01/01/88         TIME:  19:45:50
000011 //*
000012 //*********************************************
000013 //*
000014 //DSNUPROC.SYSCOPY DD DSN=USERID1.FULL.BACKUP.DATA,
000015 //     DISP=(MOD,CATLG),
000016 //     SPACE=(4000,(20,20),,,ROUND),
000017 //     UNIT=SYSDA
000018 //DSNUPROC.SYSIN   DD  *
000019   COPY TABLESPACE DBDNAM01.SPACE001 DEVT 3480 COPYDDN SYSCOPY
000020          SHRLEVEL CHANGE  FULL YES  DSNUM ALL
000021 //
```

Contents of USERID1.DB2I.CONTROL.CARDS(COPY):

```
COPY TABLESPACE DBDNAM01.SPACE001 DEVT 3480  COPYDDN SYSCOPY
SHRLEVEL CHANGE  FULL YES  DSNUM ALL
```

TABLESPACE names the tablespace to be backed up. Since tablespace name alone is not unique, it is prefixed by the database name (DBDNAM01).

DEVT is the device type of the sequential dataset.

COPYDDN is the ddname referring to the sequential dataset name.

SHRLEVEL indicates the status of the tablespace when the copy utility is executing. CHANGE allows other applications to read and update tables in the tablespace being copied. REFERENCE implies that the tablespace is available to read only applications. Use REFERENCE if you have a need to restore a tablespace to a specific point in time. CHANGE allows you to backup tablespaces being updated, but may cause problems if recovery to a specific point in time is needed. If an application was executing while a COPY using

CHANGE was being run, a recovery to only the point in time of the copy may reflect only partial updates performed by the application.

FULL reflects which pages in the tablespace are to be copied. YES implies all pages are to be copied, while NO implies that only pages modified since the last copy are to copied (INCREMENTAL). INCREMENTAL image copies can be used for faster recoveries since DB2 logs will not have to be passed for the period in time prior to the incremental image copy.

DSNUM indicates which tablespace datasets of a partitioned tablespace are to be copied. ALL implies that all partitioned tablespace datasets are to be copied. If you wish to just copy one partition, specify the partition number in place of the ALL.

Utility Example: MERGECOPY

The MERGECOPY goes hand in hand with the COPY utility when incremental image copies have been taken. The MERGECOPY utility can combine several incremental image copies into one or combine incremental image copies with a full image copy to produce a new full image copy.

```
                        DB2 UTILITIES
===
    Select from the following:


    1 FUNCTION  === EDITJCL (SUBMIT job, EDITJCL, DISPLAY, or TERMINATE)
    2 JOB ID    === USERID1    (A unique job identifier string)
    3 UTILITY   === MERGECOPY (LOAD,REORG,COPY,MERGECOPY,RECOVER,REPAIR,
                               RUNSTATS, STOSPACE, CHECK, or MODIFY)


    4 CONTROL CARDS DATA SET    === DB2I.CONTROL.CARDS(MERGECPY)
    5 RECDSN   (LOAD, REORG)    ===
    6 DISCDSN  (LOAD)           ===
    7 COPYDSN  (COPY, MERGECOPY) === PARTIAL.BACKUP.DATA


    To RESTART a utility, specify starting point, otherwise enter NO.
    8 RESTART  === NO  (NO, At CURRENT position, or beginning of PHASE)


    PRESS:  ENTER to process      END to exit    HELP for more information
```

```
DSNU EXEC:
>  MERGE/COPY UTILITY REQUESTED WITH
>     CONTROL=NONE, EDIT=SPF, COPYDSN=USERID1.PARTIAL.BACKUP.DATA,
>     INDSN=USERID1.DB2I.CONTROL.CARDS(MERGECPY),
>     RECDSN=**NOT REQUIRED**, RESTART=NO,
>     SYSTEM=DBXX, SUBMIT=NO, UID=USERID1,
>     UNIT=SYSDA, VOLUME="OMITTED", DB2I=YES,
>     DISCDSN="OMITTED".
>  THE RESULTING JCL WILL BE WRITTEN TO DSNUMER.CNTL
>SPF EDITING FACILITY INVOKED TO EDIT DSNUMER.CNTL
>  WHEN *** APPEAR, PLEASE PRESS ENTER
>  TO TERMINATE SPF:
>     PRESS PF3    - RETURN TO CLIST WITH CHANGES
>     PRESS PF4    - RETURN TO CLIST WITH CHANGES THEN
>                    RETURN TO MAIN MENU
>  ENTER CANCEL - RETURN TO CLIST WITH NO CHANGES
```

```
EDIT ---- USERID1.DSNUMER.CNTL
COMMAND ===                                          SCROLL === CSR
000001 //JOB CARD ...
000005 //UTIL EXEC DSNUPROC,SYSTEM=DBXX,UID='USERID1',UTPROC=''
000007 //************************************************
000008 //*
000009 //*  GENERATING JCL FOR THE MERGE/COPY UTILITY
000010 //*  DATE:  01/01/88          TIME:  19:46:43
000012 //************************************************
000013 //*
000014 //DSNUPROC.SYSCOPY DD DSN=USERID1.PARTIAL.BACKUP.DATA,
000015 //      DISP=(MOD,CATLG),
000016 //      SPACE=(4000,(20,20),,,ROUND),
000017 //      UNIT=SYSDA
000018 //DSNUPROC.SYSIN    DD  *
000019  MERGECOPY TABLESPACE DBDNAM01.SPACE001 DEVT 3480
000020  WORKDDN SYSUT1 DSNUM ALL NEWCOPY NO COPYDDN SYSCOPY
000021 //
```

Contents of USERID1.DB2I.CONTROL.CARDS(MERGECPY):

```
MERGECOPY TABLESPACE DBDNAM01.SPACE001 DEVT 3480
WORKDDN SYSUT1 DSNUM ALL NEWCOPY NO COPYDDN SYSCOPY
```

TABLESPACE, DEVT, DSNUM, and COPYDDN (same as for COPY).
WORKDDN is the ddname for a dataset used to contain the intermediate
results of merging incremental image copies and/or full image copies.
NEWCOPY indicates what the output sequential dataset will be. NO implies that incremental image copies are just being merged with incremental
image copies to produce a single incremental image copy. YES implies incremental image copies are being combined with a full image copy to produce
a new full image copy.

Before discussing the recovery utility, we need to identify how DB2 keeps
track of changes to the objects it manages. During the course of processing,
DB2's Resource Manager detects information needing to be recorded for
database and system recovery. This could be caused by performing a simple
update operation to a table. The Resource Manager collects this information
into what is called a *log record* and passes it on to DB2's Log Manager. As
each log record is written, it is assigned an increasing relative byte number,
commonly referred to as RBA. It is the function of the Log Manager to
manage all log records created by the system.

When the Log Manager receives a log record, it places it into VSAM
datasets called log buffers. When all of the log buffers become full, or a log
write ahead request has been received, or an installation defined number of
log buffers are full, the buffers are written to what is referred to as an *active
log* dataset. The log buffer areas are then reusable.

The active log dataset is a VSAM ESDS. Once an active log dataset becomes
full, it is off loaded to what is referred to as an *archive log* dataset. Once off
loaded, the active log dataset is reusable.

Archive log datasets are nothing more than sequential datasets. DB2 can
manage up to 1000 archive log datasets. DB2 keeps track of the RBA ranges
contained in each log dataset. This information is contained in a VSAM KSDS
dataset called the Boot Strap Data Set or BSDS.

The BSDS contains an inventory of all log datasets and can map any given
log RBA to an active log dataset or an archived log dataset. When a full
recovery is performed, the appropriate log datasets are dynamically allocated
by the DB2 Log Manager by using the BSDS. As a result, the individual performing the recovery does not need to be concerned about which log datasets
are required.

Utility Example: RECOVER

The RECOVER utility is used to restore a tablespace from its backup dataset generated by the COPY. Several options are available when performing a recovery. The options are:

1. Recover tablespace from last backup and apply all DB2 logs written since the last backup (FULL RECOVERY).
2. Recover tablespace from a backup dataset and do not apply any log (Point-in-time-recovery/partial recovery).
3. Recover tablespace from last backup and apply DB2 logs with a RBA (Relative Byte Address) less than some byte-string. (Also a partial recovery)
4. Recover tablespace pages contained in an error range.

In addition to recovering tablespaces, the RECOVER utility can be used to recover indexes. Indexes are *not* image copied. Instead, they are reconstructed from the table data during a recovery. If a tablespace and an index both need to be recovered, the tablespace recovery needs to completed prior to recovering the index.

```
                        DB2 UTILITIES
===
Select from the following:


1 FUNCTION  === EDITJCL (SUBMIT job, EDITJCL, DISPLAY, or TERMINATE)
2 JOB ID    === USERID1  (A unique job identifier string)
3 UTILITY   === RECOVER   (LOAD,REORG,COPY,MERGECOPY,RECOVER,REPAIR,
                          RUNSTATS,STOSPACE,CHECK, or MODIFY)
4 CONTROL CARDS DATA SET    === DB2I.CONTROL.CARDS(RECOVER)
5 RECDSN  (LOAD, REORG)     ===
6 DISCDSN (LOAD)            ===
7 COPYDSN (COPY, MERGECOPY) ===


To RESTART a utility, specify starting point, otherwise enter NO.
8 RESTART  === NO  (NO, At CURRENT position, or beginning of PHASE)


PRESS:  ENTER to process     END to exit    HELP for more information
```

```
DSNU EXEC:
>  RECOVERY UTILITY REQUESTED WITH
>     CONTROL=NONE, EDIT=SPF, COPYDSN=**NOT REQUIRED**,
>     INDSN=USERID1.DB2I.CONTROL.CARDS(RECOVER),
>     RECDSN=**NOT REQUIRED**, RESTART=NO,
>     SYSTEM=DBXX, SUBMIT=NO, UID=USERID1,
>     UNIT=SYSDA, VOLUME="OMITTED", DB2I=YES,
>     DISCDSN="OMITTED".
>  THE RESULTING JCL WILL BE WRITTEN TO DSNUREC.CNTL
>SPF EDITING FACILITY INVOKED TO EDIT DSNUREC.CNTL
>  WHEN *** APPEAR, PLEASE PRESS ENTER
>  TO TERMINATE SPF:
>     PRESS PF3     - RETURN TO CLIST WITH CHANGES
>     PRESS PF4     - RETURN TO CLIST WITH CHANGES THEN
>                     RETURN TO MAIN MENU
>     ENTER CANCEL - RETURN TO CLIST WITH NO CHANGES
```

```
EDIT ---- USERID1.DSNUREC.CNTL
 COMMAND ===                                    SCROLL === CSR
****** ************************** TOP OF DATA ********************
000001 //JOB CARD ...
000005 //UTIL EXEC DSNUPROC,SYSTEM=DBXX,UID='USERID1',UTPROC=''
000007 //***********************************************
 000009 //*  GENERATING JCL FOR THE RECOVERY UTILITY
000010 //*  DATE:  01/01/88         TIME:  19:47:45
000012 //***********************************************
000013 //*
000014 //DSNUPROC.SYSIN     DD  *
000015    RECOVER TABLESPACE  DBDNAM01.SPACE001 DSNUM ALL
000016 //
****** ************************** BOTTOM OF DATA *****************
```

Contents of USERID1.DB2I.CONTROL.CARDS(RECOVER):

```
RECOVER TABLESPACE   DBDNAM01.SPACE001 DSNUM ALL
```

Utility Example: REPAIR

The REPAIR utility is used to change the values in a page without using SQL. In general, the repair should not be used by anyone outside of those responsible for recovering tablespaces. You should have a complete under-standing of page structures before attempting this. I am mentioning this utility here for one reason — to turn off the image copy needed flag. Should you have a situation where the table can be updated and copies are not needed, then this might apply to you.

```
                          DB2 UTILITIES
===


Select from the following:


1 FUNCTION  === EDITJCL (SUBMIT job, EDITJCL, DISPLAY, or TERMINATE)
2 JOB ID    === USERID1  (A unique job identifier string)
3 UTILITY   === REPAIR   (LOAD,REORG,COPY,MERGECOPY,RECOVER, REPAIR,
                          RUNSTATS,STOSPACE,CHECK, or MODIFY)


4 CONTROL CARDS DATA SET    === DB2I.CONTROL.CARDS(REPAIR)
5 RECDSN   (LOAD, REORG)    ===
6 DISCDSN  (LOAD)           ===
7 COPYDSN  (COPY, MERGECOPY) ===


To RESTART a utility, specify starting point, otherwise enter NO.
8 RESTART  === NO  (NO, At CURRENT position, or beginning of PHASE)


PRESS: ENTER to process     END to exit     HELP for more information
```

```
DSNU EXEC:
>  REPAIR UTILITY REQUESTED WITH
>     CONTROL=NONE, EDIT=SPF, COPYDSN=**NOT REQUIRED**,
>     INDSN=USERID1.DB2I.CONTROL.CARDS(REPAIR),
>     RECDSN=**NOT REQUIRED**, RESTART=NO,
>     SYSTEM=DBXX, SUBMIT=NO, UID=USERID1,
>     UNIT=SYSDA, VOLUME="OMITTED", DB2I=YES,
>     DISCDSN="OMITTED".
>  THE RESULTING JCL WILL BE WRITTEN TO DSNUREP.CNTL
>SPF EDITING FACILITY INVOKED TO EDIT DSNUREP.CNTL
>  WHEN *** APPEAR, PLEASE PRESS ENTER
>  TO TERMINATE SPF:
>     PRESS PF3    - RETURN TO CLIST WITH CHANGES
>     PRESS PF4    - RETURN TO CLIST WITH CHANGES THEN
>                    RETURN TO MAIN MENU
>     ENTER CANCEL - RETURN TO CLIST WITH NO CHANGES
```

```
EDIT ---- USERID1.DSNUREP.CNTL
COMMAND ===                                       SCROLL === CSR
****** ************************** TOP OF DATA ********************
000001 //JOB CARD ...
000005 //UTIL EXEC DSNUPROC,SYSTEM=DBXX,UID='USERID1',UTPROC=''
000006 //*
000007 //***********************************************
000008 //*
000009 //*   GENERATING JCL FOR THE REPAIR UTILITY
000010 //*   DATE: 01/01/88            TIME:  19:48:29
000011 //*
000012 //***********************************************
000013 //*
000014 //DSNUPROC.SYSIN    DD  *
000015    REPAIR SET   TABLESPACE DBDNAM01.SPACE001 NOCOPYPEND
000016 //
****** ************************** BOTTOM OF DATA *****************
```

Contents of USERID1.DB2I.CONTROL.CARDS(REPAIR):

```
REPAIR SET  TABLESPACE DBDNAM01.SPACE001 NOCOPYPEND
```

TABLESPACE (same as copy).
NOCOPYPEND causes a copy needed flag in the DB2 Catalog to be turned off. DB2 keeps a record of the utilities processing against a tablespace. If one of the utilities runs with a LOG(NO), the tablespace is not fully recoverable until a full image copy is run. To prevent you from unknowingly turning an unrecoverable tablespace over to users for updating, DB2 checks a COPY PENDING flag before the update is allowed. Image copying the tablespace with SHRLEVEL=REFERENCE will also turn off the copy pending flag.

Utility Example: RUNSTATS

The RUNSTATS utility plays a very important role in the performance of your applications. This utility records information about your tablespaces and indexes in the DB2 Catalog. Some of this information is very detailed, like the number of unique values of a key column and the number of rows in a table. This information is often used to monitor tablespace growth and to determine need for reorganization. The DB2 Optimizer also uses the information in determining access strategy. The RUNSTATS utility does not produce a report. Since the information is in the Catalog, you can at any time write queries to retrieve this information. When is a good time to run this utility? It should be run after REORGs if clustered indexes are defined on tables in the tablespace. If clustering is not involved, you may want to consider running it when characteristics of the data have changed such as after inserting additional data, after removing large volumes of data and addition of what would appear to be usable indexes.

```
                         DB2 UTILITIES
=== >
Select from the following:


 1 FUNCTION === EDITJCL (SUBMIT job, EDITJCL, DISPLAY, or TERMINATE)
 2 JOB ID   === USERID1   (A unique job identifier string)
 3 UTILITY  === RUNSTATS  (LOAD,REORG,COPY,MERGECOPY,RECOVER,REPAIR,
                           RUNSTATS,STOSPACE,CHECK, or MODIFY)
 4 CONTROL CARDS DATA SET  === DB2I.CONTROL.CARDS(RUNSTATS)
 5 RECDSN  (LOAD, REORG)   ===
 6 DISCDSN (LOAD)          ===
 7 COPYDSN (COPY, MERGECOPY) ===


To RESTART a utility, specify starting point, otherwise enter NO.
 8 RESTART  === NO  (NO, At CURRENT position, or beginning of PHASE)


PRESS: ENTER to process    END to exit    HELP for more information
```

```
DSNU EXEC:
>  RUNSTATS UTILITY REQUESTED WITH
>     CONTROL=NONE, EDIT=SPF, COPYDSN=**NOT REQUIRED**,
>     INDSN=USERID1.DB2I.CONTROL.CARDS(RUNSTATS),
>     RECDSN=**NOT REQUIRED**, RESTART=NO,
>     SYSTEM=DBXX, SUBMIT=NO, UID=USERID1,
>     UNIT=SYSDA, VOLUME="OMITTED", DB2I=YES,
>     DISCDSN="OMITTED".
>  THE RESULTING JCL WILL BE WRITTEN TO DSNURUN.CNTL
>SPF EDITING FACILITY INVOKED TO EDIT DSNURUN.CNTL
>  WHEN *** APPEAR, PLEASE PRESS ENTER
>  TO TERMINATE SPF:
>     PRESS PF3   - RETURN TO CLIST WITH CHANGES
>     PRESS PF4   - RETURN TO CLIST WITH CHANGES THEN
>                   RETURN TO MAIN MENU
>     ENTER CANCEL - RETURN TO CLIST WITH NO CHANGES
```

```
EDIT ---- USERID1.DSNURUN.CNTL
COMMAND ===                                    SCROLL === CSR
****** ************************** TOP OF DATA ********************
000001 //JOB CARD ...
000005 //UTIL EXEC DSNUPROC,SYSTEM=DBXX,UID='USERID1',UTPROC=''
000006 //*
000007 //**********************************************
000008 //*
000009 //*  GENERATING JCL FOR THE RUNSTATS UTILITY
000010 //*  DATE:  01/01/88          TIME:  19:49:07
000011 //*
000012 //**********************************************
000013 //*
000014 //DSNUPROC.SYSIN    DD  *
000015     RUNSTATS TABLESPACE DBDNAM01.SPACE001 INDEX
000016          SHRLEVEL CHANGE
000017 //
****** ************************** BOTTOM OF DATA *****************
```

Contents of USERID1.DB2I.CONTROL.CARDS(RUNSTATS):

```
RUNSTATS TABLESPACE DBDNAM01.SPACE001 INDEX
         SHRLEVEL CHANGE
```

TABLESPACE is the name of the tablespace for which information is to be collected. The columns updated in the DB2 Catalog are:

SYSIBM.SYSCOLUMNS	SYSIBM.SYSTABLES	SYSIBM.SYSTABLESPACE
HIGH2KEY	CARD	NACTIVE
LOW2KEY	NPAGES	
COLCARD	PCTPAGES	

SHRLEVEL (same as COPY).

INDEX indicates information is also to be collected about indexes and recorded in the Catalog. The columns updated in the Catalog are:

SYSIBM.SYSINDEXES

CLUSTERED
FIRSTKEYCARD
FULLKEYCARD
NLEAF
NLEVELS

Utility Example: STOSPACE

The STOSPACE utility, similar to the RUNSTATS, collects information and records it in the Catalog. The information collected pertains to the space used in direct access storage devices defined in storage groups.

```
                    DB2 UTILITIES
===


Select from the following:

1 FUNCTION === EDITJCL (SUBMIT job, EDITJCL, DISPLAY, or TERMINATE)
2 JOB ID   === USERID1  (A unique job identifier string)
3 UTILITY  === STOSPACE (LOAD,REORG,COPY,MERGECOPY,RECOVER,REPAIR,
                         RUNSTATS,STOSPACE,CHECK, or MODIFY)


4 CONTROL CARDS DATA SET    === DB2I.CONTROL.CARDS(STOSPACE)
5 RECDSN  (LOAD, REORG)    ===
6 DISCDSN (LOAD)           ===
7 COPYDSN (COPY, MERGECOPY) ===


To RESTART a utility, specify starting point, otherwise enter NO.
8 RESTART === NO  (NO, At CURRENT position, or beginning of PHASE)


PRESS: ENTER to process     END to exit    HELP for more information
```

```
DSNU EXEC:
>   STOSPACE UTILITY REQUESTED WITH
>     CONTROL=NONE, EDIT=SPF, COPYDSN=**NOT REQUIRED**,
>     INDSN=USERID1.DB2I.CONTROL.CARDS(STOSPACE),
>     RECDSN=**NOT REQUIRED**, RESTART=NO,
>     SYSTEM=DBXX, SUBMIT=NO, UID=USERID1,
>     UNIT=SYSDA, VOLUME="OMITTED", DB2I=YES,
>     DISCDSN="OMITTED".
>   THE RESULTING JCL WILL BE WRITTEN TO DSNUSTO.CNTL
>SPF EDITING FACILITY INVOKED TO EDIT DSNUSTO.CNTL
>   WHEN *** APPEAR, PLEASE PRESS ENTER
>   TO TERMINATE SPF:
>       PRESS PF3    - RETURN TO CLIST WITH CHANGES
>       PRESS PF4    - RETURN TO CLIST WITH CHANGES THEN
>                      RETURN TO MAIN MENU
>       ENTER CANCEL - RETURN TO CLIST WITH NO CHANGES
```

```
EDIT ---- USERID1.DSNUSTO.CNTL
 COMMAND ===                                        SCROLL === CSR
****** ************************** TOP OF DATA ********************
000001 //JOB CARD ...
000005 //UTIL EXEC DSNUPROC,SYSTEM=DBXX,UID='USERID1',UTPROC=''
000006 //*
000007 //************************************************
000008 //*
000009 //*   GENERATING JCL FOR THE STOSPACE UTILITY
000010 //*   DATE:  01/01/88            TIME:  19:49:41
000011 //*
000012 //************************************************
000013 //*
000014 //DSNUPROC.SYSIN    DD   *
000015 STOSPACE STOGROUP (PROD001)
000016 //
****** ************************** BOTTOM OF DATA *****************
```

Contents of USERID1.DB2I.CONTROL.CARDS(STOSPACE):

```
STOSPACE STOGROUP (PROD001)
```

STOGROUP lists the storage group or storage groups for which information
is to be collected. The information collected is stored in the following Catalog
tables:

SYSIBM.SYSINDEXES   SYSIBM.SYSTABLESPACE   SYSIBM.SYSSTOGROUP

SPACE   SPACE   SPACE
                                              SPCDATE

Utility Example: <u>CHECK</u>

If you have some doubt that an index does not match the data, the CHECK
utility can be used to verify the index entries are in sync with the rows in the
table. If not, error messages are issued.

```
DB2 UTILITIES
===


Select from the following:

1 FUNCTION === EDITJCL (SUBMIT job, EDITJCL, DISPLAY, or TERMINATE)
2 JOB ID   === USERID1  (A unique job identifier string)
3 UTILITY  === CHECK    (LOAD,REORG,COPY,MERGECOPY,RECOVER,REPAIR,
                         RUNSTATS,STOSPACE,CHECK, or MODIFY)
4 CONTROL CARDS DATA SET    === DB2I.CONTROL.CARDS(CHECK)
5 RECDSN  (LOAD, REORG)    ===
6 DISCDSN (LOAD)           ===
7 COPYDSN (COPY, MERGECOPY) ===


To RESTART a utility, specify starting point, otherwise enter NO.
8 RESTART  === NO  (NO, At CURRENT position, or beginning of PHASE)

PRESS: ENTER to process     END to exit     HELP for more information
```

```
                        DSNU EXEC:
>   CHECK UTILITY REQUESTED WITH
>      CONTROL=NONE, EDIT=SPF, COPYDSN=**NOT REQUIRED**,
>      INDSN=USERID1.DB2I.CONTROL.CARDS(CHECK),
>      RECDSN=**NOT REQUIRED**, RESTART=NO,
>      SYSTEM=DBXX, SUBMIT=NO, UID=USERID1,
>      UNIT=SYSDA, VOLUME="OMITTED", DB2I=YES,
>      DISCDSN="OMITTED".
>   THE RESULTING JCL WILL BE WRITTEN TO DSNUCHE.CNTL
>SPF EDITING FACILITY INVOKED TO EDIT DSNUCHE.CNTL
>   WHEN *** APPEAR, PLEASE PRESS ENTER
>   TO TERMINATE SPF:
>      PRESS PF3    - RETURN TO CLIST WITH CHANGES
>      PRESS PF4    - RETURN TO CLIST WITH CHANGES THEN
>                     RETURN TO MAIN MENU
>      ENTER CANCEL - RETURN TO CLIST WITH NO CHANGES
```

```
EDIT ---- USERID1.DSNUCHE.CNTL
COMMAND ===                                        SCROLL === CSR
****** ******************** TOP OF DATA ************************
000001 //JOB CARD ...
000005 //UTIL EXEC DSNUPROC,SYSTEM=DBXX,UID='USERID1',UTPROC=''
000006 //*
000007 //************************************************
000008 //*
000009 //*  GENERATING JCL FOR THE CHECK UTILITY
000010 //*  DATE:  01/01/88          TIME:  19:50:17
000011 //*
000012 //************************************************
000013 //*
000014 //DSNUPROC.SORTWK01 DD DSN=USERID1.SORTWK01,
000015 //       DISP=(MOD,DELETE,CATLG),
000016 //       SPACE=(4000,(20,20),,,ROUND),
000017 //       UNIT=SYSDA
000018 //DSNUPROC.SORTWK02 DD DSN=USERID1.SORTWK02,
000019 //       DISP=(MOD,DELETE,CATLG),
000020 //       SPACE=(4000,(20,20),,,ROUND),
000021 //       UNIT=SYSDA
000022 //DSNUPROC.SORTWK03 DD DSN=USERID1.SORTWK03,
000023 //       DISP=(MOD,DELETE,CATLG),
000024 //       SPACE=(4000,(20,20),,,ROUND),
000025 //       UNIT=SYSDA
000026 //DSNUPROC.SORTWK04 DD DSN=USERID1.SORTWK04,
000027 //       DISP=(MOD,DELETE,CATLG),
000028 //       SPACE=(4000,(20,20),,,ROUND),
000029 //       UNIT=SYSDA
000030 //DSNUPROC.SYSUT1 DD DSN=USERID1.SYSUT1,
000031 //       DISP=(MOD,DELETE,CATLG),
000032 //       SPACE=(4000,(20,20),,,ROUND),
000033 //       UNIT=SYSDA
000034 //DSNUPROC.SORTOUT DD DSN=USERID1.SORTOUT,
000035 //       DISP=(MOD,DELETE,CATLG),
000036 //       SPACE=(4000,(20,20),,,ROUND),
000037 //       UNIT=SYSDA
000038 //DSNUPROC.SYSIN    DD  *
000039 CHECK INDEX NAME(X_AUTO_SALES)
000040          TABLESPACE DBDNAM01.SPACE004
000041          WORKDDN SYSUT1 SORTDEVT 3380 SORTNUM 4
000042 //
****** ************************ BOTTOM OF DATA ******************
```

Contents of USERID1.DB2I.CONTROL.CARDS(CHECK):

```
CHECK INDEX NAME(X_AUTO_SALES)
      TABLESPACE DBDNAM01.SPACE004
      WORKDDN SYSUT1 SORTDEVT (3380 SORTNUM 4
```

INDEX NAME is the index to be checked. If you are not the creator of the index, prefixed it with the creator.
TABLESPACE is the tablespace referenced by the index.
WORKDDN is the name of a temporary work file.
SORTDEVT is the direct-access device type to be used when allocating temporary datasets.
SORTNUM is the number of temporary datasets to be generated by the utility for sorting index entries. (Similar to LOAD and REORG)

Utility Example: MODIFY

MODIFY is used to remove unwanted information contained in the SYSIBM.SYSCOPY Catalog table pertaining to a tablespace. The corresponding information about the tablespace contained in SYSIBM.SYSLGRNG directory is also deleted. You can remove entries older than a certain date or entries older than a certain number of days.

```
                        DB2 UTILITIES
     Select from the following:
     1 FUNCTION === EDITJCL (SUBMIT job, EDITJCL, DISPLAY, or TERMINATE)
     2 JOB ID   === USERID1   (A unique job identifier string)
     3 UTILITY  === MODIFY    (LOAD, REORG, COPY, MERGECOPY, RECOVER, REPAIR,
                               RUNSTATS, STOSPACE, CHECK, or MODIFY)
     4 CONTROL CARDS DATA SET   === DB2I.CONTROL.CARDS(MODIFY)
     5 RECDSN  (LOAD, REORG)    ===
     6 DISCDSN (LOAD)           ===
     7 COPYDSN (COPY, MERGECOPY) ===
     To RESTART a utility, specify starting point, otherwise enter NO.
     8 RESTART  === NO  (NO, At CURRENT position, or beginning of PHASE)


     PRESS: ENTER to process     END to exit     HELP for more information
```

```
DSNU EXEC:
>  MODIFY UTILITY REQUESTED WITH
>     CONTROL=NONE, EDIT=SPF, COPYDSN=**NOT REQUIRED**,
>     INDSN=USERID1.DB2I.CONTROL.CARDS(MODIFY),
>     RECDSN=**NOT REQUIRED**, RESTART=NO,
>     SYSTEM=DBXX, SUBMIT=NO, UID=USERID1,
>     UNIT=SYSDA, VOLUME="OMITTED", DB2I=YES,
>     DISCDSN="OMITTED".
>  THE RESULTING JCL WILL BE WRITTEN TO DSNUMOD.CNTL
>SPF EDITING FACILITY INVOKED TO EDIT DSNUMOD.CNTL
>  WHEN *** APPEAR, PLEASE PRESS ENTER
>  TO TERMINATE SPF:
>     PRESS PF3    - RETURN TO CLIST WITH CHANGES
>     PRESS PF4    - RETURN TO CLIST WITH CHANGES THEN
>                    RETURN TO MAIN MENU
>     ENTER CANCEL - RETURN TO CLIST WITH NO CHANGES
```

```
EDIT ---- USERID1.DSNUMOD.CNTL
COMMAND ===                                      SCROLL === CSR
****** *************************** TOP OF DATA ********************
000001 //JOB CARD ...
000005 //UTIL EXEC DSNUPROC,SYSTEM=DBXX,UID='USERID1',UTPROC=''
000006 //*
000007 //************************************************
000008 //*
000009 //*   GENERATING JCL FOR THE MODIFY UTILITY
000010 //*   DATE:   01/01/88          TIME:   19:51:02
000011 //*
000012 //************************************************
000013 //*
000014 //DSNUPROC.SYSIN    DD   *
000015   MODIFY RECOVERY TABLESPACE DBDNAM01.SPACE001 DELETE
000016   AGE(880601)
000017 //
****** *************************** BOTTOM OF DATA *****************
```

Contents of USERID1.DB2I.CONTROL.CARDS(MODIFY):

```
MODIFY RECOVERY TABLESPACE DBDNAM01.SPACE001
DELETE DATE(880601)
```

TABLESPACE is the name of the tablespace for which information is to be
deleted.
DELETE specifies time frame for which entries are to be deleted.
DATE(880601) implies that all entries older than JUNE 1, 1988 are to be
deleted.
AGE(30) would imply that all entries older than 30 days are to be deleted.
The following utilities cannot be generated by DB2I.

DSNTIAUL — is an application program allowing the user to unload table
data. This utility has an advantage over DBMAUI in that it does not expand
numeric data types. This could drastically reduce unload record length if a lot
of numeric data types are defined for columns in the table. Like DBMAUI, it
has the capability to create the corresponding LOAD control cards for reloading the data unloaded.

```
//*
//************************************************************
//**    UNLOAD EMPLOYEES_TABLE.                            **
//************************************************************
//*
//UNLOAD EXEC PGM=IKJEFT01,DYNAMNBR=100
//SYSTSPRT DD SYSOUT=*
//SYSPRINT DD SYSOUT=*
//LISTING  DD SYSOUT=*
//SYSUDUMP DD SYSOUT=*
//SYSPUNCH DD DSN=USERID1.LOAD.CNTL,
//     DISP=(NEW,CATLG,DELETE),
//     DCB=(RECFM=FB,LRECL=80,BLKSIZE=6400),
//     SPACE=(TRK,(1,1)),
//     UNIT=DISK
//SYSREC00 DD DSN=USERID1.UNLOAD.EMPLOYEE.DATA,
//     DISP=(NEW,CATLG,DELETE),
//     SPACE=(TRK,(1,1)),
//     UNIT=DISK
//SYSREC01 DD DSN=USERID1.UNLOAD.AUTOSALE.DATA,
//     DISP=(NEW,CATLG,DELETE),
```

```
//       SPACE=(TRK,(1,1)),
//       UNIT=DISK
//SYSTSIN DD *
   DSN SYSTEM(DB39)
   RUN PROGRAM(DSNTIAUL) PLAN(DSNTIAU2) LIB('DBXX.RUNLIB.LOAD')
//SYSIN   DD *
   USERID1.EMPLOYEES_TABLE WHERE DEPT='D890' ORDER BY EMPLOYEE_NO
   AUTO_INS_SALES WHERE SALES_REGION = 'MIDWEST' ORDER BY YTD_SALES
//*
```

SYSPUNCH dataset will contain load control cards for the data unloaded.
SYSREC00 is the unload dataset for the first table specified in SYSIN.
SYSREC01 is the unload dataset for the second table specified in SYSIN.
SYSTSIN contains the DB2 commands to execute program DSNTIAUL
using Plan name DSNTIAU2. DBXX.RUNLIB.LOAD should be replaced by
the library containing the executable load module DSNTIAUL.
SYSIN contains the control cards describing which table and rows should
be unloaded. Only 72 characters can be specified for one statement. The
WHERE and ORDER BY clauses are allowed if desired. Whatever is coded for
the control statement is prefixed by SELECT * FROM when executed.

Output summary provided by program DSNTIAUL:

```
SUCCESSFUL UNLOAD 6 ROWS OF TABLE     USERID1.EMPLOYEES_TABLE
           WHERE DEPT='D890' ORDER BY EMPLOYEE_NO
SUCCESSFUL UNLOAD 2 ROWS OF TABLE     AUTO_INS_SALES
           WHERE SALES_REGION = 'MIDWEST' ORDER BY YTD_SALES
```

Contents of USERID1.LOAD.CNTL after execution:

```
LOAD DATA INDDN SYSREC00 INTO TABLE
     USERID1.EMPLOYEES_TABLE WHERE DEPT='D890' ORDER BY EMPLOYEE_NO
   (
   EMPLOYEE_NO        POSITION(      1          )
   INTEGER                        ,
   EMPLOYEE_NAME      POSITION(      5          )
   CHAR(                      16) ,
   ADDRESS_STATE      POSITION(     21          )
   CHAR(                       2) ,
   DEPT               POSITION(     23          )
   CHAR(                       4) ,
```

```
SALARY                POSITION(      27:        30)
DECIMAL
)
LOAD DATA INDDN SYSREC01 INTO TABLE
AUTO_INS_SALES WHERE SALES_REGION = 'MIDWEST' ORDER BY YTD_SALES
(
SALES_PERSON_NO       POSITION(       1              )
INTEGER                          ,
SALES_REGION          POSITION(       5              )
CHAR(                          9) ,
YTD_SALES             POSITION(      14:        18)
DECIMAL                          ,
BONUS                 POSITION(      19:        22)
DECIMAL
)
```

Contents of EMPLOYEES_TABLE from which data was to be unloaded:

EMPLOYEES_TABLE

EMPLOYEE NO	EMPLOYEE NAME	ADDRESS STATE	DEPT	SALARY
150	JONES	UT	D600	70000.00
175	MURPHY	IA	D900	40000.00
200	LARSON	IL	D890	60000.00
250	CASPER	MN	D890	70000.00
300	SMITH	WI	D900	50000.00
350	JORDAN	FL	D890	50000.00
400	BLACK	MO	D600	60000.00
450	NICKELS	OH	D500	35000.00
495	GREEN	ND	D700	40000.00
500	EINERSON	UT	D890	80000.00
550	WILLMORE	TX	D500	45000.00
600	GRAVES	CA	D890	30000.00
650	SMITH	NC	D500	40000.00
700	ROCKY	SC	D890	40000.00
750	GRAY	TX	D500	45000.00
850	NELSON	IL	D700	35000.00
900	SHANK	NY	D700	35000.00

Contents of AUTO_INS_SALES TABLE from which data was to be unloaded:

```
SALES
PERSON   SALES               YTD
NO       REGION              SALES        BONUS
-------  ---------   ------------  ----------
   415   MIDWEST        200000.00     2000.00
   350   SOUTHEAST      500000.00     5000.00
   800   MIDWEST        500000.00     5000.00
   425   NORTHEAST      750000.00     7500.00
   500   NORTHWEST     1000000.00    10000.00
```

```
B2 Column Name DB2 Data Type      Unload Position   Unload format
-------------- -------------      ------------------  -------------
ALES_PERSON_NO INTEGER      = Positions (1-4)    BINARY
ALES_REGION    CHAR         = Positions (5-13)   CHARACTER
TD_SALES       DECIMAL(9,2) = Positions (14,18)  PACKED DECIMAL
ONUS           DECIMAL(7,2) = Positions (19-22)  PACKED DECIMAL
```

Hex contents of USERID1.UNLOAD.AUTOSALE.DATA:

```
0000000001111111111212
1234567890123456789012     Unload data positions
----------------------
....MIDWEST   .........
0009DCCECEE44000000000
001F4946523002000C200C
----------------------
....MIDWEST   .........
0002DCCECEE44000000000
00304946523005000C500C
----------------------
```

```
B2 Column Name DB2 Data Type      Unload Position   Unload format
-------------- -------------      ------------------  -------------
MPLOYEE_NO     INTEGER      = Positions (1-4)    BINARY
MPLOYEE_NAME   CHAR         = Positions (5-20)   CHARACTER
DDRESS_STATE   CHAR         = Positions (21,22)  CHARACTER
EPT            CHAR         = Positions (23,26)  CHARACTER
ALARY          DECIMAL(7,2) = Positions (27-30)  PACKED DECIMAL
```

Hex Contents of USERID1.UNLOAD.EMPLOYEE.DATA:

```
000000000111111111122222222223
1234567890123456789012 34567890
------------------------------
...HLARSON          ILD890-...
000CDCDEDD4444444444CDCFFF6000
00083192650000000000934890000C
------------------------------
....CASPER          MND890....
000FCCEDCD4444444444DDCFFF7000
000A31275900000000000454890000C
------------------------------
...;JORDAN          FLD890&...
0005DDDCCD4444444444CDCFFF5000
001E16941500000000000634890000C
------------------------------
...4EINERSON        UTD890....
000FCCDCDEDD44444444EECFFF8000
00145955926500000000434890000C
------------------------------
....GRAVES          CAD890....
0005CDCECE4444444444CCCFFF3000
00287915520000000000314890000C
------------------------------
....ROCKY           SCD890 ...
000BDDCDE44444444444ECCFFF4000
002C96328000000000000234890000C
------------------------------
```

DSN1COPY — is a program quite useful in copying and moving DB2 tablespace or indexspace datasets. It does not run under DB2's control. As a result, it can be run even if DB2 is nonoperational. It works with either the tablespace or its backup. It can also be used to analyze pages in tablespaces and indexspaces for validity. It is used to expand tablespace and indexspace datasets unless storage groups are being used. If you are using storage groups, the primary and/or secondary quantity in the DB2 catalog needs to be altered (not yet available) in order to keep the expanded dataset through the reorganization or recovery processes. Currently, to change the primary and secondary allocation for storage groups, you need to drop the tablespace and recreate everything subordinate or do some tricky repairs on the catalog and directory.

Before this utility is executed, the tablespaces or indexspaces to be restored or copied should be stopped. Caution should be taken when using this utility since the DB2 safeguards are disabled when tablespaces and indexspaces are stopped.

In the following example, a copy of tablespace dataset SPACE001 on DB2 System (DBXX) will be restored to another DB2 System (DBYY). Before beginning, we need to inquire into the DB2 Catalog on each of the DB2 Systems to determine the internal identifiers assigned by DB2 for the required objects. It is because of these identifiers that moving copies directly or reorg unloads to other DB2 Systems are not allowed. The DSN1COPY utility has an option to translate the internal identifiers during the copy process. To determine the internal identifiers, you need to inquire into the SYSIBM.SYSTABLESPACE and SYSIBM.SYSTABLES tables in the DB2 Catalog. In the following examples, DBXX is the "from" or "source" DB2 System, and DBYY is the "to" or "target" DB2 System.

SOURCE SYSTEM (DBXX) :   SYSIBM.SYSTABLESPACE

NAME	CREATOR	DBNAME	DBID	PSID
SPACE001	USERID1	DBDNAM01	331	2

SOURCE SYSTEM (DBXX) :   SYSIBM.SYSTABLES

TSNAME	NAME	CREATOR	OBID
SPACE001	TEST_TABLE	USERID1	3

TARGET SYSTEM (DBYY) :   SYSIBM.SYSTABLESPACE

NAME	CREATOR	DBNAME	DBID	PSID
SPACE001	USERID1	DBDNAM01	309	2

TARGET SYSTEM (DBYY) :   SYSIBM.SYSTABLE

TSNAME	NAME	CREATOR	OBID
SPACE001	TEST_TABLE	USERID1	3

```
//STEP010   EXEC PGM=DSN1COPY,
//         PARM='FULLCOPY,OBIDXLAT,RESET,PRINT(1,5)'
//STEPLIB     DD DSN=load.library(DSN1COPY),DISP=SHR
//SYSUT1 DD DSN=DB2BKUP.DBDNAM01.SPACE001,
//         DISP=OLD,
//         UNIT=TAPE,
//         VOL=SER=volume1
//SYSUT2 DD DSN=DB2YY.DSNDBD.DBDNAM01.SPACE001.I0001.A001,
//         DISP=OLD
//SYSPRINT    DD SYSOUT=*
//****************************************************************
//**    FIRST RECORD IS  DATABASE IDENTIFIER.              **
//**    SECOND RECORD IS TABLESPACE OR INDEXSPACE IDENTIFIER  **
//**    THIRD AND FOLLOWING RECORDS ARE TABLE IDENTIFIERS.  **
//**                                                        **
//**  SOURCE OBJECTS          TARGET OBJECTS               **
//**     DBID=331                 DBID=309                 **
//**     PSID=2                   PSID=2                   **
//**     OBID=3                   OBID=3                   **
//****************************************************************
//SYSXLAT     DD
331 309
2 2
3 3
//UTPRINT     DD SYSOUT=*
//SYSUDUMP    DD SYSOUT=*
//*
```

PARM=FULLCOPY,OBIDXLAT,RESET,PRINT(1,5) is a parameter list indicating what the utility is to perform. FULLCOPY implies that a full copy of
the tablespace is being used. OBIDXLAT implies that translation of internal
identifiers will be occurring. The dataset specifying how the internal identifiers are to be translated is SYSXLAT. RESET will reset log RBAs in the
tablespace or index space being copied to. You should plan on running a DB2

opy after transferring if DB2 recovery will be needed. PRINT(1,5) signifies
ages 1 through 5 are to be dumped to print also.
SYSUT1 is the backup of SPACE001 taken on System DBXX.
SYSUT2 is the tablespace dataset on System DBYY where the file SYSUT1
; to be copied.
SYSXLAT is the dataset specifying how the internal object identifiers are to
e translated.

DSN1PRNT — will print the contents of DB2 tablespace and indexspace
ages. The contents can be printed even if located on a copy dataset or any
ataset created by DSN1COPY utility. You are allowed to specify a range of
ages to print or just pages containing specific characters. Like the
)SN1COPY utility, make sure the tablespace or indexspaces are stopped.

```
//************************************************************
//* *   DISPLAY CONTENTS OF TABLESPACE.                     *
//************************************************************
//     EXEC PGM=DSN1PRNT
//          PARM='PRINT(1,5),FORMAT'
//SYSUT1 DD DSN=DBXX.DSNDBD.DBDNAM01.XREMPLOY.I0001.A001,
//         DISP=SHR
//SYSPRINT DD SYSOUT=*
```

PARM values:

PRINT(n,m) for specifying a range of pages to be printed. Beginning
page=(n), ending page=(m).
VALUE(ccccc) where ccccc is a character string to be searched for, causes
all pages containing the character string to be printed.
FORMAT instructs the utility to provide a special format for the printed
pages. If the page contains an error, it will not be formatted.
NUMPARTS(n) identifies the number of partitions to be printed if the
utility is processing against an image copy dataset. If you recall, the copy
utility can copy one partition or all partitions of a tablespace.

Recovery Scenario

Let's assume the following events occurred against the table or tables in a
ablespace.

Event (A) — Full backup is taken, using SHRLEVEL=REFERENCE
Event (B) — Users interactively update and delete rows from the tables.
Event (C) — Batch program PROGRM1C performs mass updates on tabl
rows.
Event (D) — Head crash!

The recovery JCL for all of the following recoveries would be identical. Th
differences between the recoveries are contained in the control cards creater
Based on this, the following questions might be valid.

1. Can I restore to the point of the head crash so that the data appears jus
    as it did prior to the head crash?
    For the most part, Yes. You can recover up to the last unit of wor
    committed. If an application was updating during the head crash an
    was not issuing commits, the updates would have to be reapplied.
    Control Card:

    ```
    RECOVER TABLESPACE database.tablespace
    ```

2. Can I restore back to a previous image copy without applying any of th
    changes made since? All of the changes should be redone.
    Yes, you may. This is called recovering to a prior point of consistency
    If you have several tables needing to be kept in sync, copying them a
    at the same time will allow you to restore an entire application syster
    back to a specific point in time. This is considered a partial recovery. A
    full image copy will be required after the recovery before the tablespac
    can be updated.
    Control Card:

    ```
    RECOVER TABLESPACE database.tablespace
        TOCOPY copy-dataset-name
    ```

    or if copy-dataset-name not recorded in SYSIBM.SYSCOPY

    ```
    RECOVER TABLESPACE database.tablespace
        TOCOPY copy-dataset-name
            TOVOLUME volume-name
                TOSEQNO sequence-number
    ```

3. A program, PROGRM1C, performing mass updates contained severe logic errors. Can I roll the tables back to a point just prior to the program's execution and save all other updates made prior to the program executing?

This one is a little more difficult to do. You will have to find a log RBA (Relative Byte Address) prior to the program's execution. You can recover a tablespace up to but not including a specific log RBA. Once again, this is a partial recovery and will require a full image copy to follow.

Control Card:

```
RECOVER TABLESPACE database.tablespace
    TORBA X'log-relative-byte-address'
```

Questions:

1. Utility used to combine incremental image copies: _____
2. Parameter specified in copy utility to indicate the partition being backed up: _____
3. DB2 Subcommand used to display status of a database: _____
4. DB2 Subcommand used to display status of a utility: _____
5. To find out who has a resource locked and with what plan, you could execute the _____ and _____ subcommands.
6. The utility that updates the DB2 Catalog with information about your tablespaces and indexes: _____

True or False:

7. DB2 needs to be operational for all utilities generated by DB2I?
8. DSN1COPY can be used to transport data from one DB2 System to another?
9. Tablespace and index spaces can be removed from DB2's control by starting them in utility mode.
0. A failed utility should be terminated before restarting a specific phase.
1. Copying with SHRLEVEL=CHANGE allows users to be updating while the image copy is running.
2. In the load control cards, you need to specify the column data types.

Answers:

1. MERGECOPY
2. DSNUM
3. -DISPLAY DATABASE(database-name)
4. -DISPLAY UTIL(*)
5. -DISPLAY DATABASE(database-name) LOCKS, -DISPLAY THREAD
6. RUNSTATS
7. True
8. True
9. False, you need to issue the -STOP DATABASE command.
10. False, a terminated utility would not be restartable.
11. True
12. False, you only mention the column names of the table being loaded. All references to data types describe the input data.

8

DB2 Performance and Monitoring

The first thing that comes up in conversations concerning DB2 is performance. DB2 had some bad publicity early on and is still suffering the repercussions. One should be quick to note that every new release and round of maintenance contains performance improvements.

Why is it that some users of DB2 are having performance problems, while others are not? DB2 and relational concepts are still very new to most of the industry. The cookbook approach for developing high-performance applications of traditional database managers is not yet established for DB2. Instead, what you see are a series of guidelines that vary according to the application's requirements.

One of the difficult things for DB2 users to define is what good and bad performance is. With traditional database management systems, subsecond response times were considered a requirement. With DB2 subsecond response times can also be achieved. But now, an ad hoc query running for 10 minutes might be considered a good performer if it replaced a process that was taking 10 hours.

When discussing DB2 performance, more than just response time needs to be discussed. One should take into account how applications are to be developed to achieve good performance. Good performance begins with the design process. Improperly designed tables are one of the most difficult and expensive items to correct. Poorly designed tables can make writing good performing queries very difficult, if not impossible. One also needs to take into account the number of concurrent users and the types of locks to be issued by the applications. In addition, performance can be severely impacted by how query processing is performed. Efforts to improve query processing can vary from simply restructuring a query to the addition of temporary tables or creation of indexes. Another area where performance is important, but not always recognized, is in utility processing.

Although each application developed may have different processing requirements, much of the following information still applies.

PERFORMANCE TUNING THROUGH DESIGN: Items affecting performance begin in the design phase. The number of tables being joined, row size, primary key uniqueness, and whether or not the tables have been normalized all have a direct bearing on how well the pursuing applications will perform.

DATABASE: Applications issuing DDL (CREATE,DROP,ALTER) for tablespaces, tables, and indexes should have their own database. Some types of processing within a database are restricted until DDL query execution is completed. Dynamic SQL cannot be simultaneously performed with DDL execution. Likewise, binds cannot be performed or utilities executed during DDL execution. Since personal data is more susceptible to changes requiring DDL executions than shared data, it is a good idea to separate shared data from personal data at least by database.

If all tablespaces in the database are similar in usage, they can be stopped and started at the database level as opposed to the individual tablespace level. If an entire application system is contained in the same database, the entire system can be stopped or started with one DB2 command.

TABLESPACE: Unless very small tables are being developed, use the guideline of only one table per tablespace. Many of the utilities operate at the tablespace level, and thus when one table is being processed, all tables in the tablespace are unavailable. Also, locking of a table actually locks at the tablespace level, and once again all of the tables in the tablespace are impacted. Another reason to avoid placing more than one table in a tablespace is because of possible tablespace scans. If indexes are not used for a query, the entire tablespace is scanned. This implies that every row of every table is processed regardless of the table referenced in the query. One last reason is the space occupied by deleted tables in the tablespace. The space is not reclaimed until reorganization. If only one table resides in the tablespace, the tablespace can be deleted and redefined to reclaim unusable space.

Small interrelated tables are candidates to be placed in the same tablespace if there is high probability that the data needed for all tables will be retrieved in the same I/O. Thus the total I/Os would be reduced. Small control tables used almost exclusively for "read only" might be potential candidates to include into one tablespace. Caution: If you are planning on using the LOAD

REPLACE to reload tables contained in the same tablespace, don't. The LOAD REPLACE will delete all rows from all tables in the tablespace and replace with just the table being loaded.

You should attempt to keep all of the data in a tablespace within its primary allocation. Processing the data in secondary allocations tends to be more expensive.

Tables used for read only processing should have PCTFREE and FREEPAGE set to zero in both the tablespace and all associated indexes. This will allow more data to be retrieved per I/O. Applications having high random insert activity should have adequate free space available throughout the tablespace. The additional free space allows better clustering of rows by reducing the number of page overflows. Increasing the FREEPAGE and PCTFREE specifications is a technique used to reduce concurrent page lock problems. The more free space in a page, the less rows stored in the page and, thus, fewer rows are locked when a page is locked. The disadvantages of specifying free space in tablespaces are that more DASD is required and less data will be retrieved when a page is read.

Lock size of ANY can be used for most tablespaces. It defaults to page locks initially and if the total number of locks held exceeds your system-defined limit (NUMLKTS & NUMLKUS DSNZPARMS), the lock granularity is escalated from PAGE locks to TABLESPACE lock. NUMLKTS is a parameter set during installation and is used to limit the number of locks any one thread can hold against any one tablespace. NUMLKUS is a parameter set during installation limiting the number of locks any one user can have against all tablespaces. If applications should not be allowed to escalate to tablespace locks, choose the lock size of PAGE. Specifying PAGE locks on the tablespace will deny the executing applications the ability to escalate from page to tablespace locks. This does not imply applications cannot issue table locks explicitly. If only one user is accessing the tablespace at any given time, then by all means lock at the TABLESPACE level. This will reduce the additional overhead incurred by page locking.

If large tables are being developed, you may want to consider tablespace partitioning. Partitioning allows you to process one portion of a table independently of all other portions. You have the flexibility to reorg, copy, or recover at the partition level as well as at the tablespace level. There are some disadvantages of partitioning that should be taken into account. Clustering indexes are required for partitioned tablespaces, and thus an indexspace dataset will be created for each tablespace partition. Since clustering indexes determine in which partition rows are to be placed, you do not have the ability to redistribute data easily. You cannot arbitrarily add and delete partitions with ease.

Specifying CLOSE NO instead of CLOSE YES will improve the response times for applications opening and closing tablespace and indexspace datasets. Tablespace datasets defined with "CLOSE YES" are opened when accessed by a thread and closed when the last thread accessing the tablespace is terminated. The frequent opening and closing of the dataset not only adds to application response times, but also increases the amount of entries main tained in a DB2 System dataset called SYSIBM.SYSLGRGN with regard to what logs were available when the datasets were open.

It is much easier with the current release of DB2 to expand and move tablespace datasets if they are defined explicitly (Storage Group not used) Implicit ones (Storage Group used) require the tablespace to be dropped and recreated. This would include recreating all of the tables in the tablespace and their corresponding indexes and synonyms. Plus, the authority granted on the dropped objects would have to be regranted. Any plan invalidated by a dropped object should be rebound to eliminate an automatic rebind the first time the plan is accessed after having been invalidated. When an object that a plan depends on (such as table, index, etc.) is dropped, DB2 flags the plan as being invalid or, in other words, nonexecutable. When a user attempts to ac cess the invalid plan, DB2 tries to validate the plan (Automatic Rebind). If the dropped object was an index, DB2 will determine a new access strategy and continue on with the execution using the newly bound plan. There are two problems associated with the automatic rebind. First, the user has to wait for all of the bind functions to complete prior to the application being executed Second, you may not like the access method chosen. Since index usage may have been lost, you might prefer to have another index created prior to rebinding the application plan.

TABLES: Table design affects how efficiently queries can be constructed You should keep the table row length less than 4K. Rows larger than 4K are required to use 32K buffer pools. Consider splitting the table into multiple tables as opposed to exceeding the 4K row length.

On the other hand, eliminate tables used to look up a code's value when there is little to be gained from being in a separate table. If the table row length is less than 30 bytes, consider placing the code and its corresponding value in the base table. You can take advantage of SQL's set processing capabilities to maintain the codes. For example, changing department D980 in all instances to D988 could be done with the following update statement:

```
UPDATE EMPLOYEES_TABLE
    SET DEPT = 'D988'
    WHERE DEPT = 'D980'
```

When defining columns, consider NOT NULL WITH DEFAULT over NULL when data is not initially available. Not only is an extra byte included for nulls, but special handling of the null columns will be required as was noted in the application programming chapter. Be aware that NOT NULL WITH DEFAULT can have an effect on built-in functions, such as average. The fol lowing is an example of how two tables would produce different results depending on how the Grade column is defined. Table A has Grade defined as "null," while Table B has Grade defined as "not null with default."

	Table A		Table B
Name	Grade	Name	Grade
Jones	100	Jones	100
Smith	75	Smith	75
Doe	-	Doe	0
Average Grade	87.5	Average Grade	58.3

Minimize the use of variable-length columns unless you are saving an average of 20 bytes per row. Variable length columns should be placed at the end of the row. This allows the fixed-length columns to be accessed more efficiently. Be aware that if the row length increases because the variable column has increased in length and DB2 cannot find space for the updated row, the row will be stored in another page with sufficient space, and a pointer from the original page to the new page is created. Now at least two I/Os are required to access the row. If a variable character column is defined in an index, the index entry is padded to the maximum length of the column. As a result, you could end up having an index larger than the actual base table. Additional processing is also required by DB2 to handle variable character columns. DB2 has to issue two cross-memory calls as opposed to one for columns that are of fixed length and do not contain nulls. One is required to retrieve the length of the column and one to actually get the column value.

Efficiency can be improved by avoiding even-number specifications on DECIMAL columns. For example, a column's values appearing as 999999.99 would be best defined as DECIMAL(9,2) rather than DECIMAL(8,2). Be consistent with data types used in various tables. For example, if part number is a character length of 16 in one table and 12 in another, queries accessing both tables for the same part number run the risk of not being able to use an index when joining. When DB2 has to convert data types to be consistent, you run the risk of losing index usage.

Small tables with small row sizes can have lock concurrency problems. An alternative to coding free space in the tablespace is to pad the row length such that only one row will fit per page. Inserted rows will also benefit by being placed in their own page.

INDEXES: Indexes are created for two basic reasons: The first is for performance and the second is to enforce column uniqueness. Small tables (less than 15 pages) are not usually candidates to have indexes defined. If indexes are being created for a table, consider creating one as a clustering index. The

DB2 Optimizer greatly favors clustering indexes over all others in many cir
cumstances.

Start with a small number of subpages (1) and increase if concurrency
problems exist with the index. Although you can specify up to 16 subpages, it
might be more desirable to increase the number of free pages (FREEPAGE
and percent of each page to be left free (PCTFREE). This will force less index
entries to be contained in a subpage. As a result, concurrency is improved.

Specifying CLOSE NO and keeping data within its primary allocation ap
plies to indexes as well as tablespaces.

What columns should you index? The following are the most frequently
found in indexes:

1. Columns used to test for existence (NOT EXISTS, EXIST):

```
SELECT EMPLOYEE_NO FROM EMPLOYEES_TABLE A
  WHERE EMPLOYEE_NO NOT EXISTS
  (SELECT * FROM AUTO_LIF_SALES
    WHERE SALES_PERSON_NO = A.EMPLOYEE_NO
```

2. Columns used frequently as predicates in WHERE clauses:

```
SELECT EMPLOYEE_NO FROM EMPLOYEES_TABLE
  WHERE DEPT IN ('D500','D600','D890')
```

3. Columns used in JOINS:

```
SELECT EMPLOYEE_NO,YTD_SALES
  FROM EMPLOYEE_TABLE,AUTO_LIF_SALES
  WHERE EMPLOYEE_NO=SALES_PERSON_NO AND
  EMPLOYEE_NO=00010
  AND SALES_PERSON_NO = 00010
```

4. Columns used in ORDER BY:

```
SELECT EMPLOYEE_NO,DEPT FROM EMPLOYEES_TABLE
  WHERE DEPT IN ('D500','D600','D890')
  ORDER BY DEPT
```

5. Columns by which rows are frequently processed:

```
SELECT EMPLOYEE_NO,DEPT FROM EMPLOYEES_TABLE
WHERE DEPT BETWEEN 'D500' AND 'D890'
```

6. Columns frequently referenced with high cardinality that are most often referenced by =:

```
SELECT EMPLOYEE_NO,DEPT FROM EMPLOYEES_TABLE
WHERE EMPLOYEE_NO=&VAR AND DEPT='D980'
```

Use the Explain query to ensure that anticipated index usage is achieved. ndexes not referenced are strictly overhead. For seldom executed applications requiring index usage, consider creating indexes prior to running the application and removing when done. The additional overhead of maintaining he index between executions is avoided, even though it is more efficient to reate the indexes prior to loading.

If multiple columns are contained in an index and both columns are usually eferenced by =, place the column with the highest cardinality first in the ndex. This improves the probability that the index will be selected.

Once you have created an efficient access path, you can incorporate it into a iew and grant access to the view rather than the table. The view then serves he purpose of providing the best access to the data. Views can also be used to imit the amount of data transferred. Users specifying SELECT * against the iew could receive a much smaller subset of rows and columns than if issued gainst the base table.

QUERY STRUCTURING: Multiple queries can produce the same result but nay perform very differently in achieving the desired result. You have no irect control on index usage, only influence. Through the structuring of a uery you can influence the optimizer's decision as to whether an index is sable or not. There are five basic strategies used by the optimizer to access ata:

1. Tablespace scan
2. Matching index scan
3. Nonmatching index scan
4. Matching index scan without data reference
5. Nonmatching index scan without data references

Good performing queries are often those achieving the desired index usage. he following material contains tips to help you achieve index usage.

Keep updates to columns used in indexes to a minimum. An index containing the updated column cannot be used for the update. In the following example

```
UPDATE EMPLOYEES_TABLE
   SET SALARY = SALARY * 1.12
   WHERE SALARY > 30000
   AND DEPT='D890'
```

an index created on SALARY for this query is not usable, because updating SALARY would cause the index entry to be deleted and moved further down into the index. It would then be processed again, possibly creating a loop. However, an index on DEPT could be used if it does not also contain the column SALARY. It's a good idea to keep to a minimum the number of applications updating columns contained in indexes.

Avoid specifying not equal. It will cause a tablespace scan. For example:

```
SELECT * FROM EMPLOYEES_TABLE
   WHERE DEPT ^= 'D890'
```

If many items are contained in an IN list and index usage is not being considered, try using the BETWEEN. For example:

```
SELECT * FROM EMPLOYEES_TABLE
   WHERE EMPLOYEE_NO IN
   (00010,00011,00012,00013,00014,00015,00016)
```

could also be constructed accordingly

```
SELECT * FROM EMPLOYEES_TABLE
   WHERE EMPLOYEE_NO BETWEEN 00010 and 00016
```

and have a better chance of using a clustered index.

Can the query be written to use the UNION? For example,

```
SELECT * FROM EMPLOYEES_TABLE
   WHERE DEPT='D500' or DEPT='D600' or DEPT='D890'
```

could be constructed like the following to improve the probability of using an index on the DEPT column.

```
SELECT * FROM EMPLOYEES_TABLE
   WHERE DEPT='D500'
   UNION ALL
SELECT * FROM EMPLOYEES_TABLE
```

```
        WHERE DEPT='D600'
    UNION ALL
    SELECT * FROM EMPLOYEES_TABLE
        WHERE DEPT='D600'
```

Joins should be favored over subselects. For example:

```
SELECT EMPLOYEE_NO FROM EMPLOYEES_TABLE A
    WHERE EMPLOYEE_NO EXISTS
        (SELECT * FROM AUTO_LIF_INS
            WHERE SALES_PERSON_NO = A.EMPLOYEE_NO)
```

could be replaced by the following.

```
SELECT EMPLOYEE_NO
    FROM EMPLOYEES_TABLE, AUTO_LIF_INS
    WHERE EMPLOYEE_NO = SALES_PERSON_NO
```

Also, joins can usually outperform issuing the SELECTS individually. For example:

```
SELECT EMPLOYEE_NO,SALARY FROM EMPLOYEES_TABLE
    WHERE EMPLOYEE_NO = 00010
SELECT SALES_PERSON_NO,REGION FROM AUTO_LIF_INS
    WHERE SALES_PERSON_NO = 00010
```

could be replaced by the following.

```
SELECT EMPLOYEE_NO,SALARY,REGION
    FROM EMPLOYEES_TABLE,AUTO_LIF_INS
    WHERE EMPLOYEE_NO=SALES_PERSON_NUMBER
    AND  EMPLOYEE_NO = 00010 AND SALES_PERSON_NO = 00010
```

Explain all queries when index usage is expected.

Don't select columns you don't need. Executing a query sweeping an entire table and returning all columns in the row when just a few rows or columns are needed causes unnecessary CPU consumption. Each column retrieved requires DB2 to issue a cross-memory call.

Commit DDL (Data Definition Queries) as soon as possible to reduce Catalog contention and reduce the probability of deadlocks.

Avoid requesting DB2 to perform data conversions when comparing columns to other columns or constants. Make sure they are of the same data type, scale, and precision. Index usage may be ignored when data conversions are required. If you are comparing literal constants against a column, make sure they are the same length. Plus, avoid placing arithmetic expressions on columns where index usage is desired. For example, an index on YTD_SALES would not be used in the following:

```
SELECT SALES_PERSON_NO, YTD_SALES
    FROM AUTO_LIF_INS
    WHERE YTD_SALES = :HOSTVAR + 10000
```

PERFORMANCE TUNING FOR APPLICATION PROGRAMMING: If no other users are accessing the table during a program's execution, consider issuing the lock table statement to reduce CPU consumption caused by page locks.

Avoid using subroutines for I/O if possible. It is difficult to construct a query meeting the needs of many applications. As a result, there is a tendency to transfer more data, which also means more cross-memory calls. You may find that changing the SQL statements is more desirable than having application programs contain logic to discard unwanted columns and rows returned.

The parameters specified during the BIND process can have a major impact on the performance of your application program. VALIDATE at BIND time is preferred over VALIDATE at RUN time. The tables and columns will be checked for existence and the individual binder is checked to determine if he or she has the authority to execute the SQL statements contained in the program being prepared for execution. Validation at RUN time causes the validation process to be delayed until the first time the plan is accessed. The first user will then experience delays while the validation process is performed.

Use isolation level of CS (cursor stability) for higher concurrency. It should be used mainly by programs that read and process a row or rows only once. Use RR (repeatable read) when the application must process a row more than once. Applications that process a group of rows and then go back and update the rows based on information obtained should use RR. This ensures that the rows have not changed since the first time they were selected and that other applications have not placed locks on the rows previously selected.

Acquiring resources at allocation (ALLOCATE) and releasing them at deallocation (DEALLOCATE) is preferred for applications executing all of the queries contained in the program. Database descriptors describing objects used by the application are retrieved at thread creation. All tablespaces and indexspaces not already opened are opened. Freeing resources at deallocation time instructs DB2 to release the resources acquired when the thread is terminated.

Acquiring resources when used (USE) and releasing them at commit time COMMIT) is preferred for applications containing a lot of queries, but only a ew are executed in any one execution.

Thread creation cost is significant. For high transaction processing, you hould try to use an existing thread to avoid the high thread creation costs. This is what makes CICS and IMS attractive for processing high transaction volumes. Be careful when designing high volume transaction processing applications using TSO. A lot of the applications written operate in such a manner that each transaction is a new thread. To reduce thread creation costs, onsider having the program control the input and output of screens. In this manner the user can enter multiple transactions while using the existing hread.

Use static SQL over dynamic SQL whenever possible. Dynamic SQL has to go through the same BIND functions associated with static SQL for every execution. Dynamic SQL has to be read, verified, prepared for execution, authorization of the binder checked, and then executed. There is significant ost for the SQL flexibility associated to it. If you have to use dynamic SQL, avoid views if possible because SYSIBM.SYSTABLES and SYSIBM.SYS-COLUMNS are accessed once for the view and again for the base table.

Since cursors are used to process selects returning more than one row, consider saving information necessary to restart the application and committing occasionally. Frequently an application program will complete a logical unit of work, such as the processing of a sales order, and not have a need to keep the esources currently allocated or locked from others. Completing the processing for one sales order could represent a logical unit of work. The next sales order would signify another unit of work. By saving information to restart with the next sales order, you can then commit (which frees the locks held) and thus make the previous sales order available to other applications. Completion of the commit also provides you with a recoverable unit of work.

Declaring a SELECT ... FOR UPDATE OF avoids potential deadlocks with other applications processing concurrently, which would not be the case if you issued updates independent of the select. If performing multiple row updates and deletes, issuing queries to do set processing is the most efficient. Cursors would be the next choice followed by multiple update and delete statements. If the column you are updating is contained in an index, you may want to consider deleting the row and reinserting it. Unless the update can use another index, a scan would be required.

Finally, explain all queries in the application plan to ensure that the appropriate access methods were chosen or have not changed since the last execution.

PERFORMANCE TUNING FOR UTILITY PROCESSING: An area often overlooked as far as making performance improvements is the area of utility processing. When you consider how much time is actually spent processing utilities, you can see how it could have a major impact on your processing cost. In the course of migrating to relational systems, you will often encounter the need to load data into DB2 tables on both a permanent and temporary basis.

The load utility can be used to load data into DB2 tables in a more efficient manner than the corresponding SQL insert statements. You can load data into empty tables as well as existing ones. When large volumes of data are to be loaded, you can enhance the load process by specifying LOG NO. DB2 will not log the inserts and thus omit the excessive logging that would have been done with LOG YES. Specifying LOG YES could potentially flood the DB2 logs. Even with LOG NO, the load utility is still restartable. Since the rows loaded are not logged by DB2, you are required to run a COPY with SHRLEVEL REFERENCE before the tables can be updated.

If you have a unique index defined on a table being loaded, make sure you remove all duplicate rows. DB2 does not prevent duplicates from being loaded because the rows are inserted before the indexes are updated.

If a clustered index has been defined, sort the load data by the clustering index columns. By doing this, the rows will be physically stored in the same sequence as the index. The DB2 Optimizer will be able to make better access path selections.

You can load existing data into a table by specifying RESUME YES. Assuming that indexes are defined, this can still be efficient if the data loaded has a key value higher than the previously loaded data. If not, you may want to unload the existing data, merge in the new data, sort, and load using the REPLACE option providing only one table per tablespace. The replace option allows you to refresh an existing table with new data. You do not have to drop the table, tablespace, or indexes. The previously loaded data is replaced (not merged) with the new data.

If you are planning mass deletes, consider unloading the rows to be kept and reloading with the replace option. Since the delete query is one of the more expensive queries, this could save considerable amounts of resources.

When indexes are defined for tables being loaded or reorganized, temporary datasets are created to handle the index processing. SYSUT1, SORTOUT, and the sort work files SORTWKn should be allocated in cylinders and blocked at half track for large table loads and reorganizations.

If partitioned tablespaces are being loaded, all of the partitions are unavailable during the load processing. You can reorganize, copy, and recover by individual partitions, but, like the load, all partitions are unavailable until the utility processing has completed.

The block size used for the backup dataset created by the COPY utility can be increased. It needs to be a multiple of two. If the medium used for the backup is cartridge or tape, consider increasing the block size to 16,384 for 3380s.

Don't arbitrarily assume RUNSTATS and REORG utilities need to be executed without first determining what impact they will have. Utilities, in general, make data unavailable to the applications. When running these utilities against large tables, they can be expensive and time consuming. You may find situations where only an index needs to be reorganized, rather than an entire table.

PERFORMANCE MONITORING: Monitoring the applications running on a DB2 system can require the use of many different tools. The first such tool is the -DISPLAY command. The -DISPLAY THREAD command can be used to display the status of a thread or connection to DB2. Coupled with the -DISPLAY DATABASE command, you can determine what plan a particular user is executing and the kind of locks held on the tablespace and indexspace datasets. For monitoring utilities, the -DISPLAY UTIL command is very useful in following the progress of a large load or reorg. It provides information on which of the several phases are currently being executed. In the UNLOAD and RELOAD phases, the number of rows processed is recorded and made available to the DB2 command processor.

The EXPLAIN statement is an excellent tool to analyze a query prior to execution. It displays the access method to be used, what indexes if any will be used, the order in which tables and composite tables are accessed, the order in which multiple tables will be joined, which of the join methods will be used, whether the sort needs to be invoked, and the type of locks to be issued. All queries where index usage is expected should be explained. On large tables, even ad hoc queries should be carefully coded and checked with the EXPLAIN. This reduces the risk of surprises.

The RUNSTATS utility records detailed information about tablespaces and indexes in the DB2 Catalog, while the STOSPACE utility records information about storage groups. From this information you can determine from the DB2 Catalog:

1. What percentage of the rows have been relocated from where they were originally placed in a table. Runstats must have previously been executed for the tablespace and in the following example the tablespace must contain at least one thousand rows. Consider reorganizing the tablespace if more than 10% of the rows have been moved from where they were originally placed. NEARINDREF indicates how many rows were relocated near the page where they were initially placed. FARINDREF indicates how many rows were relocated far from the page where they were initially placed.

```
SELECT TSNAME, NEARINDREF, FARINDREF, CARD,
         (NEARINDREF+FARINDREF) * 100 / CARD
    FROM SYSIBM.SYSTABLEPART
       WHERE CARD > 1000
       ORDER BY 5 DESC
```

2. To determine the number of times the next row fetched will be in another page, execute the following select. NEAROFFPOS indicates the number of times the row would be fetched from a page nearby and FAROFFPOS indicates the number of times the next row fetched has been placed in a page far away.

```
SELECT IXNAME, NEAROFFPOS, FAROFFPOS, CARD,
           FAROFFPOS*100/CARD
    FROM SYSIBM.SYSINDEXPART
    WHERE CARD > 1000
    ORDER BY 5 DESC 3.
```

3. Find tables where more than 5 percent of the rows are not in the same sequence as their clustered index.

```
SELECT NAME, TBNAME
    FROM SYSIBM.SYSINDEXES
        WHERE CLUSTERING = 'Y' AND CLUSTERED = 'N'
```

4. Find tablespaces where over 10 percent of the space is occupied by deleted rows.

```
SELECT TSNAME, DBNAME, PERCDROP
    FROM SYSIBM.SYSTABLEPART
    WHERE PERCDROP > 10
    ORDER BY PERCDROP DESC
```

Not all performance problems can be resolved from the preceding. Occasionally a problem will arise where everything appears to be designed correctly. In situations such as this, you may have to rely on DB2 traces. This is not something that should be done on a regular basis, because there is increased CPU usage associated with tracing. There are four types of traces available:

1. Accounting Trace can be used for tuning a specific program.
2. Statistics Trace is used to tune the entire DB2 System.
3. Performance Trace is designed to monitor specific components of the DB2 System.
4. Global Trace is used in conjunction with servicing the DB2 system. It tracks entry and exits from the various DB2 modules.

The use of traces should be restricted to trained individuals. Seldom is a race of every event desired or even needed. One needs to take into account he features to be traced and schedule the corresponding type of trace in the east disruptive manner possible.

Questions:

1. Indexes are created primarily for _____ and _____.
2. FREEPAGE and PCTFREE should be set to _____ for read only tables.
3. Applications executing a small portion of the SQL contained in the program should allocate resources at _____ time and release resources at _____ time.
4. _____ _____ provides more concurrency than Repeatable Read (RR).
5. Tablespaces with CLOSE YES are closed when the last _____ allocated to the tablespace has been terminated.
6. The _____ can be used to determine index usage prior to the query being executed.

True or False:

7. Columns used in Joins are candidates for being included in an index.
8. Plans should be validated at RUN time to avoid delays when the plan is executed by a user.
9. Static SQL should be coded in application programs rather than dynamic SQL if possible.
10. The Runstats utility records information about tablespaces and indexes in the DB2 Catalog.
11. The STOSPACE utility records information about plans in the DB2 Catalog.
12. Stopping a database stops all of the tablespaces and indexes associated with the database.

Answers:

1. Performance and Column uniqueness
2. Zero
3. USE, COMMIT
4. CS or Cursor Stability
5. Thread
6. EXPLAIN
7. True
8. False; At Bind time
9. True
10. True

11. False; Storage groups
12. True

9

DB2 Security and Authorizations

DB2's security structure has changed very little since first being introduced. Computer auditing and security personnel have struggled addressing two basic issues when administering security. The first is that no audit trail is provided by DB2 to keep track of the security administered. As a result, other vendors introduced applications not only to administer security but also to construct audit trails. The second issue deals with administrative privileges having access to the data.

The GRANT and REVOKE SQL statements control the creation of and access to all DB2 resources. The structure to administer security within DB2 is much like a hierarchy. Each level of the hierarchy has less authority than the previous level. DB2 allows certain privileges to be grouped for administrative purposes, as shown in Figure 9-1. Before you can execute a CREATE query, you first must have the authority to create the object specified in the SQL statement. You cannot grant authority to use an object until the object has been created. The creator of the DB2 object always has the ability to use the created object. Before anyone else can use the object, authority to access it must also be granted. For example, before you can create a table in someone else's database, you must have the privilege to create tables in the database along with the authority to access tablespaces in which the tables are to be placed.

The creator of a DB2 object initially determines who can access the created object. This can take place in one of two formats. The first consists of granting the privilege to another without allowing them to pass the privilege on. The

PRIVILEGES ASSOCIATED WITH ADMINISTRATIVE AUTHORITIES

. SYSADM
. DBADM
. DBCTRL
. DBMAINT
. SYSOPR

Install DB2

Super-SYSADM

SYSADM: Perform, access and grant the following
  Grant bind function for application development (BINDADD)
  Recover BSDS (BSDS)
  Create new databases with DBADM control (CREATEDBA)
  Create new databases with DBCTRL control (CREATEDBC)
  Create storage groups (CREATESG)
  Execute STOSPACE utility (STOSPACE)

authority over databases   authority over DB2 System

DBADM: Total authority within database including access
  Alter tablespace, table, index (ALTER)
  Delete rows from all tables in DB (DELETE)
  Create indexes on tables in DB (INDEX)
  Insert rows into database tables (INSERT)
  Select rows from tables in DB (SELECT)
  Update rows in DB tables (UPDATE)

DBCTRL: Control database without access to data
  Drop database (DROP)
  Run table load utility for tables (LOAD)
  Recover tablespaces and indexes (RECOVERDB)
  Reorg tablespaces in database (REORG)
  Repair tablespaces and indexes (REPAIR)

DBMAINT: Maintain database functions
  Create tables in database (CREATETAB)
  Create tablespaces in DB (CREATETS)
  Display database status (DISPLAYDB)
  Image Copy tablespaces (IMAGCOPY)
  Start database for processing (STARTDB)
  Execute Runstats & Check Util (STATS)
  Issue database stop command (STOPDB)

SYSOPR: System Operator
  Issue Display commands (DISPLAY
  Recover indoubt threads (RECOVER)
  Issue the stop DB2 command (STOPALL)
  Issue the start and stop trace commands (TRACE)

Figure 9-1 DB2 Administrative Authorities

second format consists of granting the privilege to another, allowing them to pass the privilege on to others. The later format contains a WITH GRANT OPTION. If the privilege to use or access an object is global in nature, the keyword PUBLIC can be used as opposed to specifying a list of individuals.

The GRANT statement is used to establish privileges, while the REVOKE is used to remove the privileges granted. DB2 privileges have been organized into five areas. They are Database Privileges, Plan Privileges, System Privileges, Table Privileges, and Use Privileges. Each of these areas will be discussed.

Upon the successful completion of the Grant statement, information pertaining to the privileges granted are recorded in the DB2 Catalog authorization tables. The corresponding tables containing this information are:

```
SYSIBM.SYSCOLAUTH
SYSIBM.SYSDBAUTH
SYSIBM.SYSPLANAUTH
SYSIBM.SYSRESAUTH
SYSIBM.SYSTABAUTH
SYSIBM.SYSUSERAUTH
```

An authorization table contains rows consisting of columns that reflect the various privileges granted to an individual. The columns contain one of the following values:

' ' = privilege not granted
'Y' = privilege has been granted, but cannot be passed to others
'G' = privilege has been granted and the individual has the authority to pass this privilege on to others

GRANT DATABASE PRIVILEGES: These are privileges used to control the creation and management of objects associated to a database. The associated objects are tablespaces and tables. The individual performing the grant is recorded as the GRANTOR in the appropriate DB2 Catalog tables. The person receiving the privilege is recorded as the GRANTEE. The format for granting database privileges follows.

```
GRANT DBADM,
      DBCTRL,
      DBMAINT,
      CREATETAB,
      CREATETS,
      DISPLAYDB,
      DROP,
      IMAGCOPY,
      LOAD,
```

```
                    RECOVERDB,
                    REORG,
                    REPAIR,
                    STARTDB
                    STATS,
                    STOPDB
                ON DATABASE database-name TO userid1, ... ,useridn
or
                ON DATABASE database-name TO PUBLIC
or
                ON DATABASE database-name TO userid1, ... ,useridn
                    WITH GRANT OPTION
```

DBADM through STOPDB are considered authorization specifications. You will need to determine which authorization specifications meet your needs. Descriptions of the authorization specifications follow:

CREATETAB — Allows the grantee to create new tables in the named database. The grantee will also need the ability to create a tablespace to place the table in or the use of an existing tablespace in the database.
CREATETS — Allows grantee to create new tablespaces in the named database.
DISPLAYDB — Allows the grantee to issue the DISPLAY DATABASE command. The DISPLAY command can be used to display the current status of the tablespaces and indexspaces in the database.
DROP — Allows the grantee to issue SQL that will drop the database.
IMAGCOPY — Allows the grantee to run the copy utility for tablespaces contained in the database.
LOAD — Allows the grantee to execute the load utility for tables in the named database.
RECOVERDB — Allows grantee to recover the tablespaces and indexes associated to the named database.
REORG — Allows the grantee to execute reorganization utilities for tablespaces and indexes in the named database.
REPAIR — Allows the grantee to execute the REPAIR utility against tablespaces and indexes.
STARTDB — Allows grantee to issue the DB2 START DATABASE command. This goes hand in hand with the DB2 DISPLAY DATABASE and STOP DATABASE commands.
STATS — Allows the grantee to execute the RUNSTATS and CHECK utilities against tablespaces and indexes contained in the named database.
STOPDB — Allows the grantee to issue the STOP DATABASE command.

All of the previous authorization specifications serve one specific function. The last three authorization specifications are designed for granting multiple authorization privileges to an individual.

DBADM — Allows the grantee to perform all of the privileges allowed by the previous authorizations for the named database. Someone could obtain total authority over a database without creating it by receiving DBADM authority. In order to create a database, one has to have CREATEDBA authority. DBADM authority only pertains to an already existing database. The creator of the database automatically receives DBADM authority over any database he or she creates.

DBCTRL — Is the same as DBADM, except the grantee does not have access to the data in the tables.

DBMAINT — Allows the grantee to perform only the functions that are read only. This authority is reserved for individuals allowed to execute COPY and RUNSTATS utilities. Omitted are the RECOVERDB, REORG, DROP, LOAD, and REPAIR authorizations.

Examples:

When a database is created, a row is inserted into SYSIBM.SYSDBAUTH. In this row, the grantor and grantee are the same as the individual that created the database. The following items have been numbered for reference in a following report.

Database DBDNAM01 was created by USERID1.

```
(0)    CREATE DATABASE DBONAME01 USING STOGROUP PROD0001
```

USERID1 can grant DBADM authority to USERID2 for database DBDNAM01:

```
(1)    GRANT DBADM ON DATABASE DBDNAM01 TO USERID2
       WITH GRANT OPTION
```

USERID1 grants Database Control authority to USERID3.

```
(2)    GRANT DBCTRL ON DATABASE DBDNAM01 TO USERID3
```

USERID1 grants Database Maintenance authority to USERID4.

```
(3)    GRANT DBMAINT ON DATABASE DBDNAM01 TO USERID4
```

USERID1 grants functions individually. In this example, the create tablespace, create table, and load are to be granted separately.

```
(4)    GRANT CREATETS,CREATETAB,LOAD ON DATABASE DBDNAM01 TO
       USERID5
```

Since USERID2 has DBADM with grant option, USERID2 can grant the same privilege to others.

(5)   GRANT DBADM ON DATABASE DBDNAM01 TO USERID6,USERID7
       WITH GRANT OPTION

USERID7 has the authority to grant privileges to others. The privileges can be granted individually if desired, as in the following:

(6)   GRANT STOPDB,STARTDB ON DATABASE DBDNAM01 TO USERID8

Table SYSIBM.SYSDBAUTH can be inquired to view the privileges granted on a database. The following select was constructed to view the database privileges granted on database DBDNAM01 as a result of the previous examples.

```
SELECT GRANTOR,GRANTEE,NAME,DATEGRANTED,TIMEGRANTED,
CREATETABAUTH,CREATETSAUTH,DBADMAUTH,DBCTRLAUTH,
DBMAINTAUTH,DISPLAYDBAUTH,DROPAUTH,IMAGCOPYAUTH,
LOADAUTH,REORGAUTH,RECOVERDBAUTH,REPAIRAUTH,STARTDBAUTH,
      STATSAUTH,STOPAUTH
   FROM SYSIBM.SYSTABAUTH
      WHERE NAME='DBDNAM01'
      ORDER BY DATEGRANTED,TIMEGRANTED
```

```
                                    C C       D
                                    R R       I   I               R
                                    E E       D S M       R   S U
                                    A A   D B P A       E R T N
                                    T T D B M L G   R C E A S
                                    E S B C A A D C L E O P R T S
                                    T P A T I Y R O O V A T A T
                        DATE   TIME A A D R N D O P A R E I D T O
GRANTOR GRANTEE       GRANTED GRANTED B C M L T B P Y D G R R B S P
------- -------       ------- ------- - - - - - - - - - - - - - - -

USERID1 USERID1       880203 14131429 G G G G G G G G G G G G G G G (0)

USERID1 USERID2       880228 10103484 G G G G G G G G G G G G G G G (1)

USERID1 USERID3       880331 10105881 Y Y   Y Y Y Y Y Y Y Y Y Y Y Y (2)

USERID1 USERID4       880331 10112499 Y Y   Y Y   Y       Y Y Y (3)

USERID1 USERID5       880331 10121210 Y Y           Y           (4)

USERID2 USERID6       880428 10103484 G G G G G G G G G G G G G G G (5)
USERID2 USERID7       880428 10103484 G G G G G G G G G G G G G G G (5)

USERID7 USERID8 DBDNAM01 880530 10121210                   Y   Y (6)
```

GRANT PLAN PRIVILEGES: In Chapter 6, we discussed the steps required to prepare a program for execution. One of these steps consisted of binding the application. The output of the bind process is a PLAN. The ability to execute a program containing SQL statements is controlled by granting and revoking execution privileges on the PLAN. The privileges can be divided into two areas. The first centers around who can execute the application PLAN, and the second focuses on who can maintain the application PLAN or perform rebinds. The format for granting these privileges is as follows.

For execution of the application:

```
GRANT EXECUTE ON PLAN plan-name1, ... ,plan-namen
                TO useridl, .... ,useridn
```
or
```
GRANT EXECUTE ON PLAN plan-name1, ... ,plan-namen
                TO PUBLIC
```
or
```
GRANT EXECUTE ON PLAN plan-name1, ... ,plan-namen
                TO useridl, ... ,useridn
                WITH GRANT OPTION
```

For maintenance of the application:

```
GRANT BIND     ON PLAN plan-name1, ... ,plan-namen
                TO useridl, .... ,useridn
```
or
```
GRANT BIND     ON PLAN plan-name1, ... ,plan-namen
                TO PUBLIC
```
or
```
GRANT BIND     ON PLAN plan-name1, ... ,plan-namen
                TO useridl, ... ,useridn
                WITH GRANT OPTION
```

Plan-name(1 – n) are the names of the application plans upon which execution or rebind privileges are being granted.

Userid(1 – n), depending on the function being granted, is the list of users who can either execute the application plan or perform maintenance (rebind) to the plan.

Examples:

```
(0)  Original plan was created by USERID1.
(1)  GRANT EXECUTE ON PLAN PROGRM1C,PROGRM1P,PROGRM1F TO PUBLIC
(2)  GRANT EXECUTE ON PLAN PROGRM1C,PROGRM1P TO USERID2,USERID3
(3)  GRANT EXECUTE ON PLAN PROGRM1C,PROGRM1P TO USERID3,USERID4
                WITH GRANT OPTION
```

```
(4)  GRANT BIND ON PLAN PROGRM1C,PROGRM1P TO USERID5,USERID6
(5)  GRANT BIND ON PLAN PROGRM1C,PROGRM1P TO USERID5,USERID6
        WITH GRANT OPTION
```

Table SYSIBM.SYSPLANAUTH can be inquired for information pertaining to plan grants.

```
SELECT GRANTOR,GRANTEE,NAME,DATEGRANTED,TIMEGRANTED
             ,BINDAUTH,EXECUTEAUTH
       FROM SYSIBM.SYSPLANAUTH
       WHERE NAME LIKE 'PROGRM1%'
```

GRANTOR	GRANTEE	PLAN NAME	DATE GRANTED	TIME GRANTED	BIND AUTH	EXECUTE AUTH	
USERID1	USERID1	PROGRM1F	871002	22224707	G	G	(0)
USERID1	USERID1	PROGRM1P	871002	22295702	G	G	(0)
USERID1	USERID1	PROGRM1C	871002	22143850	G	G	(0)
USERID1	PUBLIC	PROGRM1C	871031	10384212		Y	(1)
USERID1	PUBLIC	PROGRM1P	871031	10384212		Y	(1)
USERID1	PUBLIC	PROGRM1F	871031	10384212		Y	(1)
USERID1	USERID2	PROGRM1P	871031	10391519		Y	(2)
USERID1	USERID3	PROGRM1P	871031	10391519		Y	(2)
USERID1	USERID2	PROGRM1C	871031	10391519		Y	(2)
USERID1	USERID3	PROGRM1C	871031	10391519		Y	(2)
USERID1	USERID3	PROGRM1P	871031	10394131	G		(3)
USERID1	USERID4	PROGRM1C	871031	10394131	G		(3)
USERID1	USERID3	PROGRM1P	871031	10394131	G		(3)
USERID1	USERID4	PROGRM1C	871031	10394131	G		(3)
USERID1	USERID5	PROGRM1C	871031	10401838		Y	(4)
USERID1	USERID6	PROGRM1C	871031	10401838		Y	(4)
USERID1	USERID5	PROGRM1P	871031	10401838		Y	(4)
USERID1	USERID6	PROGRM1P	871031	10401838		Y	(4)
USERID1	USERID5	PROGRM1C	871031	10404449		G	(5)
USERID1	USERID6	PROGRM1C	871031	10404449		G	(5)
USERID1	USERID5	PROGRM1P	871031	10404449		G	(5)
USERID1	USERID6	PROGRM1P	871031	10404449		G	(5)

If the plan/program will be executed from IMS, consider granting execute to the public. You may then use your existing IMS security scheme for controlling all access.

GRANT SYSTEM PRIVILEGES: These are privileges pertaining to DB2 system resources and their creation, as opposed to privileges on databases or applications. The system privileges determine who can create databases and issue BIND commands for new applications and thus control the application development process. They also control who can create storage groups, perform system traces, plus stop and start the DB2 system.

The following is the format for granting system privileges:

```
GRANT SYSADM,
      SYSOPER,
      BINDADD,
      BSDS,
      CREATEDBA,
      CREATEDBC
      CREATESG,
      DISPLAY,
      RECOVER,
      STOPALL,
      STOSPACE,
      TRACE
   TO useridl, ... ,useridn
```

or

```
   TO useridl, ... ,useridn WITH GRANT OPTION
```

or

```
   TO PUBLIC
```

SYSADM through TRACE are considered authorization specifications. Pick the authorization specifications that meet your needs. The authorization specification descriptions follow:

BINDADD — Implies the grantee can issue the BIND command and thus create new application plans.

BSDS — Allows the grantee to recover the boot strap data set which contains an inventory of all DB2 system logs.

CREATEDBA — Allows the grantee to create new databases. The creator will automatically obtain DBADM authority over the created database.

CREATEDBC — Allows the grantee to create new databases, but the grantee will only have DBCTRL authority over the database.

CREATESG — Allows the grantee to create new storage groups. By being the creator of the storage group, the grantee will also be able to add and remove volumes from the storage group.

DISPLAY — Allows the grantee to issue the DISPLAY commands to monitor the DB2 system. The grantee will be able to display all threads to DB2 from other MVS subsystems, as well as the status of all databases.

RECOVER — Allows the grantee to recover threads to other subsystems when one or more of the connecting subsystems failed and left the status of a thread in doubt.
STOPALL — Grantee can issue the STOP DB2 command to stop all processing on the DB2 system.
TRACE — Grantee can issue the START TRACE and STOP TRACE commands to assist in gathering information for resolving problems.

Should an individual need all or some of the above authorization specifications, then the following may be used:

SYSADM — A person granted this authority has control over all authority. This is a very powerful level and should be restricted to as few people as possible. Accountability for these individuals must be high. An individual with this authority can delete any object or inquire into any table.
SYSOPER — recipients of this authority can issue system operation commands such as DISPLAY, STOPALL, RECOVER, and TRACE. They are not allowed access to tables, nor can they create DB2 objects.

Examples:

```
(0)    Assuming USERID1 has SYSADM privileges, the following
       may be issued.
(1)    GRANT SYSADM TO USERID2
(2)    GRANT DISPLAY TO PUBLIC
(3)    GRANT CREATEDBA TO USERID2,USERID3 WITH GRANT OPTION
(4)    GRANT BINDADD TO PUBLIC


SYSIBM.SYSUSERAUTH:
SELECT GRANTOR, GRANTEE
     , DATEGRANTED, TIMEGRANTED
     , ALTERBPAUTH, BINDADDAUTH
     , BSDSAUTH, CREATEDBAAUTH
     , CREATEDBCAUTH, CREATESGAUTH
     , DISPLAYAUTH, RECOVERAUTH, STOPALLAUTH
     , STOSPACEAUTH, SYSADMAUTH, SYSOPRAUTH
     , TRACEAUTH
FROM SYSIBM.SYSUSERAUTH
WHERE GRANTOR = USER
```

```
                                  C C
                                  R R C           S
                                  E E R D R S T
                                  A A E I E T O S S
                                  T T A S C O S Y Y T
                                  E D B E E T P O P P S S R
                                  R A S D D E L V A A A O A
                  DATE    TIME    B D D B B S A E L C D P C
GRANTOR GRANTEE GRANTED GRANTED   P D S A C G Y R L E M R E
------- ------- ------- --------- - - - - - - - - - - - - -

USERID1 USERID1 871031  10470429  G G G G G G G G G G G G G  (0)

USERID1 USERID2 871031  11060429                      Y      (1)

USERID1 PUBLIC  871031  11070423                    Y        (2)

USERID1 USERID2 880103  12130303            G                (3)
USERID1 USERID3 880103  12130303            G                (3)

USERID1 PUBLIC  880213  09091411  Y                          (4)
```

GRANT TABLE PRIVILEGES: By far the bulk of the DB2 privileges granted will be on the actual table or view. This is performed through table grant privileges. Privileges granted against tables can be done at the table level or on a column-by-column basis. You may grant the privileges to an individual or individuals or all. The format for granting table privileges follows:

```
        GRANT ALL PRIVILEGES ON TABLE tablename1, ... ,tablenamen,
                                      ,viewname1, ... ,viewnamen
                TO userid1, ... ,useridn
or
        GRANT ALL PRIVILEGES ON TABLE tablename1, ... ,tablenamen,
                                      ,viewname1, ... ,viewnamen
                TO userid1, ... ,useridn  WITH GRANT OPTION
or
        GRANT ALTER,DELETE,INDEX,INSERT,SELECT,UPDATE
                ON TABLE tablename1, ... ,tablenamen,
                                      ,viewname1, ... ,viewnamen
                TO userid1, ... ,useridn
or
        GRANT ALTER,DELETE,INDEX,INSERT,SELECT,UPDATE
                ON TABLE tablename1, ... ,tablenamen,
                                      ,viewname1, ... ,viewnamen
                TO userid1, ... ,useridn  WITH GRANT OPTION
```

Tablename(1 – n) is the list of tables to which access is being granted. Tables and views can be granted simultaneously in the same grant. *Viewname(1 – n)* is the list of views for which access is to be granted.

Userid(1 – n) is the list of grantees to receive the authority. PUBLIC implies that the table or view can be accessed by anyone.

ALTER through UPDATE represent the different authorization specifications allowed. If you wish to grant all the privileges, specify ALL or ALL PRIVILEGES. Otherwise, list the ones desired individually.

ALTER — If an individual is allowed to add additional columns to an existing table, the ALTER privilege can be granted to the individual. The individual can then issue ALTER TABLE SQL statements for the named table.

DELETE — Allows the grantee to issue the SQL DELETE statement and thus delete rows from tables or from tables specified in views.

INDEX — Allows the grantee to create indexes on the named tables.

SELECT — Allows the grantee to issue SELECT SQL statements to retrieve rows/columns from the named tables or views. It does not imply update, delete, or insert authority.

UPDATE — Allows the grantee to issue the SQL UPDATE statement to update all columns in the named tables.

UPDATE *(column1, ... ,column)* — Allows grantee to update only specific columns in a table. The grantor can have select privileges on all of the columns but is restricted to updating only one.

Examples:

```
(0)  Signifies privileges established by being the creator
     of the table.
(1)  GRANT SELECT ON TABLE LIF_INS_SALES TO PUBLIC
(2)  GRANT SELECT ON LIF_INS_SALES TO PUBLIC
(3)  GRANT UPDATE ON LIF_INS_SALES TO USERID6 WITH GRANT
     OPTION
(4)  GRANT UPDATE (YTD_SALES) ON LIF_INS_SALES TO USERID2
(5)  GRANT SELECT,DELETE,UPDATE,INSERT ON LIF_INS_SALES
     TO USERID2,USERID3
(6)  GRANT ALTER,INDEX ON LIF_INS_SALES TO USERID5
```

SYSIBM.SYSTABAUTH can be inquired against to display the results from the previous grants. This query produced the following report. If UPDATE authority has been granted on individual columns, view SYSIBM.SYS-COLAUTH.

```
SYSIBM.SYSTABAUTH:
        SELECT GRANTOR, GRANTEE
           , STNAME
           , DATEGRANTED
```

```
        , TIMEGRANTED, UPDATECOLS, ALTERAUTH
        , DELETEAUTH, INDEXAUTH, INSERTAUTH
        , SELECTAUTH, UPDATEAUTH
  FROM SYSIBM.SYSTABAUTH
  WHERE GRANTOR='USERID1'
        AND STNAME='LIF_INS_SALES'
  ORDER BY DATEGRANTED,TIMEGRANTED
```

```
                                              U
                                              P
                                              D
                                    A    D    I  S  U
                                    T  A E    I  N  E P
                                    E  L L    N  S  L D
                                    C  T E    D  E  E A
                          DATE   TIME O  E T    E  R  C T
GRANTOR GRANTEE STNAME    GRANTED GRANTED L R E X T T E
------- ------- --------------- ------- -------- - - - - - - -
USERID1 USERID1 LIF_INS_SALES   870704  08445318  G G G G G G (0)

USERID1 PUBLIC  LIF_INS_SALES   880103  11055217          Y   (1)

USERID1 PUBLIC  LIF_INS_SALES   880103  11064916          Y   (2)

USERID1 USERID6 LIF_INS_SALES   880331  11252899            G (3)

USERID1 USERID2 LIF_INS_SALES   880401  11252899 *        Y   (4)

USERID1 USERID2 LIF_INS_SALES   880430  11262790     Y   Y Y Y (5)
USERID1 USERID3 LIF_INS_SALES   880430  11262790     Y   Y Y Y (5)

USERID1 USERID5 LIF_INS_SALES   880501  11265418 Y   Y       (6)
```

```
SYSIBM.SYSCOLAUTH:
SELECT GRANTOR, GRANTEE
     , CREATOR, TNAME
     , DATEGRANTED, TIMEGRANTED, COLNAME
  FROM SYSIBM.SYSCOLAUTH
  WHERE TNAME='LIF_INS_SALES'
```

```
                                         DATE    TIME
GRANTOR GRANTEE CREATOR TNAME          GRANTED GRANTED  COLNAME
------- ------- ------- -------------  ------- -------- ---------
USERID1 USERID2 USERID1 LIF_INS_SALES 880401  11252899 YTD_SALES
```

GRANT USE PRIVILEGES: Authority to use certain DB2 objects, such a buffer pools, storage groups, and tablespaces, must be granted to those wh are to use objects after they have been created. Through usage grants tablespaces can be directed into certain buffer pools and storage groups. Also tables can be directed into specific tablespaces. The format for this type c grant is as follows.

```
        GRANT USE OF BUFFERPOOL buffer-pool-number1, ..
                        ,buffer-pool-numbern
            TO userid1, ... ,useridn
            WITH GRANT OPTION
or
        GRANT USE OF BUFFERPOOL buffer-pool-number1, ...
                        ,buffer-pool-numbern
            TO userid1, ... ,useridn
or
        GRANT USE OF BUFFERPOOL buffer-pool-number1, ...
                        ,buffer-pool-numbern
            TO PUBLIC


        GRANT USE OF STOGROUP stogroup-name1, ... ,stogroup-namen
            TO userid1, ... ,useridn
            WITH GRANT  OPTION
or
        GRANT USE OF STOGROUP stogroup-name1, ... ,stogroup-namen
            TO userid1, ... ,useridn
or
        GRANT USE OF STOGROUP stogroup-name1, ... ,stogroup-namen
            TO PUBLIC


        GRANT USE OF TABLESPACE database1.tablespace1, ...
                        databasen.tablespacen
            TO userid1, ... ,useridn
            WITH GRANT  OPTION
or
        GRANT USE OF TABLESPACE database1.tablespace1, ...
                        databasen.tablespacen
            TO userid1, ... ,useridn
or
        GRANT USE OF TABLESPACE database1.tablespace1, ...
                        databasen.tablespacen
            TO PUBLIC
```

Buffer-pool(1 – n) represents a list of the already existing buffer pools i which access is to be granted. Your choices are BP0, BP1, BP2 and BP32K.

Userid(1 – n) is a list of users who are to be able to use the resource bein granted.

Stogroup(1 – n) is the list of storage groups in which use is being granted.
Database(1 – n).tablespace(1 – n) is a list of the tablespaces upon which use
is being granted.

Examples:

```
(1)    GRANT USE OF BUFFERPOOL BP0,BP1,BP2 TO PUBLIC
(2)    GRANT USE OF STOGROUP PROD0001
              TO USERID2,USERID3,USERID4
              WITH GRANT OPTION
(3)    GRANT USE OF TABLESPACE DBDNAM01.SPACE001,
           DBDNAM01.SPACE0002, DBDNAM02.SPACE001,DBDNAM02.SPACE0002
              TO USERID2,USERID3
```

Table SYSIBM.SYSRESAUTH may be inquired against to view the results
of the above grants.

```
SYSIBM.SYSRESAUTH:
SELECT GRANTOR,GRANTEE,NAME,OBTYPE,DATEGRANTED,TIMEGRANTED,USEAUTH
          FROM SYSIBM.SYSRESAUTH
     WHERE GRANTOR = 'userid1'
     ORDER BY DATEGRANTED,TIMEGRANTED
```

GRANTOR	GRANTEE	QUALIFIER	NAME	OBTYPE	DATE GRANTED	TIME GRANTED	USE AUTH	
USERID1	PUBLIC		BP0	B	880103	11010112	Y	(1)
USERID1	PUBLIC		BP1	B	880103	11010112	Y	(1)
USERID1	PUBLIC		BP2	B	880103	11010112	Y	(1)
USERID1	USERID2		PROD0001	S	880105	09081242	G	(2)
USERID1	USERID3		PROD0001	S	880105	09081242	G	(2)
USERID1	USERID4		PROD0001	S	880105	09081242	G	(2)
USERID1	USERID2	DBDNAM01	SPACE001	R	880331	10101225	Y	(3)
USERID1	USERID2	DBDNAM01	SPACE002	R	880331	10101225	Y	(3)
USERID1	USERID2	DBDNAM02	SPACE001	R	880331	10101225	Y	(3)
USERID1	USERID2	DBDNAM02	SPACE002	R	880331	10101225	Y	(3)
USERID1	USERID3	DBDNAM01	SPACE001	R	880331	10101225	Y	(3)
USERID1	USERID3	DBDNAM01	SPACE002	R	880331	10101225	Y	(3)
USERID1	USERID3	DBDNAM02	SPACE001	R	880331	10101225	Y	(3)
USERID1	USERID3	DBDNAM02	SPACE002	R	880331	10101225	Y	(3)

The REVOKE SQL statement will undo the privileges obtained by the
GRANT SQL statement. If privileges are granted using the WITH GRANT
OPTION, it is possible for a chain reaction to occur when a REVOKE is is-
sued. Let's take a case where USERID1 granted SELECT on a table to

USERID2 (with grant option) and USERID2 turned around and granted SELECT to USERID3. If USERID1 revokes SELECT from USERID2 then USERID3 also loses SELECT because it was based on USERID2 having the privilege. For each type of grant there is a corresponding REVOKE.

REVOKE DATABASE PRIVILEGES: These SQL statements are designed to remove the privileges granted on existing databases. The actual database and its associated objects are left intact. Only the database authorizations are dropped. The format for the REVOKE is very similar to that used in granting the privilege. It is as follows:

```
REVOKE DBADM,
       DBCTRL,
       DBMAINT,
       CREATETAB,
       CREATETS,
       DISPLAYDB,
       DROP,
       IMAGCOPY,
       LOAD,
       RECOVERDB,
       REORG,
       REPAIR,
       STARTDB,
       STATS,
       STOPDB
    ON DATABASE database-name FROM userid1, ... ,useridn
or
    ON DATABASE database-name FROM PUBLIC
```

DBADM through STOPDB are considered authorization specifications. You cannot revoke a specific privilege contained within the DBADM, DBCTRL, or DBMAINT administrative authorities. If you do not want an individual to have a certain privilege, you should grant the privileges individually. For example, if an individual was not to have IMAGCOPY privileges on a database, DBADM, DBCTRL, or DBMAINT authorization specifications cannot be used. The authorization specifications being revoked are the same ones listed under the GRANT DATABASE PRIVILEGES.

Examples:

```
REVOKE DBADM ON DATABASE DBDNAM01 FROM USERID2,USERID3
REVOKE IMAGCOPY,STATS ON DBDNAM01 FROM USERID6,USERID7
REVOKE DBMAINT ON DATABASE DBDNAM01,DBDNAM02 FROM
       USERID2
REVOKE STATS ON DATABASE DBDNAM01 FROM PUBLIC
```

REVOKE PLAN PRIVILEGES: The ability to execute a plan or rebind an application can be removed from an individual.
For revoking execution of application plans:

```
REVOKE EXECUTE ON PLAN plan-name1, ... ,plan-namen
              FROM userid1, .... ,useridn
```
or
```
REVOKE EXECUTE ON PLAN plan-name1, ... ,plan-namen
              FROM PUBLIC
```
or
```
REVOKE EXECUTE ON PLAN plan-name1, ... ,plan-namen
              FROM userid1, .... ,useridn  BY ALL
```
or
```
REVOKE EXECUTE ON PLAN plan-name1, ... ,plan-namen
       FROM userid1, .... ,useridn  BY userid1, .... ,useridn
```

For revoking the ability to maintain existing applications:

```
REVOKE BIND    ON PLAN plan-name1, ... ,plan-namen
               FROM userid1, .... ,useridn
```
or
```
REVOKE BIND    ON PLAN plan-name1, ... ,plan-namen
               FROM PUBLIC
```
or
```
REVOKE BIND    ON PLAN plan-name1, ... ,plan-namen
               FROM userid1, ... ,useridn  BY ALL
```
or
```
REVOKE BIND    ON PLAN plan-name1, ... ,plan-namen
       FROM userid1, ... ,useridn  BY userid1, ... ,useridn
```

Plan-name(1 − n) are the names of the application plans for which the authority is to be removed.
Userid(1 − n) in the FROM clause, it is the list of users who will lose the privilege. If specified in the BY clause, it represents a list of the users who had granted the privilege being revoked. The BY clause is only available to those with SYSADM authority. It provides those with SYSADM authority the ability to revoke security granted by others.

```
REVOKE EXECUTE ON PLAN PROGRM1C,PROGRM1P,PROGRM1F FROM PUBLIC
REVOKE EXECUTE ON PLAN PROGRM1C,PROGRM1P FROM USERID2,USERID3
REVOKE BIND    ON PLAN PROGRM1C,PROGRM1P FROM USERID5,USERID6
```

REVOKE SYSTEM PRIVILEGES: Allows system privileges granted to individuals to be revoked. The following is the format for revoking system privileges.

```
        REVOKE  SYSADM,
                SYSOPER,
                BINDADD,
                BSDS,
                CREATEDBA,
                CREATEDBC
                CREATESG,
                DISPLAY,
                RECOVER,
                STOPALL,
                STOSPACE,
                TRACE
            FROM useridl, ... ,useridn
or
            FROM PUBLIC
or
            FROM useridl, ... ,useridn BY ALL
or
            FROM useridl, ... ,useridn BY useridl, ... ,useridn
```

Examples:

```
    REVOKE BINDADD,CREATEDBA FROM USERID2,USERID3
    REVOKE DISPLAY FROM PUBLIC
```

REVOKE TABLE PRIVILEGES: Allows the table privileges granted to be revoked. Although you can grant update on individual columns, you must revoke the column updates at the table level.

```
    REVOKE ALL PRIVILEGES ON TABLE tablenamel, ... ,tablenamen,
                                    ,viewnamel, ... ,viewnamen
            FROM useridl, ... ,useridn
or
            FROM useridl, ... ,useridn  BY ALL
or
            FROM useridl, ... ,useridn  BY useridl,
                                    ... ,useridn
or
    REVOKE ALTER,DELETE,INDEX,INSERT,SELECT,UPDATE
            ON TABLE tablenamel, ... ,tablenamen,
                        ,viewnamel, ... ,viewnamen
            FROM useridl, ... ,useridn
or
            FROM useridl, ... ,useridn  BY ALL
```

)r

```
       FROM userid1, ... ,useridn  BY userid1,
                   ...,useridn
```

Examples:

```
     REVOKE SELECT ON TABLE LIF_INS_SALES FROM PUBLIC
     REVOKE SELECT ON LIF_INS_SALES FROM PUBLIC
     REVOKE UPDATE ON LIF_INS_SALES FROM USERID6
     REVOKE UPDATE ON LIF_INS_SALES FROM USERID2
     REVOKE SELECT,DELETE,UPDATE,INSERT ON LIF_INS_SALES
            FROM USERID2,USERID3
     REVOKE ALTER,INDEX ON LIF_INS_SALES FROM USERID5
```

REVOKE USE PRIVILEGES: Is used to remove the use of resources such as buffer pools, storage groups, and tablespaces from individuals.

```
   REVOKE USE OF BUFFERPOOL buffer-pool-number1, ...
                         ,buffer-pool-numbern
           FROM userid1, ... ,useridn
```

)r

```
           FROM userid1, ... ,useridn  BY ALL
```

)r

```
           FROM userid1, ... ,useridn  BY userid1,
                   ... ,useridn
```

or

```
           FROM PUBLIC
```

```
   REVOKE USE OF STOGROUP stogroup-name1, ... ,stogroup-namen
           FROM userid1, ... ,useridn
```

or

```
           FROM userid1, ... ,useridn  BY ALL
```

or

```
           FROM userid1, ... ,useridn  BY userid1,
                   ... ,useridn
```

or

```
           FROM PUBLIC
```

```
   REVOKE USE OF TABLESPACE database1.tablespace1, ...
                        databasen.tablespacen
           FROM userid1, ... ,useridn
```

or

```
           FROM userid1, ... ,useridn  BY ALL
```

or

        FROM *useridl,* ... *,useridn*   BY *useridl,*
               ... *,useridn*

or

        FROM PUBLIC

Examples:

```
REVOKE USE OF BUFFERPOOL BP0,BP1,BP2 FROM PUBLIC
REVOKE USE STOGROUP PROD0001,PROD0002,PROD0003
       FROM USERID2,USERID3,USERID3
REVOKE USE OF TABLESPACE DBDNAM01.SPACE001,
   DBDNAM01.SPACE0002,DBDNAM02.SPACE001, DBDNAM02.SPACE0002
       FROM USERID2,USERID3
REVOKE USE OF STOGROUP PROD0001,PROD0002,PROD0003
       FROM USERID3,USERID4,USERID5
```

Here are some items you should be aware of when managing authorizations:

1. DB2 provides no audit trail. Once a privilege is revoked, all traces of it disappear.
2. Dropping a DB2 object, whether directly or indirectly, causes all authority granted on the dropped object to be removed. DBMAUI or something similar should be used to reconstruct the authority prior to dropping the object.
3. DB2 does not stop you from regranting a privilege. Granting the same privilege 20 times to an individual causes 20 rows to be inserted into the appropriate table. On the other hand, revoking the privilege would cause all 20 rows to be deleted from the authorization table.
4. An individual can receive the same authority from multiple users. Should one of these users revoke their granted authority, a chain of rows may be deleted from the authorization table. DB2 not only keeps track of the privilege granted, but also when it was granted. Figure 9-2 illustrates how the date and time a grant takes place can have a rather dramatic effect on the existing authorizations.
5. If you use personal TSOIDs to create objects, what are you going to do when the individual leaves? Functional, generic, and user exits have been used with some degree of success to handle such problems.
6. Individuals with SYSADM and DBADM authority have the ability to view even the most sensitive table data.

To develop applications, the following authorizations or privileges are needed. Since SYSADM has the authority to perform all of the following, I will exclude it.

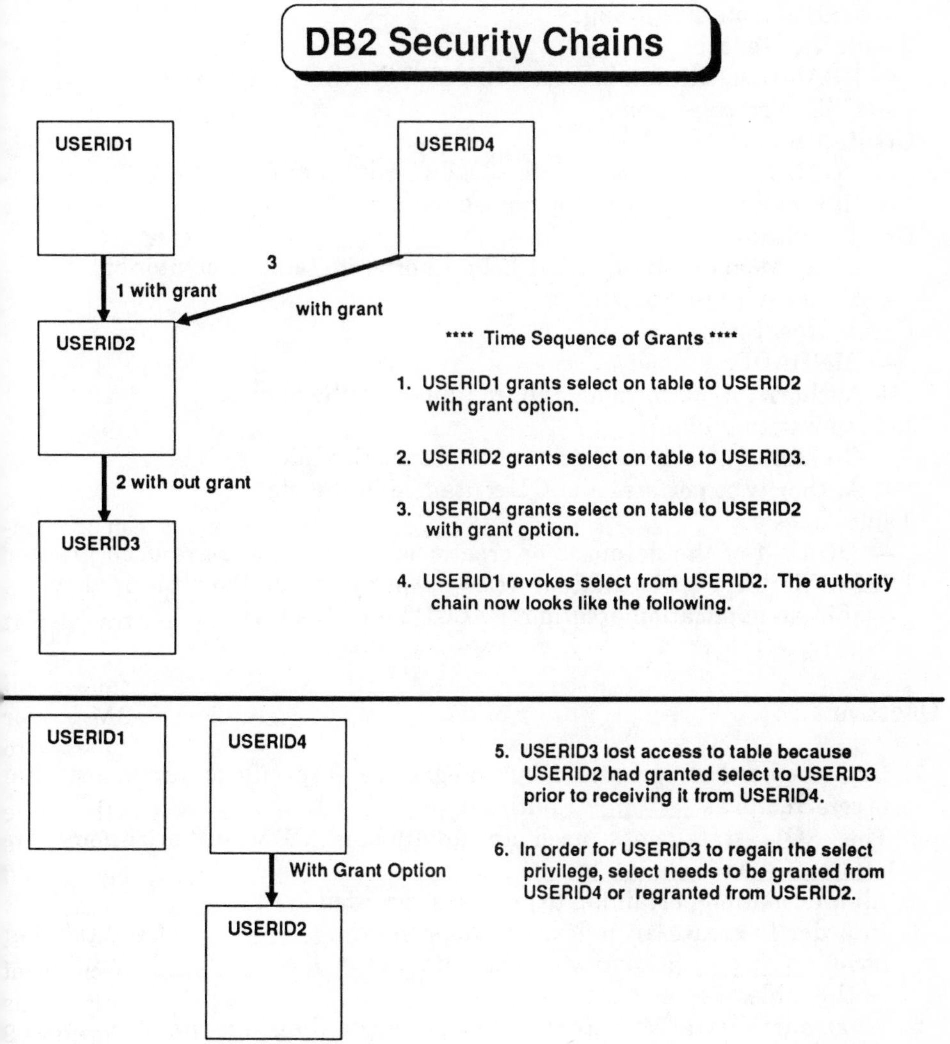

DB2 Security Chains

USERID1

USERID4

3

1 with grant

with grant

USERID2

**** Time Sequence of Grants ****

1. USERID1 grants select on table to USERID2 with grant option.

2. USERID2 grants select on table to USERID3.

2 with out grant

3. USERID4 grants select on table to USERID2 with grant option.

USERID3

4. USERID1 revokes select from USERID2. The authority chain now looks like the following.

USERID1

USERID4

5. USERID3 lost access to table because USERID2 had granted select to USERID3 prior to receiving it from USERID4.

With Grant Option

6. In order for USERID3 to regain the select privilege, select needs to be granted from USERID4 or regranted from USERID2.

USERID2

Figure 9-2 DB2 Security Chain Example

Create Databases:
— CREATEDBA or CREATEDBC
— USE of a storage group
Create Tablespaces:
— DBADM on the database or CREATETS within a database
— USE of storage group
Create Table:
— DBADM on database or CREATETAB within tablespace
— USE of a tablespace in the named database
Create Index:
— DBADM on database or INDEX authority on table or creator of table
— Use of storage group
Create New Plan:
— BINDADD
— Authority to perform all SQL contained in the plan
Rebind Existing Plan:
— Creator of plan or authority to bind specific plan
— Authority to perform all SQL contained in the plan
Table Access:
— DBADM of the database or creator of the table or have been granted
INSERT,UPDATE,DELETE, or SELECT privileges on the table or view
— If in an application program, EXECUTE on the plan

Questions:

1. One who has been granted all privileges over a specific database has what is referred to as _____ authority.
2. The SQL statements used to administer DB2 authorizations are _____ and _____.
3. All information pertaining to grants is recorded in the ____ _____.
4. In order to create an index, you must be the _____ of the table or have _____ authority on the database or have _____ authority on the table.
5. What administrative authorities can execute the Runstats for a specific database?

True or False:

6. DB2 objects have to exist prior to granting authority on them.
7. The same privilege can be granted to an individual more than once.
8. Dropping a DB2 object automatically removes all of the authority granted on the dropped object.
9. Updates to a row are restricted to all columns in the row.
10. DBMAUI can reconstruct the grants issued on a dropped object.
11. The creator of a database automatically has DBADM authority over the database.

2. If the GRANTOR and GRANTEE are the same in the DB2 Catalog table, the grantor is the creator of the object since you cannot grant authority to yourself.

nswers:

1. DBADM
2. Grant, revoke
3. DB2 catalog
4. Creator, DBADM, INDEX
5. SYSADM, DBADM, DBCTRL, and DBMAINT
6. True
7. True
8. True
9. False; authority to update can be granted on a column by column basis;
10. False; before being dropped, not after
11. True
12. True

Chapter

10

Database Design

Many of the steps involved with designing applications for Database 2 are identical to those used with the traditional database management systems. The following items should be included in your design process, plus any others you are accustomed to performing at your installation. The order in which the following steps can be performed may vary depending on your special situations. One such situation includes whether or not a data dictionary is available for relational. With DB2, the database is used to identify a collection of tablespaces, tables, indexspaces, and indexes. In reality, designing for relational should be perceived as table design rather than database design. The following is a list of design steps that, for the most part, will be common to most DB2 installations.

— Determine System Requirements
— Collect Data Requirements
— Classify Data to be Collected into Entities
— Place Data Elements Describing the Same Entity into a Table
— Analyze Table Columns
— Identify all Table Relationships
— Normalize Tables
— Examine Performance Implications of the Design
— Determine Table Integrity Requirements
— Determine Table Access
— Identify Data Sources for Load Purposes

345

DETERMINE SYSTEM REQUIREMENTS AND COLLECTING DATA REQUIREMENTS: The methods of determining a system's requirements and the gathering of the data requirements are processes that are in place in many installations already. How they are performed can vary dramatically from one installation to another. Since many installations already have methodology in place for these processes, I will limit the discussion to the areas that are new or need to be re-evaluated for DB2 development.

CLASSIFY DATA INTO ENTITIES: Once the data elements needing to be collected have been identified, classify these data elements into entities. An entity is anything for which information is to be collected. It could be a salesperson, an engineering decision, a manufacturing process, a marketing concept, or even a specific point in time. Throughout much of this book, employees was an entity for which information was being collected. The information collected about an entity is considered data or data elements.

PLACE DATA ELEMENTS DESCRIBING THE SAME ENTITY INTO A TABLE: All data collected should be grouped with the entity it describes. The entity on which information is collected becomes a base table, and the individual data elements describing the entity become columns in the table. In the following illustration, consider Sales Person an entity for which data is to be collected.

Sales Person:
    Address
    Salary
    Hire Date
    SS No.
    Age
    Bonus

The following table could be derived from the above entity and associated data elements.

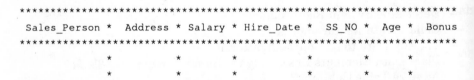

```
************************************************************************
 Sales_Person *  Address * Salary * Hire_Date *  SS_NO *  Age *  Bonus
************************************************************************
            *          *        *          *        *      *
            *          *        *          *        *      *
```

ANALYZE TABLE COLUMNS: Column names should be assigned to the data elements that will be contained in the tables. Although all column names within a table must be unique, the column name of a foreign key may be the same name as its primary key in another table. Attempt to keep the names meaningful to the users. These are the names users and developers will be referencing when constructing queries. At the same time you are determining the column name, avoid using reserved words contained in the application programming languages being used. Date is one that frequently catches COBOL programmers off guard.

Identify the columns comprising the primary key. These are the columns that uniquely identify one row describing the entity from others. If foreign key columns are defined in a base table, ensure they are defined with the same data type and precision found in their corresponding primary table.

Analyze the data to ensure that you have not included two or more columns containing similar data such as Sales Region and Territory as seen in the following example:

Sales Person	Sales Region	Address	Salary	Dept	Territory
Jones	Northeast	Chicago	60,000	800	NE
Smith	Southeast	Tampa	70,000	890	SE
Brown	Northwest	Portland	65,000	800	NW

If Sales Region and Territory appear to contain the same kind of data values, consider removing one or the other of the columns.

Ensure that two or more columns having the same name do not in actuality represent totally different data elements, such as Name in the following example:

Sales Person	Name	Date of Origin	Policy Amount	Policy Type	Name
Jones	J. Black	03/30/88	50,000	Life	M. Black
Smith	K. Smith	03/31/88	20,000	Term	L. Smith
Brown	A. Jordan	04/01/88	10,000	Life	S. Jordan

Name in the above example should represent two different data elements. The first Name column represents the originator of the insurance policy, while the second Name represents the beneficiary of the policy. The column names should be altered, as in the following example, to represent the actual data element being collected.

Sales Person	Policy Owner	Date of Origin	Policy Amount	Policy Type	Policy Beneficiary
Jones	J. Black	03/30/88	50,000	Life	M. Black
Smith	K. Smith	03/31/88	20,000	Term	L. Smith
Brown	A. Jordan	04/01/88	10,000	Life	S. Jordan

Determine what columns, if any, need to contain unique values. If this uniqueness needs to be enforced through the design, create unique indexes for the columns requiring uniqueness.

IDENTIFY TABLE RELATIONSHIPS: There are four basic relationships that can exist between tables:

* One to Many
* Many to One
* Many to Many
* One to One

Figure 10-1, (A) through (D), illustrates the types of relationships found between tables. Although a table can contain many columns, the examples reflect only columns contained in primary and foreign keys.

A One-to-Many relationship, as seen in Figure 10-1(A), implies that you have a case where the primary key in one table is related to multiple primary keys of another table. For example, a salesperson (Jones) has sold three policies. They are 90988, 09090, and 98765. A salesperson can sell many policies, but each policy in the Sales Policy table is associated to only one salesperson. With the One-to-Many relationship, place a foreign key in the many Table that is the primary key of the one Table. The result of this is shown in Figure 10-2(A).

A Many-to-One relationship, illustrated in Figure 10-1(B), is identical to the One-to-Many relationship. Once again, place a foreign key in the Many Table that is the primary key in the One Table, as seen in Figure 10-2(B).

Figure 10-1(C) identifies a Many-to-Many relationship where the primary key of one table is related to multiple primary keys of another table and vice versa. In the example, a salesperson can take more than one class, and one class can have more than one salesperson enrolled. In these situations, you may find the solution consists of creating a new table containing just the relationships between the two tables. Data that pertains only to the relationship between the tables, such as grade in Figure 10-2(C), is called "intersection data" and should be contained only in the new table.

The last relationship, One-to-One, pertains to situations similar to the one shown in Figure 10-1(D), where there is a one-to-one relationship between two tables. Each salesperson was required to maintain one and only one escrow account to prevent the commingling of his or her funds with the clients. Likewise, the salesperson has sole responsibility over the escrow account. In these situations the primary key of one table should be placed as a foreign key in the other. Since it is a one-to-one relationship, you will have to decide which table should contain the foreign key. The table chosen to contain the foreign key could have an impact on your performance. If most applications access one table far more than the other and the foreign key is frequently the only column needed from the other, the frequently accessed table is the likely candidate to contain the foreign key. If access is not a factor, using the table whose primary key is the shortest as the foreign key in the other table can save space. Figure 10-2(D) illustrates the two possibilities.

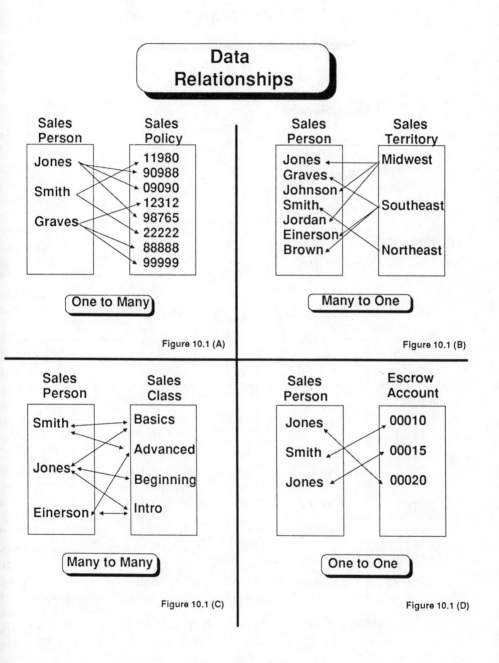

Figure 10-1 Types of Data Relationships

Data Relationships
One to Many

Sales Person Table

Sales Person		
Jones		
Smith		
Graves		

Primary Key

Sales Policy Table

Sales Policy	Sales Person		
11980	Smith		
90988	Jones		
09090	Jones		
12312	Graves		
98765	Jones		
22222	Smith		
88888	Graves		
99999	Graves		

Primary Key   Foreign Key

Figure 10-2A One-to-Many Data Relationship

Data Relationships
Many to One

Sales Territory

Sales Territory		
Midwest		
Southeast		
Northeast		

Primary Key

Sales Person

Sales Person	Sales Territory		
Jones	Midwest		
Graves	Southeast		
Johnson	Midwest		
Smith	Northeast		
Jordan	Midwest		
Einerson	Southeast		
Brown	Southeast		

Primary Key   Foreign Key

Figure 10-2B Many-to-One Data Relationship

Data Relationships
Many to Many

Sales Person

Sales Person		
Smith		
Jones		
Einerson		

Primary Key

Sales Class

Sales Class		
Basics		
Advanced		
Beginning		
Intro		

Primary Key

Sales Class Roster

Sales Person	Sales Class	Grade	
Smith	Basics	B+	
Smith	Advanced	B-	
Jones	Basics	B	
Jones	Beginning	A+	
Jones	Intro	A+	
Einerson	Advanced	C+	
Einerson	Intro	A+	

Primary Key

Intersection Data

Figure 10-2C Many-to-Many Data Relationship

Data Relationships
One to One

Sales Person Table

Sales Person	Escrow Account		
Smith	00010		
Jones	00015		
Einerson	00020		

Primary Key   Foreign Key

Escrow Account Table

Escrow Account		
00010		
00015		
00020		

Primary Key

- OR -

Sales Person Table

Sales Person		
Smith		
Jones		
Einerson		

Primary Key

Primary Key

Escrow Account Table

Escrow Account	Sales Person		
00010	Smith		
00015	Jones		
00020	Einerson		

Foreign Key

Figure 10-2D One-to-One Data Relationship

NORMALIZE TABLES: Unnormalized tables can lead to inefficient query construction. The steps involved to normalize your tables provide the foundation for obtaining correctly designed tables.

The first step in the normalization process is to eliminate situations where a row contains a set of values. In Figure 10-3, columns Territory1, Territory2, and Territory3 were designed to contain multiple values within a row for a salesperson's territories. This technique can lead to problems. You will have to analyze the columns to determine if data exists or not. What should be done if a salesperson is allowed four territories? Rather than this design, remove the territory columns and place them in a new table called Sales Territory. The new table should contain both a Territory column and a Salesperson column. The Salesperson column in the new table is a foreign key referring back to a specific row in the Salesperson table.

The second step is to eliminate redundant data values across rows. If the data value is updated for one row, what impact does it have on other rows. Note the Dept No and Sales Dept columns in Figure 10-4. Notice that everywhere a department number is specified, a corresponding sales department name follows. As a result, the name of the sales department could potentially be stored in the table many times. If there were 100 employees in department 800, Life Ins name would also be stored 100 times in the table. To avoid this, consider creating a new table called Dept. The new table will contain a department number and its corresponding department name. Leave the department name in the Salesperson table as a foreign key to the Dept table. As a result, the department name will only be stored once for each department number.

The third step in normalizing tables is to eliminate columns from the table that are not a dependent of the primary key. In Figure 10-5 we can determine that salespersons have been provided with a company car. Although the salesperson has a car with a particular vehicle identification number, this information is not directly dependent on the key of the table, which is Salesperson. Ask yourself the question: What happens when a salesperson leaves the company? Does the car also go away? Few companies would knowingly give away cars to employees leaving a job. If you wish to keep track of which car is assigned to a salesperson, create a new table called Company Cars. The new table should contain the Vehicle id, Car Model, and any other information pertaining to the vehicle. Remove the Car Model column from the Salesperson table. The Vehicle id column should be left in the Salesperson table to serve as a foreign key pointing to a row in the Company Car table. Now if a salesperson's row is deleted from the table, the information describing the car will still remain intact.

The fourth and last step consists of eliminating situations where independent, multivalued attributes exist within a row. In Figure 10-6, we have a situation where information is to be retained about the responsibilities assigned to a manager, as well as the user manuals his or her department supports. Queries to access this kind of table are very difficult to construct, because the column sometimes has values and sometimes does not. Instead, consider placing the independent multivalued columns "Responsibilities" and

Normalize Step 1
Eliminate Sets of Columns within a row

Remove columns with repeating data elements and place into their own table.

Sales Person

Sales Person	Address	Dept No	Sales Dept	Car Model	Vehicle Id	Territory1	Territory2	Territory3
Smith	Ohio	800	Life Ins	Ford	A010	Southeast		
Jones	Calif	890	Auto Ins	Chevy	A020	Southwest	Southeast	
Jordan	Maine	900	Term Ins	Subaru	A030	Northwest		
Brown	Ohio	890	Auto Ins	Ford	A040	Southeast	Northeast	Midwest
Black	Texas	890	Auto Ins	Chevy	A012	Midwest	Northeast	
Larson	Iowa	900	Term Ins	Ford	B012	Midwest		

Sales Person

Sales Person	Address	Dept No	Sales Dept	Car Model	Vehicle Id	Territory1	Territory2	Territory3
Smith	Ohio	800	Life Ins	Ford	A010	Southeast		
Jones	Calif	890	Auto Ins	Chevy	A020	Southwest	Southeast	
Jordan	Maine	900	Term Ins	Subaru	A030	Northwest		
Brown	Ohio	890	Auto Ins	Ford	A040	Southeast	Northeast	Midwest
Black	Texas	890	Auto Ins	Chevy	A012	Midwest	Northeast	
Larson	Iowa	900	Term Ins	Ford	B012	Midwest		

Figure 10-3 Normalization Step 1 (Sets of Columns)

Normalize Step 2
Eliminate Redundant Values Across Rows

Sales Person

Sales Person	Address	Dept No	Sales Dept	Car Model	Vehicle Id	Territory1	Territory2	Territory3
Smith	Ohio	800	Life Ins	Ford	A010	Southeast		
Jones	Calif	890	Auto Ins	Chevy	A020	Southwest	Southeast	
Jordan	Maine	900	Term Ins	Subaru	A030	Northwest		
Brown	Ohio	890	Auto Ins	Ford	A040	Southeast	Northeast	Midwest
Black	Texas	890	Auto Ins	Chevy	A012	Midwest	Northeast	
Larson	Iowa	900	Term Ins	Ford	B012	Midwest		

Sales Person

Sales Person	Address	Dept No	Sales Dept	Car Model	Vehicle Id	Territory1	Territory2	Territory3
Smith	Ohio	800	Life Ins	Ford	A010	Southeast		
Jones	Calif	890	Auto Ins	Chevy	A020	Southwest	Southeast	
Jordan	Maine	900	Term Ins	Subaru	A030	Northwest		
Brown	Ohio	890	Auto Ins	Ford	A040	Southeast	Northeast	Midwest
Black	Texas	890	Auto Ins	Chevy	A012	Midwest	Northeast	
Larson	Iowa	900	Term Ins	Ford	B012	Midwest		

Figure 10-4 Normalization Step 2 (Redundant Values)

Normalize Step 3
Eliminate Columns not Dependent on Key

Should the deletion of a sales person cause information about sales cars to disappear also? Probably not?

Sales Person

Sales Person	Address	Dept No	Sales Dept	Car Model	Vehicle Id	Territory1	Territory2	Territory3
Smith	Ohio	800	Life Ins	Ford	A010	Southeast		
Jones	Calif	890	Auto Ins	Chevy	A020	Southwest	Southeast	
Jordan	Maine	900	Term Ins	Subaru	A030	Northwest		
Brown	Ohio	890	Auto Ins	Ford	A040	Southeast	Northeast	Midwest
Black	Texas	890	Auto Ins	Chevy	A012	Midwest	Northeast	
Larson	Iowa	900	Term Ins	Ford	B012	Midwest		

Sales Person

Sales Person	Address	Dept No	Sales Dept	Car Model	Vehicle Id	Territory1	Territory2	Territory3
Smith	Ohio	800	Life Ins	Ford	A010	Southeast		
Jones	Calif	890	Auto Ins	Chevy	A020	Southwest	Southeast	
Jordan	Maine	900	Term Ins	Subaru	A030	Northwest		
Brown	Ohio	890	Auto Ins	Ford	A040	Southeast	Northeast	Midwest
Black	Texas	890	Auto Ins	Chevy	A012	Midwest	Northeast	
Larson	Iowa	900	Term Ins	Ford	B012	Midwest		

Figure 10-5 Normalization Step 3 (Key Dependency)

> **Normalize Step 4**
> **Eliminate independent multi-valued**
> **attributes about the entity**

Manager	Responsibilities	User Manuals
Williams	DB2 Installations	
Williams	QMF Installations	
Williams	DBMAUI Installations	
Williams		How to Use IMS
Williams		How to Use VSAM
Jordan	MVS Installations	
Jordan	JES Installations	
Parsons	Payroll Conversion	
Parsons		W2 Statements Process

By devising the following table, queries can be constructed
to retrieve the results much more efficiently.

Manager	Responsibilities
Williams	DB2 Installations
Williams	QMF Installations
Williams	DBMAUI Installations
Jordan	MVS Installations
Jordan	JES Installations
Parsons	Payroll Conversion

Manager	User Manuals
Williams	How to Use IMS
Williams	How to Use VSAM
Parsons	W2 Statements Process

Figure 10-6 Normalization Step 4 (Multi-valued Attributes)

"User Manuals" in separate tables. The Manager column should also be included in both. Figure 10-7 depicts the design after the normalization steps have been performed.

EXAMINE PERFORMANCE IMPLICATIONS OF DESIGN: Performing all four steps of normalization does not necessarily imply that you have the optimum design for performance. After performing normalization of the tables, you need to determine the performance implications of your design. If you have split columns into separate tables, how many rows will be in the tables? How long are the rows? If you are constructing tables with row lengths of less than 30 bytes, you may want to consider performing what is called denormalization of your tables. This implies placing redundant data back into a table and eliminating some of the tables to avoid an excessive number of table joins in the queries.

DETERMINE TABLE INTEGRITY REQUIREMENTS: As of this publication, DB2 provides little assistance in maintaining data integrity. Frequently, application programs are developed solely to enforce the integrity concerns. If two base tables contain columns whose values must match, the values must be entered, updated, and deleted in a consistent manner or you will get misleading results when performing table joins on the columns. Ensuring columns contain the correct range of values is enforcement of domain integrity. In addition, you need to ask yourself how insert, delete, and update processing should be handled between related columns of one or more tables. Refer to Figure 10-8 when asking yourself the following questions:

1. What impact does the deletion of a row from one table have on the other? Should a user be allowed to delete a department from the Dept table if it referenced in the Salesperson table?
2. What impact does the update of a column in one table have on the other? If department 800 is changed to 810 in the Salesperson table, we have individuals working in a department not defined in the Dept table.
3. What impact does inserting a row into one table have on the related table? Is it valid to insert a row into the Dept table without anyone working in the department?

Although application programs can be written to address the domain and referential integrity aspects lacking at this time, there are steps you should take to minimize the impact. First, limit the number of programs performing updates, deletes, and inserts. This will reduce the number of programs having to contain the logic to enforce integrity. Storing data redundantly can also complicate maintaining data integrity. To ensure that domain and referential integrity are being enforced, consider constructing queries and/or design application programs to verify the consistency between related tables.

Be cautious as to how the table can be maintained. There are many products available in the market that will allow updates as well as selects. Many of these products allow you to include audits but require the authoriza-

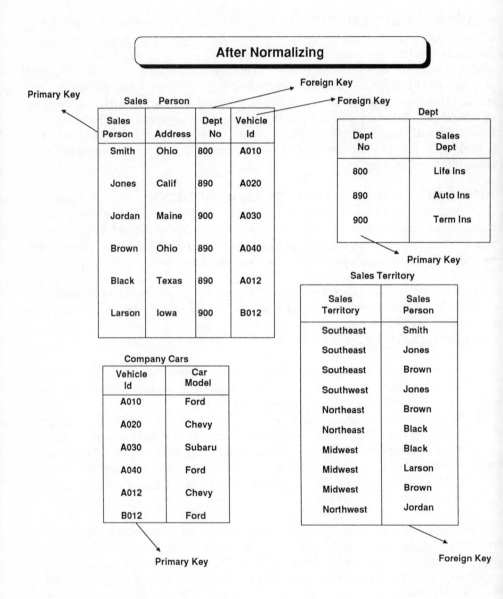

Figure 10-7 Normalization Final Result

Referential Integrity

Sales Person

Sales Person	Salary	Dept	Sales Territory
Jones	60,000	800	Northeast
Smith	50,000	890	Northwest
Johnson	65,000	900	Southeast
Graves	80,000	800	Midwest

Update 800 to 810 (2)

Dept

Delete (1)

Dept	Dept	Manager
800	Auto Ins	Black
890	Life Ins	Jordan
900	Home Ins	Brown
999	Term Ins	Gray

Insert (3)

Figure 10-8 Referential Integrity

tion to be granted at the table level. If you grant update authority on a table to an individual for the use with one of these products, what would prevent the user from going into QMF or something similar and issuing the update and thus bypass all integrity aspects?

DETERMINE TABLE ACCESS: Although an entire row may be returned to an application, frequently only a few columns are used in determining which rows will satisfy a particular query. Identify all columns by which the tables will be accessed and the frequency in which they will be accessed. Identify columns used in joining tables, ORDER BY clauses, and WHERE predicates. In order to appropriately construct the required indexes, you need to thoroughly identify how the data will be accessed and at what frequency.

IDENTIFY DATA SOURCES: Much of the data currently being placed in DB2 is coming from existing systems. Identify where the data to be loaded can be found and how, if necessary, it should be formatted. The approach used to load the data should also be reviewed. Data is normally placed into tables in one of two fashions: It may be inserted through applications using inserts or loaded via the load utility. The load utility is the more efficient process of the two but does not allow for concurrent usage.

CASE STUDY: Design a set of tables to satisfy the following requirements.

You have been given the task of monitoring how many people have attended or will be attending the computer system courses being taught at your installation. Enrollment is open to all employees. In addition to scheduling the students, you must also find instructors for the courses and provide the instructors with a schedule for when they will be teaching. The instructors teaching the courses will vary from time to time. A course may be taught more than once per any given day. With different instructors, it could even be taught at the same time. Although no grades are given, a student must attend the entire class in order to receive credit for it. Periodically you will be asked to provide a composite list of courses completed by an individual. Students starting a course but failing to complete it are given 60 days to make up the material either independently or by being scheduled in another class. Otherwise, they will be treated as if they had never attended.

SAMPLE REPORT 1: The number of students who have either completed or are currently enrolled in the classes.

CLASS NUMBER	CLASS NAME	Students Enrolled
10	DB2 CONCEPTS	11
20	IMS CONCEPTS	4
30	CICS CONCEPTS	4
40	DB2 DESIGN	7
.	.	.

SAMPLE REPORT 2: Provide course schedules for the instructors.

INSTRUCTOR NAME	CLASS NUMBER	CLASS NAME	DATE SCHEDULED	CLASS LOCATION
JORDAN, B	40	DB2 DESIGN	23DEC87	ROOM 130
	40	DB2 DESIGN	08JAN88	ROOM 130
LARSEN, S	10	DB2 CONCEPTS	07JAN88	ROOM 120
LARSON, S	10	DB2 CONCEPTS	21DEC87	ROOM 115
	10	DB2 CONCEPTS	06JAN88	ROOM 115
SMITH, F	20	IMS CONCEPTS	21DEC87	ROOM 110
	30	CICS CONCEPTS	22DEC87	ROOM 110
.	. .		.	. .
.	. .		.	. .
.	. .		.	. .

SAMPLE REPORT 3: Report on classes taken by employees. Sequence by date attended.

EMPL NO.	EMPLOYEE NAME	DEPT	DEPT LOCATION	CLASS No	CLASS NAME	DATE SCHDL	WHERE TAUGHT
1000	JONES, K	800	ACCOUNTING	20	IMS CONCEPTS	21DEC87	ROOM 110
				10	DB2 CONCEPTS	06JAN88	ROOM 115

							2
1001	JONES, C	800	ACCOUNTING	30	CICS CONCEPT	22DEC87	ROOM 110
				10	DB2 CONCEPTS	07JAN88	ROOM 120

							2
1002	JONES, A	800	ACCOUNTING	30	CICS CONCEPT	22DEC87	ROOM 110
				10	DB2 CONCEPTS	07JAN88	ROOM 120
				40	DB2 DESIGN	08JAN88	ROOM 130

							3
1003	LARSON, B	801	MARKETING	30	CICS CONCEPT	22DEC87	ROOM 110
				10	DB2 CONCEPTS	07JAN88	ROOM 120
				40	DB2 DESIGN	08JAN88	ROOM 130

							3

```
1004 LARSON, C   802  TRAINING     40 DB2 DESIGN   08JAN88   ROOM 130
                                                             ---------
                                                                     1


1007 EINERSON, D 802  TRAINING     40 DB2 DESIGN   23DEC87   ROOM 130
                                   40 DB2 DESIGN   08JAN88   ROOM 130
                                                             ---------
                                                                     2


1008 EINERSON, S 800  ACCOUNTING   40 DB2 DESIGN   23DEC87   ROOM 130
                                                             ---------
                                                                     1
```

  .   .   .   .

  .   .   .   .

  .   .   .   .

CASE STUDY SOLUTION:

Determine entities:
Classes
Employees

Group data elements by entity:
Classes:
    Class number
    Class name
    Date scheduled
    Class location
    Instructor

Employees:
    Employee identifier
    Employee name
    Department
    Department location

IDENTIFY TABLE RELATIONSHIPS: Since a course can have multiple students and a student can take multiple courses, we have a many-to-many relationship. A third table should be designed to identify the relationships between classes and employees. Since we were asked to keep track of whether an employee completed the course or not, intersection data containing this information will need to be defined. The new table consists of the primary keys from the related tables plus any intersection data. The third table looks like the following:

Class roster:
    Class number
    Date scheduled
    Employee number
    Completed?

Analyze Table Columns: Assign column names to the data elements. It appears that the instructor column is a foreign key for the employee number
column in the employee table. Instructor and employee number should be
defined with the same precision. Identify primary keys of both tables. Determine attributes of columns.

```
CLASS:
        CLASS_NUMBER    SMALLINT NOT NULL, <---- Primary Key (Not unique)
        CLASS_NAME      CHAR(20) NOT NULL,
        DATE_SCHEDULED  DATE     NOT NULL, <---- Primary Key (Not unique)
        LOCATION        CHAR(10) NOT NULL,
        INSTRUCTOR      SMALLINT NOT NULL) <--- Foreign Key


EMPLOYEE:
        EMPLOYEE_NUMBER SMALLINT NOT NULL, <----- Primary Key (Unique)
        EMPLOYEE_NAME   CHAR(15) NOT NULL,
        DEPT            SMALLINT NOT NULL,
        LOCATION        CHAR(15) NOT NULL)


CLASS ROSTER:
        CLASS_NUMBER    SMALLINT NOT NULL <----- Key
        DATE_SCHEDULED  DATE     NOT NULL <----- Key
        EMPLOYEE_NUMBER SMALLINT NOT NULL <----- Key
        COMPLETED       CHAR(3)  NOT NULL <----- Intersection data
```

Identify Table Accesses: Extensive joins will be required on the columns
identified as either primary or foreign keys. The following columns are potential candidates for indexes.

```
        CLASS:
            1)  CLASS_NUMBER and DATE_SCHEDULED

        EMPLOYEE:
            1)  EMPLOYEE_NUMBER

        CLASS_ROSTER:
            1)  EMPLOYEE_NUMBER
            2)  CLASS_NUMBER, DATE_SCHEDULED and EMPLOYEE_NUMBER
```

Appendix A:
Database 2 Catalog Tables

SYSCOLAUTH

Records the UPDATE privileges held by users on individual columns of a table or view.

GRANTOR	GRANTEE	GRANTEETYPE	CREATOR
TNAME	TIMESTAMP	DATEGRANTED	TIMEGRANTED
COLNAME	IBMREQD		

SYSCOLUMNS

Contains one row for every column of each table and view, including the columns of the DB2 catalog tables.

NAME	TBNAME	TBCREATOR	COLNO
COLTYPE	LENGTH	SCALE	NULLS
COLCARD	HIGH2KEY	LOW2KEY	UPDATES
IBMREQD	REMARKS	DEFAULT	KEYSEQ
FOREIGNKEY	FLDPROC	LABEL	

SYSCOPY

Contains information needed for recovery.

DBNAME	TSNAME	DSNUM	ICTYPE
ICDATE	START_RBA	FILESEQNO	DEVTYPE
IBMREQD	DSNAME	ICTIME	SHRLEVEL
DSVOLSER			

SYSDATABASE

Contains one row for each data base, except for data base DSNDB01.

NAME	CREATOR	STGROUP	BPOOL
DBID	IBMREQD		

SYSDBAUTH

Records the privileges held by users over databases.

GRANTOR	GRANTEE	NAME	TIMESTAMP
DATEGRANTED	TIMEGRANTED	GRANTEETYPE	AUTHHOWGOT
CREATETABAUTH	CREATETSAUTH	DBADMAUTH	DBCTRLAUTH
DBMAINTAUTH	DISPLAYDBAUTH	DROPAUTH	IMAGCOPYAUTH
LOADAUTH	REORGAUTH	RECOVERDBAUTH	REPAIRAUTH
STARTDBAUTH	STATSAUTH	STOPAUTH	IBMREQD

SYSDBRM   Contains one row for each DBRM of each application plan.

NAME	TIMESTAMP	PDSNAME	PLNAME
PLCREATOR	PRECOMPTIME	PRECOMPDATE	QUOTE
COMMA	HOSTLANG	IBMREQD	

SYSFIELDS   Contains one row for every column that has a field procedure.

TBCREATOR	TBNAME	COLNO	NAME
FLDTYPE	LENGTH	SCALE	FLDPROC
WORKAREA	IBMREQD	EXITPARML	PARMLIST
EXITPARM			

SYSFOREIGNKEYS   Contains one row for every column of every foreign key.

CREATOR	TBNAME	RELNAME	COLNAME
COLNO	COLSEQ	IBMREQD	

SYSINDEXES   Contains one row for every index, including indexes on catalog tables.

NAME	CREATOR	TBNAME	TBCREATOR
UNIQUERULE	COLCOUNT	CLUSTERING	CLUSTERED
DBID	OBID	ISOBID	DBNAME
INDEXSPACE	FIRSTKEYCARD	FULLKEYCARD	NLEAF
NLEVELS	BPOOL	PGSIZE	ERASERULE
DSETPASS	CLOSERULE	SPACE	IBMREQD

SYSINDEXPART   Contains one row for each unpartitioned index and one row for each partition of a partitioned index.

PARTITION	IXNAME	IXCREATOR	PQTY
SQTY	STORTYPE	STORNAME	VCATNAME
CARD	FAROFFPOS	LEAFDIST	NEAROFFPOS
IBMREQD	LIMITKEY	FREEPAGE	PCTFREE

SYSKEYS   Contains one row for each column of an index key.

IXNAME	IXCREATOR	COLNAME	COLNO
COLSEQ	ORDERING	IBMREQD	

SYSLINKS   Contains one row for every link between tables. (In each link, the parent and children are cata tables.)

CREATOR	TBNAME	LINKNAME	PARENTNAME
PARENTCREATOR	CHILDSEQ	DBNAME	DBID
OBID	COLCOUNT	INSERTRULE	IBMREQD

SYSPLAN   Contains one row for each application plan.

NAME	CREATOR	BINDDATE	VALIDATE
ISOLATION	VALID	OPERATIVE	BINDTIME
PLSIZE	IBMREQD	AVGSIZE	ACQUIRE
RELEASE	EXREFERENCE	EXSTRUCTURE	EXCOST
EXPLAN	EXPREDICATE		

SYSPLANAUTH   Records the privileges held by users over application plans.

GRANTOR	GRANTEE	NAME	TIMESTAMP
DATEGRANTED	TIMEGRANTED	GRANTEETYPE	AUTHHOWGOT
BINDAUTH	EXECUTEAUTH	IBMREQD	

SYSPLANDEP   Records the dependencies of plans on tables, views, synonyms, table spaces, and indexes.

BNAME	BCREATOR	BTYPE	DNAME
IBMREQD			

SYSRELS   Contains one row for every link.

CREATOR	TBNAME	RELNAME	REFTBNAME
REFTBCREATOR	COLCOUNT	DELETERULE	IBMREQD

SYSRESAUTH   Records the privileges held by users over buffer pools, storage groups, and table spaces.

GRANTOR	GRANTEE	QUALIFIER	NAME
GRANTEETYPE	AUTHHOWGOT	OBTYPE	TIMESTAMP
DATEGRANTED	TIMEGRANTED	USEAUTH	IBMREQD

SYSSTMT   Contains one or more rows for each SQL statement of each DBRM.

NAME	PLNAME	PLCREATOR	SEQNO
STMTNO	SECTNO	IBMREQD	TEXT

SYSSTOGROUP   Contains one row for each storage group.

NAME	CREATOR	VCATNAME	VPASSWORD
SPACE	SPCDATE	IBMREQD	

SYSSYNONYMS   Contains one row for each synonym of a table or view.

NAME	CREATOR	TBNAME	TBCREATOR
IBMREQD			

SYSTABAUTH   Records the privileges held by users on tables and views.

GRANTOR	GRANTEE	GRANTEETYPE	DBNAME
SCREATOR	STNAME	TCREATOR	TTNAME
AUTHHOWGOT	TIMESTAMP	DATEGRANTED	TIMEGRANTED
UPDATECOLS	ALTERAUTH	DELETEAUTH	INDEXAUTH
INSERTAUTH	SELECTAUTH	UPDATEAUTH	IBMREQD

SYSTABLEPART   Contains one row for each unpartitioned table space and one row for each partition of a partitioned table space.

PARTITION	TSNAME	DBNAME	IXNAME
IXCREATOR	PQTY	SQTY	STORTYPE
STORNAME	VCATNAME	CARD	FARINDREF
NEARINDREF	PERCACTIVE	PERCDROP	IBMREQD
LIMITKEY	FREEPAGE	PCTFREE	

SYSTABLES   Contains one row for each table and view.

NAME	CREATOR	TYPE	DBNAME
TSNAME	DBID	OBID	COLCOUNT
EDPROC	VALPROC	CLUSTERTYPE	CLUSTERRID
CARD	NPAGES	PCTPAGES	IBMREQD
REMARKS	PARENTS	CHILDREN	KEYCOLUMNS
RECLENGTH	STATUS	KEYOBID	LABEL

SYSTABLESPACE   Contains one row for each table space.

NAME	CREATOR	DBNAME	DBID
OBID	PSID	BPOOL	PARTITIONS
LOCKRULE	PGSIZE	ERASERULE	STATUS
IMPLICIT	NTABLES	NACTIVE	DSETPASS
CLOSERULE	SPACE	IBMREQD	ROOTNAME
ROOTCREATOR			

SYSUSERAUTH   Records the system privileges held by users.

GRANTOR	GRANTEE	TIMESTAMP	DATEGRANTED
TIMEGRANTED	GRANTEETYPE	AUTHHOWGOT	ALTERBPAUTH
BINDADDAUTH	BSDSAUTH	CREATEDBAAUTH	CREATEDBCAUTH
CREATESGAUTH	DISPLAYAUTH	RECOVERAUTH	STOPALLAUTH
STOSPACEAUTH	SYSADMAUTH	SYSOPRAUTH	TRACEAUTH
IBMREQD			

SYSVIEWDEP   Records the dependencies of views on tables and other views.

BNAME	BCREATOR	BTYPE	DNAME
DCREATOR	IBMREQD		

SYSVIEWS

Contains one or more rows for each view.

NAME	CREATOR	SEQNO	CHECK
IBMREQD	TEXT		

SYSVLTREE

Contains the remaining part, if any, of the parse tree representation of views.

IBMREQD	VTREE

SYSVOLUMES

Contains one row for each volume of each storage group.

SGNAME	SGCREATOR	VOLID	IBMREQD

SYSVTREE

Contains a row for each view. Each row contains the parse tree of the view. If the parse tree is longer than 4000 bytes, the rest of the parse tree is saved in the SYSVLTREE table.

NAME	CREATOR	TOTLEN	IBMREQD
VTREE			

Appendix B: Database 2 Data Types

Numeric Data Types:

INTEGER   Large whole numbers (full word)

SMALLINT   Small whole numbers (less that 32,767, half word)

FLOAT   Floating point number

DECIMAL(n1,n2)   A number with "n1" total digits of which
"n2" are to the right of the decimal point

Character Data Types:

CHAR(n)   Fixed character string of "n"

VARCHAR(n)   Variable length character string with a
maximum length of "n"

LONG VARCHAR   Variable length string of characters equal
to the number of bytes left in a page

Graphic Data Types:

GRAPHIC(n)   Fixed length string of double byte characters
of lenth "n" where "n" ranges from 1 to 127

VARGRAPHIC(n)   Varying length string of double-byte
characters, of maximum length of "n".

LONG VARGRAPHIC   Varying length string of double-byte
characters whose maximum length is
determined by amount of space available
in page.

DATE/TIME Data Types:

DATE (For dates)

TIME (For times)

TIMESTAMP(For date and time timestamps)

Data Types can allow for nulls by specifying:

NOT NULL   Prevents column from containing nulls

NOT NULL WITH DEFAULT   Forces a column to take on a
default value in no data is present
The default values for:
Numeric = 0
Fixed-length string = blank
Varying length string = a string of length 0
(Appendix B)

Appendix C: PLAN Table

Contains output from the EXPLAIN SQL statement and the
EXPLAIN parameter if used in the BIND process.

Column Name	Data Type	Description
QUERYNO	INTEGER	n, if SET QUERYNO = n was used; otherwise a number assigned by DB2, unique within each DBRM.
QBLOCKNO	SMALLINT	A number to identify subselects in explainable – sql – statement. The top – level subselect is 1.
APPNAME	CHAR(8)	Application plan name. If the EXPLAIN statement is created dynamically, this is blank.
PROGNAME	CHAR(8)	Name of the DBRM in which the EXPLAIN statement is embedded.
PLANNO	SMALLINT	A number indicating the step of the application plan in which the subselect identified by QBLOCKNO is processed. Each new table accessed requires a new step in the PLAN.
METHOD	SMALLINT	A number indicating the method used in the step: 0 = Access a first table (PLANNO is 1) 1 = Nested loop join. 2 = Merge scan join. 3 = Additional sorts (needed by ORDER BY, GROUP BY, or SELECT DISTINCT).
CREATOR	CHAR(8)	Creator of the new table accessed in this step; Blank for METHOD = 3.
TNAME	CHAR(18)	Name of the new table accessed in this step; Blank for METHOD = 3.
TABNO	SMALLINT	A number to distinguish different references to the same table.
ACCESSTYPE	CHAR(2)	Method of accessing the new table: I = By an index identified in ACCESSNAME R = By sequential scan of pages ' ' = Either: If INSERT statement the access is by the first index created on the table. UPDATE and DELETE that use WHERE CURRENT of cursor, are accessed by the cursor.
MATCHCOLS	SMALLINT	For ACCESSTYPE = I, the number of columns of the index that are used selectively to match the predicate. 0 if no columns are used or if ACCESSTYPE is not I.

Column Name	Data Type	Description
ACCESSCREATOR	CHAR(8)	For ACCESSTYPE I, the creator of the index, else blank.
ACCESSNAME	CHAR(18)	For ACCESSTYPE I, the name of the index, else blank.
INDEXONLY	CHAR(1)	Y if only index must be accessed. N if data must also be accessed
SORTN_UNIQ	CHAR(1)	Whether a sort is perfomed on the new table to remove duplicate rows. Y = yes; N = no.
SORTN_JOIN	CHAR(1)	Whether a sort is performed on the new table for METHOD = 2 join. Y = yes; N = no.
SORTN_ORDERBY	CHAR(1)	Whether a sort is performed on the new table for ORDER BY. Y = yes; N = no.
SORTN_GROUPBY	CHAR(1)	Whether a sort is performed on the new table for GROUP BY. Y = yes; N = no;
SORTC_UNIQ	CHAR(1)	Whether a sort is performed on the composite table to remove duplicate rows. Y = yes; N = no.
SORTC_JOIN	CHAR(1)	Whether a sort is performed on the composite table for METHOD = 2 join. Y = yes; N = no.
SORTC_ORDERBY	CHAR(1)	Whether a sort is performed on the composite table for ORDER BY. Y = yes; N = no.
SORTC_GROUPBY	CHAR(1)	Whether a sort is performed on the composite table for GROUP BY. Y = yes; N = no.
TSLOCKMODE	CHAR(3)	Lock mode applied to the tablespace containing the table. (IS, IX, S, X, SIX)
TIMESTAMP	CHAR(16)	Date and time EXPLAIN was executed. (YYYYMMDDHHMMSSTH)
REMARKS	VARCHAR(254)	User documentation .

Appendix D: Host Language Declarations

COBOL Declarations for Host Variables

DB2 DATA TYPE	COBOL Equivalent	Explanatory Notes
CHAR (Character string)	01 identifier PIC X(n). or 01 identifier PICTURE IS X(n).	"n" is a positive integer and should equal the length of the CHAR column value assigned to the host variable. Anything other than Xs in the PICTURE clause will make the data item unacceptable as a host variable.
VARCHAR (Varying-length character string)	01 identifier 49 identifier PIC S9(ni) COMP. 49 identifier PIC X(nc).	"ni" is a positive integer from 1 to 4. "nc" is a positive integer and should equal the length of the largest VARCHAR column value that can be assigned to the host variable.
GRAPHIC (Fixed-length graphic string)	01 identifier PIC G(n) DISPLAY-1	"n" is a positive integer from 1 to 127. "n" refers to the number of double byte characters, not to the number of bytes.
VARGRAPHIC (Varying-length graphic string)	01 identifier 49 identifier PIC S9(ni) COMP. 49 identifier PIC G(nc) DISPLAY-1	"ni" is a positive integer from 1 to 4. "nc" is a positive integer and should equal the length in double byte characters of the largest VARGRAPHIC column value that can be assigned to the host variable.
SMALLINT (Halfword integer)	01 identifier PIC S9(4) COMP. or 01 identifier PIC S9(n) COMP. or 01 identifier PICTURE S9(n) USAGE IS COMPUTATIONAL.	"n" is a positive integer from 1 to 4. No decimal point is allowed. Anything other than a 9 will make the data item unacceptable as a host variable. "PIC S" and "COMP" are required.

375

DB2 DATA TYPE	COBOL Equivalent	Explanatory Notes
INTEGER (Fullword integer)	01 identifier PIC S9(9) COMP. or 01 identifier PIC S9(n) COMP. or 01 identifier PICTURE S9(n) USAGE IS COMPUTATIONAL.	"n" is a positive integer from 5 to 9. No decimal point is allowed. Anything other than a 9 will make the data item unacceptable as a host variable. "PIC S" and "COMP" are required.
DECIMAL (Decimal value)	01 identifier PIC S9V COMP-3. or 01 identifier PIC S9(n)V COMP-3. or 01 identifier PIC S9(n)V9(m) COMP-3. or 01 identifier PIC S9(n)V9(m) USAGE IS COMPUTATIONAL-3.	"n" and "m" are positive integers; "n+m" cannot exceed 15. You must include a "V" to denote the decimal point. Anything other than a 9 and a V will make the data item unacceptable as a host variable. "PIC S" and "COMP-3" are required.
FLOAT(21) (Single precision floating-point)	01 identifier COMP-1. or 01 identifier USAGE IS COMPUTATIONAL-1.	"COMP-1" is required.
FLOAT(53) (Double precision floating-point)	01 identifier COMP-2. or 01 identifier USAGE IS COMPUTATIONAL-2.	"COMP-2" is required.
DATE	01 identifier PIC X(n). or 01 identifier PICTURE IS X(n).	If you are using a date exit routine, "n" is determined by that routine; otherwise, "n" must be at least 10.
TIME	01 identifier PIC X(n). or 01 identifier PICTURE IS X(n).	If you are using a time exit routine, "n" is determined by that routine. Otherwise, "n" must be at least 6; to include seconds, "n" must be at least 8.
TIMESTAMP	01 identifier PIC X(n). or 01 identifier PICTURE IS X(n).	"n" must be at least 19. To include microseconds, "n" must be 26; if "n" is less than 26, truncation occurs on the microseconds part.

PL/I Declarations for Host Variables

DB2 DATA TYPE	PL/I Equivalent	Explanatory Notes
CHAR (Character string)	DCL identifier CHAR(n);	"n" is a positive integer and should equal the length of the CHAR column value assigned to the host variable.
VARCHAR (Varying-length character string)	DCL identifier CHAR(n) VAR;	"n" is a positive integer and should equal the length of the largest VARCHAR column value that can be assigned to the host variable.
GRAPHIC (Fixed-length graphic string)	DCL identifier GRAPHIC(n);	"n" is a positive integer from 1 to 127. "n" refers to the number of double byte characters, not to the number of bytes.
VARGRAPHIC (Varying-length graphic string)	DCL identifier GRAPHIC(n) VAR;	"n" is a positive integer and refers to the number of double byte characters, not to the number of bytes.

SMALLINT
(Halfword integer)
	DCL identifier BIN FIXED;
	  or
	DCL identifier FIXED BIN;
	  or
	DCL identifier BIN FIXED(15);
	  or
	DCL identifier FIXED BIN(15);	

INTEGER (Fullword integer)	DCL identifier BIN FIXED(31); or DCL identifier FIXED BIN(31);	

DB2 DATA TYPE	PL/I Equivalent	Explanatory Notes
DECIMAL (Decimal value)	DCL identifier DEC FIXED(s); or DCL identifier FIXED DEC(s); or DCL identifier DEC FIXED(s,p); or DCL identifier FIXED DEC(s,p);	"s" (the scale factor) and "p" (the precision) are positive inte- gers. "s" cannot be larger than "p". "p" is 15 or less.
FLOAT(21) (Single precision floating-point)	DCL identifier BIN FLOAT(n); or DCL identifier FLOAT BIN(n); or DCL identifier DEC FLOAT(m); or DCL identifier FLOAT DEC(m);	"n" is a positive integer from 1 to 21, however DB2 will recog- nize it as FLOAT(21). "m" is a positive integer from 1 to 6, however DB2 will recog- nize it as FLOAT(21).
FLOAT(53) (Double precision floating-point)	DCL identifier BIN FLOAT(n); or DCL identifier FLOAT BIN(n); or DCL identifier DEC FLOAT(m); or DCL identifier FLOAT DEC(m);	"n" is a positive integer from 22 to 53, however DB2 will recog- nize it as FLOAT(53). "m" is a positive integer from 7 to 16, however DB2 will it as FLOAT(53).
DATE	DCL identifier CHAR(n);	If you are using a date exit routine, "n" is determined by that routine; otherwise, "n" must be at least 10.
TIME	DCL identifier CHAR(n);	If you are using a time exit routine, "n" is determined by that routine. Otherwise, "n" must be at least 6; to include seconds, "n" must be at least 8.
TIMESTAMP	DCL identifier CHAR(n);	"n" must be at least 19. To include microseconds, "n" must be 26; if "n" is less than 26, truncation occurs on the micro- seconds part.

FORTRAN Declarations for Host Variables

DB2 DATA TYPE	FORTRAN Equivalent	Explanatory Notes
CHAR (Character string)	CHARACTER*n identifier	"n" is a positive integer value and should equal the length of the CHAR column value assigned to the host variable.
VARCHAR (Varying-length character string)	CHARACTER*n identifier	Because FORTRAN doesn't allow varying-length character strings, code a varying-length character host variable as a CHARACTER host variable large enough to contain the largest expected VARCHAR value. "n" is a positive integer and should equal the length of the largest VARCHAR column value that can be assigned to the host variable.
SMALLINT (Halfword integer)	INTEGER*2 identifier	
INTEGER (Fullword integer)	INTEGER*4 identifier	
DECIMAL (Decimal value)	REAL*8 identifier	Because FORTRAN doesn't support decimal numbers, code a decimal host variable as a REAL variable.
FLOAT(21) (Single precision floating-point)	REAL identifier or REAL*4 identifier	
FLOAT(53) (Double precision floating-point)	REAL*8 identifier or DOUBLE PRECISION identifier	
DATE	CHARACTER*n identifier	If you are using a date exit routine, "n" is determined by that routine; otherwise, "n" must be at least 10.
TIME	CHARACTER*n identifier	If you are using a time exit routine, "n" is determined by that routine. Otherwise, "n" must be at least 6; to include seconds, "n" must be at least 8.
TIMESTAMP	CHARACTER*n identifier	"n" must be at least 19. To include microseconds, "n" must be 26; if "n" is less than 26, truncation occurs on the microseconds part.

Appendix E: SQL Communication and Description Areas

SQLCA for COBOL:

```
01 SQLCA.
            05 SQLCAID    PIC X(8).
            05 SQLCABC    PIC S9(9) COMP-4.
            05 SQLCODE    PIC S9(9) COMP-4.
            05 SQLERRM.
               49 SQLERRML PIC S9(4) COMP-4.
               49 SQLERRMC PIC X(70).
            05 SQLERRP    PIC X(8).
            05 SQLERRD    OCCURS 6 TIMES
                          PIC S9(9) COMP-4.

            05 SQLWARN.
               10 SQLWARN0 PIC X.
               10 SQLWARN1 PIC X.
               10 SQLWARN2 PIC X.
               10 SQLWARN3 PIC X.
               10 SQLWARN4 PIC X.
               10 SQLWARN5 PIC X.
               10 SQLWARN6 PIC X.
               10 SQLWARN7 PIC X.
            05 SQLEXT     PIC X(8).
```

SQLCA for PL/I:

```
DECLARE
    1 SQLCA,
      2 SQLCAID CHAR(8),
      2 SQLCABC FIXED(31) BINARY,
```

```
2 SQLCODE FIXED(31) BINARY,
2 SQLERRM CHAR(70) VAR,
2 SQLERRP CHAR(8),
2 SQLERRD(6) FIXED(31) BINARY,
2 SQLWARN,
    3 SQLWARN0 CHAR(1),
    3 SQLWARN1 CHAR(1),
    3 SQLWARN2 CHAR(1),
    3 SQLWARN3 CHAR(1),
    3 SQLWARN4 CHAR(1),
    3 SQLWARN5 CHAR(1),
    3 SQLWARN6 CHAR(1),
    3 SQLWARN7 CHAR(1),
2 SQLEXT CHAR(8);
```

SQLCA for FORTRAN:

```
EXTERNAL SQLADD,DSNHFT,SQVCHR
        INTEGER*4 SQLADD,SQVCHR
        INTEGER   SQSHHW /65536/,SQTIME(2) /330115187,242274828/
        INTEGER   SQC002(10) /10*0/
        INTEGER   SQC003(10) /10*0/
        INTEGER   SQD004(3,6) /18*0/
        INTEGER   SQC004(10) /10*0/
        INTEGER   SQC005(10) /10*0/
*       THE SQL COMMUNICATIONS AREA
        INTEGER   SQLCOD,
    C             SQLERR(6),
    C             SQLTXL*2
        COMMON /SQLCA1/SQLCOD,SQLERR,SQLTXL
        CHARACTER SQLERP*8,
    C             SQLWRN(0:7)*1,
    C             SQLTXT*70,
    C             SQLEXT*8
        COMMON /SQLCA2/SQLERP,SQLWRN,SQLTXT,SQLEXT
```

SQLDA for PL/I Dynamic Varying-List-Select:

```
DECLARE
    1 SQLDA BASED(SQLDAPTR),
        2 SQLDAID CHAR(8),
```

```
    2 SQLDABC FIXED(31) BINARY,
    2 SQLN    FIXED(15) BINARY,
    2 SQLD    FIXED(15) BINARY,
    2 SQLVAR(SQLSIZE REFER(SQLN)),
      3 SQLTYPE FIXED(15) BINARY,
      3 SQLLEN FIXED(15) BINARY,
      3 SQLDATA POINTER,
      3 SQLIND POINTER,
      3 SQLNAME CHAR(30) VAR;
DECLARE SQLSIZE FIXED(15) BINARY;
DECLARE SQLDAPTR POINTER;
```

Appendix F:
Application Program Examples

COBOL PROGRAM PROGRM1C: CURSOR with Static Select

```
ID DIVISION.
   PROGRAM-ID.  PROGRM1C.
   AUTHOR.      BRUCE LARSON
   ENVIRONMENT DIVISION.
   CONFIGURATION SECTION.
   INPUT-OUTPUT SECTION.
   FILE-CONTROL.
   DATA DIVISION.
   FILE SECTION.
   WORKING-STORAGE SECTION.

01  DCLEMPLOYEES-TABLE.
    10 EMPLOYEE-NO        PIC S9(9) USAGE COMP.
    10 EMPLOYEE-NAME      PIC X(16).
    10 ADDRESS-STATE      PIC X(2).
    10 DEPT               PIC X(4).
    10 SALARY             PIC S99999V99 USAGE COMP-3.

01  SQLCA.
    05 SQLCAID            PIC X(8).
    05 SQLCABC            PIC S9(9) COMP-4.

    05 SQLCODE            PIC S9(9) COMP-4.
    05 SQLERRM.
       49 SQLERRML        PIC S9(4) COMP-4.
       49 SQLERRMC        PIC X(70).
    05 SQLERRP            PIC X(8).
```

```
       05 SQLERRD                    OCCURS 6 TIMES
                                     PIC S9(9) COMP-4.
       05 SQLWARN.
          10 SQLWARN0                PIC X.
          10 SQLWARN1                PIC X.
          10 SQLWARN2                PIC X.
          10 SQLWARN3                PIC X.
          10 SQLWARN4                PIC X.
          10 SQLWARN5                PIC X.
          10 SQLWARN6                PIC X.
          10 SQLWARN7                PIC X.
       05 SQLEXT                     PIC X(8).


   01  SALARY-DISPLAY                           PIC Z(6).ZZ.
   01  RC                                       PIC +99999.
   01  HOST-DEPT                                PIC X(4).


   PROCEDURE DIVISION.
   001-MAINLINE.
       DISPLAY ' '.
       DISPLAY '******* BEGIN EXECUTION OF PROGRM1C.********'.
       DISPLAY ' '.
  *------------------------------------------------------------
       EXEC SQL
         DECLARE CURSOR1 CURSOR
         FOR SELECT EMPLOYEE_NO, EMPLOYEE_NAME,
             ADDRESS_STATE, DEPT, SALARY
             FROM EMPLOYEES_TABLE
             WHERE DEPT = :HOST-DEPT
       END-EXEC.
  *------------------------------------------------------------
       MOVE 'D890' TO HOST-DEPT.
  *------------------------------------------------------------
       DISPLAY 'OPEN CURSOR NAMED: CURSOR1 '
       DISPLAY ' '
       EXEC SQL
         OPEN CURSOR1
       END-EXEC.
       IF SQLCODE NOT = 0
           DISPLAY 'OPEN ERROR FOR CURSOR NAMED = CURSOR1'
           DISPLAY ' '
```

```
          PERFORM 250-DISPLAY-SQLCA THRU 250-EXIT
          GO TO 500-EXIT.
*------------------------------------------------------------
      DISPLAY 'DISPLAY ROWS FETCHED FOR CURSOR
         NAMED = CURSOR1'.
      DISPLAY ' '.
      PERFORM 200-FETCH-EMPLOYEE-ROWS THRU 200-EXIT
        UNTIL SQLCODE NOT = 0.
      IF SQLCODE <  0
          DISPLAY 'FETCH ERROR USING CURSOR NAMED: CURSOR1.'
          DISPLAY ' '
          PERFORM 250-DISPLAY-SQLCA THRU 250-EXIT
          GO TO 500-EXIT.
      MOVE SQLCODE TO RC.
      DISPLAY ' '.
      DISPLAY 'SQLCODE = '  RC.
      DISPLAY ' '.
      DISPLAY 'END OF FETCH USING CURSOR NAMED: CURSOR1.'.
      DISPLAY ' '.
*------------------------------------------------------------
      DISPLAY 'CLOSE CURSOR NAMED: CURSOR1'.
      DISPLAY ' '.
      EXEC SQL
        CLOSE CURSOR1
      END-EXEC.
      IF SQLCODE NOT = 0
          DISPLAY 'CLOSE ERROR ON CURSOR NAMED: CURSOR1'
          DISPLAY ' '

          PERFORM 250-DISPLAY-SQLCA THRU 250-EXIT
          GO TO 500-EXIT.
      GO TO 500-EXIT.
*------------------------------------------------------------
  200-FETCH-EMPLOYEE-ROWS.
      EXEC SQL
        FETCH CURSOR1
          INTO :DCLEMPLOYEES-TABLE
      END-EXEC.
      IF SQLCODE < 0
          DISPLAY 'BAD SQLCODE ON FETCH = ' RC
          DISPLAY ' '
```

```
            PERFORM 250-DISPLAY-SQLCA THRU 250-EXIT
            GO TO 500-EXIT.
        IF SQLCODE NOT = 0
            GO TO 200-EXIT.
        MOVE SALARY TO SALARY-DISPLAY.
        DISPLAY 'EMPLOYEE NUMBER = ' EMPLOYEE-NO.
        DISPLAY '                   EMPLOYEE NAME = '
            EMPLOYEE-NAME.
        DISPLAY '                   STATE = '
            ADDRESS-STATE.
        DISPLAY '                   DEPARTMENT = '
            DEPT.
        DISPLAY '                   SALARY = '
            SALARY-DISPLAY.
        DISPLAY ' '.
    200-EXIT.  EXIT.


    250-DISPLAY-SQLCA.
        DISPLAY ' '.
        DISPLAY 'DISPLAY SQLCA AREA.'.
        DISPLAY 'SQLCAID = '  SQLCAID.

        MOVE SQLCODE TO RC.
        DISPLAY 'SQLCODE = '  RC.
        DISPLAY 'SQLERRMC= '  SQLERRMC.
        DISPLAY 'SQLWARN0 = ' SQLWARN0.
        IF SQLWARN0 NOT EQUAL TO 'W'
            DISPLAY 'SQLWARN1 = ' SQLWARN1
            DISPLAY 'SQLWARN2 = ' SQLWARN2
            DISPLAY 'SQLWARN3 = ' SQLWARN3
            DISPLAY 'SQLWARN4 = ' SQLWARN4
            DISPLAY 'SQLWARN5 = ' SQLWARN5
            DISPLAY 'SQLWARN6 = ' SQLWARN6
            DISPLAY 'SQLWARN7 = ' SQLWARN7.
    250-EXIT.  EXIT.


    500-EXIT.
```

```
       DISPLAY '******** END EXECUTION OF PROGRM1C. ********'.
       GOBACK.
```

FORTRAN PROGRAM PROGRM1F: CURSOR with Static Select

```
C-------- ALLOCATE FI(FT03F001) FOR OUTPUT. ------------------
       EXEC SQL INCLUDE SQLCA
       INTEGER EMPLNO*4
       CHARACTER NAME*16, STATE*2, DEPT*4, HTDEPT*4
       REAL SALARY*8
       EXEC SQL
     + DECLARE CURSOR1 CURSOR
     + FOR SELECT EMPLOYEE_NO,EMPLOYEE_NAME,
     +         ADDRESS_STATE,DEPT,SALARY
     +         FROM EMPLOYEES_TABLE
     +         WHERE DEPT = :HTDEPT
       WRITE (3,500)
500    FORMAT(' ********* BEGIN EXECUTION OF PROGRM1F **********')
       WRITE (3,510)
510    FORMAT(' ')
       HTDEPT = 'D890'
       WRITE (3,1010)
1010   FORMAT(' OPEN CURSOR NAMED: CURSOR1 ')
       WRITE (3,1030)
1030   FORMAT(' ')
       EXEC SQL
     + OPEN CURSOR1
       IF (SQLCOD.LT.0) THEN
           WRITE(3,1040)
1040       FORMAT(' OPEN ERROR FOR CURSOR NAMED: CURSOR1')
           GO TO 9990
       ENDIF
       WRITE (3,2010)
2010   FORMAT(' DISPLAY ROWS FETCHED FOR CURSOR NAMED: CURSOR1')
       WRITE (3,2020)
2020   FORMAT(' ')
2030   CONTINUE
       EXEC SQL
     + FETCH CURSOR1
     +     INTO :EMPLNO, :NAME, :STATE, :DEPT, :SALARY
       IF (SQLCOD.EQ.100) GO TO 9000
```

```
      IF (SQLCOD.NE.0) GO TO 9990
      WRITE(3,3010) EMPLNO
3010  FORMAT(' EMPLOYEE NUMBER = ',I4)
      WRITE(3,3020) NAME
3020  FORMAT('                          EMPLOYEE NAME = ',A16)
      WRITE(3,3030) STATE
3030  FORMAT('                          STATE = ',A2)
      WRITE(3,3040) DEPT
3040  FORMAT('                          DEPARTMENT = ',A4)
      WRITE(3,3050) SALARY
3050  FORMAT('                          SALARY = ',F8.2)
      WRITE(3,3055)
3055  FORMAT(' ')
      GO TO 2030
9000     WRITE(3,9010) SQLCOD
9010     FORMAT(' SQLCODE = ',I4)
         WRITE(3,9020)
9020     FORMAT(' ')
         WRITE(3,9030)
9030     FORMAT(' END OF FETCH USING CURSOR NAMED: CURSOR1')
      WRITE(3,9040)
9040  FORMAT(' CLOSE CURSOR NAMED: CURSOR1')
         WRITE(3,9045)
9045     FORMAT(' ')
      EXEC SQL
    +   CLOSE CURSOR1
      IF (SQLCOD.LT.0) THEN
         WRITE(3,9050)
9050     FORMAT(' CLOSE ERROR ON CURSOR NAMED: CURSOR1')
         WRITE(3,9055)
9055     FORMAT(' ')
         GO TO 9990
      ENDIF
      IF (SQLCOD.EQ.0) GO TO 9995
9990  WRITE(3,9991) SQLCOD
9991  FORMAT(' SQLCODE: ',I4)
      WRITE(3,9992) SQLTXT
9992  FORMAT(' SQLTXT = ',A70)
9995  WRITE(3,9999)
9999  FORMAT(' ********** END EXECUTION OF PROGRM1F. **********')
```

```
      STOP
      END
```

PL/I PROGRAM PROGRM1P: CURSOR with Static Select

```
PROGRM1: PROCEDURE OPTIONS (MAIN);
  /*                                                               */
  /*   INCLUDE SQLCA AND EMPLOYEE TABLE DECLARATION.               */
  /*                                                               */
  DCL
     WARNING BIN FIXED(15) INIT(0),
     ZERO  BIN FIXED(15) INIT(0);
  EXEC SQL INCLUDE EMPLOYEE;
  EXEC SQL INCLUDE SQLCA;
  /*                                                               */
  /*                                                               */
  DCL
     SQLWORK CHAR(110) VARYING;
  DCL
     RETCODE FIXED(31) BIN,
     HOSTDEPT CHAR(4);
  DCL
     (ADDR,PLIRETC)
     BUILTIN;
  DCL
     SYSPRINT FILE STREAM OUTPUT ENV(FB,RECSIZE(133),BLKSIZE(133));
  /*                                                               */
  /*                                                               */
  /***************************************************************/
  PUT SKIP EDIT (' ') (A);
  PUT SKIP EDIT('***** BEGIN EXECUTION OF PROGRM1P *****') (A(43));
  PUT SKIP EDIT (' ') (A);
  /***************************************************************/
  /*                                                               */
  /*   DECLARE CURSOR1.                                            */
  /*                                                               */
  PUT SKIP EDIT ('DECLARE CURSOR1') (A(15));
  PUT SKIP EDIT (' ') (A);
  EXEC SQL
     DECLARE CURSOR1 CURSOR
     FOR SELECT EMPLOYEE_NO,EMPLOYEE_NAME,
```

```
                   ADDRESS_STATE, DEPT, SALARY
              FROM EMPLOYEES_TABLE
              WHERE DEPT= :HOSTDEPT;
/************************************************************/
RETCODE = ZERO;
HOSTDEPT = 'D890';
/************************************************************/
/*                                                       */
/*  OPEN CURSOR.                                         */
/*                                                       */
PUT SKIP EDIT ('OPEN CURSOR1') (A(12));
PUT SKIP EDIT (' ') (A);
EXEC SQL OPEN CURSOR1;
IF SQLCODE = 0 THEN GOTO DISPERR;
/************************************************************/
/*                                                       */
/*  FETCH ROWS USING CURSOR.                             */
/*                                                       */
PUT SKIP EDIT ('FETCH USING CURSOR1') (A(19));
PUT SKIP EDIT (' ') (A);
   DO UNTIL (SQLCODE =ZERO);
      EXEC SQL FETCH CURSOR1 INTO ROWAREA;
        IF SQLCODE < 0 THEN GOTO DISPERR;
        PUT SKIP EDIT ('EMPLOYEE NUMBER = ',EMPLNO) (A(18),F(8));
        PUT SKIP EDIT ('EMPLOYEE NAME = ',EMPLNAME) (A(16),A(16));
        PUT SKIP EDIT ('STATE = ',STATE) (A(8),A(2));
        PUT SKIP EDIT ('DEPT = ',DEPT) (A(7),A(4));
        PUT SKIP EDIT ('SALARY = ',SALARY) (A(9),F(8));
        PUT SKIP EDIT (' ') (A);
   END;
/************************************************************/
/*                                                       */
/*  CLOSE CURSOR.                                        */
/*                                                       */
PUT SKIP EDIT ('CLOSE CURSOR1') (A(13));
PUT SKIP EDIT (' ') (A);
EXEC SQL CLOSE CURSOR1;
IF SQLCODE < 0 THEN GOTO DISPERR;
IF SQLCODE = 0 THEN GOTO STOPRUN;
/*                                                       */
/*  ERROR ENCOUNTERED, DISPLAY CONTENTS OF SQLCA AREA.   */
```

```
/*                                                               */
DISPERR:
RETCODE = WARNING;
PUT SKIP EDIT (' ') (A);
PUT SKIP EDIT ('DISPLAY SQLCA AREA=') ( A(19));
PUT SKIP EDIT ('SQLCAID = ',SQLCAID) (A(11), A(8));
PUT SKIP EDIT ('SQLCODE = ',SQLCODE) (A(11), F(8));
PUT SKIP EDIT ('SQLERRMC= ',SQLERRM) (A(11), A(70));
PUT SKIP EDIT ('SQLWARN0 = ',SQLWARN0) (A(11), A);
   IF SQLWARN0 = 'W'
      THEN DO;
         PUT SKIP EDIT ('SQLWARN1 = ',SQLWARN1) (A(11),A);
         PUT SKIP EDIT ('SQLWARN2 = ',SQLWARN2) (A(11),A);
         PUT SKIP EDIT ('SQLWARN3 = ',SQLWARN3) (A(11),A);
         PUT SKIP EDIT ('SQLWARN4 = ',SQLWARN4) (A(11),A);
         PUT SKIP EDIT ('SQLWARN5 = ',SQLWARN5) (A(11),A);
         PUT SKIP EDIT ('SQLWARN6 = ',SQLWARN6) (A(11),A);
         PUT SKIP EDIT ('SQLWARN7 = ',SQLWARN7) (A(11),A);
         PUT SKIP EDIT (' ') (A);
      END;
/*                                                               */
/*      STOP RUN                                                 */
/*                                                               */
STOPRUN:
PUT SKIP EDIT ('******* END EXECUTION OF PROGRM1P ******')
(A(40));
```

```
CALL PLIRETC(RETCODE);
END PROGRM1;
```

COBOL PROGRAM PROGRM2C: Static SQL Update

```
ID DIVISION.
            PROGRAM-ID.  PROGRM2C.
            AUTHOR.         BRUCE LARSON
        ENVIRONMENT DIVISION.
        CONFIGURATION SECTION.
        INPUT-OUTPUT SECTION.
        FILE-CONTROL.
        DATA DIVISION.
        FILE SECTION.
        WORKING-STORAGE SECTION.

            EXEC SQL
                INCLUDE EMPLOYEE
            END-EXEC.

            EXEC SQL
                INCLUDE SQLCA
            END-EXEC.

        01  SALARY-DISPLAY                        PIC Z(6).ZZ.
        01  RC                                    PIC +99999.
        01  UPDATED-ROWS                          PIC +99999.
        01  HOST-DEPT                             PIC X(4).

        PROCEDURE DIVISION.
        001-MAINLINE.
            DISPLAY ' '.
            DISPLAY '******* BEGIN EXECUTION OF PROGRM2C.********'.
            DISPLAY ' '.
    *------------------------------------------------------------
            MOVE 'D700' TO HOST-DEPT.
            DISPLAY 'EMPLOYEES IN DEPARTMENT D700 PRIOR TO UP-
    DATE.'.
            DISPLAY ' '.
    *------------------------------------------------------------
            EXEC SQL
```

```
    SELECT EMPLOYEE_NO, EMPLOYEE_NAME,
        ADDRESS_STATE, DEPT, SALARY
    INTO :DCLEMPLOYEES-TABLE
        FROM EMPLOYEES_TABLE
    WHERE DEPT = :HOST-DEPT AND EMPLOYEE_NO = 495
END-EXEC.
IF SQLCODE < 0
    DISPLAY 'SELECT ERROR FOR EMPLOYEE NUMBER 495.'
    DISPLAY ' '
    PERFORM 250-DISPLAY-SQLCA THRU 250-EXIT
    GO TO 500-EXIT.
IF SQLCODE > 0 GO TO 500-EXIT.
DISPLAY 'EMPLOYEE NUMBER = ' EMPLOYEE-NO.
DISPLAY '                  EMPLOYEE NAME = '
    EMPLOYEE-NAME.
DISPLAY '                      STATE = '
    ADDRESS-STATE.
DISPLAY '                      DEPARTMENT = '
    DEPT.
MOVE SALARY TO SALARY-DISPLAY.
DISPLAY '                      SALARY = '
    SALARY-DISPLAY.
DISPLAY ' '.
*-----------------------------------------------------------
EXEC SQL
    SELECT EMPLOYEE_NO, EMPLOYEE_NAME,
        ADDRESS_STATE, DEPT, SALARY
    INTO :EMPLOYEE-NO, :EMPLOYEE-NAME,
            :ADDRESS-STATE, :DEPT, :SALARY
        FROM EMPLOYEES_TABLE
    WHERE DEPT = :HOST-DEPT AND EMPLOYEE_NO = 850
END-EXEC.
IF SQLCODE < 0
    DISPLAY 'SELECT ERROR FOR EMPLOYEE NUMBER 850.'
    DISPLAY ' '
    PERFORM 250-DISPLAY-SQLCA THRU 250-EXIT
    GO TO 500-EXIT.
IF SQLCODE > 0 GO TO 500-EXIT.
DISPLAY 'EMPLOYEE NUMBER = ' EMPLOYEE-NO.
DISPLAY '                  EMPLOYEE NAME = '
    EMPLOYEE-NAME.
```

```
        DISPLAY '                      STATE = '
           ADDRESS-STATE.
        DISPLAY '                      DEPARTMENT = '
           DEPT.
        MOVE SALARY TO SALARY-DISPLAY.
        DISPLAY '                      SALARY = '
           SALARY-DISPLAY.
        DISPLAY ' '.
   *-------------------------------------------------------------
        EXEC SQL
           SELECT EMPLOYEE_NO, EMPLOYEE_NAME,
                  ADDRESS_STATE, DEPT, SALARY
             INTO :DCLEMPLOYEES-TABLE
                  FROM EMPLOYEES_TABLE
             WHERE DEPT = :HOST-DEPT AND EMPLOYEE_NO = 900
        END-EXEC.
        IF SQLCODE < 0
           DISPLAY 'SELECT ERROR FOR EMPLOYEE NUMBER 900.'
           DISPLAY '  '
           PERFORM 250-DISPLAY-SQLCA THRU 250-EXIT
           GO TO 500-EXIT.
        IF SQLCODE > 0 GO TO 500-EXIT.
        DISPLAY 'EMPLOYEE NUMBER = ' EMPLOYEE-NO.
        DISPLAY '                      EMPLOYEE NAME = '
           EMPLOYEE-NAME.
        DISPLAY '                      STATE = '
           ADDRESS-STATE.
        DISPLAY '                      DEPARTMENT = '
           DEPT.
        MOVE SALARY TO SALARY-DISPLAY.
        DISPLAY '                      SALARY = '
           SALARY-DISPLAY.
        DISPLAY ' '.
   *-------------------------------------------------------------
        DISPLAY 'INCREASE ALL SALARIES IN DEPT 700 BY 1000.'.
        DISPLAY ' '.
        EXEC SQL
           UPDATE EMPLOYEES_TABLE
              SET SALARY = SALARY + 1000.00
              WHERE DEPT='D700'
        END-EXEC.
```

```
    IF SQLCODE < 0
        DISPLAY 'SALARY UPDATE ERROR FOR INCREASES.'
        DISPLAY ' '
        PERFORM 250-DISPLAY-SQLCA THRU 250-EXIT
        GO TO 500-EXIT.
    IF SQLCODE > 0 GO TO 500-EXIT.
    MOVE SQLERRD(3) TO UPDATED-ROWS.
    DISPLAY 'ROWS UPDATED DURING INCREASE = ',
        UPDATED-ROWS.
    DISPLAY ' '.
*--------------------------------------------------------------
    DISPLAY 'DISPLAY ROWS AFTER UPDATE.'.
    DISPLAY ' '.
*--------------------------------------------------------------
    EXEC SQL
        SELECT EMPLOYEE_NO, EMPLOYEE_NAME,
               ADDRESS_STATE, DEPT, SALARY
        INTO :DCLEMPLOYEES-TABLE
             FROM EMPLOYEES_TABLE
        WHERE DEPT = :HOST-DEPT AND EMPLOYEE_NO = 495
    END-EXEC.
    IF SQLCODE < 0
        DISPLAY 'SELECT ERROR FOR EMPLOYEE NUMBER 495.'
        DISPLAY ' '
        PERFORM 250-DISPLAY-SQLCA THRU 250-EXIT
        GO TO 500-EXIT.
    IF SQLCODE > 0 GO TO 500-EXIT.
    DISPLAY 'EMPLOYEE NUMBER = ' EMPLOYEE-NO.
    DISPLAY '                     EMPLOYEE NAME = '
        EMPLOYEE-NAME.
    DISPLAY '                         STATE = '
        ADDRESS-STATE.
    DISPLAY '                     DEPARTMENT = '
        DEPT.
    MOVE SALARY TO SALARY-DISPLAY.
    DISPLAY '                         SALARY = '
        SALARY-DISPLAY.
    DISPLAY ' '.
*--------------------------------------------------------------
    EXEC SQL
        SELECT EMPLOYEE_NO, EMPLOYEE_NAME,
```

```
              ADDRESS_STATE, DEPT, SALARY
     INTO :EMPLOYEE-NO, :EMPLOYEE-NAME,
              :ADDRESS-STATE, :DEPT, :SALARY
          FROM EMPLOYEES_TABLE
     WHERE DEPT = :HOST-DEPT AND EMPLOYEE_NO = 850
END-EXEC.
IF SQLCODE < 0
    DISPLAY 'SELECT ERROR FOR EMPLOYEE NUMBER 850.'
    DISPLAY ' '
    PERFORM 250-DISPLAY-SQLCA THRU 250-EXIT
    GO TO 500-EXIT.
IF SQLCODE > 0 GO TO 500-EXIT.
DISPLAY 'EMPLOYEE NUMBER = ' EMPLOYEE-NO.
DISPLAY '                  EMPLOYEE NAME = '
    EMPLOYEE-NAME.
DISPLAY '                         STATE = '
    ADDRESS-STATE.
DISPLAY '                    DEPARTMENT = '
    DEPT.
MOVE SALARY TO SALARY-DISPLAY.
DISPLAY '                        SALARY = '
    SALARY-DISPLAY.
DISPLAY ' '.
*-------------------------------------------------------------------
EXEC SQL
    SELECT EMPLOYEE_NO, EMPLOYEE_NAME,
           ADDRESS_STATE, DEPT, SALARY
      INTO :DCLEMPLOYEES-TABLE
           FROM EMPLOYEES_TABLE
     WHERE DEPT = :HOST-DEPT AND EMPLOYEE_NO = 900
END-EXEC.
IF SQLCODE < 0
    DISPLAY 'SELECT ERROR FOR EMPLOYEE NUMBER 900.'
    DISPLAY ' '
    PERFORM 250-DISPLAY-SQLCA THRU 250-EXIT
    GO TO 500-EXIT.
IF SQLCODE > 0 GO TO 500-EXIT.
DISPLAY 'EMPLOYEE NUMBER = ' EMPLOYEE-NO.
DISPLAY '                  EMPLOYEE NAME = '
    EMPLOYEE-NAME.
DISPLAY '                         STATE = '
```

```
            ADDRESS-STATE.
       DISPLAY '                    DEPARTMENT = '
            DEPT.
       MOVE SALARY TO SALARY-DISPLAY.
       DISPLAY '                    SALARY = '
            SALARY-DISPLAY.
       DISPLAY ' '.
*------------------------------------------------------------
   DISPLAY 'REDUCE SALARY FOR EMPLOYEES IN DEPT D700 BY 1000'.
       DISPLAY ' '.
       EXEC SQL
          UPDATE EMPLOYEES_TABLE
            SET SALARY = SALARY - 1000.00
            WHERE DEPT='D700'
       END-EXEC.
       IF SQLCODE < 0
            DISPLAY 'SALARY UPDATE ERROR FOR DECREASES.'
            DISPLAY ' '
            PERFORM 250-DISPLAY-SQLCA THRU 250-EXIT
            GO TO 500-EXIT.
       IF SQLCODE > 0 GO TO 500-EXIT.
       MOVE SQLERRD(3) TO UPDATED-ROWS.
     DISPLAY 'ROWS UPDATED DURING DECREASE = ', UPDATED-ROWS.
       DISPLAY ' '.
*------------------------------------------------------------
       DISPLAY 'EMPLOYEES IN DEPARTMENT D700 AFTER UPDATE.'.
       DISPLAY ' '.
       EXEC SQL
          SELECT EMPLOYEE_NO, EMPLOYEE_NAME,
                ADDRESS_STATE, DEPT, SALARY
            INTO :DCLEMPLOYEES-TABLE
                FROM EMPLOYEES_TABLE
          WHERE DEPT = :HOST-DEPT AND EMPLOYEE_NO = 495
       END-EXEC.
       IF SQLCODE < 0
            DISPLAY 'SELECT ERROR FOR EMPLOYEE NUMBER 495.'
            DISPLAY ' '
            PERFORM 250-DISPLAY-SQLCA THRU 250-EXIT
            GO TO 500-EXIT.
       IF SQLCODE > 0 GO TO 500-EXIT.
       DISPLAY 'EMPLOYEE NUMBER = ' EMPLOYEE-NO.
```

```
        DISPLAY '                         EMPLOYEE NAME = '
           EMPLOYEE-NAME.
        DISPLAY '                      STATE = '
           ADDRESS-STATE.
        DISPLAY '                         DEPARTMENT = '
           DEPT.
        MOVE SALARY TO SALARY-DISPLAY.
        DISPLAY '                         SALARY = '
           SALARY-DISPLAY.
        DISPLAY ' '.
*------------------------------------------------------------
        EXEC SQL
           SELECT EMPLOYEE_NO, EMPLOYEE_NAME,
               ADDRESS_STATE, DEPT, SALARY
           INTO :EMPLOYEE-NO, :EMPLOYEE-NAME,
                  :ADDRESS-STATE, :DEPT, :SALARY
               FROM EMPLOYEES_TABLE
           WHERE DEPT = :HOST-DEPT AND EMPLOYEE_NO = 850
        END-EXEC.
        IF SQLCODE < 0
           DISPLAY 'SELECT ERROR FOR EMPLOYEE NUMBER 850.'
           DISPLAY ' '
           PERFORM 250-DISPLAY-SQLCA THRU 250-EXIT
           GO TO 500-EXIT.
        IF SQLCODE > 0 GO TO 500-EXIT.
        DISPLAY 'EMPLOYEE NUMBER = ' EMPLOYEE-NO.
        DISPLAY '                         EMPLOYEE NAME = '
           EMPLOYEE-NAME.
        DISPLAY '                      STATE = '
           ADDRESS-STATE.
        DISPLAY '                         DEPARTMENT = '
           DEPT.
        MOVE SALARY TO SALARY-DISPLAY.
        DISPLAY '                         SALARY = '
           SALARY-DISPLAY.
        DISPLAY ' '.
*------------------------------------------------------------
        EXEC SQL
           SELECT EMPLOYEE_NO, EMPLOYEE_NAME,
               ADDRESS_STATE, DEPT, SALARY
           INTO :DCLEMPLOYEES-TABLE
```

```
            FROM EMPLOYEES_TABLE
      WHERE DEPT = :HOST-DEPT AND EMPLOYEE_NO = 900
    END-EXEC.
    IF SQLCODE < 0
        DISPLAY 'SELECT ERROR FOR EMPLOYEE NUMBER 900.'
        DISPLAY ' '
        PERFORM 250-DISPLAY-SQLCA THRU 250-EXIT
        GO TO 500-EXIT.
    IF SQLCODE > 0 GO TO 500-EXIT.
    DISPLAY 'EMPLOYEE NUMBER = ' EMPLOYEE-NO.
    DISPLAY '                  EMPLOYEE NAME = '
        EMPLOYEE-NAME.
    DISPLAY '                  STATE = '
        ADDRESS-STATE.
    DISPLAY '                  DEPARTMENT = '
        DEPT.
    MOVE SALARY TO SALARY-DISPLAY.
    DISPLAY '                  SALARY = '
        SALARY-DISPLAY.
    DISPLAY ' '.
    GO TO 500-EXIT.
*-------------------------------------------------------------
250-DISPLAY-SQLCA.
    DISPLAY ' '.
    DISPLAY 'DISPLAY SQLCA AREA.'.
    DISPLAY 'SQLCAID = ' SQLCAID.
    MOVE SQLCODE TO RC.
    DISPLAY 'SQLCODE = ' RC.
    DISPLAY 'SQLERRMC= ' SQLERRMC.

    DISPLAY 'SQLWARN0 = ' SQLWARN0.
    IF SQLWARN0 NOT EQUAL TO 'W'
        DISPLAY 'SQLWARN1 = ' SQLWARN1
        DISPLAY 'SQLWARN2 = ' SQLWARN2
        DISPLAY 'SQLWARN3 = ' SQLWARN3
        DISPLAY 'SQLWARN4 = ' SQLWARN4
        DISPLAY 'SQLWARN5 = ' SQLWARN5
        DISPLAY 'SQLWARN6 = ' SQLWARN6
        DISPLAY 'SQLWARN7 = ' SQLWARN7.
250-EXIT.  EXIT.
```

```
      500-EXIT.
          DISPLAY '******** END EXECUTION OF PROGRM2C. ********'.
          GOBACK.
```

FORTRAN PROGRAM PROGM2F: Static SQL Update

```
C-------- ALLOCATE FI(FT03F001) FOR OUTPUT. ------------------
      EXEC SQL INCLUDE SQLCA
      INTEGER EMPLNO*4
      CHARACTER NAME*16, STATE*2, DEPT*4, HTDEPT*4
      REAL SALARY*8
      WRITE (3,100)
100   FORMAT(' ********** BEGIN EXECUTION OF PROGRM2F **********')
      WRITE (3,110)
110   FORMAT(' ')
      HTDEPT = 'D700'
      WRITE (3,120)
120   FORMAT(' EMPLOYEES IN DEPARTMENT D700 PRIOR TO UPDATE.')
      WRITE (3,130)
130   FORMAT(' ')
      EXEC SQL
    +   SELECT EMPLOYEE_NO, EMPLOYEE_NAME,
    +        ADDRESS_STATE,DEPT,SALARY
    +        INTO :EMPLNO, :NAME, :STATE, :DEPT, :SALARY
    +        FROM EMPLOYEES_TABLE
    +        WHERE DEPT = :HTDEPT AND EMPLOYEE_NO= 495
      IF (SQLCOD.LT.0) THEN
          WRITE(3,200)
200       FORMAT('SELECT ERROR FOR EMPLOYEE_NO = 495.')
          WRITE(3,210)
210       FORMAT(' ')
          GO TO 9990
      ENDIF
      WRITE(3,220) EMPLNO
220   FORMAT(' EMPLOYEE NUMBER = ',I4)
      WRITE(3,230) NAME
230   FORMAT('                        EMPLOYEE NAME = ',A16)
      WRITE(3,240) STATE
240   FORMAT('                        STATE = ',A2)
      WRITE(3,250) DEPT
250   FORMAT('                        DEPARTMENT = ',A4)
      WRITE(3,260) SALARY
```

```
260   FORMAT ('                      SALARY = ',F8.2)
      WRITE(3,270)
270   FORMAT(' ')
      EXEC SQL
    +  SELECT EMPLOYEE_NO, EMPLOYEE_NAME,
    +         ADDRESS_STATE,DEPT,SALARY
    +      INTO :EMPLNO, :NAME, :STATE, :DEPT, :SALARY
    +         FROM EMPLOYEES_TABLE
    +      WHERE DEPT = :HTDEPT AND EMPLOYEE_NO= 850
      IF (SQLCOD.LT.0) THEN
         WRITE(3,300)
300      FORMAT('SELECT ERROR FOR EMPLOYEE_NO = 850.')
         WRITE(3,310)
310      FORMAT(' ')
         GO TO 9990
      ENDIF
      WRITE(3,330) EMPLNO
330   FORMAT(' EMPLOYEE NUMBER = ',I4)
      WRITE(3,340) NAME
340   FORMAT('                   EMPLOYEE NAME = ',A16)
      WRITE(3,350) STATE
350   FORMAT('                      STATE = ',A2)
      WRITE(3,360) DEPT
360   FORMAT('                   DEPARTMENT = ',A4)
      WRITE(3,370) SALARY
370   FORMAT('                      SALARY = ',F8.2)
      WRITE(3,380)
380   FORMAT(' ')
      EXEC SQL
    +  SELECT EMPLOYEE_NO, EMPLOYEE_NAME,
    +         ADDRESS_STATE,DEPT,SALARY
    +      INTO :EMPLNO, :NAME, :STATE, :DEPT, :SALARY
    +         FROM EMPLOYEES_TABLE
    +      WHERE DEPT = :HTDEPT AND EMPLOYEE_NO= 900
      IF (SQLCOD.LT.0) THEN
         WRITE(3,400)
400      FORMAT('SELECT ERROR FOR EMPLOYEE_NO = 900.')
         WRITE(3,410)
410      FORMAT(' ')
         GO TO 9990
      ENDIF
```

```
      WRITE(3,420) EMPLNO
 420  FORMAT(' EMPLOYEE NUMBER = ',I4)
      WRITE(3,430) NAME
 430  FORMAT('                        EMPLOYEE NAME = ',A16)
      WRITE(3,440) STATE
 440  FORMAT('                        STATE = ',A2)
      WRITE(3,450) DEPT
 450  FORMAT('                        DEPARTMENT = ',A4)
      WRITE(3,460) SALARY
 460  FORMAT('                        SALARY = ',F8.2)
      WRITE(3,470)
 470  FORMAT(' ')
C------------------------------------------------------------
      WRITE (3,500)
 500  FORMAT(' INCREASE ALL SALARIES IN DEPT 700 BY 1000.')
      WRITE (3,510)
 510  FORMAT(' ')
C------------------------------------------------------------
      EXEC SQL
     +  UPDATE EMPLOYEES_TABLE
     +     SET SALARY = SALARY + 1000.00
     +        WHERE DEPT ='D700'
      IF (SQLCOD.LT.0) GO TO 9990
C------------------------------------------------------------
      WRITE (3,600)
 600  FORMAT(' DISPLAY ROWS AFTER UPDATE.')
      WRITE (3,610)
 610  FORMAT(' ')
C------------------------------------------------------------
      EXEC SQL
     +  SELECT EMPLOYEE_NO, EMPLOYEE_NAME,
     +        ADDRESS_STATE,DEPT,SALARY
     +     INTO :EMPLNO, :NAME, :STATE, :DEPT, :SALARY
     +        FROM EMPLOYEES_TABLE
     +        WHERE DEPT = :HTDEPT AND EMPLOYEE_NO= 495
      IF (SQLCOD.LT.0) THEN
         WRITE(3,700)
 700     FORMAT('SELECT ERROR FOR EMPLOYEE_NO = 495.')
         WRITE(3,710)
 710     FORMAT(' ')
         GO TO 9990
```

```
      ENDIF
      WRITE(3,720) EMPLNO
720   FORMAT(' EMPLOYEE NUMBER = ',I4)
      WRITE(3,730) NAME
730   FORMAT('               EMPLOYEE NAME = ',A16)
      WRITE(3,740) STATE
740   FORMAT('                       STATE = ',A2)
      WRITE(3,750) DEPT
750   FORMAT('                  DEPARTMENT = ',A4)

      WRITE(3,760) SALARY
760   FORMAT('                      SALARY = ',F8.2)
      WRITE(3,770)
770   FORMAT(' ')
      EXEC SQL
   +  SELECT EMPLOYEE_NO, EMPLOYEE_NAME,
   +         ADDRESS_STATE,DEPT,SALARY
   +      INTO :EMPLNO, :NAME, :STATE, :DEPT, :SALARY
   +         FROM EMPLOYEES_TABLE
   +      WHERE DEPT = :HTDEPT AND EMPLOYEE_NO= 850
      IF (SQLCOD.LT.0) THEN
         WRITE(3,800)
800      FORMAT('SELECT ERROR FOR EMPLOYEE_NO = 850.')
         WRITE(3,810)
810      FORMAT(' ')
         GO TO 9990
      ENDIF
      WRITE(3,830) EMPLNO
830   FORMAT(' EMPLOYEE NUMBER = ',I4)
      WRITE(3,840) NAME
840   FORMAT('               EMPLOYEE NAME = ',A16)
      WRITE(3,850) STATE
850   FORMAT('                       STATE = ',A2)
      WRITE(3,860) DEPT
860   FORMAT('                  DEPARTMENT = ',A4)
      WRITE(3,870) SALARY
870   FORMAT('                      SALARY = ',F8.2)
      WRITE(3,880)
880   FORMAT(' ')
      EXEC SQL
   +  SELECT EMPLOYEE_NO, EMPLOYEE_NAME,
```

```
     +          ADDRESS_STATE,DEPT,SALARY
     +        INTO :EMPLNO, :NAME, :STATE, :DEPT, :SALARY
     +        FROM EMPLOYEES_TABLE
     +        WHERE DEPT = :HTDEPT AND EMPLOYEE_NO= 900
       IF (SQLCOD.LT.0) THEN
          WRITE(3,900)
900       FORMAT('SELECT ERROR FOR EMPLOYEE_NO = 900.')
          WRITE(3,910)
910       FORMAT(' ')
          GO TO 9990
       ENDIF
       WRITE(3,920) EMPLNO
920    FORMAT(' EMPLOYEE NUMBER = ',I4)
       WRITE(3,930) NAME
930    FORMAT('                  EMPLOYEE NAME = ',A16)
       WRITE(3,940) STATE
940    FORMAT('                  STATE = ',A2)
       WRITE(3,950) DEPT
950    FORMAT('                  DEPARTMENT = ',A4)
       WRITE(3,960) SALARY
960    FORMAT('                  SALARY = ',F8.2)
       WRITE(3,970)
970    FORMAT(' ')
C------------------------------------------------------------------
       WRITE(3,1000)
1000 FORMAT(' ISSUE SQL ROLLBACK TO UNDUE CHANGES MADE')
       EXEC SQL ROLLBACK
       IF (SQLCOD.LT.0) GO TO 9990
C------------------------------------------------------------------
9000      WRITE(3,9010) SQLCOD
9010      FORMAT(' SQLCODE = ',I4)
          WRITE(3,9020)
9020 FORMAT(' ')
          GO TO 9995
C------------------------------------------------------------------
9990 WRITE(3,9991) SQLCOD
9991 FORMAT(' SQLCODE: ',I4)
       WRITE(3,9992) SQLTXT
9992 FORMAT(' SQLTXT = ',A70)
C------------------------------------------------------------------
9995 WRITE(3,9999)
```

```
9999 FORMAT(' ********* END EXECUTION OF PROGRM2F. **********')
     STOP
     END
```

PL/I PROGRAM PROGRM2P: Static SQL Update.

```
PROGRM2: PROCEDURE OPTIONS(MAIN);
/*  INCLUDE SQLCA AND EMPLOYEE TABLE DECLARATION.                */
DCL
  WARNING BIN FIXED(15) INIT(0),
  ZERO  BIN FIXED(15) INIT(0);
EXEC SQL INCLUDE EMPLOYEE;
EXEC SQL INCLUDE SQLCA;
DCL
  RETCODE FIXED(31) BIN,
  HOSTDEPT CHAR(4);
DCL
  (ADDR,PLIRETC)
  BUILTIN;
DCL
  SYSPRINT FILE STREAM OUTPUT ENV(FB,RECSIZE(133),BLKSIZE(133));
/*************************************************************/
PUT SKIP EDIT (' ') (A);
PUT SKIP EDIT('***** BEGIN EXECUTION OF PROGRM2P *******')
(A(43));
PUT SKIP EDIT (' ') (A);
RETCODE = ZERO;
HOSTDEPT = 'D700';
/*************************************************************/
/*                                                          */
/*    DISPLAY  EMPLOYEES IN DEPARTMENT D700.                */
PUT SKIP EDIT ('EMPLOYEES IN DEPT D700 PRIOR TO UPDATE') (A(38));
PUT SKIP EDIT (' ') (A);
EXEC SQL
      SELECT EMPLOYEE_NO,EMPLOYEE_NAME,
             ADDRESS_STATE, DEPT, SALARY
        INTO :ROWAREA
         FROM EMPLOYEES_TABLE
         WHERE DEPT= :HOSTDEPT AND EMPLOYEE_NO = 495;
IF SQLCODE < 0 THEN GOTO DISPERR;
IF SQLCODE > 0 THEN GOTO NEXT001;
PUT SKIP EDIT ('EMPLOYEE NUMBER = ',EMPLNO) (A(18),F(8));
```

```
PUT SKIP EDIT ('EMPLOYEE NAME = ',EMPLNAME) (A(16),A(16));
PUT SKIP EDIT ('STATE = ',STATE) (A(8),A(2));
PUT SKIP EDIT ('DEPT = ',DEPT) (A(7),A(4));
PUT SKIP EDIT ('SALARY = ',SALARY) (A(9),F(8));
PUT SKIP EDIT (' ') (A);
NEXT001:
EXEC SQL
      SELECT EMPLOYEE_NO,EMPLOYEE_NAME,
             ADDRESS_STATE, DEPT, SALARY
         INTO :ROWAREA
           FROM EMPLOYEES_TABLE
           WHERE DEPT= :HOSTDEPT AND EMPLOYEE_NO = 850;
IF SQLCODE < 0 THEN GOTO DISPERR;
IF SQLCODE > 0 THEN GOTO NEXT002;
PUT SKIP EDIT ('EMPLOYEE NUMBER = ',EMPLNO) (A(18),F(8));
PUT SKIP EDIT ('EMPLOYEE NAME = ',EMPLNAME) (A(16),A(16));
PUT SKIP EDIT ('STATE = ',STATE) (A(8),A(2));
PUT SKIP EDIT ('DEPT = ',DEPT) (A(7),A(4));
PUT SKIP EDIT ('SALARY = ',SALARY) (A(9),F(8));
PUT SKIP EDIT (' ') (A);
NEXT002:
EXEC SQL
      SELECT EMPLOYEE_NO,EMPLOYEE_NAME,
             ADDRESS_STATE, DEPT, SALARY
         INTO :ROWAREA
           FROM EMPLOYEES_TABLE
           WHERE DEPT= :HOSTDEPT AND EMPLOYEE_NO = 900;
IF SQLCODE < 0 THEN GOTO DISPERR;
IF SQLCODE > 0 THEN GOTO NEXT003;
PUT SKIP EDIT ('EMPLOYEE NUMBER = ',EMPLNO) (A(18),F(8));
PUT SKIP EDIT ('EMPLOYEE NAME = ',EMPLNAME) (A(16),A(16));
PUT SKIP EDIT ('STATE = ',STATE) (A(8),A(2));
PUT SKIP EDIT ('DEPT = ',DEPT) (A(7),A(4));
PUT SKIP EDIT ('SALARY = ',SALARY) (A(9),F(8));
PUT SKIP EDIT (' ') (A);
NEXT003:
/*******************************************************************
EXEC SQL
      UPDATE EMPLOYEES_TABLE
             SET SALARY = SALARY + 1000.00
             WHERE DEPT ='D700';
```

```
IF SQLCODE = 0 THEN GOTO DISPERR;
/****************************************************************/
/*    DISPLAY  EMPLOYEES IN DEPARTMENT. AFTER UPDATES.         */
PUT SKIP EDIT ('EMPLOYEES IN DEPT D700 AFTER UPDATE') (A(35));
PUT SKIP EDIT (' ') (A);
EXEC SQL
      SELECT EMPLOYEE_NO,EMPLOYEE_NAME,
             ADDRESS_STATE, DEPT, SALARY
      INTO :ROWAREA
        FROM EMPLOYEES_TABLE
        WHERE DEPT= :HOSTDEPT AND EMPLOYEE_NO = 495;
IF SQLCODE < 0 THEN GOTO DISPERR;
IF SQLCODE > 0 THEN GOTO NEXT011;
PUT SKIP EDIT ('EMPLOYEE NUMBER = ',EMPLNO) (A(18),F(8));
PUT SKIP EDIT ('EMPLOYEE NAME = ',EMPLNAME) (A(16),A(16));
PUT SKIP EDIT ('STATE = ',STATE) (A(8),A(2));
PUT SKIP EDIT ('DEPT = ',DEPT) (A(7),A(4));
PUT SKIP EDIT ('SALARY = ',SALARY) (A(9),F(8));
PUT SKIP EDIT (' ') (A);
NEXT011:
EXEC SQL
      SELECT EMPLOYEE_NO,EMPLOYEE_NAME,
             ADDRESS_STATE, DEPT, SALARY
      INTO :ROWAREA
        FROM EMPLOYEES_TABLE
        WHERE DEPT= :HOSTDEPT AND EMPLOYEE_NO = 850;
IF SQLCODE < 0 THEN GOTO DISPERR;
IF SQLCODE > 0 THEN GOTO NEXT012;
PUT SKIP EDIT ('EMPLOYEE NUMBER = ',EMPLNO) (A(18),F(8));
PUT SKIP EDIT ('EMPLOYEE NAME = ',EMPLNAME) (A(16),A(16));
PUT SKIP EDIT ('STATE = ',STATE) (A(8),A(2));
PUT SKIP EDIT ('DEPT = ',DEPT) (A(7),A(4));
PUT SKIP EDIT ('SALARY = ',SALARY) (A(9),F(8));
PUT SKIP EDIT (' ') (A);
NEXT012:
EXEC SQL
      SELECT EMPLOYEE_NO,EMPLOYEE_NAME,
             ADDRESS_STATE, DEPT, SALARY
      INTO :ROWAREA
        FROM EMPLOYEES_TABLE
        WHERE DEPT= :HOSTDEPT AND EMPLOYEE_NO = 900;
```

```
IF SQLCODE < 0 THEN GOTO DISPERR;
IF SQLCODE > 0 THEN GOTO NEXT013;
PUT SKIP EDIT ('EMPLOYEE NUMBER = ',EMPLNO) (A(18),F(8));
PUT SKIP EDIT ('EMPLOYEE NAME = ',EMPLNAME) (A(16),A(16));
PUT SKIP EDIT ('STATE = ',STATE) (A(8),A(2));
PUT SKIP EDIT ('DEPT = ',DEPT) (A(7),A(4));
PUT SKIP EDIT ('SALARY = ',SALARY) (A(9),F(8));
PUT SKIP EDIT (' ') (A);
NEXT013:
/********************************************************************/
PUT SKIP EDIT ('ISSUE ROLLBACK TO UNDUE CHANGES.') (A(38));
PUT SKIP EDIT (' ') (A);
EXEC SQL
      ROLLBACK;
IF SQLCODE = 0 THEN GOTO DISPERR;
/********************************************************************/
GOTO STOPRUN;
/********************************************************************/
/*   ERROR ENCOUNTERED, DISPLAY CONTENTS OF SQLCA AREA.          */
DISPERR:
RETCODE = SQLCODE;
PUT SKIP EDIT (' ') (A);
PUT SKIP EDIT ('DISPLAY SQLCA AREA=') ( A(19));
PUT SKIP EDIT ('SQLCAID =  ',SQLCAID) (A(11), A(8));
PUT SKIP EDIT ('SQLCODE =  ',SQLCODE) (A(11), F(8));
PUT SKIP EDIT ('SQLERRMC=  ',SQLERRM) (A(11), A(70));
PUT SKIP EDIT ('SQLWARN0 = ',SQLWARN0) (A(11), A);
   IF SQLWARN0 = 'W'
     THEN DO;
        PUT SKIP EDIT ('SQLWARN1 = ',SQLWARN1) (A(11),A);
        PUT SKIP EDIT ('SQLWARN2 = ',SQLWARN2) (A(11),A);
        PUT SKIP EDIT ('SQLWARN3 = ',SQLWARN3) (A(11),A);
        PUT SKIP EDIT ('SQLWARN4 = ',SQLWARN4) (A(11),A);
        PUT SKIP EDIT ('SQLWARN5 = ',SQLWARN5) (A(11),A);
        PUT SKIP EDIT ('SQLWARN6 = ',SQLWARN6) (A(11),A);
        PUT SKIP EDIT ('SQLWARN7 = ',SQLWARN7) (A(11),A);
        PUT SKIP EDIT (' ') (A);
     END;
   /*   STOP RUN                                                  */
STOPRUN:
PUT SKIP EDIT ('******* END EXECUTION OF PROGRM2P ******')
```

```
(A(40));
 CALL PLIRETC(RETCODE);
 END PROGRM2;
```

COBOL PROGRAM PROGRM3C: Cursor with Dynamic Fixed-List-Select

```
ID DIVISION.
          PROGRAM-ID.  PROGRM3C.

          AUTHOR.       BRUCE LARSON
          ENVIRONMENT DIVISION.
          CONFIGURATION SECTION.
          INPUT-OUTPUT SECTION.
          FILE-CONTROL.
          DATA DIVISION.
          FILE SECTION.
          WORKING-STORAGE SECTION.

     01   DCLEMPLOYEES-TABLE.
          10 EMPLOYEE-NO          PIC S9(9) USAGE COMP.
          10 EMPLOYEE-NAME        PIC X(16).
          10 ADDRESS-STATE        PIC X(2).
          10 DEPT                 PIC X(4).
          10 SALARY               PIC S99999V99 USAGE COMP-3.
     01   SQLCA.
          05 SQLCAID                  PIC X(8).
          05 SQLCABC                  PIC S9(9) COMP-4.
          05 SQLCODE                  PIC S9(9) COMP-4.
          05 SQLERRM.
             49 SQLERRML               PIC S9(4) COMP-4.
             49 SQLERRMC               PIC X(70).
          05 SQLERRP                  PIC X(8).
          05 SQLERRD                  OCCURS 6 TIMES
                                      PIC S9(9) COMP-4.

          05 SQLWARN.
             10 SQLWARN0               PIC X.
             10 SQLWARN1               PIC X.
             10 SQLWARN2               PIC X.
             10 SQLWARN3               PIC X.
             10 SQLWARN4               PIC X.
             10 SQLWARN5               PIC X.
             10 SQLWARN6               PIC X.
```

```
        10 SQLWARN7              PIC X.
     05 SQLEXT                   PIC X(8).
  01 SALARY-DISPLAY                          PIC Z(6).ZZ.
  01 RC                                      PIC +99999.
  01 HOST-DYNAMIC-SELECT.
     49 HOST-SQL-LENGTH          PIC S9(4) COMP VALUE +110.
     49 HOST-SQL-STATEMENT       PIC X(110) VALUE SPACES.
  01 Q1                          PIC X(1) VALUE QUOTE.
  01 HOST-DEPT                   PIC X(4).
  01 DISPLAY-SQL-STATEMENT       PIC X(110) VALUE SPACES.


PROCEDURE DIVISION.
001-MAINLINE.
    DISPLAY ' '.
    DISPLAY '******* BEGIN EXECUTION OF PROGRM3C.********'.
    DISPLAY ' '.
    MOVE 'D890' TO HOST-DEPT.
   STRING 'SELECT EMPLOYEE_NO,EMPLOYEE_NAME,ADDRESS_STATE,'
      'DEPT,SALARY FROM EMPLOYEES_TABLE '
      'WHERE DEPT = '
      Q1 HOST-DEPT Q1
      DELIMITED BY SIZE INTO HOST-SQL-STATEMENT.
    MOVE HOST-SQL-STATEMENT  TO DISPLAY-SQL-STATEMENT.
    DISPLAY 'DISPLAY DYNAMIC SELECT: '.
    DISPLAY DISPLAY-SQL-STATEMENT.
    DISPLAY ' '
    DISPLAY 'DECLARE SQL STATEMENT: CURSOR1'.
    DISPLAY ' '
    EXEC SQL
       DECLARE CURSOR1 CURSOR FOR STATEMENT01
    END-EXEC.
    IF SQLCODE NOT = 0
        DISPLAY 'CLOSE ERROR ON CURSOR NAMED: CURSOR1'
        DISPLAY ' '
        PERFORM 250-DISPLAY-SQLCA THRU 250-EXIT
        GO TO 500-EXIT.
    DISPLAY 'PREPARE SQL STATEMENT: CURSOR1'.
    DISPLAY ' '.
    EXEC SQL
       PREPARE STATEMENT01 FROM :HOST-DYNAMIC-SELECT
    END-EXEC.
```

```
        IF SQLCODE NOT = 0
            DISPLAY 'CLOSE ERROR ON CURSOR NAMED: CURSOR1'
            DISPLAY ' '
            PERFORM 250-DISPLAY-SQLCA THRU 250-EXIT
            GO TO 500-EXIT.
        DISPLAY 'OPEN CURSOR NAMED: CURSOR1 '
        DISPLAY ' '
        EXEC SQL
          OPEN CURSOR1
        END-EXEC.
        IF SQLCODE NOT = 0
            DISPLAY 'OPEN ERROR FOR CURSOR NAMED = CURSOR1'
            DISPLAY ' '
            PERFORM 250-DISPLAY-SQLCA THRU 250-EXIT
            GO TO 500-EXIT.
    DISPLAY 'DISPLAY ROWS FETCHED FOR CURSOR NAMED = CURSOR1'.
        DISPLAY ' '.
        PERFORM 200-FETCH-EMPLOYEE-ROWS THRU 200-EXIT
          UNTIL SQLCODE NOT = 0.
        IF SQLCODE <  0
            DISPLAY 'FETCH ERROR USING CURSOR NAMED: CURSOR1.'
            DISPLAY '  '
            PERFORM 250-DISPLAY-SQLCA THRU 250-EXIT
            GO TO 500-EXIT.
        MOVE SQLCODE TO RC.
        DISPLAY ' '.
        DISPLAY 'SQLCODE = '   RC.
        DISPLAY ' '.
        DISPLAY 'END OF FETCH USING CURSOR NAMED: CURSOR1.'.
        DISPLAY ' '.
        DISPLAY 'CLOSE CURSOR NAMED: CURSOR1'.
        DISPLAY ' '.
        EXEC SQL
          CLOSE CURSOR1
        END-EXEC.
        IF SQLCODE NOT = 0
            DISPLAY 'CLOSE ERROR ON CURSOR NAMED: CURSOR1'
            DISPLAY ' '
            PERFORM 250-DISPLAY-SQLCA THRU 250-EXIT
            GO TO 500-EXIT.
        GO TO 500-EXIT.
```

```
200-FETCH-EMPLOYEE-ROWS.
    EXEC SQL
      FETCH CURSOR1
        INTO :DCLEMPLOYEES-TABLE
    END-EXEC.
    IF SQLCODE < 0
        DISPLAY 'BAD SQLCODE ON FETCH = ' RC
        DISPLAY ' '
        PERFORM 250-DISPLAY-SQLCA THRU 250-EXIT
        GO TO 500-EXIT.
    IF SQLCODE NOT = 0
        GO TO 200-EXIT.
    MOVE SALARY TO SALARY-DISPLAY.
    DISPLAY 'EMPLOYEE NUMBER = ' EMPLOYEE-NO.
    DISPLAY '                        EMPLOYEE NAME = '
        EMPLOYEE-NAME.
    DISPLAY '                        STATE = '
        ADDRESS-STATE.
    DISPLAY '                        DEPARTMENT = '
        DEPT.
    DISPLAY '                        SALARY = '
        SALARY-DISPLAY.
    DISPLAY ' '.
200-EXIT.  EXIT.


250-DISPLAY-SQLCA.
    DISPLAY ' '.
    DISPLAY 'DISPLAY SQLCA AREA.'.
    DISPLAY 'SQLCAID = '  SQLCAID.
    MOVE SQLCODE TO RC.
    DISPLAY 'SQLCODE = '  RC.
    DISPLAY 'SQLERRMC= '  SQLERRMC.
    DISPLAY 'SQLWARN0 = ' SQLWARN0.
    IF SQLWARN0 NOT EQUAL TO 'W'
        DISPLAY 'SQLWARN1 = ' SQLWARN1
        DISPLAY 'SQLWARN2 = ' SQLWARN2
        DISPLAY 'SQLWARN3 = ' SQLWARN3
        DISPLAY 'SQLWARN4 = ' SQLWARN4
        DISPLAY 'SQLWARN5 = ' SQLWARN5
```

```
             DISPLAY 'SQLWARN6 = ' SQLWARN6
             DISPLAY 'SQLWARN7 = ' SQLWARN7.
     250-EXIT.  EXIT.
     500-EXIT.
             DISPLAY '******* END EXECUTION OF PROGRM3C. **********'.
             GOBACK.
```

FORTRAN PROGRAM PROGRM3F: CURSOR with Dynamic Fixed-list-Select

```
C----------- PROGRM3F  ------------------------------------
      EXEC SQL INCLUDE SQLCA
C-----------------------------------------------------------
      INTEGER EMPLNO*4
      CHARACTER NAME*16, STATE*2, DEPT*4, HTDEPT*4
      REAL SALARY*8
C-----------------------------------------------------------
      CHARACTER SQL001*33, SQL002*31, SQL003*29
      CHARACTER HQUOTE*1
      CHARACTER HSTSQL*99
C-----------------------------------------------------------
      DATA HQUOTE
     C/''''/
C-----------------------------------------------------------
      WRITE (3,500)
  500 FORMAT(' ********** BEGIN EXECUTION OF PROGRM3F **********')
      WRITE (3,510)
  510 FORMAT(' ')
      SQLCOD = -1
      HTDEPT = 'D890'
      SQL001 = 'SELECT EMPLOYEE_NO,EMPLOYEE_NAME,'
      SQL002 = 'ADDRESS_STATE,DEPT,SALARY FROM '
      SQL003 = 'EMPLOYEES_TABLE WHERE DEPT = '
      HSTSQL = SQL001//SQL002//SQL003//HQUOTE//HTDEPT//HQUOTE
C-----------------------------------------------------------
```

```
      WRITE (3,515)
 515  FORMAT(' DISPLAY DYNAMIC SQL STATEMENT')
      WRITE (3,516)
 516  FORMAT(' ')
      WRITE(3,520) HSTSQL
 520  FORMAT(' ',A99)
      WRITE (3,521)
 521  FORMAT(' ')
C------------------------------------------------------------
      WRITE (3,530)
 530  FORMAT(' DECLARE DYNAMIC FIXED LIST SELECT SQL STATEMENT')
      WRITE (3,540)
 540  FORMAT(' ')
      EXEC SQL
    +   DECLARE CURSOR1 CURSOR FOR STATEMENT1
C------------------------------------------------------------
      WRITE (3,560)
 560  FORMAT(' PREPARE DYNAMIC FIXED LIST SELECT FROM HSTSQL')
      WRITE (3,570)
 570  FORMAT(' ')
      EXEC SQL
    +   PREPARE STATEMENT1 FROM :HSTSQL
      IF (SQLCOD.NE.0) GO TO 9990
C------------------------------------------------------------
      WRITE (3,1010)
1010  FORMAT(' OPEN CURSOR NAMED: CURSOR1 ')
      WRITE (3,1030)
1030  FORMAT(' ')
      EXEC SQL
    +   OPEN CURSOR1
      IF (SQLCOD.NE.0) GO TO 9990
C------------------------------------------------------------
      WRITE (3,2010)
2010  FORMAT(' DISPLAY ROWS FETCHED FOR CURSOR NAMED: CURSOR1')
      WRITE (3,2020)
2020  FORMAT(' ')
2030  CONTINUE
      EXEC SQL
    +   FETCH CURSOR1
    +     INTO :EMPLNO, :NAME, :STATE, :DEPT, :SALARY
```

```
      IF (SQLCOD.EQ.100) GO TO 9000
      IF (SQLCOD.NE.0) GO TO 9990
      WRITE(3,3010) EMPLNO
 3010 FORMAT(' EMPLOYEE NUMBER = ',I6)
      WRITE(3,3020) NAME
 3020 FORMAT('                         EMPLOYEE NAME = ',A16)
      WRITE(3,3030) STATE
 3030 FORMAT('                         STATE = ',A2)
      WRITE(3,3040) DEPT
 3040 FORMAT('                         DEPARTMENT = ',A4)
      WRITE(3,3050) SALARY
 3050 FORMAT('                         SALARY = ',F8.2)
      WRITE(3,3055)
 3055 FORMAT(' ')
      GO TO 2030
C----------------------------------------------------------------
 9000    WRITE(3,9010) SQLCOD
 9010    FORMAT(' SQLCODE = ',I4)
         WRITE(3,9020)
 9020    FORMAT(' ')
         WRITE(3,9030)
 9030    FORMAT(' END OF FETCH USING CURSOR NAMED: CURSOR1')
         WRITE(3,9031)
 9031    FORMAT(' ')
C------------------------------------------------------------
      WRITE(3,9040)
 9040 FORMAT(' CLOSE CURSOR NAMED: CURSOR1')
      WRITE(3,9041)
 9041 FORMAT(' ')
      EXEC SQL
    +   CLOSE CURSOR1
      IF (SQLCOD.EQ.0) GO TO 9995
      GO TO 9995
C----------------------------------------------------------------
 9990 WRITE(3,9991) SQLCOD
 9991 FORMAT(' SQLCODE: ',I4)
      WRITE(3,9992) SQLTXT
 9992 FORMAT(' SQLTXT = ',A70)
C----------------------------------------------------------------
 9995 WRITE(3,9999)
```

```
9999 FORMAT(' ********* END EXECUTION OF PROGRM3F. **********')
     STOP
     END
```

PL/I PROGRAM PROGRM3P: CURSOR with Dynamic Fixed-List-Select

```
PROGRM3: PROCEDURE OPTIONS(MAIN);
/*  INCLUDE SQLCA AND EMPLOYEE TABLE DECLARATION.              */
DCL
   WARNING BIN FIXED(15) INIT(0),
   ZERO  BIN FIXED(15) INIT(0),
   QUOTE CHAR(1) INIT('''');
EXEC SQL INCLUDE EMPLOYEE;
EXEC SQL INCLUDE SQLCA;
DCL
   SQLWORK CHAR(99) VARYING;
DCL
   RETCODE FIXED(31) BIN,
   HOSTDEPT CHAR(4),
   SQL001   CHAR(33),
   SQL002   CHAR(31),
   SQL003   CHAR(29);
DCL
   (ADDR,PLIRETC)
   BUILTIN;
DCL
   SYSPRINT FILE STREAM OUTPUT ENV(FB,RECSIZE(133),BLKSIZE(133));
/***********************************************************************/
PUT SKIP EDIT (' ') (A);
PUT SKIP EDIT('****** BEGIN EXECUTION OF PROGRM3P *******')
(A(43));
PUT SKIP EDIT (' ') (A);
/***********************************************************************/
/*   CONSTRUCT SQL STATEMENT.                                  */
RETCODE = ZERO;
HOSTDEPT = 'D890';

SQL001 = 'SELECT EMPLOYEE_NO,EMPLOYEE_NAME,';
SQL002 = 'ADDRESS_STATE,DEPT,SALARY FROM ';
SQL003 = 'EMPLOYEES_TABLE WHERE DEPT = ';
SQLWORK = SQL001SQL002SQL003QUOTEHOSTDEPTQUOTE;
PUT SKIP EDIT('DYNAMIC SQL STATEMENT CONSTRUCTED') (A(33));
```

```
PUT SKIP EDIT (' ') (A);
PUT SKIP EDIT(SQLWORK) (A(99));
PUT SKIP EDIT (' ') (A);
/****************************************************************/
/*                                                            */
/*    DECLARE SQL STATEMENT.                                   */
/*                                                            */
PUT SKIP EDIT ('DECLARE DYNAMIC FIXED LENGTH SELECT') (A(35));
PUT SKIP EDIT (' ') (A);
EXEC SQL
   DECLARE CURSOR1 CURSOR FOR STATEMENT1;
/****************************************************************/
/*                                                            */
/*    PREPARE SQL STATEMENT.                                   */
/*                                                            */
PUT SKIP EDIT ('PREPARE DYNAMIC FIXED LENGTH SELECT') (A(35));
PUT SKIP EDIT (' ') (A);
EXEC SQL PREPARE STATEMENT1 FROM :SQLWORK;
IF SQLCODE = 0 THEN GOTO DISPERR;
/****************************************************************/
/*                                                            */
/*   OPEN CURSOR.                                              */
/*                                                            */
PUT SKIP EDIT ('OPEN CURSOR: CURSOR1') (A(20));
PUT SKIP EDIT (' ') (A);
EXEC SQL OPEN CURSOR1;
IF SQLCODE = 0 THEN GOTO DISPERR;
/****************************************************************/
/*                                                            */
/*   FETCH ROWS USING CURSOR.                                 */
/*                        o                                   */
PUT SKIP EDIT ('FETCH USING CURSOR: CURSOR1') (A(27));
PUT SKIP EDIT (' ') (A);
   DO UNTIL (SQLCODE =ZERO);
      EXEC SQL FETCH CURSOR1 INTO ROWAREA;
         IF SQLCODE < 0 THEN GOTO DISPERR;
         PUT SKIP EDIT ('EMPLOYEE NUMBER = ',EMPLNO) (A(18),F(8));
         PUT SKIP EDIT ('EMPLOYEE NAME = ',EMPLNAME) (A(16),A(16));
         Po SKIP EDIT ('STATE = ',STATE) (A(8),A(2));
         PUT SKIP EDIT ('DEPT = ',DEPT) (A(7),A(4));
         PUT SKIP EDIT ('SALARY = ',SALARY) (A(9),F(8));
```

```
          PUT SKIP EDIT (' ') (A);
     END;
/**************************************************************/
/*                                                          */
/*   CLOSE CURSOR.                                          */
/*                                                          */
PUT SKIP EDIT ('CLOSE CURSOR: CURSOR1') (A(21));
PUT SKIP EDIT (' ') (A);
EXEC SQL CLOSE CURSOR1;
IF SQLCODE < 0 THEN GOTO DISPERR;
IF SQLCODE = 0 THEN GOTO STOPRUN;
/*                                                          */
/*   ERROR ENCOUNTERED, DISPLAY CONTENTS OF SQLCA AREA.     */
/*                                                          */
DISPERR:
RETCODE = WARNING;
PUT SKIP EDIT (' ') (A);
PUT SKIP EDIT ('DISPLAY SQLCA AREA=') ( A(19));
PUT SKIP EDIT (' SQLCAID =  ',SQLCAID) (A(11), A(8));
PUT SKIP EDIT (' SQLCODE =  ',SQLCODE) (A(11), F(8));

PUT SKIP EDIT (' SQLERRMC= ',SQLERRM) (A(11), A(70));
PUT SKIP EDIT (' SQLWARN0 = ',SQLWARN0) (A(11), A);
   IF SQLWARN0 = 'W'
      THEN DO;
         PUT SKIP EDIT ('SQLWARN1 = ',SQLWARN1) (A(11),A);
         PUT SKIP EDIT ('SQLWARN2 = ',SQLWARN2) (A(11),A);
         PUT SKIP EDIT ('SQLWARN3 = ',SQLWARN3) (A(11),A);
         PUT SKIP EDIT ('SQLWARN4 = ',SQLWARN4) (A(11),A);
         PUT SKIP EDIT ('SQLWARN5 = ',SQLWARN5) (A(11),A);
         PUT SKIP EDIT ('SQLWARN6 = ',SQLWARN6) (A(11),A);
         PUT SKIP EDIT ('SQLWARN7 = ',SQLWARN7) (A(11),A);
         PUT SKIP EDIT (' ') (A);
      END;
/*                                                          */
/*      STOP RUN                                            */
/*                                                          */
STOPRUN:
PUT SKIP EDIT ('******* END EXECUTION OF PROGRM3P ******')
(A(40));
```

```
CALL PLIRETC(RETCODE);
END PROGRM3;
```

COBOL PROGRAM PROGRM4C: EXECUTE IMMEDIATE of NON-Select SQL

```
ID DIVISION.
        PROGRAM-ID.  PROGRM4C.
        AUTHOR.       BRUCE LARSON
      ENVIRONMENT DIVISION.
      CONFIGURATION SECTION.
      INPUT-OUTPUT SECTION.
      FILE-CONTROL.
      DATA DIVISION.
      FILE SECTION.
      WORKING-STORAGE SECTION.
      01  SQLCA.
          05 SQLCAID            PIC X(8).
          05 SQLCABC            PIC S9(9) COMP-4.
          05 SQLCODE            PIC S9(9) COMP-4.
          05 SQLERRM.
             49 SQLERRML         PIC S9(4) COMP-4.
             49 SQLERRMC         PIC X(70).
          05 SQLERRP            PIC X(8).
          05 SQLERRD            OCCURS 6 TIMES
                                PIC S9(9) COMP-4.

          05 SQLWARN.
             10 SQLWARN0         PIC X.
             10 SQLWARN1         PIC X.
             10 SQLWARN2         PIC X.
             10 SQLWARN3         PIC X.
             10 SQLWARN4         PIC X.
             10 SQLWARN5         PIC X.
             10 SQLWARN6         PIC X.
             10 SQLWARN7         PIC X.
          05 SQLEXT             PIC X(8).

      01  SALARY-DISPLAY                      PIC Z(6).ZZ.
      01  RC                                  PIC +9999999.
      01  HOST-DYNAMIC-SQL.
          49 HOST-SQL-LENGTH     PIC S9(4) COMP VALUE +50.
```

```
       49 HOST-SQL-STATEMENT      PIC X(50) VALUE SPACES.
 01   Q1                          PIC X(1) VALUE QUOTE.
 01   DISPLAY-SQL-STATEMENT       PIC X(50) VALUE SPACES.
 PROCEDURE DIVISION.
 001-MAINLINE.
     DISPLAY ' '.
     DISPLAY '******* BEGIN EXECUTION OF PROGRM4C.********'.
     DISPLAY ' '.
*-------------------------------------------------------------
     STRING 'CREATE DATABASE DBNAME01'
        DELIMITED BY SIZE INTO HOST-SQL-STATEMENT.
     MOVE HOST-SQL-STATEMENT  TO DISPLAY-SQL-STATEMENT.
     DISPLAY 'DISPLAY DYNAMIC SQL: '.
     DISPLAY DISPLAY-SQL-STATEMENT.
     DISPLAY ' '.
     DISPLAY 'EXECUTE IMMEDIATE:'.
     DISPLAY ' '.
     EXEC SQL
        EXECUTE IMMEDIATE :HOST-DYNAMIC-SQL
     END-EXEC.
     IF SQLCODE NOT = 0
        DISPLAY 'EXECUTE IMMEDIATE ERROR ON CREATE!'
        DISPLAY ' '
        PERFORM 250-DISPLAY-SQLCA THRU 250-EXIT
        GO TO 500-EXIT.
*-------------------------------------------------------------
     MOVE SPACES TO HOST-SQL-STATEMENT.
     STRING 'DROP DATABASE DBNAME01'
        DELIMITED BY SIZE INTO HOST-SQL-STATEMENT.
     MOVE HOST-SQL-STATEMENT  TO DISPLAY-SQL-STATEMENT.
     DISPLAY 'DISPLAY DYNAMIC SQL: '.
     DISPLAY DISPLAY-SQL-STATEMENT.
     DISPLAY ' '.
     DISPLAY 'EXECUTE IMMEDIATE:'.
     DISPLAY ' '.
     EXEC SQL
        EXECUTE IMMEDIATE :HOST-DYNAMIC-SQL
     END-EXEC.
     IF SQLCODE NOT = 0
        DISPLAY 'EXECUTE IMMEDIATE ERROR ON DROP!'
        DISPLAY ' '
```

```
        PERFORM 250-DISPLAY-SQLCA THRU 250-EXIT
        GO TO 500-EXIT.
     GO TO 500-EXIT.
*---------------------------------------------------------------
  250-DISPLAY-SQLCA.
     DISPLAY ' '.
     DISPLAY 'DISPLAY SQLCA AREA.'.
     DISPLAY 'SQLCAID = '  SQLCAID.
     MOVE SQLCODE TO RC.
     DISPLAY 'SQLCODE = '  RC.
     DISPLAY 'SQLERRMC= '  SQLERRMC.

     DISPLAY 'SQLWARN0 = '  SQLWARN0.
     IF SQLWARN0 NOT EQUAL TO 'W'
        DISPLAY 'SQLWARN1 = '  SQLWARN1
        DISPLAY 'SQLWARN2 = '  SQLWARN2
        DISPLAY 'SQLWARN3 = '  SQLWARN3
        DISPLAY 'SQLWARN4 = '  SQLWARN4
        DISPLAY 'SQLWARN5 = '  SQLWARN5
        DISPLAY 'SQLWARN6 = '  SQLWARN6
        DISPLAY 'SQLWARN7 = '  SQLWARN7.
  250-EXIT.  EXIT.

  500-EXIT.
     DISPLAY '******** END EXECUTION OF PROGRM4C. ********'.
     GOBACK.
```

FORTRAN PROGRAM PROGRM4F: EXECUTE IMMEDIATE of NON-Select SQL

```
C----------  PROGRM4F  ---------------------------------------
      EXEC SQL INCLUDE SQLCA
C-----------------------------------------------------------
      CHARACTER HSTSQL*24
      WRITE (3,100)
 100  FORMAT(' ********** BEGIN EXECUTION OF PROGRM4F **********')
      WRITE (3,110)
```

```
110   FORMAT(' ')
      SQLCOD = -1
      HSTSQL = 'CREATE DATABASE DBNAME01'
      WRITE (3,200)
200   FORMAT(' DISPLAY DYNAMIC SQL STATEMENT')
      WRITE (3,210)
210   FORMAT(' ')
      WRITE(3,220) HSTSQL
220   FORMAT(' ',A24)
      WRITE (3,230)
230   FORMAT(' ')
      WRITE (3,330)
330   FORMAT(' EXECUTE IMMEDIATE ON DYNAMIC SQL STATEMENT')
      WRITE (3,340)
340   FORMAT(' ')
      EXEC SQL
    +   EXECUTE IMMEDIATE :HSTSQL
      IF (SQLCOD.NE.0) GO TO 9990
      HSTSQL = 'DROP    DATABASE DBNAME01'
      WRITE (3,400)
400   FORMAT(' DISPLAY DYNAMIC SQL STATEMENT')
      WRITE (3,410)
410   FORMAT(' ')
      WRITE(3,420) HSTSQL
420   FORMAT(' ',A24)
      WRITE (3,430)
430   FORMAT(' ')
      WRITE (3,440)
440   FORMAT(' EXECUTE IMMEDIATE ON DYNAMIC SQL STATEMENT')
      WRITE (3,450)
450   FORMAT(' ')
      EXEC SQL
    +   EXECUTE IMMEDIATE :HSTSQL
      IF (SQLCOD.NE.0) GO TO 9990
      GO TO 9995
9990  WRITE(3,9991) SQLCOD
9991  FORMAT(' SQLCODE: ',I4)
      WRITE(3,9992) SQLTXT
9992  FORMAT(' SQLTXT = ',A70)
9995  WRITE(3,9999)
9999  FORMAT(' ********** END EXECUTION OF PROGRM4F. **********')
```

```
     STOP
     END
```

PL/I PROGRAM PROGRM4P: EXECUTE IMMEDIATE of NON-Select SQL

```
PROGRM4: PROCEDURE OPTIONS(MAIN);
 /*                                                              */
 /*   INCLUDE SQLCA AND EMPLOYEE TABLE DECLARATION.              */
 /*                                                              */
 EXEC SQL INCLUDE SQLCA;
 /*                                                              */
 /*                                                              */
 DCL
    SQLWORK CHAR(24) VARYING;
 DCL
    RETCODE FIXED(31) BIN;
 DCL
    SYSPRINT FILE STREAM OUTPUT ENV(FB,RECSIZE(133),BLKSIZE(133));
 /*                                                              */
 /*                                                              */
 /****************************************************************/
 PUT SKIP EDIT (' ') (A);
 PUT SKIP EDIT('****** BEGIN EXECUTION OF PROGRM4P ******')
 (A(43));
 PUT SKIP EDIT (' ') (A);
 /****************************************************************/
 /*                                                              */
 /*   CONSTRUCT SQL STATEMENT.                                   */
 /*                                                              */
 /****************************************************************/
 SQLWORK = 'CREATE DATABASE DBNAME01';
 PUT SKIP EDIT('DYNAMIC SQL STATEMENT') (A(21));
 PUT SKIP EDIT (' ') (A);
 PUT SKIP EDIT(SQLWORK) (A(24));
 PUT SKIP EDIT (' ') (A);
 /****************************************************************/
 /*                                                              */
 /*   EXECUTE IMMEDIATE                                          */
 /*                                                              */
 PUT SKIP EDIT ('EXECUTE IMMEDIATE ON DYNAMIC SQL') (A(32));
```

```
PUT SKIP EDIT (' ') (A);
EXEC SQL EXECUTE IMMEDIATE :SQLWORK;
IF SQLCODE = 0 THEN GOTO DISPERR;
/***********************************************************************/
 SQLWORK = 'DROP    DATABASE DBNAME01';
 PUT SKIP EDIT('DYNAMIC SQL STATEMENT') (A(21));
 PUT SKIP EDIT (' ') (A);
 PUT SKIP EDIT(SQLWORK) (A(24));
 PUT SKIP EDIT (' ') (A);
/***********************************************************************/
 /*                                                                 */
 /*    EXECUTE IMMEDIATE                                            */
 /*                                                                 */
 PUT SKIP EDIT ('EXECUTE IMMEDIATE ON DYNAMIC SQL') (A(32));
 PUT SKIP EDIT (' ') (A);
EXEC SQL EXECUTE IMMEDIATE :SQLWORK;
 IF SQLCODE = 0 THEN GOTO DISPERR;
 IF SQLCODE = 0 THEN GOTO STOPRUN;
/***********************************************************************/
 /*                                                                 */
 /*   ERROR ENCOUNTERED, DISPLAY CONTENTS OF SQLCA AREA.            */
 /*                                                                 */
 DISPERR:
 RETCODE = SQLCODE;
 PUT SKIP EDIT (' ') (A);
 PUT SKIP EDIT ('DISPLAY SQLCA AREA=') ( A(19));
 PUT SKIP EDIT ('SQLCAID = ',SQLCAID) (A(11), A(8));
 PUT SKIP EDIT ('SQLCODE = ',SQLCODE) (A(11), F(8));
 PUT SKIP EDIT ('SQLERRMC= ',SQLERRM) (A(11), A(70));
 PUT SKIP EDIT (' SQLWARN0 = ',SQLWARN0) (A(11), A);
    IF SQLWARN0 = 'W'
      THEN DO;
        PUT SKIP EDIT ('SQLWARN1 = ',SQLWARN1) (A(11),A);
        PUT SKIP EDIT ('SQLWARN2 = ',SQLWARN2) (A(11),A);
        PUT SKIP EDIT ('SQLWARN3 = ',SQLWARN3) (A(11),A);
        PUT SKIP EDIT ('SQLWARN4 = ',SQLWARN4) (A(11),A);
        PUT SKIP EDIT ('SQLWARN5 = ',SQLWARN5) (A(11),A);
        PUT SKIP EDIT ('SQLWARN6 = ',SQLWARN6) (A(11),A);
        PUT SKIP EDIT ('SQLWARN7 = ',SQLWARN7) (A(11),A);
        PUT SKIP EDIT (' ') (A);
      END;
```

```
/*                                                                */
/*      STOP RUN                                                  */
/*                                                                */
STOPRUN:
PUT SKIP EDIT ('******* END EXECUTION OF PROGRM4P ******')
(A(40));
CALL PLIRETC(RETCODE);
END PROGRM4;
```

Appendix G:
Program Execution Results

Output from execution of program PROGRM1C:

```
********* BEGIN EXECUTION OF PROGRM1C.**********

OPEN CURSOR NAMED: CURSOR1

DISPLAY ROWS FETCHED FOR CURSOR NAMED = CURSOR1

EMPLOYEE NUMBER = 000000200
                    EMPLOYEE NAME = LARSON
                    STATE = IL
                    DEPARTMENT = D890
                    SALARY =   60000.00

EMPLOYEE NUMBER = 000000500
                    EMPLOYEE NAME = EINERSON
                    STATE = UT
                    DEPARTMENT = D890
                    SALARY =   80000.00

EMPLOYEE NUMBER = 000000250
                    EMPLOYEE NAME = CASPER
                    STATE = MN
                    DEPARTMENT = D890
                    SALARY =   70000.00

EMPLOYEE NUMBER = 000000600
                    EMPLOYEE NAME = GRAVES
                    STATE = CA
```

```
                          DEPARTMENT = D890
                          SALARY =   30000.00
EMPLOYEE NUMBER = 000000350
                          EMPLOYEE NAME = JORDAN
                          STATE = FL
                          DEPARTMENT = D890
                          SALARY =   50000.00


EMPLOYEE NUMBER = 000000700
                          EMPLOYEE NAME = ROCKY
                          STATE = SC
                          DEPARTMENT = D890
                          SALARY =   40000.00


SQLCODE = +00100

END OF FETCH USING CURSOR NAMED: CURSOR1.

CLOSE CURSOR NAMED: CURSOR1

********** END EXECUTION OF PROGRM1C. **********
```

Output from execution of program PROGRM1F:

```
********** BEGIN EXECUTION OF PROGRM1F **********

OPEN CURSOR NAMED: CURSOR1

DISPLAY ROWS FETCHED FOR CURSOR NAMED: CURSOR1

EMPLOYEE NUMBER =   200
                          EMPLOYEE NAME = LARSON
                          STATE = IL
                          DEPARTMENT = D890
                          SALARY = 60000.00

EMPLOYEE NUMBER =   500
                          EMPLOYEE NAME = EINERSON
                          STATE = UT
                          DEPARTMENT = D890
                          SALARY = 80000.00
```

```
EMPLOYEE NUMBER =   250
                    EMPLOYEE NAME = CASPER
                    STATE = MN
                    DEPARTMENT = D890
                    SALARY = 70000.00

EMPLOYEE NUMBER =   600
                    EMPLOYEE NAME = GRAVES
                    STATE = CA
                    DEPARTMENT = D890
                    SALARY = 30000.00

EMPLOYEE NUMBER =   350
                    EMPLOYEE NAME = JORDAN
                    STATE = FL
                    DEPARTMENT = D890
                    SALARY = 50000.00

EMPLOYEE NUMBER =   700
                    EMPLOYEE NAME = ROCKY
                    STATE = SC
                    DEPARTMENT = D890
                    SALARY = 40000.00

SQLCODE =   100

END OF FETCH USING CURSOR NAMED: CURSOR1
CLOSE CURSOR NAMED: CURSOR1

********** END EXECUTION OF PROGRM1F. **********
```

Output from execution of program PROGRM1P:

```
****** BEGIN EXECUTION OF PROGRM1P *******

DECLARE CURSOR1

OPEN CURSOR1

FETCH USING CURSOR1
```

```
EMPLOYEE NUMBER =        200
EMPLOYEE NAME = LARSON
STATE = IL
DEPT = D890
SALARY =      60000

EMPLOYEE NUMBER =        500
EMPLOYEE NAME = EINERSON
STATE = UT
DEPT = D890
SALARY =      80000

EMPLOYEE NUMBER =        250
EMPLOYEE NAME = CASPER
STATE = MN
DEPT = D890
SALARY =      70000

EMPLOYEE NUMBER =        600
EMPLOYEE NAME = GRAVES

STATE = CA
DEPT = D890
SALARY =      30000

EMPLOYEE NUMBER =        350
EMPLOYEE NAME = JORDAN
STATE = FL
DEPT = D890
SALARY =      50000

EMPLOYEE NUMBER =        700
EMPLOYEE NAME = ROCKY
STATE = SC
DEPT = D890
SALARY =      40000

EMPLOYEE NUMBER =        700
EMPLOYEE NAME = ROCKY
STATE = SC
DEPT = D890
```

```
SALARY =      40000
CLOSE CURSOR1


******* END EXECUTION OF PROGRM1P ******
```

Output from execution of program PROGRM2C:

```
********* BEGIN EXECUTION OF PROGRM2C.**********

EMPLOYEES IN DEPARTMENT D700 PRIOR TO UPDATE.

EMPLOYEE NUMBER = 000000495
                  EMPLOYEE NAME = GREEN
                  STATE = ND
                  DEPARTMENT = D700
                  SALARY =    40000.00

EMPLOYEE NUMBER = 000000850
                  EMPLOYEE NAME = NELSON
                  STATE = IL
                  DEPARTMENT = D700
                  SALARY =    35000.00

EMPLOYEE NUMBER = 000000900
                  EMPLOYEE NAME = SHANK
                  STATE = NY
                  DEPARTMENT = D700
                  SALARY =    35000.00

INCREASE ALL SALARIES IN DEPT 700 BY 1000.

ROWS UPDATED DURING INCREASE = +00003

DISPLAY ROWS AFTER UPDATE.

EMPLOYEE NUMBER = 000000495
                  EMPLOYEE NAME = GREEN
                  STATE = ND
                  DEPARTMENT = D700
                  SALARY =    41000.00
EMPLOYEE NUMBER = 000000850
```

```
                EMPLOYEE NAME = NELSON
                STATE = IL
                DEPARTMENT = D700
                SALARY =   36000.00

EMPLOYEE NUMBER = 000000900
                EMPLOYEE NAME = SHANK
                STATE = NY
                DEPARTMENT = D700
                SALARY =   36000.00

REDUCE SALARY FOR EMPLOYEES IN DEPT D700 BY 1000.

ROWS UPDATED DURING DECREASE = +00003

EMPLOYEES IN DEPARTMENT D700 AFTER UPDATE.

EMPLOYEE NUMBER = 000000495
                EMPLOYEE NAME = GREEN
                STATE = ND
                DEPARTMENT = D700
                SALARY =   40000.00

EMPLOYEE NUMBER = 000000850
                EMPLOYEE NAME = NELSON
                STATE = IL
                DEPARTMENT = D700
                SALARY =   35000.00

EMPLOYEE NUMBER = 000000900
                EMPLOYEE NAME = SHANK
                STATE = NY
                DEPARTMENT = D700
                SALARY =   35000.00

********** END EXECUTION OF PROGRM2C. **********
```

Output from execution of program PROGRM2F:

```
********** BEGIN EXECUTION OF PROGRM2F **********

EMPLOYEES IN DEPARTMENT D700 PRIOR TO UPDATE.

EMPLOYEE NUMBER =   495
                    EMPLOYEE NAME = GREEN
                    STATE = ND
                    DEPARTMENT = D700
                    SALARY = 40000.00

EMPLOYEE NUMBER =   850
                    EMPLOYEE NAME = NELSON
                    STATE = IL
                    DEPARTMENT = D700
                    SALARY = 35000.00

EMPLOYEE NUMBER =   900
                    EMPLOYEE NAME = SHANK
                    STATE = NY
                    DEPARTMENT = D700
                    SALARY = 35000.00

INCREASE ALL SALARIES IN DEPT 700 BY 1000.

DISPLAY ROWS AFTER UPDATE.

EMPLOYEE NUMBER =   495
                    EMPLOYEE NAME = GREEN
                    STATE = ND
                    DEPARTMENT = D700
                    SALARY = 41000.00

EMPLOYEE NUMBER =   850
                    EMPLOYEE NAME = NELSON
                    STATE = IL
                    DEPARTMENT = D700
                    SALARY = 36000.00

EMPLOYEE NUMBER =   900
                    EMPLOYEE NAME = SHANK
                    STATE = NY
```

```
                    DEPARTMENT = D700
                    SALARY = 36000.00

ISSUE SQL ROLLBACK TO UNDUE CHANGES MADE
SQLCODE =    0

********** END EXECUTION OF PROGRM2F. **********
```

Output from execution of program PROGRM2P:

```
****** BEGIN EXECUTION OF PROGRM2P *******

EMPLOYEES IN DEPT D700 PRIOR TO UPDATE

EMPLOYEE NUMBER =        495
EMPLOYEE NAME = GREEN
STATE = ND
DEPT = D700
SALARY =    40000

EMPLOYEE NUMBER =        850
EMPLOYEE NAME = NELSON
STATE = IL
DEPT = D700
SALARY =    35000

EMPLOYEE NUMBER =        900
EMPLOYEE NAME = SHANK
STATE = NY
DEPT = D700
SALARY =    35000

EMPLOYEES IN DEPT D700 AFTER UPDATE

EMPLOYEE NUMBER =        495
EMPLOYEE NAME = GREEN
STATE = ND
DEPT = D700
SALARY =    41000

EMPLOYEE NUMBER =        850
```

```
EMPLOYEE NAME = NELSON
STATE = IL
DEPT = D700
SALARY =    36000

EMPLOYEE NUMBER =       900
EMPLOYEE NAME = SHANK
STATE = NY
DEPT = D700
SALARY =    36000

ISSUE ROLLBACK TO UNDUE CHANGES.

******* END EXECUTION OF PROGRM2P ******
```

Output from execution of program PROGRM3C:

```
********* BEGIN EXECUTION OF PROGRM3C.**********

DISPLAY DYNAMIC SELECT:
SELECT EMPLOYEE_NO,EMPLOYEE_NAME,ADDRESS_STATE,DEPT,SALARY
FROM EMPLOYEES_TABLE

DECLARE SQL STATEMENT: CURSOR1

PREPARE SQL STATEMENT: CURSOR1

OPEN CURSOR NAMED: CURSOR1

DISPLAY ROWS FETCHED FOR CURSOR NAMED = CURSOR1

EMPLOYEE NUMBER = 000000200
                  EMPLOYEE NAME = LARSON
                  STATE = IL
                  DEPARTMENT = D890
                  SALARY =  60000.00
EMPLOYEE NUMBER = 000000500
                  EMPLOYEE NAME = EINERSON
                  STATE = UT
                  DEPARTMENT = D890
                  SALARY =  80000.00
```

```
EMPLOYEE NUMBER = 000000250
                  EMPLOYEE NAME = CASPER
                  STATE = MN
                  DEPARTMENT = D890
                  SALARY =  70000.00

EMPLOYEE NUMBER = 000000600
                  EMPLOYEE NAME = GRAVES
                  STATE = CA
                  DEPARTMENT = D890
                  SALARY =  30000.00

EMPLOYEE NUMBER = 000000350
                  EMPLOYEE NAME = JORDAN
                  STATE = FL
                  DEPARTMENT = D890
                  SALARY =  50000.00

EMPLOYEE NUMBER = 000000700
                  EMPLOYEE NAME = ROCKY
                  STATE = SC
                  DEPARTMENT = D890
                  SALARY =  40000.00

SQLCODE = +00100

END OF FETCH USING CURSOR NAMED: CURSOR1.
CLOSE CURSOR NAMED: CURSOR1

********** END EXECUTION OF PROGRM3C. **********
```

Output from execution of program PROGRM3F:

```
********** BEGIN EXECUTION OF PROGRM3F **********

DISPLAY DYNAMIC SQL STATEMENT

SELECT EMPLOYEE_NO,EMPLOYEE_NAME,ADDRESS_STATE,DEPT,SALARY
FROM EMPLOYEES_TABLE
```

DECLARE DYNAMIC FIXED LIST SELECT SQL STATEMENT

PREPARE DYNAMIC FIXED LIST SELECT FROM HSTSQL

OPEN CURSOR NAMED: CURSOR1

DISPLAY ROWS FETCHED FOR CURSOR NAMED: CURSOR1

```
EMPLOYEE NUMBER =    200
                     EMPLOYEE NAME = LARSON
                     STATE = IL
                     DEPARTMENT = D890
                     SALARY = 60000.00


EMPLOYEE NUMBER =    500
                     EMPLOYEE NAME = EINERSON
                     STATE = UT
                     DEPARTMENT = D890
                     SALARY = 80000.00


EMPLOYEE NUMBER =    250
                     EMPLOYEE NAME = CASPER
                     STATE = MN
                     DEPARTMENT = D890
                     SALARY = 70000.00
EMPLOYEE NUMBER =    600
                     EMPLOYEE NAME = GRAVES
                     STATE = CA
                     DEPARTMENT = D890
                     SALARY = 30000.00


EMPLOYEE NUMBER =    350
                     EMPLOYEE NAME = JORDAN
                     STATE = FL
                     DEPARTMENT = D890
                     SALARY = 50000.00


EMPLOYEE NUMBER =    700
                     EMPLOYEE NAME = ROCKY
                     STATE = SC
                     DEPARTMENT = D890
```

```
                      SALARY = 40000.00

SQLCODE =  100

END OF FETCH USING CURSOR NAMED: CURSOR1

CLOSE CURSOR NAMED: CURSOR1

********** END EXECUTION OF PROGRM3F. **********
```

Output from execution of program PROGRM3P:

```
****** BEGIN EXECUTION OF PROGRM3P *******

DYNAMIC SQL STATEMENT CONSTRUCTED

SELECT EMPLOYEE_NO,EMPLOYEE_NAME,ADDRESS_STATE,DEPT,SALARY
FROM EMPLOYEES_TABLE

DECLARE DYNAMIC FIXED LENGTH SELECT

PREPARE DYNAMIC FIXED LENGTH SELECT

OPEN CURSOR: CURSOR1
FETCH USING CURSOR: CURSOR1

EMPLOYEE NUMBER =        200
EMPLOYEE NAME = LARSON
STATE = IL
DEPT = D890
SALARY =     60000
EMPLOYEE NUMBER =        500
EMPLOYEE NAME = EINERSON
STATE = UT
DEPT = D890
SALARY =     80000

EMPLOYEE NUMBER =        250
EMPLOYEE NAME = CASPER
STATE = MN
DEPT = D890
```

```
SALARY =      70000

EMPLOYEE NUMBER =        600
EMPLOYEE NAME = GRAVES
STATE = CA
DEPT = D890
SALARY =      30000

EMPLOYEE NUMBER =        350
EMPLOYEE NAME = JORDAN
STATE = FL
DEPT = D890
SALARY =      50000

EMPLOYEE NUMBER =        700

EMPLOYEE NAME = ROCKY
STATE = SC
DEPT = D890
SALARY =    40000

EMPLOYEE NUMBER =        700
EMPLOYEE NAME = ROCKY
STATE = SC
DEPT = D890
SALARY =    40000

CLOSE CURSOR: CURSOR1

******* END EXECUTION OF PROGRM3P ******
```

Output from execution of program PROGRM4C:

```
********* BEGIN EXECUTION OF PROGRM4C.**********

DISPLAY DYNAMIC SQL:
CREATE DATABASE DBNAME01

EXECUTE IMMEDIATE:

DISPLAY DYNAMIC SQL:
```

```
DROP DATABASE DBNAME01

EXECUTE IMMEDIATE:

********** END EXECUTION OF PROGRM4C. **********
```

Output from execution of program PROGRM4F:

```
********** BEGIN EXECUTION OF PROGRM4F **********

DISPLAY DYNAMIC SQL STATEMENT

CREATE DATABASE DBNAME01

EXECUTE IMMEDIATE ON DYNAMIC SQL STATEMENT

DISPLAY DYNAMIC SQL STATEMENT

DROP    DATABASE DBNAME01

EXECUTE IMMEDIATE ON DYNAMIC SQL STATEMENT

********** END EXECUTION OF PROGRM4F. **********
```

Output from execution of program PROGRM4P:

```
****** BEGIN EXECUTION OF PROGRM4P ******

DYNAMIC SQL STATEMENT

CREATE DATABASE DBNAME01

EXECUTE IMMEDIATE ON DYNAMIC SQL

DYNAMIC SQL STATEMENT

DROP    DATABASE DBNAME01

EXECUTE IMMEDIATE ON DYNAMIC SQL

******* END EXECUTION OF PROGRM4P ******
```